The Clean Water Act
TMDL Program: Law,
Policy, and Implementation

The Clean Water Act TMDL Program: Law, Policy, and Implementation

Oliver A. Houck

Environmental Law Institute
Washington, D.C.

2nd Edition

Acknowledgements

The author would like to acknowledge, with gratitude, the research assistance of Tulane law students Andrew L. Adams, Eileen Budd, Deborah A. Clarke, Danielle R. Cover, Scott M. Galante, Ann-Marie Johnson, Adriana Lopez, Christopher Moore, Shannon Skinner, Louis Spencer, Erik Van Hespen, and R. Brent Walton in the preparation of the four articles underlying this monograph. In addition, he is grateful for the insights of many attorneys, scientists, administrators, and others involved in the TMDL process, including but by no means limited to Robert Adler, Professor of Law, University of Utah College of Law; John Barrett, Texas Farm Bureau; William Cooter, Research Environmental Scientist, Research Triangle Institute; Geoff Grubbs, Office of Water Programs, U.S. Environmental Protection Agency; Eric Huber, Earthjustice Legal Defense Fund; Jessica Landman, Natural Resources Defense Council; and Rick Parrish, Southern Environmental Law Center.

About the Author

Oliver A. Houck is a Professor of Law at Tulane University where he directs the Environmental Law Program. A graduate of Harvard College and Georgetown Law Center, prior to joining the Tulane faculty in 1981, he was an Assistant U.S. Attorney in Washington, D.C. and then General Counsel to the National Wildlife Federation, also in Washington. He has served on the Board of Directors of the Environmental Law Institute and the Defenders of Wildlife and on the Litigation Review Committee of the Environmental Defense Fund. He has also served on the Environmental Advisory Board of the U.S. Army Corps of Engineers and on two panels of the National Academy of Sciences. He has published widely on water pollution, endangered species, biological diversity, and public interest law.

Contents

Foreword

For the past quarter century, the Clean Water Act has relied primarily on technological standards to abate point source pollution and achieve national clean water goals. The U.S. Environmental Protection Agency (EPA) and its state counterparts have labored to adopt, apply, and enforce technology-based limits on water dischargers, and by all accounts, the technology approach has produced significant results. Industrial pollution has plummeted and municipal loadings have dropped. Meanwhile, water quality standards, as set out in the total maximum daily load (TMDL) program of §303(d) of the Clean Water Act, lay largely dormant—at least until the 1990s, when they were activated by citizen suits demanding implementation in order to control pollution from nonpoint sources which cumulatively are impairing waters nationwide. The TMDL litigation has set off a flurry of activity at EPA, in the states, and in our nation's courtrooms and has brought up questions concerning federalism, science, and policital will. In order to make sense of this activity and to address these questions, the Environmental Law Institute (ELI) has turned to Professor Oliver A. Houck, one of the country's leading experts in water quality law, to author *The Clean Water Act TMDL Program: Law, Policy, and Implementation*.

Professor Houck begins this monograph by providing a thorough political history of clean water legislation from 1948 to the present. This history includes discussion and analysis of congressional testimony and committee reports concerning the 1972 amendments to the Clean Water Act and a detailed analysis of the Water Quality Act of 1987. He then moves on to present the tale of EPA's inaction in implementing TMDLs and the lawsuits that inevitably followed. From here Professor Houck provides an in-depth discussion of the roles of the recent TMDL litigation, the TMDL guidance issued by EPA, the Federal Advisory Committee Act report on TMDLs, the standards for nonpoint source pollution under other federal water-related programs, and the state responses in addressing nonpoint source pollution.

He then explores two remaining obstacles to the successful implementation of the TMDL program: the limits of science and the limits of political will. Next, he examines the TMDL rules that were issued in 2000. Professor Houck completes his analysis with reflections on where the TMDL program is going, whether it makes sense, and what can be done to improve its chances of success. He concludes that while TMDLs are a highly resource-intensive and indirect way to approach the significant remaining water pollution problems of this country, they hold the promise of progress with sufficient time and money, more active state leadership, and the retention of elements that have proven key to the success of the Act's point source discharge program as well: numerical targets, fixed plans, and the ability of people concerned about clean water to ensure that they are met.

At ELI, a dedicated and talented team of editors and production staff contributed to this project. Rachel L. Jean-Baptiste edited the manuscript; Linda Johnson, William Straub, and Carolyn Fischer worked on the production of the book; and Kim Goldberg led the marketing effort. As a national environmental research and publishing organization dedicated to the development of more effective and more efficient environmental protection efforts, ELI is pleased to present *The Clean Water Act TMDL Program: Law, Policy, and Implementation*. We hope that those dedicated to improving the quality of our country's water will find it to be a valuable resource.

—J. William Futrell, President
Environmental Law Institute

Chapter 1:
Introduction

> Almost 25 years after the passage of the [Clean Water Act], the national water program is at a defining moment. We—meaning each of you, each of our State, local, and Tribal partners, and all of us in the Office of Water—are making the transition from a clean water program based primarily on technology-based controls to water quality-based controls implemented on a watershed basis. . . . The [total maximum daily load (TMDL)] program is crucial to success because it brings rigor, accountability, and statutory authority to the process.

> —Robert Perciasepe, Assistant Administrator for Water,
> U.S. Environmental Protection Agency [1]

The Clean Water Act (CWA) [2] is changing course. Originally predicated on state programs to achieve water quality standards, the Act was overhauled in 1972 [3] to require national technology standards for point source dischargers, an approach that would go on to revolutionize environmental law. [4] After long debate, however, the Congress also retained a water quality-based strategy for waters that remained polluted after the application of technology standards—§303(d). [5] Eclipsed by more action-forcing provisions of the Act, §303(d) would lie dormant for the next 20 years.

The 1972 Amendments worked. Industrial pollution plummeted [6]; rates of wetland loss slowed, and in some regions even reversed [7]; and municipal loadings, the subject of $128 billion in public funding for treatment works, dropped by nearly 50% while their populations served were doubling in size. [8] Oft-criticized for its "impossible" goals (e.g., zero discharge), "unrealistic" deadlines, and "command-and-control" mechanisms, the unavoidable fact is that the Act's fixed deadlines, best-you-can-do technology standards, individual permits, and multiple enforcement mechanisms generated widespread compliance, new and improved technologies, source reduction, waste recycling, and a growing number of voluntary, quasi-voluntary, and alternative abatement schemes. [9] By any measure—number of dischargers on permit, [10] pounds of pollution abated, [11] stream segments improved, [12] fisheries restored to waters where they had not been seen for decades [13]—the Act has made its case in court and, by its imitation, to the world. [14]

Yet, we do not have clean water. To be sure, we have improved water quality since circa 1972—when rivers and harbors were so contaminated they were actually catching fire [15]—but, taken as a whole, we have not had clean water in America in the lifetime of anyone living. Moreover, the more we learn about the actual quality of America's waters today, the worse, in the aggregate, the news. We have been spared knowing how polluted our waters are by the simple fact that we have not made a serious effort to find out. Only 19% of the nation's rivers, lakes, and estuaries have been assessed for pollution, [16] and these for, in most cases, only the most rudimentary contaminants. The data available have led to the rote conclusion that approximately one-third of America's waters do not meet water quality standards. [17] That number may be high, more likely it is low, but if it is even in the ballpark it is bad news for a country that has poured billions of dollars and countless work-years into programs intended to do no less than eliminate pollution and secure clean water nationwide.

What has gone wrong, of course, is that pollution sources not regulated by the Act have bloomed like algae to swallow the gains. A regional story might serve as an example. The Gulf of Mexico is one of the richest marine environments on earth, hosting two-fifths of America's coastal wetlands, [18] one-third of its commercial seafood, [19] and one-half of its migratory waterfowl. [20] Gulf fisheries weigh in at nearly two billion pounds per year, stimulating $26 billion in commerce. [21] More than 100 hundred communities with unique histories and cultures live on the Gulf and from these resources. [22] In recent decades, the Gulf has begun to die. At the mouth of the Mississippi River and spreading west to Texas is an 8,000 square mile "dead zone" of water too anaerobic to support life. [23] Bottom-dwellers die, menhaden and shrimp move out, [24] and with them go the rest of the food chain up to and including humans. The die-off is from animal waters and fertilizers, the lion's share of which enter the Mississippi from lands above its confluence with the Ohio, [25] more than 975 river miles away. [26]

Every state and every major watershed in America can tell a similar story. [27] The waters in northern Wisconsin are polluted by dairy farms, [28] in North Carolina by hogs, [29] in Maryland by chickens, [30] in South Florida by sugar, [31] in Wyoming by beef cattle, [32] in Oregon by clearcuts, [33] in Maine by logging roads, [34] in California by irrigation return flows, [35] and across suburban America by an expanding and irreversible crop of tract housing and subdivisions, [36] all of which have several characteristics in common. Individually small, it is their cumulative impacts that are the problem, and we have not yet in any medium found an easy way to persuade people to fix problems for which they are only a contributing factor. Furthermore, although individually small, these sources are supported by industries with a political lock on state legislatures and, in some cases, on Congress as well. Most importantly, they are by nature diffuse, not outfalls from fixed points, and therefore long considered to be beyond those requirements of the CWA that have led to its success. [37]

Which would end the story, but for the remarkable resurrection of §303(d), which has returned to the CWA and its players like Banquo's ghost. Its idea is not new. Regulating water discharges by gauging their impacts on receiving water quality was America's original approach to pollution control, and it has continued as the approach of choice for states and dischargers ever since. [38] The attraction of this approach might be surprising, given the fact that it never really worked for water pollution or anything else. It has remained popular, however, because of its emphasis on state and local management, and because of the illusion it offers that reduction measures can be calibrated by, and limited to, only those necessary to offset undesirable environmental effects. Section 303(d) provided a structure for water quality-based regulation. States would identify waters that remained polluted after the application of technology standards, they would determine the total maximum daily loads (TMDLs) of pollutants that would bring these waters up to grade, and they would then allocate these loads among discharge sources in discharge permits and state water quality plans. [39] If the states did not do it, EPA would. [40]

Only the states did none of it, and neither did EPA–until a series of federal court cases in the late 1980s and early 1990s began to crack the defenses, catching EPA and the states by surprise. [41] A wave of litigation followed, state by state, compelling listings of impaired waters and schedules for first-ever TMDLs. The listings were daunting. Idaho rose from 16 impaired waters to 962. The schedules were tight, as early as five years. EPA scrambled forward with §303(d) guidance and memoranda as fast as they could be proposed and convened a Federal Advisory Committee Act panel of state agencies, industry dischargers, and environmentalists to seek a consensus on goals, mechanisms, and timetables for the program. Consensus would not be easy. Nonpoint sources, largely responsible for the pollution at issue and largely immune to date from the requirements of the CWA, were openly hostile to abatement requirements. Municipal and industrial sources were no happier with the prospect of being tagged with nonpoint sources' share. Environmentalists, meanwhile, were spurring the action forward. A few states accepted the challenge. Others bunkered down and looked to Congress for relief. As the heat turned up on the TMDL program it was easy to forget that the reason the CWA retained such an approach, and directed its use for the upgrade of polluted waters, is that both the states and pollution dischargers insisted on it. In a very real sense, this is the ghost they wanted.

At journey's end is a new water pollution control program. Its scope is ambitious—at last count nearly 40% of the nation's waters remain impaired. Its players are lukewarm to reluctant, and there are some who will fight it to the end. And its basic assumptions—that pollution can be controlled by calibrating sources and effects, and that state and local authorities have the will to do so—are, at best, unproven. On the other hand, this is a program that Congress enacted. It has the potential to succeed where others have not, and it has the power of a citizenry concerned about clean water and determined to take it forward. And it is at the door.

This monograph attempts to explain where the TMDL program came from, to examine what its issues are, and to consider how it will fare. Chapter 2 presents a history of water quality-based regulation, the legislative struggle leading to §303(d), and its aftermath in the Congress. Chapter 3 describes EPA's early implementation of §303(d), the hiatus between its theory and its practice, the litigation that forced the program forward, and the legal issues ahead. Chapter 4 treats EPA's subsequent efforts to manage the program, its address of the issues, the companion initiatives of the Administration and other federal agencies, and the first state TMDLs to emerge. Chapter 5 reflects on where this program has been, where it is going, and its prospects for success. Chapter 6 concludes with a summary of the events leading to the adoption of the final TMDL rules in the year 2000 and an assessment of the program. Separate appendices present §§303(d) and (e) and 319 of the CWA (Appendix A), an outline of TMDL litigation (Appendix B), an evaluation of 55 state TMDLs (Appendix C), and EPA's July 2000 TMDL regulations (Appendix D).

Welcome to TMDLs.

Notes to Chapter 1

1. Memorandum from Robert Perciasepe, Assistant Administrator for Water, U.S. EPA, to Regional Administrators and Regional Water Division Administrators, U.S. EPA, *New Policies for Establishing and Implementing Total Maximum Daily Loads (TMDLs)* (Aug. 8, 1997) http://www.epa.gov/owowwtr1/watershed/ratepace.html.

2. 33 U.S.C. §§1251-1387, ELR STAT. FWPCA §§101-607. Technically the "Federal Water Pollution Control Act," in 1977 Congress ceded to common usage and recognized the "Clean Water Act" as well. *See* Clean Water Act of 1977, Pub. L. No. 95-217, §2, 91 Stat. 1566 (1977) ("This Act may be cited as the 'Federal Water Pollution Control Act' (commonly referred to as the Clean Water Act).").

3. Federal Water Pollution Control Act Amendments of 1972, Pub. L. No. 92-500, 86 Stat. 816 (codified as amended in scattered sections of 33 U.S.C.).

4. The CWA's technology standards approach has been subsequently adopted by, inter alia, the Clean Air Act, 42 U.S.C. §§7401-7671q, ELR STAT. CAA §§101-618 (technology standards for stationary sources in nonattainment areas, *id.* §7503, ELR STAT. CAA §173); by the Resource Conservation and Recovery Act, 42 U.S.C. §§6901-6992k, ELR STAT. RCRA §§1001-11012 (technology standards for land disposal, 51 Fed. Reg. 40572 (Nov. 7, 1986)); and the pollution control programs of the European Union, *see* Council Directive 76/464, 1976 O.J. (L 129/23) (technology standards for toxic water discharges). For a discussion of the coalescing of environmental law around technology standards, see Oliver A. Houck, *Of Bats, Birds and BAT: The Convergent Evolution of Environmental Law,* 63 Miss. L.J. 403 (1994).

5. Section 303 of the Federal Water Pollution Control Act Amendments of 1972 retained the water quality standards-based regulatory approach of earlier federal legislation, with significant strengthening provisions, chief among them was §303(d). 33 U.S.C. §1313(d), ELR STAT. FWPCA §303(d).

6. Between 1987 and 1990 alone, during which time technology standards for toxic pollutants were first implemented for many industrial categories, direct toxic discharges dropped from 417 to 197 million pounds per year, and indirect discharges into municipal sewage systems fell from 610 to 447 million pounds. ROBERT W. ADLER ET AL., THE CLEAN WATER ACT 20 YEARS LATER 18 (1993). A 1989 EPA study showed post-best available technology (BAT) loadings from the pulp and paper industry dropping from 10 to 0.9 million pounds per day for suspended solids, from 8 to 0.5 million for biological oxygen demand, and from 32,000 to 3,000 for organic toxins; similarly dramatic reductions were recorded for aluminum, coal, iron and steel, leather, and other major source categories. U.S. EPA, WATER IMPROVEMENT STUDY, tbl. 1-2 (1989) ("Comparison of RAW and BAT Pollutant loadings for BAT Industries").

7. COUNCIL ON ENVIRONMENTAL QUALITY, ENVIRONMENTAL QUALITY 1994-1995, at 271-73 (1997).

8. *Id.* at 14.

9. For examples of emerging quasi-voluntary and alternative emission limitations, see *Comments Sought by EPA on Alternatives to Proposed Industrial Laundry Standards,* 29 Env't Rep. (BNA) 1697 (Jan. 1, 1999) (discussing a nonregulation option for industrial laundries); *EPA to Propose Less Stringent Metal Effluent Guidelines,* INSIDE EPA WKLY. REP., Apr. 23, 1999, at 6 (discussing the U.S. Environmental Protection Agency's (EPA's) plan to propose optional guidelines for the metal products and machinery industry). In large part stimulated by the increased pressure of technology standards, EPA and industry have been experimenting with "pollution prevention" initiatives since the early 1990s. *See* Blueprint for National Pollution Prevention Study, 56 Fed. Reg. 7549 (Feb. 26, 1991); *see also More Than 600 Firms Asked to Reduce Releases of 17 Toxic Chemicals Voluntarily,* [21 Current Developments] Env't Rep. (BNA) 1838 (Feb. 15, 1991).

10. ADLER ET AL., *supra* note 6, at 137.

11. *Id.* at 16; *see also supra* note 6.

12. *Id.* at 224-45; *see also* WATER IMPROVEMENT STUDY, *supra* note 6, at tbl. 3-1 ("Summary of Water Quality Monitoring Results: Compliance With Criteria") and fig. 3-1 ("Summary of Water Quality Modeling: Overall Results") (showing a 29% increase in waters attaining water quality standards after the implementation of BAT).

13. For a discussion of these and other CWA successes, see U.S. EPA & U.S. DEP'T OF AGRIC., CLEAN WATER ACTION PLAN: RESTORING AND PROTECTING AMERICA'S WATERS, EPA 840-R-98-001, at 1-2 (Feb. 1998) [hereinafter CWAP] (discussing the Williamette River, where the "mighty salmon perished," which now supports "boating, skiing, swimming, and fishing").

14. The European Union has adopted a water pollution control program modeled on the CWA. *See* Council Directive 76/464 on Pollution Caused by Certain Dangerous Substances Discharged Into the Aquatic Environment of the Community, 1976 O.J. (L 129) 23 (providing technology-based emission limitations for toxic discharges, supplemented by a water quality standards approach).

15. *See* Patricia Howard, *A Happier Cleveland,* HOUS. POST, Oct. 24, 1990, at A2 (describing the 1969 fire on the Cuyahoga River in Cleveland, Ohio).

16. TMDL FEDERAL ADVISORY COMMITTEE ACT COMMITTEE, FINAL REPORT 3 (May 20, 1998) [hereinafter FACA REPORT].

17. *See id.* The draft National Water Quality Inventory Report to Congress for 1996 indicated that 35% of the nation's assessed rivers, streams, and estuaries, and 39% of the nation's assessed lakes, ponds, and reservoirs, do not fully support water quality standards. *Id.* For a troubling critique of these assessments, see PUBLIC EMPLOYEES FOR ENVIRONMENTAL RESPONSIBILITY, MURKY WATERS, OFFICIAL WATER QUALITY REPORTS ARE ALL WET; AN INSIDE LOOK AT EPA'S IMPLEMENTATION OF THE CLEAN WATER ACT (1999).

18. MISSISSIPPI RIVER COMM'N, U.S. ARMY CORPS OF ENG'RS, MISSISSIPPI RIVER AND TRIBUTARIES PROJECT, CAIRO TO THE GULF (1977).

19. Nancy N. Rabalais & Donald E. Harper Jr., *Studies of Benthic Biota in Areas Affected by Severe Hypoxia, in* COASTAL OCEAN PROGRAM OFFICE, NATIONAL OCEANIC & ATMOSPHERIC ADMINISTRATION, PROCEEDINGS OF NUTRIENT ENHANCED COASTAL OCEAN PRODUCTIVITY WORKSHOP, LOUISIANA UNIVERSITIES MARINE CONSERVATION 150 (Oct. 1991).

20. *Id.*

21. Carol Kaesuk Yoon, *A "Dead Zone" Grows in the Gulf of Mexico*, N.Y. TIMES, Jan. 20, 1998, at F-1.

22. U.S. DEP'T OF COMMERCE & LOUISIANA DEP'T OF NATURAL RESOURCES, LOUISIANA COASTAL RESOURCES PROGRAM FINAL ENVIRONMENTAL IMPACT STATEMENT 22-30 (1980).

23. *See* Yoon, *supra* note 21.

24. *Id*; *see also* Rabalais & Harper, *supra* note 19.

25. U.S. EPA, SOURCES AND QUANTITIES OF NUTRIENTS ENTERING THE GULF OF MEXICO FROM SURFACE WATERS OF THE UNITED STATES, EPA 800-4-02-002, at 1 (Sept. 1992) (attributing three-quarters of dead zone nutrient loadings to sources above the Ohio River).

26. Telephone Conversation with John Hall, Public Affairs Office, U.S. Army Corps of Engineers, New Orleans, La. (June 3, 1999).

27. Particularly well-documented studies of hypoxia are available for Long Island Sound, *see A Total Maximum Daily Load (TMDL) for Long Island Sound: Charting a Course to Clean Water* (Apr. 25, 1999) http://www.soundkeeper.org/tmdl/, and the Chesapeake Bay, *see* Elaine Bueschen, Pfiesteria Piscicida: *A Regional Symptom of a National Problem*, 28 ELR 10317 (June 1998).

28. CWAP, *supra* note 13, at 10.

29. John Burns, *The Eight Million Little Pigs—A Cautionary Tale: Statutory and Regulatory Responses to Hog Farming*, 31 WAKE FOREST L. REV. 851 (1996) (analysis of the North Carolina hog farming industry).

30. Margaret Kriz, *Pfiesteria Hysteria*, 29 NAT'L J. 1783 (1997); Margaret Kriz, *Fish and Fowl*, 30 NAT'L J. 450 (1998).

31. *Everglades Pact Pledges Aid to Threatened Area*, TIMES PICAYUNE (NEW ORLEANS), July 11, 1991, at A-20.

32. ADLER ET AL., *supra* note 6, at 180-81 (discussing grazing effects in Wyoming); *see also* Debra L. Donahue, *The Untapped Power of the Clean Water Act Section 401*, 23 ECOLOGY L.Q. 201, 279-80 (1996).

33. ADLER ET AL., *supra* note 6, at 182-83.

34. *Id.* at 183.

35. *Id.*

36. *See id.* at 193-98 (discussing the growing problem of urban runoff).

37. For a general discussion of difficulties in managing nonpoint source pollution under the CWA, *see, e.g.*, WILLIAM H. RODGERS JR., ENVIRONMENTAL LAW 292-318 (2d ed. 1994); for more specifics, see David Zaring, *Agriculture, Nonpoint Source Pollution and Regulatory Control: The Clean Water Act's Bleak Present and Future*, 20 HARV. ENVTL. L. REV. 515 (1996).

38. For this history and the attachment of states to the water quality approach, see Chapter 2 *infra.*

39. More specifically, this section requires states to (1) identify waters that will remain in violation of water quality standards after the imposition of technology controls, 33 U.S.C. §1313(d)(1)(A), ELR STAT. FWPCA §303(d)(1)(A); (2) prioritize those waters for remedial action, *id.*; (3) identify TMDL allocations that will meet water quality standards, *id.* §1313(d)(1)(C), ELR STAT. FWPCA §303(d)(1)(C); and (4) incorporate these allocations into discharge permits and state water quality plans, *id.* §1313(e)(3)(C), (F), ELR STAT. FWPCA §303(e)(3)(C), (F).

40. *Id.* §1313(d)(2), ELR STAT. FWPCA §303(d)(2).

41. This inaction, litigation, and the subsequent development of TMDLs are described in Chapters 3 and 4 *infra.*

Chapter 2:
The History and Evolution of §303

Water Quality Standards Regulation and TMDLs

It is, perhaps, the oldest argument in environmental law. Assuming there is a consensus that some attention should be paid to the environment, there is no consensus on why, and, therefore, by whom and how. The root question in this argument is whether we are protecting the environment or are managing it for our use. [1] This question rose to the national level early in the debate over water pollution control.

The theory of water quality standards-based regulation rests squarely on human use. [2] Water is meant to be used, as is any other natural resource, and one legitimate function is the assimilation of wastes. Decisions about water use should be made by people who use it, local communities, industries, and authorities. To control pollution, local authorities (1) determine the use they want, e.g., recreation or waste transport; (2) determine what biological criteria, e.g., four parts per million of oxygen, are needed to support this use; (3) assess the impacts of dischargers on these criteria; and (4) abate those discharges that cause the criteria to be exceeded. This was the nation's first strategy for pollution control, and it was an approach that states, municipalities, and industrial dischargers could all support. It relied on the preferences and decisions of local authorities, staffed agencies of water quality technicians, empowered water pollution control boards, and limited pollution controls to those that were needed to meet a proven problem. It was elegant, straightforward, and logical. Unfortunately, it did not work very well. [3]

By 1972, with reports on deteriorating water quality from every quarter, the nation was ready for a new strategy of pollution control. There was a new ethical premise, that water should simply be clean. There was a new political view, that pollution was a national problem and required federal intervention. And there was a new mechanism, technology standards. Retained in the Act, however, were the vestiges of a water quality standards-based program, codified in §303. [4] While the initial provisions of §303 amplified on the process of establishing state water quality standards, §303(d) added a prescription for using these standards to upgrade waters that remained polluted after the application of technology-based requirements. [5] It has become a battleground.

In brief, §303(d) requires three steps. The states will:

1. identify waters that are and will remain polluted after the application of technology standards; [6]

2. prioritize these waters, taking into account the severity of their pollution; [7] and

3. establish "total maximum daily loads" (TMDLs) for these waters at levels necessary to meet applicable water quality standards, accounting for seasonal variations and with a margin of safety to reflect lack of certainty about discharges and water quality. [8]

States are to submit their inventories and TMDLs to EPA for approval. If EPA does not approve, the Agency is to promulgate them itself for incorporation into state planning. [9] Under §303(e), [10] states are to develop plans for all waters that include, inter alia, (1) discharge limitations at least as stringent as the requirements of its water quality standards [11] and (2) TMDLs. [12]

The TMDL process represents, in the short life of environmental law, an ancient approach to pollution control. As this chapter proceeds to discuss how these requirements evolved and, in a subsequent chapter, how they have been implemented, it is useful to understand their assumptions and their constituencies. From the very first hint of federal involvement in water pollution control 50 years ago, states and pollution dischargers have fought a running battle to defend and, where lost, return to the local primacy and utilitarianism of regulation by water quality standards. Whatever else might be said about the ineffectiveness and difficulties of this regulation in practice, this has been their Camelot, the land from which we were unceremoniously wrenched and to which we should return. To their dismay, we have.

The Rise of Water Quality Standards in Federal Law

In the beginning, and for the greater part of this century, water pollution control was based on principles of nuisance and the balance of competing uses by local water boards and occasionally local courts. [13] With a growing awareness of pollution following World War II, the federal government entered these waters only lightly and with the greatest deference to state and local prerogatives. Affirming the "primary responsibilities and rights of the states" in managing water quality, [14] the Water Pollution Control Act of 1948 [15] provided money for state and municipal programs, the good offices of the U.S. Surgeon General to "coordinate" state and interstate programs, and a cumbersome abatement process for interstate pollution when it rose to the level of a public nuisance. Amendments authorizing the Surgeon General to promulgate water quality standards for interstate waters were proposed in 1956, and rejected on the grounds that many states were regulating through the use of these standards anyway; federal standards would confuse the issue and usurp state authority. [16] Federal legislation in 1956 and for the next 10 years was largely restricted to technical assistance and funding. Even in this role, the possible federal intrusion was making industrial dischargers anxious. [17]

Water quality standards came into federal law with the Water Quality Act of 1965, [18] which required federally approved standards on interstate waters. [19] In its debates, Congress rejected a national policy of "keeping waters as clean as possible," a policy heavily criticized by industry, in favor of recognizing their function for "waste assimilation" and other uses. [20] It also considered, and rejected, a proposal for federal "effluent limitations," forerunners of the 1972 amendments to come. [21] For the moment, state water quality standards were at their apex, the center of the federal-state water pollution control program. States would have first option to develop interstate standards for federal review and approval. [22] States could gear these standards to accommodate a wide latitude of permissible uses, from drinking water supply, wildlife, and recreation to "agricultural, industrial, and other legitimate uses." [23] If a state did not act, however, the U.S. Secretary of Health, Education, and Welfare could adopt standards, after further consultation with the state and the opportunity for a full administrative hearing. [24] Even this latter provision was opposed by the House, which advocated the milder sanction of precluding funding for states that failed to submit water quality standards [25]; federal standards, the House argued, would lead to federal "zoning" and discourage state initiative. [26]

In part on their own initiative, but lured forward by increased federal funding in 1966 and the threat of federal intervention if water quality standards were not forthcoming, states moved slowly over the next five years to adopt standards for interstate waters. [27] The 1965 Act, however, said little about the content of these standards and less about what came next. The standards were to be based on "water quality criteria," and have a "plan for (their) implementation and enforcement." [28] By the turn of the 1970s, minimum standards—in the eyes of some observers, subminimum [29]—had been approved for nearly all of the states. Taken alone, they might have satisfied Congress but the step that was to follow, the implementation plans, did not materialize. [30] Indeed, state implementation and enforcement exhibited a "preference," in the words of one commentator quite partial to state programs, for "education and informal persuasion to enforcement in attacking water quality problems." [31] It was this lack of progress in linking the standards to the actual abatement of pollution, coupled with the lightning-quick appearance of an alternative enforcement scheme under the federal Refuse Act, [32] that so discredited the water quality standards approach and led to its near—but not total—eclipse in 1972.

The 1972 Amendments: The States and the Regulated Community Make Their Case

The Federal Water Pollution Control Amendments of 1972 [33] were not foreordained. The product of years of wrangling in both houses of Congress, [34] they were resisted strongly by most states, by a wide spectrum of industry, and by high-level members of the Administration up to and including the President. They were enacted because of an unusual spectrum of bipartisan Senate leadership and strong public opinion. Throughout this fight, the Senate was ready for federal permits based on best available technology. The House was holding firm on state programs based on water quality standards. The legislative history of the Act has been well-written by, among others, the Congress itself and bears no repeating. [35] What is relevant today is who was arguing for state water quality programs and what they represented about their ability to do the job.

New York Governor Nelson Rockefeller was the principal witness for state interests on the House bill. He complimented the House approach that "would leave the permit granting up to the States and limit federal intervention into [sic] interstate cases." [36] As between water quality or effluent standards, he continued, "I prefer the present system of water quality standards. . . . I think the present system is a good one, because we classify waters and set standards rather than determine arbitrary emission standards." [37] The governor's written testimony elaborated: "[T]he states are in a far better position to know the numerous local and natural variables that must determine the final setting of detailed numeric standards for water quality." [38] While the federal government should set "general guidelines," states should be given a "reasonable degree of latitude" to take local and natural conditions into account in setting these standards, and the same latitude "in the implementation of State abatement orders." [39]

Governor Rockefeller's statements were accompanied by the written testimony of nearly a dozen state governors and associations, all clearly concerned with retaining their programs and authority. The first was Governor Moore of West Virginia, Chairman of the National Governor's Conference, who stated that:

In the past, States and their political subdivisions have taken the lead in environmental protection. The Governors of the States are increasingly distressed over Federal legislation which ignores the many remarkable achievements of the States and preempts their efforts to improve upon the past performances. [The Congress should be concerned with] strengthening state programs rather than their preemption. [40]

Governor Exon of Nebraska:

As I understand the proposed legislation it will extend the Federal Government's regulations over water pollution control matters which are internal to the State. Already we have seen the 1899 Refuse Act bill used far beyond the original intent as a subterfuge to encroach upon the constitutional authority of the State. The proposed legislation appears to be one more unjustified step in the road to complete Federal takeover. [41]

Governor Smith of Texas:

As now written, HR 11896 would remove the major responsibility for water pollution control from the states and place it at the federal level.... Modification of existing state standards by the EPA Administrator to make them more stringent in order to comply with the unrealistic 1981 goal could create more problems than it would cure. [42]

Governor Burns of Hawaii:

There are instances in both HR 11896 and in S 2770 in which the language is inconsistent with the important responsibility which states must have to define and direct their water pollution control programs. Hawaii, as well as other states, possesses unique characteristics in terms of problems and opportunities. Blanket standards for effluent sources control cannot logically have the same performance in each state. [43]

Governor Carter of Georgia:

The record should clearly show that the State of Georgia and Georgia people place a high priority on a quality environment.... We are in the midst of a water pollution abatement program that will, when fully implemented, restore the quality of our polluted streams to provide for multiple uses of our resources.... If the State is not provided an opportunity to conduct such a permit program without duplicative reviews by inexperienced bureaucrats who are reluctant to make decisions required for complex problems, the total pollution abatement program will be hampered. [44]

Governor Andrus of Idaho:

The virtual takeover by the federal government in the water pollution field by providing the Environmental Protection Agency
(EPA) veto power over discharge permits issued by the states
would effectively strip the states of the policy-making authority in
this field. Establishing water quality standards and implementation programs to meet these standards can best be done at the state
and local levels where personnel have full knowledge of local
conditions and problems. [45]

The National Legislative Conference concluded:

[I]t [is] unwise for Federal legislation to preempt State efforts
where these, in many cases, have been even stronger than Federal programs. [46]

These state views were supported by an impressive array of water quality
engineers and technocrats. In their view, state water quality standards regulation was not only politically optimal; it was logical, feasible, and in fact at
hand. Leading the charge was the Ad Hoc Advisory Task Force to the National Governors' Conference, which included water pollution control
managers from California, Washington, Illinois, Pennsylvania, New York,
the Western States Water Council, and the New England Interstate Pollution
Control Commission. [47] They stated:

The diversity of water quality control problems existing in the
United States today poses problems that are not amenable to the
simple, generalized solutions that generally flow from a centralized
agency. State water quality control agencies have acquired a background of information, experience and extremities in dealing with
the problems of their respective areas. This knowledge, experience
and expertise should not be bypassed by the Administrator in the
formulation of information and guidelines necessary for the
achievement of the environmental goals of the senate bill. [48]

In separate testimony, the Chairman of the California Water Resources
Control Board, accompanied by the Chairman of the Water and Power
Committee of the Los Angeles Chamber of Commerce stated:

Present water pollution law that assigns the primary responsibility
to the States is, we believe, very sound in principle and should be
expanded and strengthened. . . . National [technological] standards,
such as "secondary treatment," become fixed and therefore eliminate objective judgment based on proven fact and not emotional
rhetoric, particularly where complex environmental problems are
involved. The ability to respond to changing social, economic,
technological, and ecological constraints is mandatory we believe,
if a water quality program is to be at all viable. The jurisdiction of

the Federal Government should not extend beyond those waters included today; that is interstate and coastal waters . . . . [49]

The President of the American Water Works Association:

> We would favor both water and water pollution legislation that provides that the states establish and enforce water quality standards, with the federal government stepping in only when the states fail. . . . This policy specifically calls upon the states "to provide water quality management, including pollution abatement and control."[50]

The Director of the Dallas, Texas, Water Utilities Department:

> I would point out to you that a blanket water quality standard and permit system which is not flexible or allows for the changes in the nature of streams cannot succeed. . . . Each stream must be evaluated and reevaluated in terms of its assimilative capacity. . . . I think EPA will confirm that in the final analysis the permit system will have to be based on pounds of pollution which is placed in the streams at various points and these will be based on the ability of the stream to assimilate the residual oxygen demand of such effluents. [51]

The Deputy Secretary for Environmental Protection and Regulation for Pennsylvania:

> We are one of the states that utilize predictive mathematical models in the development of water quality implementation plans so as to do the best job possible in insuring that water quality criteria are met. . . . Our experience has been that some minimum treatment or effluent requirements are desirable but that, to meet water quality criteria, it is necessary to consider watersheds as a whole and, by mathematical modeling, determine how much treatment must be provided to protect water quality and leave room for future growth. [52]

The Administration was represented by the Chairman of the President's Council on Environmental Quality (CEQ), accompanied by the Chairman of the Council of Economic Advisors (CEA) and attaching statements of two Professors of Civil Engineering at Manhattan College, New York. CEQ Chairman Train:

> I would be truly amazed if the nation that has sent men to the moon, and achieved dazzling technological accomplishments in other areas of national concern could not within the next five years muster the ability to determine and predict relationships between what is discharged into the water and the resultant quality of the water. . . . Indeed, if we are unable to relate effluents to water quality accomplishment, it raises fundamental questions about all aspects of our water quality management efforts. . . . A permit pro-

gram unrelated to impacts of discharges on water quality simply cannot work effectively. [53]

CEA Chairman McCracken:

> CEA is in agreement with the use of water quality targets appropriate to the conditions and expected uses of water in particular areas of the country. That is basic to the concept of relating the costs of programs to the benefits received from them. To abandon that concept for a nationally legislated standard which focuses on the level of pollutants removed and is unrelated to water quality uses and standards is economically unwise because it means a necessary misallocation of our inevitably scarce economic resources. [54]

Professor Thomann:

> With the ability to relate effluent waste load to resulting water quality, the maximum allowable waste discharge to meet the objective can be estimated. Administrative and enforcement devices can be employed at this point. This procedure incorporates in a rational way the interaction between water utility and waste discharge recognizing the nature of the water body (e.g., size, configuration), the water quality goal and the amount of residue discharged. [55]

Professor O'Connor:

> What is most basically required is a comprehensive analysis of sources of pollution. . . . Given a set of water quality criteria, the model would analyze alternate engineering solutions to achieve this goal. . . . Examples of this model effort have been accomplished in many areas throughout the country in which the effects on water quality have been quantitatively determined in light of various water resources and waste treatment planning. [56]

Representatives of American industry also strongly favored water quality-based regulation. [57] The Chairman of the American Iron and Steel Institute:

> The Senate is now considering a bill that would make all streams in the country so clean that they would be suitable for fishing and swimming. This is a laudable objective, but it is unworkable and unrealistic in an industrial society like ours. We propose that the Committee specify in the bill it will shortly be drafting that the Environmental Protection Agency promulgate water quality standards for a specified water use. This could be done by classifying streams for existing uses, depending on local requirements. Thus, in highly industrialized areas, streams that are not used for public water supply could be classified for industrial use, with one set of quality criteria. [58]

The Senior Vice President of the American Petroleum Institute:

> There have been suggestions that water legislation follow the lead
> set in air legislation. We do not believe that the parallel is a valid
> one. Minimum national air quality standards for the protection of
> human health are a logical and necessary requirement. All of us
> must breath the air every single moment of the day no matter where
> we happen to be. We do not have to drink from any and all bodies of
> water, which presently serve a wide variety of uses. Rarely do we
> actually drink water directly from a river or lake. Nor must we swim
> in every available body of water. . . . This does not mean, of course,
> that we recommend being content with maintaining the quality of
> water at a stated minimum for a use category. Any state which de-
> termines that it is desirable to enhance water quality from agricul-
> tural use classification to recreational use classification should be
> free to take appropriate action. [59]

Taken as a whole, this testimony constituted a powerful plea for the continuation of a federal program based on state water quality standards. For
state governors, it respected state sovereignty. For state water quality managers, it respected their expertise. For academics, it was rational. For municipal and industrial dischargers, it avoided overkill. And for fiscal conser-
vatives, it could be done within budget. Their strong and united message
was that water quality standard-based regulation *could* be done, and was *being* done: models were out there all across the country. The states were
ready and willing to go.

For the record, not all states agreed. Governor Anderson of Minnesota,
paired somewhat awkwardly before the House Public Works Committee
with Governor Rockefeller, saw the merit, indeed the need, for uniform federal standards that would discourage a race to the bottom and the loss of industry to more accommodating states. [60] The National Farmers Union—perhaps feeling itself untouched by the issue—also testified strongly
in favor of national effluent limits and strong federal enforcement:
"[E]xperience with interstate compacts in this country shows that more often than not they have been used as a smoke screen to ward off overdue action by the Federal government, rather than as a means of solving the problems over which they are given jurisdiction." [61] At one point, responding to
testimony from the Los Angeles Chamber of Commerce, the Acting Chair
of the House Public Works Committee, a body known for its sympathies
with state interests through the debate, exploded:

> We have heard that from the Chamber of Commerce from the very
> beginning, "Don't pass any Federal law; just let us keep it at home
> in the State." So consequently, we didn't get anything done. We left

it to the States, year after year, and we didn't get a single thing but a bunch of nursery rhymes as to the Constitution, and we didn't get any clean water until the Federal Government insisted upon it and made some dollars available to the State for that use. [62]

He could have been speaking for the Senate, whose report on prior federal water pollution control legislation read like a bill of indictment against a program based on state water quality standards. [63] The Senate found the standards weak, late, widely disparate, scientifically doubtful, largely unenforced, and probably unenforceable. [64] The Senate's perspective would pass its chamber by a vote of 89-0, [65] and would go on to sweep the House conferees. Given the views of the Senate leadership on water quality standards—and the views of many in the House as well—it was no miracle that federal technology standards prevailed. If there was a surprise, it was that water quality standards stayed alive.

Congress Disposes: §303(d)

The Senate began work on a new federal water act in April of 1970. [66] By early 1971, it had a prototype bill in place and began eight days of hearings, leading by October of that year to S. 2770. [67] The Senate bill contained all the essential elements of the Federal Water Pollution Control Act (FWPCA)—its aspirational goals, technology standards, and permit and enforcement systems—save one: state water quality standards. [68] To the Senate leadership, and to Sen. Edmund Muskie (D-Me.) in particular, water quality standards had so utterly failed that they had no remaining role to play. [69] Environmentalists, however, cautious about resting the new Act on any one approach alone, secured an amendment that would reserve a role for water quality standards, although hardly an active one. [70] Under the Senate bill as amended, EPA would publish water quality criteria reflecting the "latest scientific information on factors needed" for restoring the nation's waters, [71] and, in a separate section, both the states and EPA were to prepare reports that would "correlate existing water quality with the water quality criteria" [72]; the criteria would thus become an index rather than a driver for the abatement of water pollution. However, §302 also authorized EPA to impose a more stringent discharge limitation where technology-based limits would interfere with the attainment of water quality suitable for fish, wildlife, and recreation. [73]

Playing catch up from the start, the House did not begin its markup until November 1971. [74] By this time, the Senate had passed S. 2770, and to state, administration, and industry representatives the mission now was to regain state primacy and the water quality standards program. [75] The House, perhaps by its nature, was historically more influenced by state and industry views on environmental protection. [76] As the House Public Works Committee Chairman John A. Blatnik explained of his committee members:

> They are all men of good intentions, but they get beat over the head by powerful interests back home. I won't mention any names, but say somebody is from South Carolina or Georgia, and the Georgia Power Co., gets after them. . . . You can't find finer men, or men of more integrity. But you can only go so far. [77]

They were also naturally more inclined to back state authority, and the committee leadership, Republican and Democratic alike, supported the view that water should be regulated by local uses rather than by national effluent standards. [78] Speaker after speaker emphasized the capability of the states to do the job. Public Works Committee Chairman Blatnik:

> To argue that State administration of State programs somehow weakens the legislation is to argue that the people in our State capitals, in our towns and cities across the country are not entitled to a voice in the conduct of their own affairs. [79]

Congressman Roe:

> Mr. Chairman, simply put, the amendment which we have just heard declares in loud, shrill tones that the States cannot be trusted. . . . I have had considerable experience working on this program at the State level as a cabinet officer in New Jersey, and I can attest to the fact that State officials are as capable as their counterparts in EPA. And they enjoy an advantage not shared by those who work in our Nation's Capital in that they are closer to the problems and, in many cases, have a better understanding of what has to be done. [80]

Congressman Robison:

> [H.R. 11896] retains the wealth of organization, expertise and experience that the individual States have built up over the years—while—proponents of a complete take over by the Washington bureaucracy would consign that wealth to the scrap heap. [81]

Congressman Frenzel:

> Some of us may be attracted to the "papa knows best" theory. Centralism always dies hard, I suppose, but if enough of us still believe in State land local governments—in their ability to solve local problems—we can, by passing this amendment, give our States the authority to solve their rightful responsibilities. [82]

H.R. 11896, reported by the committee and passed by the House in March 1972, retained the emphasis on state water quality standards and deflected the Senate's approach by adopting the idea of effluent limitations but postponing their implementation until the completion of a study by a congressionally appointed National Water Commission. The House leadership was careful, however, in a climate of rising public demand for environmental protection, to characterize its approach as supplemental to, and indeed stronger than, the Senate bill. Rep. William Harsha (R-Ohio), the ranking Republican member of the House committee, pointed out that H.R. 11896 required the states to adopt water quality standards for intrastate as well as interstate waters which, in conjunction with effluent limitations, made it "[i]mminently [sic] stronger than the bill before the other body." [83] He noted, further, that water quality standards would be controlling for any given discharger only "if they are more stringent than the effluent limitations" determined by best available technology. [84] In these representations, he failed to note that technology limits would be postponed until after the National Water Commission study, after which, of course, anything might happen. The only certainty for the foreseeable future would be the continuation of a federal program based on state water quality standards.

In its efforts to make its water quality standards program more defensible, however, the House committee had added provisions that strengthened the 1965 Act in several significant ways. The first, noted above, was to extend the standards, under federal review and approval, to intrastate waters. [85] A second was to require the states to submit a continuing planning process that would coordinate its pollution control efforts. [86] The third, a sleeper that lay low for the next 20 years, was §303(d). [87]

On its face, there was and is nothing remarkable about §303(d). According to the House staff member who drafted it, §303(d) was a conscious response to the perceived failings of the 1965 Act and to the barrage of criticism that state performance and water quality standards regulation were receiving from both the Senate and a strong minority of House members. [88] Representative Harsha, who would carry this end of the debate, knew that it would be a difficult sell to keep a states-only, standards-based approach in the Act; he needed both a rationale and a strategy that would work. [89] The rationale was that water quality standards would clean up waters which remained substandard after the application of technology-based limits. The strategy was (1) to involve both the states and EPA, and (2) to lay out the steps that anyone intending such a cleanup would logically take: identify the polluted waters, prioritize them, identify the maximum pollution loads they could take, and apply them. [90] To an environmentalist involved in the drafting of this section, this process was the key. [91] The 1965 Act had provided neither a mandate nor a blueprint for using standards to clean up polluted waters. Section 303(d) provided both.

The House committee report described §303(d) with care. It recognized and ruled on the difficulties involved; they would not defeat the process:

The Committee heard extensive testimony during the oversight and legislative hearings to the effect that it is extremely difficult to apportion the discharge load from all point sources along a waterway or section of a waterway. However, testimony was also heard from the more experienced States that they already have this capability. *The Committee feels that with appropriate support from the Administrator, the required analysis can be completed by the States in a timely fashion.* [92]

It also recognized the contributions of nonpoint sources; all sources would have to be abated:

Any required more stringent effluent limitations will be set on the basis of that reduction in the quantity and quality of the discharge of pollutants which would be required to make the total discharge load in the receiving waters from municipal and industrial sources consistent with water quality standards. *This should not be interpreted to mean that such more stringent industrial and municipal effluent limitations will, in themselves, bring about a meeting of water quality standards for receiving waters. The Committee clearly recognizes that non-point sources of pollution are a major contributor to water quality problems.* [93]

It, lastly, recognized the need for implementation, through plans that include "effluent limitations and schedules of compliance at least as stringent as any required to meet any applicable water quality standard," [94] including the "total maximum daily load for pollutants in accordance with Section 303(d)." [95]

It may be surprising, at first blush, that §303, and in particular the prescriptive language of §303(d), offspring of the House of Representatives, received no more attention in the House committee report or the House floor debates. The House hearings on H.R. 11896—2,343 pages in length [96]—contain virtually no discussion of, and no disagreement over, the requirements of §303(d). [97] That the process was, nonetheless, intended and deliberate is clear from both the manner of its drafting and its description in the committee report. Perhaps the best explanation for its minimal discussion is that the process was so obvious. Section 303(d) simply made the implicit explicit. It took the states at their word. States *wanted* this responsibility; they could now *take* the lead in cleaning up polluted waters. Here was how.

It would not persuade the Senate. Among the many differences at issue in the conference to reconcile the Senate and House bills, the role of state water quality standards versus technology standards was the crux of the matter. The Senate would not yield on the technology approach, but it would have to make a tradeoff. House §303 with its water quality criteria and standards, total maximum daily loads for polluted waters, and implementation plans would be retained, although relegated to a backup role where technology standards were insufficient to meet water quality goals. [98] House staff saw §303 as providing a "game plan for the next generation." [99] The Senate was less sanguine: in the words of one Senate staff member, "We didn't take it seriously and thought it would be foolish for EPA to waste time and money to implement it." [100] Senator Muskie, principal author of the Senate bill and Chair of its Public Works Committee, was equally direct, telling the EPA Administrator to "assign secondary priority" to §303 when it came to allocation of resources in the years ahead. [101] EPA—and the states, whose program, in essence, this really was—would take this advice to heart.

The Backlash: Congress Stays the Course

The passage of the 1972 Amendments did not end the water quality versus technology standards debate. Over the next few years, two prestigious national commissions would issue reports that reflected, inter alia, the continuing preference of states and the development community for a state-based water quality standards approach.

The Commission Reports

The first such report was produced by the National Water Commission, created by Congress in 1968 and authorized to study a range of water policy issues, including pollution. [102] The seven commissioners had backgrounds in public utilities, agribusiness, and state water management. [103] The commission's conclusions on pollution control were staffed and edited by a separate panel chaired by the Deputy Commissioner of the New York State Department of Conservation with representatives from water departments in California, Ohio, and Pennsylvania. [104] One is where one comes from, and the commission's final report, issued in 1973, reads like a cry of anguish from states and industry against the onset of a federal, technology-based program. Asking itself at the start, "When is water polluted?" the commission answered, in italics that emphasized the strength of its feelings:

> *Water is polluted if it is not of sufficiently high quality to be suitable for the highest uses people wish to make of it at present or in the future.* Such uses should be determined by responsible public authorities. [105]

These responsible authorities were, furthermore, local. [106] The "major advantage" of water quality standards was their "adaptation . . . to a wide variety of local needs and conditions" which should not be "lost through misguided desires for nationwide, or even statewide uniformity." [107] Granted, state water quality programs had been slow in developing, but the administrative machinery and technology for a standards-based program was now in place. State water quality standards were up to snuff, and "scientifically based predictive models" for making water quality impact calculations and relating them to dischargers were both "available" and "rapidly developing." [108] As for enforcement, "recent studies of state and local pollution control programs document[ed] a new resolve to regulate forcefully and comprehensively." [109] The 1972 Amendments made a strategic error in superimposing a federal program; "sound political theory supports the notion that the level of government closest to the problem should deal with it, if competent to do so." [110] Congress should reverse its course and "reaffirm its commitment to the water quality standards approach and economically presentable minimum treatment requirements." [111] Whatever the merits of these conclusions, they constitute a powerful statement from state agencies and the regulated community that pollution control by water quality standards was workable and that states were ready to go forward with the job.

By 1973, of course, the views of the National Water Commission were about two years behind the curve. Congress had opted for technology standards as its lead vehicle. As described above, however, Congress also retained the water quality approach and created yet another commission to study the implementation of the Act and determine if any "mid-course correction" were necessary. [112] The National Commission on Water Quality (1976 Commission) differed from its predecessor in its exclusive focus on water quality, and in its composition: chaired by the Vice President of the United States (and former Governor of New York, Nelson Rockefeller), 10 of its 15 members were also members of Congress, 2 represented industry, and 1 represented a state pollution control agency. [113] Their divergence of views is instructive.

The 1976 Commission had considerable difficulty reaching consensus, [114] and its report contained the separate concurring-in-part and dissenting-in-part views of no fewer than 13 of its 15 members. [115] Of its six principal recommendations, the two bones of contention were whether the Act's goals should be retained and whether its technology standards should go beyond the best practicable technology levels to best available technology (BAT). Overall, the commission recommended a new goal of "conservation and reuse" [116] and a delay in the adoption of BAT standards, [117] over the vigorous dissents of Senator Muskie, Sen. Howard Baker (R-Tenn.), and others [118]; Governor Rockefeller appears to have won his point, if a little late in the day. In a *Letter and Supplemental Views*, S. Ladd Davies of the Arkansas Department of Pollution Control and Ecology, the sole designated state representative on the commission, agreed "generally" with the majority, but then added his own perspective:

> Personal preference, although probably prejudiced and biased, would dictate the use of Water Quality Standards since I am strongly opposed to treatment for treatment sake. In water quality limited waters, water quality standards are the controlling factor, not effluent limitations. Effluent limited waters provide some flexibility in utilizing the waters as a resource for providing assimilative capacity for stabilizing certain waste. [119]

Assuming that Mr. Davies was a fair representative of state views at the time, states continued to view, and were willing to argue for, a return to state water quality standards as the proper basis for the national program.

These recommendations did not persuade Congress. When Congress revisited the Act in 1977, it modified only slightly its approach to technology standards, tightening the controls on toxic discharges and loosening them for conventional ones. [120] Certain conventional-but-toxic pollutants could also qualify for less stringent technology controls, but with a floor at meeting water quality standards in any given waterway. [121] This small concession to water quality impacts was as far as Congress was willing to go. But there was always the possibility of a more friendly administration.

The New Federalism, 1982

The next important movement was not what Congress did but what Congress refused to do, and then threatened to do, in the early 1980s. It was a dramatic showdown between a new administration in Washington, urged forward by state agencies and regulated industry, and a Congress that still remembered the lackluster showing of the FWPCA. At issue was a return to water quality standards.

Under the banner of "New Federalism," [122] in January 1982 the incoming EPA Administrator announced that, while the Clean Water Act was "fundamentally sound" and "without a need for major or extensive revision at this time," the Agency would "suggest changes only in those few areas where obvious statutory problems have emerged." [123] An EPA issues paper outlined what those "few areas" might be by suggesting, inter alia, waivers from treatment requirements for communities that discharge sewage into "major rivers where that discharge is diluted," and waivers for industrial dischargers "where there would be no negative impact on the quality of the receiving waters." [124] More globally, the paper asked, was the "continued development" of effluent guidelines "without respect to receiving water quality the wisest course, or should the Act be changed to allow consideration of receiving water quality?" [125] This was a question that states and industry were ready to hear.

Sensing that such a virtual repeal of the 1972 Act was not in the cards on Capitol Hill, EPA moved at the same time both to return as much of the action to water quality standards as possible, and to relax its requirements for water quality-based decisions. Speaking to an organization of state water pollution agencies, EPA's Assistant Administrator for Water declared that the Administration "strongly supports the water-quality based approach to regulating pollutants." [126] It was time to "reassess the appropriateness of technology-based standards" that "offend one's sense of fair play and stifle the intellectual curiosity that has made this nation the most advanced technological society on earth." [127] As for the standards themselves, they had been hampered by "the nature of federal involvement, the role and technical validity of water quality criteria, inadequate consideration of economic impacts and unrealistic use designations." [128] The answer, an agency official told the Water Management Association of Ohio, was "greater flexibility" for the states. [129] The new EPA was playing to a state audience, and the script would be new water quality regulations.

A January 1982 EPA draft proposed regulations that would provide considerable flexibility indeed. [130] Among the many proposals were those for downgrading existing uses, permitting degradation of water quality within existing uses, eliminating protection for outstanding "natural resource waters," allowing for "site-by-site" rather than statewide water quality criteria, and requiring benefit-cost analyses for the standards themselves. [131] These proposals were enthusiastically endorsed by the Association of State and Interstate Water Pollution Control Administrators (ASIWPCA) providing "a more workable framework" for state regulation on a site-specific basis. [132] In fact, states had played a lead role in developing the proposed revisions and, according to EPA's Assistant Administrator for Water, a subcommittee of the ASIWPCA had "revised five drafts of the regulation and met with EPA on numerous occasions." [133] The ASIWPCA was particularly intent on retaining state authority over nonpoint source pollution, and over water quality monitoring and assessments; state staffs were "knowledgeable about water quality impact assessments" that require a "high degree of technical and professional judgment." [134] The undeclared but obvious predicate to this argument was, once again, that water quality impact assessments and regulation was a drill the states were perfectly capable of executing. This said, the ASIWPCA's Executive Director also cautioned that "there must be continued recognition that fishable/swimmable water quality may not always be attainable due to natural conditions or affordability." [135] Not surprisingly, these positions were endorsed with no less enthusiasm by the Chemical Manufacturers Association ("the standards [would] reflect the realities of site-specific conditions"), [136] Union Carbide, and the American Mining Congress. [137]

Congress was not pleased. Nor was it silent. It summoned EPA officials to a steady grilling on their philosophies and proposals, returning again and again to the weaknesses of state controls. [138] Despite EPA representations that state agencies had been vigorous in cleaning up water pollution and that they now had water quality regulation technology at their fingertips, [139] the Agency's proposals were characterized in House hearings as "dangerous" and "an absolute disaster." [140] In April 1983, five senior members of Congress wrote EPA urging that its proposals be scrapped, [141] and the Senate threatened to codify its own version of water quality regulations. [142] The Agency backed down. By October 1983, EPA was under new management and had written revised regulations that retained stringent requirements for existing uses and water quality. [143] For the moment, the fight was over but the states and the regulated community had showed their hand, insisting once again that state water quality standards were a ballgame they could and should play. There was no mention of the fact that nothing in the Clean Water Act prevented them from playing it right then, to the extent that it would lead to water quality improvements. Or that, in fact, §303(d) required them to do so.

The Water Quality Act of 1987

Undeterred by their reception in Congress to date, states continued to urge modifications to the CWA that would increase their authority and flexibility to regulate based on ambient water quality. In 1985, the ASIWPCA proposed amendments to allow the substitution of "narrative" water quality criteria for numerical criteria, and the elimination of permits for stormwater discharges where they would not "impair designated water uses." [144] Against continuing state and industry complaint, however, Congress would hold the line against degradation and relaxation of the standards themselves. But by 1986, a remarkable consensus was also growing among the states, Congress, environmentalists, and industry over improvements to the CWA. Front and center among them was a return to water quality standards for the regulation of two chronic and unsolved problems of the national pollutant discharge elimination system program: toxic and nonpoint source pollution.

Fifteen years after the FWPCA of 1972, it was clear that BAT controls on limited categories of industries for a limited (if large) number of toxic pollutants was going to be insufficient for waters impacted by multiple dischargers, some technology-limited and some not, and by multiple pollutants, some regulated, some not. [145] News from the states themselves showed toxic pollution to be pandemic, with more than 124,000 stream miles, one-half million acres of lakes, and nearly 1,000 square miles of estuaries showing "acute" toxic problems [146]; information on toxicity in Boston Harbor, Puget Sound, and other high profile water bodies was even more disturbing. [147] Expressing its concern with the "historic ineffectiveness of the water quality approach," [148] the Senate proposed to upgrade technology limitations for toxins and expand the categories of industries to which they applied. [149] In keeping with its historic perspective, the House proposed to upgrade toxic water quality criteria and to address toxic "hot spots" through permit revisions based on water quality standards. [150] The bills converged as they evolved, and by the time the Administrator of EPA, his eyes dutifully focused on their budgetary impact, testified that additional toxic controls were "neither necessary nor desirable," [151] the momentum had passed him by.

The Water Quality Act of 1987 had something for everyone concerned with toxic pollution. [152] One section provided for new rounds of technology standards. [153] Another called for the development of numerical (which all knew meant, enforceable) toxic water quality criteria. [154] The third, of most relevance to this Monograph, §304(*l*), provided a blueprint with a tight, five-year timetable for the accelerated cleanup of toxic hot spots. [155] The blueprint looked familiar: states would (1) identify and list toxic polluted waters, [156] (2) identify each point source of toxic pollutants into these waters and the loadings from each source, [157] and (3) prepare an "individual control strategy" (ICS) achieving toxic standards for each listed water through additional permit limitations. [158] If states did not execute, as in §303(d), EPA would. [159] This was, of course, the same water quality-upgrade process that states were supposed to be performing under §303(d), but that had been shelved in the face of other priorities; the hot spot ICSs were TMDLs, limited to point sources and toxins. Environmentalists supported the bill. [160] The ASIWPCA supported the bill: the technology for water quality was at hand, it said. [161] The pulp and paper industry said likewise. [162] With a cheery enthusiasm perhaps influenced by the fact that the Agency perceived it as a program that, for a change, the *states* were going to have primary responsibility for implementing, EPA's Deputy Assistant Administrator for Water stated that whatever problems were experienced in the past with water quality-based permitting, "we've learned something in the last 20 years." She explained, "[O]ur monitoring technology is much better than it was 20 years ago . . . we've got a lot of information we didn't have 20 years ago." [163] In sum, "the combination of the much better information and the much better permitting and enforcement base means that I think we have a chance we didn't have then." [164]

In fact, §304(*l*) delivered a substantial number of new toxic controls, along with some lessons for §303(d). There was an enormous variation in state responses to the requirements for explicit numerical water quality criteria. Some states responded quickly; others, three years after passage of the amendments, still had no aquatic life criteria for priority pollutants. [165] The criteria adopted showed even greater variety, with permitted concentration levels for certain toxins more than 10,000 times as protective in one state than another. [166] The FWPCA experience of 20 years earlier remained: for dischargers and for the environment, water quality standards regulation would mean a highly uneven playing field.

Instructive and new, however, was the pace and output of the hot spot offense. Under prodding from environmental groups and against resistance from affected industries, EPA put states on aggressive timetables to identify toxic-polluted waters and propose ICSs. [167] Within the two-year statutory deadline, all but one state had submitted lists that, in the aggregate, identified nearly 500 toxic polluted waters (EPA would add 100 more), and more than 750 facilities contributing to their pollution. [168] By July 1994, states had converted 588 ICSs into permit limitations, with another 120 identified as outstanding. [169] As of 1997, the game all but over, more than 675 ICSs had been completed under the toxic hot spot program. [170] No records are available on the quality of these ICSs, or the pollution loadings actually abated under this program. One has to assume, if only by their number and by the vigor with which some dischargers resisted the process, [171] that in at least some cases the reductions were significant. If this conclusion is sound, then the toxic hot spot process provides some evidence that—at least for specific pollutants and for point source dischargers—water quality impact assessments could be made, traced to sources, and abated.

The 1987 Amendments provide no such evidence, yet, for the abatement of nonpoint source pollution. By the mid-1980s it had also become apparent to Congress and everyone else that, as much progress as had been made in abating point source pollution generally, nonpoint sources were outstripping these hard-won (and expensive) gains. [172] Both state and EPA reports identified nonpoint sources (e.g., farm runoff, municipal runoff, clearcuts, and logging roads) as a major—and growing—cause of water pollution nationwide. [173] A 1972 program to address this type of pollution through state and watershed planning under §208 of the CWA had produced volumes of studies and no measurable improvement. [174] In its 1984 Water Quality Inventory, EPA listed several reasons for this lack of progress, among them the diffuse nature of nonpoint sources, difficulties in tracing pollution to sources, and the lack of baseline data on stream conditions. [175] Not mentioned, perhaps out of tact, was the more fundamental political difficulty of dealing with agriculture, silviculture, and municipalities. [176]

With support, again, from both the states and the environmental community and, again, over opposition from the Administration ("[e]xperience argues against a federal responsibility in non-point source control implementation" which involves "site-specific conditions and sensitive land-use issues"), [177] Congress added §309 to the Act to fund and stimulate state nonpoint programs. [178] At first blush, this process, too, looked familiar. States would prepare reports to: (1) identify waters polluted by nonpoint sources, [179] (2) identify nonpoint sources to these waters, [180] (3) identify management practices applicable to these sources, [181] and (4) prepare a management program [182] for EPA approval. [183] Here, however, the similarities to the programs under §§303(d) and 304(*l*) end. The nonpoint management plans could include regulatory or nonregulatory methods such as training, demonstration projects, and financial assistance. [184] There were no standards or performance criteria; no abatement had to happen. [185] There were, further, no consequences if no management planning happened at all. [186] Unlike TMDLs and ICSs, the federal government would not step in. [187] This was the epitome of a voluntary program, and it produced about the same results as its predecessor had in 1972: a volume of studies, a number of voluntary programs, and little noticeable cleanup of nonpoint source pollution. [188]

The relative success of the 1987 Act in addressing toxic pollution through water quality standards, and its failure to come to grips with nonpoint pollution through a similar-looking strategy, carry an important message for the improvement of water quality in the late 1990s and beyond. As user-friendly as voluntary approaches to pollution control are, for pollution control to work something should happen when volunteerism fails. Spurred forward by the need to act because otherwise the federal government would, states adopted toxic water quality criteria and developed control strategies for toxic hot spots in a surprisingly short period of time. Without a similar spur, nonpoint controls—even though separately funded—have languished. On the ground, face to face with a source, pollution control is hard and, without technology-based limitations to support them, nonpoint sources are the hardest of all. This lesson would soon lead to pressure in another quarter: §303(d).

The Argument Continues

And so the CWA moved into the 1990s, its federal technology standards working significant reductions in pollution discharges, its state water quality standards, with a few notable exceptions, a distant and lightly attended second. As the Act came up for reauthorization in 1992 and 1993, the lead vehicle was S. 1114, [189] which provided another, 1987-like menu for strengthening both the technology and water quality programs, and for eliminating the discharge of bioaccumulative toxins altogether. [190] The water quality provisions proposed to upgrade and standardize state water quality criteria and the flow and mixing zones through which these criteria were applied to discharge permits; EPA criteria would be presumed applicable unless a state could show cause for departure. [191] The net effect would have been a more level playing field for water quality-based regulation, but a federal machine would do the leveling.

The states were not pleased. On July 1, 1993, the ASIWPCA testified on S. 1114, largely in opposition, and number one on its agenda were the water quality standards provisions. [192] The bill went "too far[,] interfering with state decision making authority." [193] States needed "flexibility to develop WQS, tailored to meet individual hydrology, geology, topography, ecosystem and climate considerations." [194] A top-down approach "inhibits innovation and thwarts aggressive and/or creative approaches" which would lead to national improvements. [195] This needed flexibility included the substitution of "narrative" criteria (e.g., "no toxics in toxic amounts," "no unreasonable adverse effects on aquatic life") for numerical criteria (e.g., 0.015 milligrams per liter of zinc), relaxation of minimum standards of "fishable/swimmable" for the nations waters, and relaxation of the antidegradation policy. [196] This same flexibility should be provided for nonpoint source programs, and requirements for technology-based, nonpoint controls should be repealed from the Coastal Zone Management Act as well. [197] Water quality management was the state's game; EPA should step out of the way and let them play. [198]

S. 1114 was overtaken by the elections of 1994, and the next proposed amendments to the CWA would look very different indeed. The lead this time came from the House, and H.R. 961 was the Contract With America's first priority for environmental law reform. [199] Industrial dischargers, state agencies, and agricultural interests liked this bill, because they largely wrote it. [200] Echoing a catch-phrase of the 1990s, the U.S. Chamber of Commerce stated that, among its greatest concerns with the CWA was its "departure from sound science" and its "unrealistic" and "rigid" numerical standards. [201] H.R. 961 introduced realism to the Act through a benefit-cost requirement for all water quality criteria and standards. [202] States were encouraged to set their standards based on "economic and social considerations" (not further defined), [203] and to publish a "cost of compliance" analysis of all new criteria [204]; EPA would need to certify that each of its standards "maximizes net benefits to society" (not further defined). [205] Specifically targeting TMDLs, states would be allowed to set their own rates of progress with an end date for load allocations by the year 2016. [206] Nonpoint sources would be addressed through a "Bi-Partisan Initiative" of federal funding for nonregulatory approaches, stretched out over the next 20 years. [207] To the ASIWPCA, testifying largely in favor of H.R. 961, this approach in particular represented a "major breakthrough" in nonpoint source management, giving states "broad flexibility" while retaining their "accountability." [208] More broadly, the states were in the "best position to define the standards and other regulatory controls" needed to achieve the goals of the Act; the states had the "vast majority of the monitoring data, stream surveys and other information" necessary for standards development. [209] The proper federal role was technical support, and more money. [210]

Does the argument ever change? H.R. 961 passed the House, but failed in the Senate and—more dramatically—before the general public. [211] Within a year it had been labeled by some of its own proponents a poster child for how not to pass environmental legislation. But the issues both H.R. 961 and S. 1114 addressed, albeit quite differently, remain. At their heart is where the CWA goes next, beyond a program applying technology limitations to industrial and municipal dischargers. Congress already spoke to this question, as early as 1972. It is, of course, why the House drafted §303(d) and held onto it throughout the conference. Section 303(d) was going to be the program for the "next generation." We are now that generation.

Reflections on Water Quality Standards Legislation and Its Stakeholders

Water quality standards regulation has more than a 25-year history in federal law, and a longer history yet in some state programs. As national attention on water pollution intensified, states resisted federal supervision of their standards in 1965, and then fought a hard battle to retain these standards in the 1972 Amendments, which became the CWA. Water quality-based permitting was the last bastion of state authority in a program that was otherwise going rapidly to EPA. State governors, state agency heads, state water quality engineers, municipal authorities, and their representatives in Congress expressed their confidence—witness by witness, over and over—that states had the technology and the expertise to regulate by water quality standards. They could do this job, if only the federal government would let them.

Industry agreed with this position, although one suspects that industry may have been motivated less by confidence that water quality standards regulation would work as by confidence that it would not. Several administrations agreed, although one suspects they were motivated more by budget considerations, and by relief that this was one less chore for the federal government. Whatever their motives, both industry and federal administrators added their opinions that water quality regulation was something the states could and should be doing.

Congress agreed, barely. It retained state water quality-based regulation, but in a fashion that has gone largely unnoticed in the literature and, until recently, almost equally unnoticed in practice. Congress did *not* simply retain the underperforming water quality program of the 1965 Act. In §303(d), it completely rewrote the program, and in the rewrite spelled out a blueprint for compliance that is as specific in its detail as any other provision of the

Act. While there was no debate on §303(d), the provision was no sleeper to either the House or the Senate. Water quality standards were the House's major issue, and the House report describes the §303(d) process with clarity and at some length. After that recitation, what was there really to debate? If a water quality-based program was going to be retained, this was, and remains, about the only way it could work.

For the next 25 years, states, industry, and various administrations have taken their runs at the CWA, and a consistent theme from these quarters has been the impropriety of "top down" controls, the wastefulness of "treatment for treatment sake," and the need to place more reliance on water quality-based regulation and provide more "flexibility" for state implementation based on the knowledge of local conditions. Whatever the merits of these arguments, they sidestep an important aspect of the CWA, which is its very explicit reservation of state authority to control water pollution more protectively than the federal program. Nothing in federal law prohibits a state from abating any discharge it wants, virtually any way it wants. This being so, and not surprisingly, the state arguments for greater flexibility invariably center on permission to *relax* criteria, use standards, testing, and monitoring requirements. Both implicit and explicit in these state, industry, and, at times, administration arguments are their representations that water quality-based regulatory programs make sense and that the states are well qualified, indeed uniquely qualified, to conduct them. Which brings this discussion to a great disconnect.

For the past 25 years, and more, states and their adherents in and out of Congress have argued for recognition of their ability and authority to regulate based on water quality standards. And for the same 25 years states have had not only the authority under §303 to do so, they have had a rather well-prescribed mandate to do so. They did not do so. By and large, they did not do anything called for under §303(d): (1) they did not submit inventories of polluted waters, (2) they did not prioritize these waters for cleanup, (3) they did not promulgate TMDLs, and (4) they did not incorporate them into point source or nonpoint source discharge controls. They did not do it in the 1970s. They did not do it in the 1980s. They did not do it at the outset of the 1990s, nor did EPA—until a series of citizen suits rocked EPA and the states into a hasty rereading of §303(d) and a scramble to comply.

Notes to Chapter 2

1. The ethical dimensions of these points of view are explored in, inter alia, MICHAEL E. ZIMMERMAN, CONTESTING EARTH'S FUTURE (University of California Press 1994), and sources cited therein. They are seen in the writings of American authors as early as Henry David Thoreau, came to the fore in the rupture between Gifford Pinchot and John Muir over "multiple-use management" of the nation's forests, *see* STEWART L. UDALL, THE QUIET CRISIS 97-125 (1963), and crop up constantly in environmental and administrative law in concepts ranging from standing-to-sue to the designation of wilderness areas. They would be seen again in the sharp division between the House and the Senate as the CWA evolved. *See infra* text accompanying notes 63-98.

2. This description of water quality-based regulation is taken from N. William Hines, *Nor Any Drop to Drink: Public Regulation of Water Quality Part I: State Pollution Control Programs*, 52 IOWA L. REV. 186 (1966) [hereinafter Hines I]. For a full discussion of the theory, *see id.*; *see generally* 2 WILLIAM H. RODGERS JR., ENVIRONMENTAL LAW: AIR & WATER (1986).

3. The failures of water quality-based regulation under the federal Water Quality Act of 1965 have been fully described by Congress, *see infra* note 63; the courts, *see* Weyerhauser Co. v. Costle, 590 F.2d 1011, 9 ELR 20284 (D.C. Cir. 1978); and commentators, *see* RODGERS, *supra* note 2, at 242-52. No step in the process worked: use determinations were highly variable, leaving protective states at a distinct disadvantage, and a race-to-the-bottom; information on those biological conditions necessary to support aquatic life was spotty and insufficient; impact assessment was equally imprecise, and the chore of tracing impacts from multiple-dischargers was overwhelming; and abatement in the face of these uncertainties was ephemeral and rarely achieved. *Id.* For two differing views on the continuing usefulness of water quality-based regulation, *compare* Jeffrey M. Gaba, *Federal Supervision of State Water Quality Standards Under the Clean Water Act*, 36 VAND. L. REV. 1167 (1983) (urging abandonment of the effort as futile), *with* William F. Pedersen Jr., *Turning the Tide on Water Quality*, 15 ECOLOGY L.Q. 69 (1988) (urging greater emphasis on water quality standards).

4. 33 U.S.C. §1313, ELR STAT. FWPCA §303.

5. *Id.* §1313(d), ELR STAT. FWPCA §303(d).

6. *Id.* §1313(d)(1)(A), ELR STAT. FWPCA §303(d)(1)(A).

7. *Id.*

8. *Id.* §1313(d)(1)(C), ELR STAT. FWPCA §303(d)(1)(C).

9. *Id.* §1313(d)(2), ELR STAT. FWPCA §303(d)(2).

10. *Id.* §1313(e), ELR STAT. FWPCA §303(e).

11. *Id.* §1313(e)(3)(A), ELR STAT. FWPCA §303(e)(3)(A).

12. *Id.* §1313(e)(3)(C), ELR STAT. FWPCA §303(e)(3)(C).

13. For comprehensive histories of local, state, and federal efforts toward water pollution control, see Hines I, *supra* note 2; N. William Hines, *Nor Any Drop to Drink: Public Regulation of Water Quality Standards Part III: The Federal Effort*, 52 IOWA L. REV. 799 (1967) [hereinafter Hines III].

14. *See* Water Quality Act, ch. 758, tit. III, §303, 62 Stat. 1155 (1948) (codified as amended in scattered sections of 33 U.S.C.).

15. *Id.*

16. *See Hearings on S. 890 & S. 923 Before a Subcomm. of the Senate on Public Works*, 84th Cong. 45 (1955); *see generally* Hines III, *supra* note 13, at 814, 815.

17. *See Hearings on H.R. 11714 Before the Subcomm. on Rivers and Harbors of the House Comm. on Public Works*, 85th Cong. 14-15 (1958). The National Association of Manufacturers advocated the termination of federal monies and the limitation of federal assistance to research and advice. *Id.*

18. Pub. L. No. 89-234, 79 Stat. 903 (1965) (codified as amended in scattered sections of 33 U.S.C.).

19. *See id.*

20. S. REP. No. 88-649, at 1 (1963). For a discussion of industry criticism, see H.R. REP. No. 86-294, at 6 (1959).

21. S. 4, 89th Cong. (1965); H. CONF. REP. No. 89-1022 (1965).

22. *See supra* note 18.

23. *See id.*

24. *See id.*

25. *See* H.R. 215, 89th Cong. (1965).

26. *See* H.R. 1885, 88th Cong. (1964).

27. The pace and rigor with which the states moved was the subject of some discussion. *See* U.S. SENATE COMM. ON PUBLIC WORKS, 93RD CONG., 2D SESS., A LEGISLATIVE HISTORY OF THE WATER POLLUTION CONTROL ACT AMENDMENTS OF 1972 (1972) [hereinafter A LEGISLATIVE HISTORY OF THE WATER POLLUTION CONTROL ACT AMENDMENTS OF 1972]. By 1972, all states had at least submitted water quality standards for EPA approval. *See* HARVEY LIEBER, FEDERALISM & CLEAN WATERS 13 (1975). In addition, 45 states had instituted some form of permit system for industrial dischargers. *See id.*

28. *Supra* note 18.

29. *See* LIEBER, *supra* note 27, at 14 (quoting Gus Speth, Natural Resources Defense Council (NRDC)).

30. RODGERS, *supra* note 2, at 242 ("The enforcement plans typically were vague directives to a particular source, such as to install secondary treatment or its equivalent, with the details of the obligation a subject of barter between state officials and plant engineers.").

31. Hines I, *supra* note 2, at 230-31.

32. Mar. 3, 1899, c. 425, §13, 30 Stat. 1152 (codified at 33 U.S.C. §407). For a discussion of the sudden appearance of the Refuse Act as a tool for water pollution control, see William H. Rodgers Jr., *Industrial Water Pollution and the Refuse Act: A Second Chance for Water Quality*, 119 U. PA. L. REV. 761 (1971); Oliver A. Houck, *The Water, the Trees, and the Land: The Nearly Forgotten Cases That Changed the American Landscape*, 70 TUL. L. REV. 2279, 2289-91 (1996).

33. Pub. L. No. 92-500, 86 Stat. 816 (codified as amended in scattered sections of 33 U.S.C.).

34. The Senate Public Works Committee held 33 days of public hearings on the 1972 legislation, resulting in 6,400 pages of testimony from 170 attorneys and 470 additional written statements; the senators met in an additional 45 executive sessions to hammer out the Committee's positions. The House Public Works Committee held 38 days of hearings, heard from 294 witnesses, and received 135 additional statements. The House committee report ran to 424 pages, and the House and Senate conferees wrangled for five more months before arriving at the final bill. The process took more than two years. *See* LIEBER, *supra* note 27, at 31-75.

35. A LEGISLATIVE HISTORY OF THE WATER POLLUTION CONTROL ACT AMENDMENTS OF 1972, *supra* note 27.

36. *Water Pollution Control Legislation—1971: Hearings on H.R. 11896, H.R. 11895 Before the Comm. on Public Works*, 92d Cong. 483 (1971) [hereinafter *House Hearings I*] (statement of Nelson A. Rockefeller, Governor of New York).

37. *Id.* at 489.

38. *Water Pollution Control Legislation—1971: Hearings on H.R. 11896, H.R. 11895 Before the Committee on Public Works*, 92d Cong., 1st Sess. 667 (1971) [hereinafter *House Hearings II*] (statement of Nelson A. Rockefeller, Governor of New York).

39. *Id.*

40. *House Hearings I, supra* note 36, at 511 (statement of Arch A. Moore Jr., Governor of West Virginia).

41. *Id.* at 52 (letter of J. James Exon, Governor of Nebraska).

42. *Id.* at 523 (letter of Preston Smith, Governor of Texas).

43. *Id.* at 525 (letter of John A. Burns, Governor of Hawaii).

44. *Id.* at 527 (letter of Jimmy Carter, Governor of Georgia).

45. *Id.* (letter of Cecil D. Andrus, Governor of Idaho).

46. LIEBER, *supra* note 27, at 66.

47. *House Hearings II, supra* note 38, at 512 (listing membership of the Ad Hoc Task Force to the National Governors' Conference).

48. *Id.* at 520.

49. *Id.* at 266 (statement of Kerry Mulligan, Chairman, Water Resources Control Board, state of California; accompanied by James Krieger, Chairman, Water and Power Committee, Los Angeles Chamber of Commerce).

50. *Id.* at 387 (statement of Charles A. Black, President, American Water Works Association).

51. *Id.* at 419 (statement of Henry J. Graeser, Director of the Dallas Water Utilities Department of the city of Dallas, Texas).

52. *Id.* at 995 (statement of Wesley E. Gilbertson, Deputy Secretary for Environmental Protection and Regulation, Department of Environmental Resources, commonwealth of Pennsylvania).

53. *House Hearings I, supra* note 36, at 202-03 (statement of a panel composed of Russell E. Train, Chairman, Council on Environmental Quality, and Paul V. McCracken, Council of Economic Advisors).

54. *Id.* at 213.

55. *Id.* at 205 (letter of Robert V. Thomann, Associate Professor of Civil Engineering, Manhattan College, Bronx, New York).

56. *Id.* at 206-08 (letter of Donald J. O'Connor, Professor of Civil Engineering, Manhattan College, Bronx, New York) (citing models for the Sacramento-San Joaquin Delta, the Delaware River, the Mohawk River, the Houston Ship Canal, and several large metropolitan areas).

57. While it may not be fair to judge an argument by the company it keeps, in this case the industry's arguments in favor of water quality standards were tied so closely to its arguments against federal oversight, citizen suits, and other implementation and enforcement requirements that it is hard not to conclude that industry, like the Senate in 1972, saw water quality standards as minimally enforceable and that it was this viewpoint—rather than considerations of federalism or state expertise—that motivated industry's full court press to retain a state water quality standards-based program. Industry knew water quality standards did not work, and that is exactly why it wanted them. For the position of the U.S. Chamber of Commerce, see generally H.E. Dunkelberger, *Federal-State Relationships in the Adoption of Water Quality Standards Under the Federal Pollution Control Act*, 2 NAT. RESOURCES L. 47 (1969).

58. *House Hearings II, supra* note 38, at 1726 (statement of Reynold C. MacDonald, Chairman, American Iron & Steel Institute).

59. *Id.* at 741 (statement of P.N. Gammelgard, Senior Vice President, Public and Environmental Affairs, American Petroleum Institute). Similar testimony was received from representatives of General Mills, Martin Marietta, the National Association of Manufacturers, and the Weyerhauser Corporation. *Id.* at 1088-33, 1796-812.

60. *House Hearings I, supra* note 36, at 484 (statement of Wendell R. Anderson, Governor of Minnesota). Governor Anderson told Congress:

> I think the greatest problem that the Governor has and members of the State legislature have is this, that any time you try to pass a tough piece of legislation in the area of the environment, that obviously could not only cost the taxpayers some money, but clearly it makes it difficult for industry to compete and the argument that we hear so often is on the part of the business community, that it will be very, very difficult to do business in Minnesota if we have these tough environmental standards because all the other States are not doing the same thing, so the only thing they need do is move to another State. They won't have to incur that expense, and they will be able to compete more easily. So it seems to me that what is absolutely necessary in my judgment is for the Congress to establish uniform standards of pollution control in all 50 states.

Id.

61. *House Hearings II, supra* note 38, at 698 (statement of Weldon Barton, Assistant Director of Legislative Services, National Farmers' Union).

62. *Id.* at 273 (question of Mr. Jones during testimony by James Krieger, Chairman Water and Power Committee, Los Angeles Chamber of Commerce).

63. S. REP. NO. 92-414 (1972), *reprinted in* 1972 U.S.C.C.A.N. 3668. This said, the committee was careful to preface its report as intending "no criticism" of the state's performance, and as seeking "to restore the balance of federal-state efforts in the program as stipulated by the 1965 and 1966 Acts." S. CONF. REP. No. 92-1236 (1971). It is difficult to swallow either statement without a tall glass of water.

64. *See* S. REP. NO. 92-414.

65. LIEBER, *supra* note 27, at 41.

66. *Id.* at 31.

67. *Id.* at 35-39.

68. S. 2770, 92d Cong. (1971).

69. LIEBER, *supra* note 27, at 39-40. A Senate member and Senator Muskie's legislative assistant at the time recall that the senator had lost faith both in the science necessary to link pollution sources to impacts and in the states' willingness to do it. Telephone Conversation with Leon Billings (Mar. 31, 1997).

70. Telephone Conversation with David Zwick, Clean Water Fund (Apr. 21, 1997). Mr. Zwick lobbied actively on behalf of the environmental community throughout the 1971-1972 reauthorization process. *See* LIEBER, *supra* note 27, at 14-16, 37, 54, 66, 88, 91. He recalls enlisting the support of Sen. John Tunney (D-Cal.) for the introduction of an amendment to keep water quality standards in the Senate bill. The Tunney Amendment was adopted in June 1971. For a discussion of Senator Tunney's proposals, see LIEBER, *supra* note 27, at 44, 51. According to Mr. Zwick, environmentalists were well aware that the amendment "lacked teeth"; it would, however, provide the opportunity for something stronger in the House.

71. S. 2770, §304.

72. *Id.* §302.

73. *Id.* These more stringent limitations were qualified, however, by required consideration of economic and social impacts. *Id.*

74. LIEBER, *supra* note 27, at 60. House efforts were thrown into disarray by the heart attack suffered by this committee chair.

75. *Id.* at 59-60. For an example of the pressure applied by the National Association of Manufacturers, see 118 CONG. REC. 10788 (1972).

76. LIEBER, *supra* note 27, at 60.

77. *See* LIEBER, *supra* note 27, at 59 (quoting Jamie Heard, *Environment Report: Water Pollution Proposals to Test Blatnik's Strength as Public Works Chairman*, 3 NAT'L J. 1719 (1971)).

78. LIEBER, *supra* note 27, at 61.

79. Heard, *supra* note 77.

80. LIEBER, *supra* note 27, at 578.

81. *Id.* at 727.

82. *Id.* at 549. This statement was made in relationship to an amendment authorizing states to regulate more stringently than federal standards.

83. *Id.* at 675.

84. A LEGISLATIVE HISTORY OF THE WATER POLLUTION CONTROL ACT AMENDMENTS OF 1972, *supra* note 27, at 245-46.

85. H.R. 11896, 92d Cong. §303(b) (1972).

86. H.R. 911, 92d Cong. §303(e) (1972).

87. *Id.* §303(d).

88. Telephone Conversation with Gordon Wood (Mar. 28, 1997). Mr. Wood was Minority Professional Staff Assistant to the House Committee on Public Works, and primarily responsible for drafting §303 of the House bill. Committee Counsel Lester Edelman recalls Mr. Wood standing at a blackboard before the committee, briefing members on the workings of this provision. Telephone Conversation with Lester Edelman (Mar. 27, 1997). Lending support to these recollections is the fact that H.R. 11846, as introduced in the House in November 1971, contained no §303(d) language. *See* H.R. 11896, 92d Cong. (Nov. 19, 1971). The section first appears in the bill reported out by the committee and voted on by the House in March 1972. *See* H.R. 11896, 92d Cong. §303(d) (Mar. 11, 1972). This is to say, §303(d) happened in committee.

89. Telephone Conversation with Gordon Wood, *supra* note 88.

90. *See supra* text accompanying notes 6 8.

91. Telephone Conversation with David Zwick, *supra* note 70. Both Mr. Wood and Mr. Zwick recall collaborating on the drafting of §303(d). *See also* Telephone Conversation with Gordon Wood, *supra* note 88. The previous year, Mr. Zwick had

published a book on the implementation of the Federal Water Pollution Control Act of 1965, identifying its shortcomings in the application of water quality standards and in their enforcement. DAVID ZWICK, WATER WASTELAND (1971). The objective was to remedy those problems.

92. H. REP. NO. 92-911, at 105 (1972) (emphasis added).

93. *Id.* (emphasis added). It is unclear from this statement alone whether the committee envisaged that the TMDLs include nonpoint sources. On the one hand, the first sentence quoted refers only to emissions limitations for municipal and industrial dischargers; they would have to be "consistent" with water quality standards, for which a reasonable paraphrase would be "not contribute to the violation" of water quality standards. *Cf* Arkansas v. Oklahoma, 503 U.S. 91, 22 ELR 20552 (1992) (states may not contribute to the violation of water quality standards of neighboring states). It is logical that the committee report describes only municipal and industrial sources as needing additional "emissions limitations" because these are the only sources directly subject to emissions limitations under the Act. The committee goes on to recognize, however, that water quality standards were also violated by nonpoint sources in a "major" way. This sentence implies the obvious: there is no way to determine the appropriate contributions from, and limitations on, municipal and industrial point sources without considering these nonpoint sources as well. How a state would choose to allocate its limits among point and nonpoint source contributors would, at least in the first instance, be up to states to decide. But the only logical interpretation of this legislative history behind §303(d) is that nonpoint sources were a big fact of life in achieving water quality standards, and they would have to be included in the assessments of polluted waters and their TMDL allocations. Were they not included, a process to ensure that municipal and industrial limits were "consistent with water quality standards" would make no sense; it, literally, could not be done.

94. H. REP. NO. 92-911, at 108.

95. *Id.* It further noted the importance of developing TMDLs for waters not yet polluted, for future permitting. *Id.* at 106; *see* 33 U.S.C. §1313(d)(3), ELR STAT. FWPCA §303(d)(3). These TMDLs have yet to materialize in fact or in litigation.

96. *See* H. REP. NO. 92-911, at 69 (report of the House Committee on Public Works).

97. The only direct reference found by this author was the remarks of Representative Harsha outlining the bill in its entirety and explaining the intent of §303 to upgrade polluted waters: "HR 11896 requires that if the application of 'best applicable control technology available' is not sufficient to meet water quality standards, further and more stringent controls must be imposed." A LEGISLATIVE HISTORY OF THE WATER POLLUTION CONTROL ACT AMENDMENTS OF 1972, *supra* note 27, at 246.

98. H.R. CONF. REP. NO. 92-1465 (1972). Incongruously, and indicative of the cut-and-paste nature of this compromise, the conference committee also retained the similar-sounding §302, allowing EPA to upgrade point source discharge per-

mits to meet with quality standards. *See supra* note 73 and accompanying text. EPA has yet to invoke its authority under this section. *See* RODGERS, *supra* note 2, at 285-88.

99. Telephone Conversation with Gordon Wood, *supra* note 88.

100. LIEBER, *supra* note 27, at 78. Another Senate staff member at the time recently stated: "there is no one more surprised than I am" by the recent renaissance of §303, given his view of the provision at the time. Telephone Conversation with Leon Billings, *supra* note 69.

101. A LEGISLATIVE HISTORY OF THE WATER POLLUTION CONTROL ACT AMENDMENTS OF 1972, *supra* note 27, at 171.

102. National Water Commission Act, Pub. L. No. 90-515, 82 Stat. 868 (1968). The commission issued a final report, *Water Policies for the Future* (June 1973), and a summary of its conclusions and recommendations, *New Directions in U.S. Water Policy* (June 1973).

103. The commission board included the Chairman and CEO of Consolidated Edison Company; the President of Independent Distributors (a wholesale farm equipment distribution firm) and former Oregon Secretary of State; an attorney and past President of the Municipal League of Seattle and King County, Washington; a consultant to the Arizona Public Service Company and President of the Central Arizona Water Conservation District; a professor of hydraulic engineering; an attorney and past member of the Missouri House of Representatives; and an attorney and Counsel to the Texas Water Quality Board. *New Directions in U.S. Water Policy*, *supra* note 102, at 109, 110.

104. The Panel on Water Pollution Control was composed of the Deputy Commissioner of the New York State Department of Environmental Conservation; a consultant to the Ohio River Valley Sanitation Commission; the Director of the Water Resources Research Institute at North Carolina State University; the Director of the Pennsylvania Bureau of Sanitary Engineering; the Chief Engineer and General Manager of the Sanitation Districts of Los Angeles, California; a professor of entomology at the University of Minnesota; and two attorneys. *Water Policies for the Future*, *supra* note 102, at 559.

105. *Id.* at 70.

106. *Id.* at 86, 91. With some inconsistency, however, the commission recommended federal standards for toxic dischargers. *Id.* at 91.

107. *Id.* at 91.

108. *Id.* at 85-86.

109. *Id.* at 86.

110. *Id.*

111. *Id.* at 88.

112. 33 U.S.C. §1325, ELR STAT. FWPCA §315. The commission's charge was to "make a full and complete investigation of all of the technological[,]. . . economic,

social, and environmental effects of achieving or not achieving" the best available technology (BAT) limitations and goals of the 1972 Act. *Id.*

113. *See* NATIONAL COMMISSION ON WATER QUALITY, COMMISSION MEMBERS, REPORT TO THE CONGRESS iv (Mar. 18, 1976). The commission was composed of five members approved by the Senate, five by the House, and five by the Administration. 33 U.S.C. §1315(b), ELR STAT. FWPCA §305(b). This composition virtually guaranteed a rehash of the arguments of 1971 and 1972.

114. "The members of the Commission have unanimously voted to submit the attached report with the understanding that the members have not necessarily endorsed every detail of the report . . . ." NATIONAL COMMISSION ON WATER QUALITY, *supra* note 113, at 2.

115. *See id., Commission Comments*, at v.

116. *Id.* at 29.

117. *Id.* at 29.

118. *Id.* at 18, 19, 124; *id.* at 43-44 (Senator Muskie), 65-66 (Senator Randolph), 69-74 (Senator Baker).

119. *Id.* at 62-63.

120. Federal Water Pollution Control Act, Pub. L. No. 95-217, 91 Stat. 1566. For a discussion of these amendments, see Oliver A. Houck, *The Regulation of Toxic Substances Under the Clean Water Act*, 21 ELR 10528, 10534-35 (1991); RODGERS, *supra* note 2, at 411-21.

121. Pub. L. No. 95-217, §43, 91 Stat. 1566 (adding §301(g), BAT waiver for conventional pollution, but not beyond water quality standards).

122. *"New Federalism," Water Act Goals Do Not Mix, House Panel Tells Hernandez*, [12 Current Developments] Env't Rep. (BNA) 1363 (Feb. 26, 1982).

123. *Gorsuch Outlines Water Act Issues in January 19 Letter to Members of Congress*, [12 Current Developments] Env't Rep. (BNA) 1211 (Jan. 22, 1982).

124. *Id.*

125. *Id.*

126. *Eidsness Says Administration Favors Water Quality-Based Pollutant Controls*, [13 Current Developments] Env't Rep. (BNA) 805 (Oct. 15, 1982).

127. *Id.*

128. *Id.*

129. *Hernandez Says EPA Seeks to Return Management of Water Programs to States*, [13 Current Developments] Env't Rep. (BNA) 850 (Oct. 22, 1982).

130. *Revisions to Water Quality Rule Moving Through EPA Review Process*, [12 Current Developments] Env't Rep. (BNA) 1391 (Mar. 5, 1982).

131. *Id.*

132. *Proposed Water Quality Standards Changes Subject of 11 Public Meetings, EPA Announces*, [13 Current Developments] Env't Rep. (BNA) 915 (Nov. 5, 1982).

133. Testimony of Eric Eidsness, EPA Assistant Administrator for Water, Before the Subcomm. of Water Resources of the Comm. on Public Works and Transportation, House of Representatives 124 (1983). It should be noted, however, that not all states supported the revisions. *See California Officials Attack Proposal by EPA to Revamp Water Quality Rules*, [13 Current Developments] Env't Rep. (BNA) 1445 (Dec. 24, 1982) (the revisions "will make it harder for them to mention the state's strong water quality protection"); *Changes to Standard-Setting for Water Would Hamper States, EPA Officials Told*, [13 Current Developments] Env't Rep. (BNA) 1616 (Jan. 21, 1983) (Assistant Director of New Jersey's EPA testifying that the revisions would make state standards "indefensible and perhaps unenforceable.").

134. *Revised Procedures for Water Standards, Local Pretreatment Option Backed by ASIWPCA*, [14 Current Developments] Env't Rep. (BNA) 811 (Sept. 9, 1983).

135. *Proposed Water Quality Standards Changes Subject of 11 Public Meetings, EPA Announces, supra* note 132, at 915.

136. *Proposed Water Quality Standards Changes Praised, Criticized at EPA Public Meetings*, [13 Current Developments] Env't Rep. (BNA) 1667 (Jan. 28, 1983).

137. *Id.*

138. *See "New Federalism," Water Act Goals Do Not Mix, House Panel Tells Hernandez, supra* note 122; *No "Mid Course Corrections" Needed in Clean Water Act, Chafee Tells EPA*, [13 Current Developments] Env't Rep. (BNA) 397 (July 23, 1982).

139. *Id.*

140. *"New Federalism," Water Act Goals Do Not Mix, House Panel Tells Hernandez, supra* note 122.

141. *Five in Congress Urge EPA to Scrap Proposed Water Quality Standard Charges*, [13 Current Developments] Env't Rep. (BNA) 2182 (Apr. 1, 1983).

142. *Id.* The congressional letter explained that withdrawing the proposal "might also avoid the need to consider corrective legislation." *Id.*

143. *Final Water Quality Rule by EPA Endorsed by Four Key Senators*, [14 Current Developments] Env't Rep. (BNA) 1246 (Nov. 4, 1983).

144. *Mattingly Offers Amendments to Water Act to Ease Cost, Management Burdens for States*, [15 Current Developments] Env't Rep. (BNA) 2120 (Apr. 5, 1985).

145. SENATE COMM. ON ENVIRONMENT AND PUBLIC WORKS, 100TH CONG., 2D SESS., A LEGISLATIVE HISTORY OF THE WATER QUALITY ACT OF 1987 1323 (1987) [hereinafter 1987 ACT LEGISLATIVE HISTORY] (remarks of Sen. Stafford).

146. *Id.; see also The Clean Water Act Amendments of 1987*, [18 Current Developments] Env't Rep. (BNA), Special Rep., 39 (Sept. 4, 1987) [hereinafter Special Report].

147. *See* Special Report, *supra* note 146, at 42-43.

148. *See* 1987 ACT LEGISLATIVE HISTORY, *supra* note 145, at 1422.

149. S. 1128, 99th Cong. (1985); 131 CONG. REC. S8030 (daily ed. June 20, 1986); *see also* Special Report, *supra* 146, at 181-82.

150. *See* Special Report, *supra* 146, at 182-83.

151. *Id.* at 27-28.

152. Pub. L. No. 100-4, 102 Stat. 1018. For a discussion of these provisions, see Houck, *supra* note 120, at 10550-59. The hot spots were to be identified within two years, and abated within three more years.

153. 33 U.S.C. §1314(m), ELR STAT. FWPCA §304(m).

154. *Id.* §1313(c)(2)(B), ELR STAT. FWPCA §303(c)(2)(B).

155. *Id.* §1314(*l*), ELR STAT. FWPCA §304(*l*).

156. *Id.* The listing process was in fact a little more complex; within two years, states were to submit three lists to EPA, a "long" list of waters not meeting water quality standards, *id.* §1314(*l*)(1)(A)(ii), ELR STAT. FWPCA §304(*l*)(1)(A)(ii); a "medium" list of waters polluted by toxins, *id.* §1314(*l*)(1)(A)(i), ELR STAT. FWPCA §304(*l*)(1)(A)(i); and a "short" list of waters polluted by toxins from past sources, *id.* §1314(*l*)(1)(B), ELR STAT. FWPCA §304(*l*)(1)(B).

157. *Id.* §1314(*l*)(1)(C), ELR STAT. FWPCA §304(*l*)(1)(C).

158. *Id.* §1314(*l*)(1)(D), ELR STAT. FWPCA §304(*l*)(1)(D).

159. *Id.* §1314(*l*)(3), ELR STAT. FWPCA §304(*l*)(3).

160. *See* Special Report, *supra* note 146, at 31 (citing an NRDC attorney).

161. *Id.*; *see also* Statement of the Association of State and Infrastructure Water Pollution Control Administrators Before the Subcomm. on Environmental Protection of the Senate Comm. on Environment and Public Works, 98th Cong., 1st Sess. 418 (Apr. 1983) ("since 1972, the states have gained more than ten years experience in water quality management"; "state water quality programs have blossomed reaching substantial levels of sophistication and effectiveness.").

162. *See Hearings Before the Subcomm. on Water Resources of the House Comm. on Public Works and Transportation*, 99th Cong. 285 (1985) (statement of Rodney C. Glover, Procter & Gamble Corporation) ("states now have a greatly expanded database and more experience.").

163. *See* Special Report, *supra* note 146, at 4 (quoting EPA Deputy Assistant Administrator for Water Rebecca Hanner).

164. *Id.*

165. Three years after the 1987 Amendments, 45 states and territories had at least "some" freshwater aquatic life criteria for toxics. *See* Houck, *supra* note 120, at 10543.

166. *Id.* at 10544.

167. *Id.* at 10547-48.

168. *Id.* at 10548.

169. *See* EPA, ICS STATUS REPORT (July 1994) (a compilation of all implemented and outstanding ICSs).

170. Telephone Conversation with Deborah Clovis, Office of Wastewater Management, EPA (Jan. 31, 1997).

171. For reference on industry opposition and litigation opposing ICS requirements, particularly that of the pulp and paper industry, see Houck, *supra* note 120, at 10548.

172. The Senate Environment and Public Works Committee concluded that "nonpoint source pollution control could no longer be ignored." As point sources are bought under control, nonpoint source pollution looms as a larger problem. The evidence of nonpoint pollution continues to grow. It has been estimated that 50% of all water pollution comes from nonpoint sources. *Report of the Senate Committee on Environment and Public Works, Clean Water Act Amendments of 1985, 99th Cong., 1st Sess., in* 1987 ACT LEGISLATIVE HISTORY, *supra* note 145, vol. 2, at 1428-29.

173. EPA's 1984 water quality inventory reports that, of 47 states surveyed, 24 have identified nonpoint source pollution as a "major source of water degradation." Special Report, *supra* note 146, at 40. A 1985 ASIWPCA survey showed 11% of the nation's rivers, 30% of its lakes, and 17% of its estuaries affected by nonpoint source pollution. *Id.*

174. 33 U.S.C. §1288, ELR STAT. FWPCA §208. For discussions of §208 and its performance, see RODGERS, *supra* note 2, at 319-30; FREDERICK R. ANDERSON ET AL., ENVIRONMENTAL PROTECTION LAW AND POLICY 384-86 (1990).

175. *See* Special Report, *supra* note 146, at 40-41.

176. *See* ANDERSON ET AL., *supra* note 174, at 385, and sources cited therein. These politics have gotten no easier. *See* David Zaring, *Agriculture, Nonpoint Source Pollution, and Regulatory Control: The Clean Water Act's Bleak Present and Future*, 20 HARV. ENVTL. L. REV. 515 (1996).

177. Special Report, *supra* note 146, at 27.

178. 33 U.S.C. §1319, ELR STAT. FWPCA §309.

179. *Id.* §1319(a)(1)(A), ELR STAT. FWPCA §309(a)(1)(A).

180. *Id.* §1319(a)(1)(B), ELR STAT. FWPCA §309(a)(1)(B).

181. *Id.* §1319(a)(1)(C), ELR STAT. FWPCA §309(a)(1)(C).

182. *Id.* §1319(a)(1)(D), (b), ELR STAT. FWPCA §309(a)(1)(D), (b).

183. *Id.* §1319(d), ELR STAT. FWPCA §309(d).

184. *Id.* §1319(b)(2)(B), ELR STAT. FWPCA §309(b)(2)(B).

185. Senate leaders expressed their concern for the lack of regulatory standards, and considered §319 to be only a first step in tackling the problem. 1987 ACT LEGISLATIVE HISTORY, *supra* note 145, at 619 (remarks of Sen. Stafford).

186. Upon receipt of a state program, EPA may approve or disapprove the program. 33 U.S.C. §1329(d)(2), ELR STAT. FWPCA §319(d)(2). If it disapproves, however, no consequences follow other than the possible loss of eligibility for nonpoint source grant funding. *Id.* §1329(h), ELR STAT. FWPCA §319(h). EPA's Assistant Administrator for Water recognized the risks of this approach in 1987, but expressed optimism that the states were up to the job; although EPA lacked authority to mandate specific approaches and would require only that states submit their proposed control plans to EPA for approval, he predicted that "this approach can succeed now because state water pollution control programs are far more developed than they were when the Water Act was enacted in 1972." *Jensen Predicts Early Loan Guidance, Cites EPA Shift to Water Quality Standards,* [17 Current Developments] Env't Rep. (BNA) 2002 (Mar. 27, 1987).

187. If a state fails to submit a nonpoint source report, EPA would undertake the first two steps only: to identify nonpoint polluted waters and to identify nonpoint sources to these waters. 33 U.S.C. §1329(d)(3), ELR STAT. FWPCA §319(d)(3). No further planning requirement follows.

188. *See* Zaring, *supra* note 176. The author concludes, "Unfortunately, Section 319 has failed to reduce nonpoint source pollution. Its failings can be characterized as not enough carrot, not enough stick, and too much of the same planning imperatives that had characterized Section 208." *Id.* at 526; *see also* ROBERT W. ADLER ET AL., THE CLEAN WATER ACT TWENTY YEARS LATER 241 (1993) ("Implementation of [§]319 has failed to stem the flow of polluted runoff; the majority of state programs are ineffective and unfocused.").

189. S. 1114, 103d Cong. (1993).

190. *Id.* §203 (toxic pollution phaseout).

191. *Id.* §202 (water quality criteria and standards).

192. *See* Testimony of the Association of State and Interstate Water Pollution Control Administrators (ASIWPCA) Before the Senate Subcomm. on Clean Water, Fisheries, and Wildlife (July 1, 1993) [hereinafter July 1993 ASIWPCA Testimony] (remarks by Bruce Baker, Director, Water Resources Management, Wisconsin Department of Natural Resources).

193. *Id.* at 3.

194. *See* Testimony of the Association of State and Interstate Water Pollution Control Administrators (ASIWPCA), Before the House of Representatives Transportation and Infrastructure Subcomm. on Water Resources and the Environment 4 (Feb. 9, 1995) [hereinafter February 1995 ASIWPCA Testimony] (remarks by Bruce J. Baker et al.).

195. July 1993 ASIWPCA Testimony, *supra* note 192, at 2.

196. *Id.* at 3, 4.

197. *See Clean Water Act Reauthorization Priorities*, February 1995 ASIWPCA Testimony, *supra* note 194, at 14, 15 (entitled *The States' Perspective on Non-point Sources (NPS)*). The Coastal Zone Management Act requires states to develop technology-based management measures for nonpoint source control in coastal areas. 16 U.S.C. §1455b(g)(2), (5), ELR Stat. CZMA §306(g)(2), (5).

198. July 1993 ASIWPCA Testimony, *supra* note 192, at 2.

199. H.R. 961, 104th Cong. (1995).

200. *See* Claudia Copeland, *Clean Water: Summary of H.R. 961* (Cong. Res. Service Apr. 11, 1995); Gary Lee, *House Transportation Panel Coalition Proposes Scaling Back of Clean Water Act*, Wash. Post, Mar. 23, 1995, at A11.

201. *Hearings Before the Subcomm. on Water Resources and the Environment, House Comm. on Transportation and Infrastructure*, 104th Cong. 221 (1995) (testimony of Carol Bennet Lindsey for the U.S. Chamber of Commerce).

202. H.R. 961 §303(a)(3) (requiring a "reasonable relationship" between costs and benefits).

203. *Id.* §303(c)(2)(A)(iv).

204. *Id.* §303(a)(12).

205. *Id.* §324(a)(1)(B).

206. *Id.* §306.

207. *Id.* §319(b)(2)(B).

208. *See Hearings of the Subcomm. on Water Resources and the Environment, House of Representatives Comm. on Transportation and Infrastructure*, 104th Cong. 86 (1996) (testimony of the ASIWPCA).

209. *Id.* at 80.

210. *Id.* at 80, 84.

211. *See Issue: Clean Water Act*, 1966 Cong. Q. News 3147 ("The wave of criticism that followed House passage of [H.R. 961] pushed Republican lawmakers to reassess their efforts to revise environmental laws and helped drown HR 961 in the process.").

Chapter 3:
The Implementation of §303

Section 303(d): The Avoidance Years

Following the passage of the FWPCA Amendments of 1972, [1] EPA was fully occupied, indeed overwhelmed, in promulgating technology standards for point sources under the CWA and defending them in court. [2] The Agency had little inclination, and indeed saw little reason, to implement the "safety net" features of §303(d) before the technology requirements were in place. After all, water quality upgrading was only required when polluted waters could not be brought up to standard through best available technology requirements. And these requirements were many years away.

EPA, further, had its hands full trying to establish a floor for state water quality standards that would at least preserve the potential for §303(d) upgrading in the future. The Agency struggled with resisting states over policies requiring that existing water quality be protected, [3] that achievable water quality be met as well, [4] that standards be set for *all* state waters, [5] that existing water uses be maintained, [6] that uses such as "waste transport" be rejected, [7] that the standards of downstream states be respected, [8] and that state criteria for the uses chosen be based on at least arguably sound science. [9] What even these rather threshold efforts for a national program based on state water quality standards showed is that, although the states were to retain "primary responsibilities" for water pollution control under the Act, [10] EPA was going to have to play a major role in keeping it honest. If states could cut a corner, many would. As for moving forward to identify polluted water bodies and establishing load limits on their own initiative, there is no evidence in the decade following the 1972 Amendments that the states were going to take this bull by the horns.

EPA took §303(d) by the horns very gently. The section's obligations were to be triggered by EPA's formal identification of pollutants appropriate for water quality analysis and TMDLs. [11] Once these pollutants were identified, the drill began: states had 180 days to submit their lists of water quality limited segments (WQLSs), priorities for cleanup, and TMDLs. [12] In October 1973, rather promptly considering its many duties under the new Act, EPA published a proposed notice of a two-volume set of pollutants appropriate for the §303(d) process. [13] Then, nothing happened. The identification languished. Lawsuits in the late 1970s attempted to challenge the absence of TMDLs on the Colorado River [14] and on waters in South Dakota [15] and failed for want of the predicate: EPA hadn't started the clock.

Instead, EPA opted to fold the TMDL process into its, in retrospect, overly ambitious regulations [16] for basin planning under §§106, 208, and 303(e). [17] Basin plans encompassing all industrial, municipal, and nonpoint source controls would also establish, inter alia, TMDLs and discharge load allocations. [18] "Substantial failure" of any plan to conform to §303(e) (requiring a state "continuing planning process" that included TMDLs) might "indicate" that the process was deficient, leading to disapproval of the process and ineligibility for state delegated programs. [19] These alarming-sounding sanctions notwithstanding, the basin planning menu attempted too much in the same sitting and would fall of its own weight in the years ahead.

EPA's occupation with basin planning was pushed forward by a court order in 1975, requiring a more comprehensive and accelerated approach to the planning process. [20] The Agency's subsequent regulations provided a three-year schedule for the approval of all state plans, and more guidance on the implementation of §303(d). [21] For each water quality segment, TMDLs would include "a total allocation for point sources" and a "gross allotment for nonpoint sources," the combined total of which would not exceed the TMDL. [22] Each load allocation would incorporate an "allowance for anticipated economic and population growth over at least a five-year period," and an "additional allowance reflecting the precision and validity of the method" used in calculating these loadings. [23]

Without EPA's identification of pollutants that would trigger TMDL planning, however, these requirements remained rhetorical. In 1978, with EPA still struggling to make basin planning work, the Agency was brought up short by another court order requiring it to publish a final identification of TMDL pollutants. [24] Regrettably, from EPA's perspective, the §303(d) process would now be set in motion. In the notice of its required regulations, the Agency explained that it did not consider such finalization of the pollutant list "a matter of high priority" because many of the "practical results" of TMDLs were already being accomplished through basin planning [25]; right or wrong, this perspective persists to the present day. There may have been another reason for EPA's reluctance as well. The EPA Assistant Administrator for Water had been a close aide to Sen. Edmund Muskie during his years of combat against water quality-based regulation and for the adoption of new technology standards [26]; one gets a strong sense from EPA's new regulations that this was a game its water program administrators did not see as worth playing. They would "provide a phased approach" to establishing TMDLs "consistent with the intent of Congress" (whatever intent Congress may have had other than the explicit language of §303(d) itself), in order to "ensure" that "current State water quality management programs will not be disrupted." [27] In not disrupting state programs, they would certainly succeed.

EPA's regulations delayed, soft-pedaled, and understated the §303(d) requirements to a remarkable degree. Seizing on the statutory language that the states' "first submissions" of polluted waters and TMDLs were due in 180 days, EPA asked states to identify "one or more" water quality-limited stream segments, and one or more TMDLs, in those first six months. [28] Priority rankings for listed state waters would await future state/EPA agreements. [29] Nonpoint source contributions would not need to be considered in setting these priorities since "the relative significance of point and nonpoint sources will in some cases not be determined until TMDLs are developed," [30] whatever that might mean. Lest even these minimal obligations seem harsh, EPA further stipulated that the "results of past or ongoing efforts" could be submitted for approval. [31] In short, one TMDL submission would suffice. When the second one was due was anyone's guess, as was what would constitute a TMDL. The stage was set for inaction.

Inaction occurred. A few states submitted a few lists. Most states submitted nothing at all. The question became: what now? EPA's answer, based on a literal reading of the Act, was: nothing. [32] Section 303(d) required only that the Agency approve or disapprove state submissions. If the states submitted something unacceptably minimal, EPA could correct the problem with its own lists and TMDLs. But if the states submitted nothing at all, there was this unfortunate disconnect: there was nothing the Agency could do.

The Constructive Submission Theory: Avoidance Might Not Work

By the early 1980s, then, the next round of citizen suits under §303(d) had to establish EPA's duty to act. It was not an easy road. In *Scott v. City of Hammond*, [33] an Illinois district court found that, although neither Indiana nor Illinois had submitted TMDLs for Lake Michigan, EPA had no power either to require the state to do so or to promulgate its own. At which point, §303(d) was a thoroughly dead letter.

On appeal, however, the Seventh Circuit reversed, [34] reasoning that the "prolonged failure" of a state to submit anything could amount to a "constructive submission" to EPA of no TMDLs, triggering EPA's duty to act. [35] In so holding, the court relied on the apparent expectation of Congress that the §303 process would actually take place to rebut EPA's insistence that Congress had nowhere given it explicit authority to intervene: "We think it unlikely that an important aspect of the federal scheme of water pollution control could be frustrated by the refusal of the states to act." [36] Under these circumstances, EPA's inaction was "tantamount to approval of state decisions that TMDL's are unneeded." [37] Remanding for the district court to decide whether in this case the states had in fact "determined not to submit TMDLs," the court made clear that this decision was not to be based on a state's motive but, rather, on whether there were sound reasons justifying the states' failure, and "persuasive evidence" that they would be moving quickly. [38] If not, EPA was going to be forced, over its obvious reluctance, off of the sidelines and into the game.

For the remainder of the 1980s, EPA treated *Scott* as an aberration and stayed with its (non)game plan. So long as the states did nothing, it could do nothing too. In 1985, the Agency consolidated its water quality management program regulations in the form that they appear today. [39] The regulations continued their emphasis on basin planning and presented the §303(d) process as a related, but separate, drill [40]—a drill, however, without a deadline. The states would submit water quality-limited segments and TMDLs, per the statute, "from time to time"; the actual schedules for these submissions would be worked out between EPA regional administrators and the states. [41] If there is any lesson to be learned across the spectrum of environmental law, it is that drills without deadlines are not performed. Its regulations written, EPA walked back off the field. It would not be able to stay on the sideline for long.

To EPA's dismay, *Scott* did not go away. The constructive submission theory took hold. A follow-up suit in Oregon, *Northwest Environmental Defense Center v. Thomas*, [42] led to a consent decree in 1987 with a timetable for federal action if Oregon did not make its, by then several years overdue, submissions of impaired waters. Starting in 1991, a series of Alaska cases [43] took the next step of requiring EPA to promulgate TMDLs for state waters, noting that no TMDLs had been submitted, nor even "attempted," nor even "promised" to be attempted. [44] The district court found EPA's "reassurances" that it had discretionary authority to act "not particularly comforting" in light of the fact that EPA had "failed to take action on this matter for over ten years" [45]; nor was the court persuaded by testimony on "EPA's other worthwhile water quality programs," or its plea for the ability to "respond to future environmental crisis by shifting available resources away from other tasks." [46] As for judicial deference to agency interpretations of law, the only interpretation EPA had shown with regard to the CWA's TMDL requirements "has been to ignore them." [47]

The message was coming home that state failure to act would bring in EPA, however reluctantly. These cases begged the question, however, of whether whatever a state might submit would suffice to forestall federal intervention. The next round of rulings seemed to indicate that virtually any state action got EPA off the hook. Following the remand in *Scott*, the states of Illinois, Indiana, and Michigan submitted rather surprising determinations that TMDLs were unnecessary for Lake Michigan; Wisconsin was a little more responsive, identifying four lake sectors for the development of wasteload allocations. EPA approved the submissions and was then challenged in *National Wildlife Federation v. Adamkus*. [48] The Federation claimed that these minimal submissions constituted, in effect, a submission of no TMDLs, triggering EPA's duty to promulgate the load allocations on its own. In 1991, the Illinois district court rejected the argument, [49] finding that since the states had submitted something and EPA had approved it, the statute was fulfilled.

In 1993, a district court in Minnesota made a similar ruling on EPA's approval of that state's progress on TMDLs in a case that previews what a grinding process full TMDL development nationwide is going to be. In 1987, Minnesota had submitted a list of five WQLSs, one of which carried a TMDL. In 1992, the state raised its list to seven river segments and scheduled TMDL development for them over the following 10 years. Citizens brought suit in *Sierra Club v. Browner*, [50] noting that Minnesota's semiannual report to EPA listed 1,116 waters as not meeting state standards, an assessment that included less than one-twentieth of the state's water bodies. [51] Clearly, in the Sierra Club's view, more WQLSs and TMDLs were called for. EPA responded by publishing its own list of 447 water quality-limited segments for Minnesota and went on to approve 43 state national pollutant discharge elimination system (NPDES) permits conditioned on wasteload allocations as TMDLs. [52] On these facts, the court could not find that there had been a constructive submission of no WQLSs or TMDLs. [53] The Sierra Club was forced to argue that the TMDL schedule was too slow, and that the permits, without nonpoint allocations, were not TMDLs at all, arguments this court was not ready to accept. [54] At trail's end for the constructive submission theory, EPA could be required to persuade the states to act or to act itself. If states did something, however, albeit minimal and on whatever schedule, they just might escape further review.

Slow Motion

In 1989, the U.S. General Accounting Office (GAO) issued a report on TMDLs entitled *More EPA Action Needed to Improve the Quality of*

Heavily Polluted Waters. [55] It was not a pretty picture. EPA Region X, the EPA office examined in depth, had received and approved only one TMDL for the 602 listed WQLSs in that region. [56] Region II had approved 4 of 168. [57] Alaska and other states had told the GAO with more candor than caution that they had no particular plans to set TMDLs, and regarded the process as a waste of time. [58] As for EPA's efforts, the report's section headings included such indictments as "EPA Action on TMDLs Was Compelled by Lawsuits," [59] "EPA Has No Way of Assessing TMDL Implementation Nationwide," [60] "EPA's Current Systems Do Not Measure TMDL Compliance," [61] and "TMDLs Not Integrated Into Reporting Requirements." [62] The report concluded that EPA had no program for TMDLs, no schedule for implementation, and no way even of knowing what was going on. [63]

One would think that this level of criticism would prompt a national response. It did not. Region X, stung most directly by the GAO analysis and by the Oregon litigation which had now spread to the state of Washington as well, began to make noises advancing the cause of TMDLs. In a series of small articles, the Region's Chief of Water Planning met the issue with remarkable optimism and candor. [64] TMDLs were "one of the most powerful, but also one of the most under-utilized" tools of the CWA, he said. [65] They were also, to many, one of the "most frightening" because of their reach to nonpoint sources of pollution. [66] Actually, TMDLs were a "very simple and surprisingly logical problem solving process." [67] Shortage of information on water quality impacts? Congress said that "ignorance is no excuse for inaction. Just add a margin of safety to compensate for the lack of knowledge and keep moving." [68] Lack of controls over nonpoint sources? A TMDL was still useful to "force managers to define both the actual amount of pollution reduction needed and the actions necessary" to achieve it, ensuring "more effective NPS [nonpoint source] programs"; indeed, "there may actually be many more control options available than are first apparent." [69]

Whatever Region X was saying, however, EPA headquarters had yet to catch the wave. [70] It was not until April 1991 that EPA began publishing guidelines for state implementation of §303(d), [71] and October 1992 that it finally set a deadline for the submission of state WQLS lists. [72] EPA's biennial reports to Congress, meanwhile, continued to paint nationwide progress on water quality improvement in glowing terms—and to say nothing, not even by way of reference, on the process or progress of TMDLs. [73] On the ground, the Agency was committing itself to the less potentially confrontational tasks of distributing grant money for state nonpoint programs and promoting consensus-based "watershed planning." [74] Section 303(d) with its more objective and enforceable requirements remained, at the federal level, a voluntary program, one more thing the states might also do. It remained that way until a third wave of lawsuits jolted the Agency back onto the field.

The Roof Falls In

The most recent litigation would challenge the quality of the state submissions under §303(d), and the adequacy of EPA's response. It would revive the question of whether "anything" as a TMDL would do. Suits filed in several venues from New York to the state of Washington began to close in, but the first to reach judgment were from Idaho and Georgia. From EPA's perspective, the roof fell in.

Idaho Sportsmen's Coalition v. Browner [75] began with the simple request that EPA develop WQLSs for a state that had submitted none until 1989, and then, in 1992, a grand total of 36. [76] On a "constructive submission" theory, this submission may have sufficed but the court went on to find EPA's approval to be arbitrary and contrary to law. [77] Under court order, EPA ultimately approved a list identifying 962 Idaho WQLSs, [78] a quantum leap in the identification of polluted waters that should shake the confidence of those reporting steady progress in the condition of the nation's waters. Phase two of the case led to another order, in 1994, that EPA proceed, in cooperation with Idaho, to develop a schedule for the development of TMDLs. [79] Phase three, in 1996, challenged the adequacy of that schedule. [80] In its 1996 decision, the court minced few words. Under the schedule offered by EPA and the state, TMDLs would not be completed for another 25 years, if then. [81] The proposed schedule set no deadlines, only "expected" dates and "targets," and assumed that the actual need for TMDLs was going to be far less than the 962 WQLSs, a conclusion to be borne out by post hoc evaluations. [82] At Idaho's proposed rate, the court noted, "the twenty-five years could easily turn into fifty or seventy-five"; "nothing in law could justify so glacial a pace." [83] The court remanded the decision to the Agency, with the "suggestion" that a completion date of five years would be "reasonable." [84]

Before EPA could even begin to eliminate this precedent on appeal, it received the same verdict, and more, in Georgia. *Sierra Club v. Hankinson* [85] challenged everything about the Georgia program from the identification of WQLSs, to water quality monitoring, to the prioritization of state waters for TMDLs, to the number, adequacy, and pace of development for the TMDLs themselves. [86] The state had, in fact, made its first submission of 123 WQLSs in 1992, augmented by the time of trial to 340 waters. [87] For these waters, the state had submitted two TMDLs, was working on two more, and was projecting a total of 28 over the next 10 years. [88] On cross-motions for summary judgment in March 1996, the court found itself unable to determine whether the WQLS list was adequate, setting it down for the unsettling prospect of trial on the merits. [89] The TMDL schedule, however, was found insufficient. [90] At Georgia's proposed pace, the court noted, it would take over 100 years to prepare TMDLs for only the waters currently on the list. [91] The few TMDLs underway, furthermore, were inadequate on their face as not considering load allocations from nonpoint sources or water conditions at other than lowest flows. [92] EPA went on to settle the WQLS issue with a new schedule agreeable to plaintiffs. [93] Then the second shoe dropped.

On August 30, 1996, the *Hankinson* court issued its order on TMDLs, requiring—where the *Idaho* court had only suggested—their completion within five years on a prescribed schedule, basin by basin. [94] CWA NPDES permits would be revised or terminated within one year following each new TMDL, and permits for new discharges into designated WQLSs would be accompanied by TMDLs to achieve water quality standards. [95] Should the state fail to comply, EPA would revise the state's delegated NPDES program to require it. [96] If the state further refused, EPA would "withdraw certification of the State NPDES program." [97] The court, finally, would retain jurisdiction over the case and would receive a detailed report on Georgia's TMDL progress, annually. [98]

EPA appealed the Georgia decision, but it could no longer afford to ignore the game. Lawsuits were pending in more than a dozen states and notice letters of intent to sue from citizen groups in a half dozen more. [99] In early 1996, EPA called for final 1996 state WQLS lists by April 1 of that year. [100] In February, the EPA Assistant Administrator for Water wrote directly to state environmental agency heads stating that TMDLs were a "critical step" and urging them to "support the TMDL program." [101] The response was not enthusiastic. By July 26, nearly four months past deadline, 34 states had not yet submitted final WQLS lists and 17 had submitted no lists at all. [102] EPA moved the deadline to October, [103] then to December. [104] EPA regional administrators were instructed to expedite their approval or disapproval of the state submissions and, where necessary, to begin preparing their own. [105]

When the dust had settled, by early 1997, all states and territories but three were in with something called a list. [106] How adequate they were, what kinds of TMDLs would follow, and in what time frame remained an open question. But at last, 25 years after the passage of §303(d), the TMDL process had actually begun.

EPA Takes the Lead

Up to this point, EPA's response to §303(d) was basically driven by lawsuits, court orders, and consent decrees. During the late fall of 1996, as the latest rulings from Georgia and Idaho were coming in, EPA's §303(d) program director was heard to wish out loud: "If only we could just win one of these cases!" [107] To which the author asked why he would want to win: What else would move the Agency or the states to do TMDLs? The question was rhetorical, but the challenge to EPA at the start of 1997 was—having put on a full-court press to obtain state WQLS lists and blunt the most immediate thrust of litigation—whether it could get ahead of the curve and map an agenda for the implementation of §303(d) that would begin to meet the statute's requirements and put some distance between itself and the courts.

To its credit—and overlooking the lateness of the hour—EPA launched several initiatives of its own, the most proactive of which were new policy guidance for its regions and the states, and a Federal Advisory Committee Act (FACA) committee. The thrust of the guidance was to try to move the process forward, ahead of the pursuing litigation. The thrust of the FACA committee was to try to achieve consensus among the states, and environmental groups, and potentially affected point and nonpoint source dischargers, over where and how the program would go. Each set a new tone for the debate.

In November 1996, impelled by a meeting with environmental litigants, EPA issued a draft *TMDL Program Implementation Strategy* [108] updating its 1991 guidelines and explaining the "vision, priorities and steps" it would take to "help States meet" TMDL program requirements [109]; if at all possible, this would remain a state game. EPA's "vision" continued to emphasize "watershed approaches," [110] but for which it now recognized TMDLs were the "technical backbone" [111]; this would remain nominally a watershed game as well, but §303(d)'s required load allocations were now the driver. The *Strategy* offered to ease state burdens by extending the frequency of reporting requirements, [112] consolidating report categories, [113] and providing more assistance on monitoring and assessments and protocols for the calculation of TMDLs. [114] EPA also offered a TMDL SWAT team to provide quick assistance on TMDL development, [115] and identified financial assistance available both from EPA sources and the programs of other agencies. [116]

This said, the *Strategy* noted but left largely unresolved several thorny policy issues of TMDL implementation, among which were the eligibility of waters for listing, the degree of certainty required for TMDL calculations, the pace for TMDL development, and "reasonable assurances" [117] that abatement strategies, particularly for nonpoint sources, would actually take place. [118] The document would answer few of these questions and raise few hackles. The tough ones would be deferred to subsequent guidance and to a committee the Agency was, at the same time, in the process of convening.

Also in November 1996, EPA appointed an advisory committee of 20 individuals with near-balanced representation of states, user groups, and the environmental community. [119] The stated purpose of the committee was to "provide consensus recommendations" on virtually every aspect of the

TMDL program. [120] To arrive at this consensus, "constructive and substantive discussion" was called for among the stakeholders. [121] Many of the issues were technical, and susceptible to relatively smooth resolution; others were more fundamental, and would take more time. Key among these were the scope of eligible waters, scientific uncertainty, implementation, and nonpoint sources.

Eligible Waters

Section 303(d) requires TMDLs for all waters for which effluent limitations are not sufficient to meet water quality standards. [122] EPA's regulations require states to prepare TMDLs for all waters that are not "expected" to meet water quality standards, [123] a criterion more in the eye of the beholder. [124] Under this guidance, some states have decided that below-standard waters did not need TMDLs because "other kinds of activities" were "planned or underway" to restore them. [125] To these states, this approach represented a reasonable allocation of resources. To environmentalists, it represented an end run around the load allocations of §303. On its face, the statute does not provide the grace of exempting below-standard waters because of the expected effects of other abatement programs, or, for that matter, the expected effects of TMDLs. Like so many jurisdictional questions in environmental law—e.g., whether an area is a "wetland," whether a species is "endangered," whether a toxin is listed for public disclosure—the scope of a program goes a long way to determining its success. What remains unlisted, remains largely unremedied.

Scientific Uncertainty

The Achilles' heel of water quality standards-based regulation has always been the difficulty of ascribing and quantifying environmental effects for particular discharge sources. There is always another possible source, or another possible reason, that the fish in Lake Pontchartrain are dying. There is always an arguable threshold level for pollutants that may not harm fish, or for oxygen levels below 5 milligrams per liter. And when we come to more complex biological impacts such as the fate and effects of nutrients, [126] particularly those effects hundreds of miles downstream, we are beyond any pretense of precise mathematics for cause and effect decisions. The question is whether we are also, for these same reasons, beyond the reach of law.

We should not be. Section 303(d) itself speaks directly to the issue in requiring a margin of safety in its TMDLs in order to accommodate the uncertainty of its underlying science. [127] Other major provisions of the CWA—and the Clean Air Act (CAA), hazardous waste laws, and wildlife and endangered species laws as well—require similar, "best guess" judgments when we are at the far edge of science and decisions need to be made. [128] Reviewing courts have been generally quite tolerant of the mix of science and best guesswork that composes most risk-based environmental decisions. [129] "Good science"—a catch phrase of the 1990s—does not mean precision; it means the best science can do at the time.

This said, legal challenges will arise over the degree of science necessary to support load calculations and their allocations to particular sources. [130] As these challenges mount, it will be important first to distinguish between the allocations and the calculations themselves. Allocation of loadings to particular sources in the TMDL process is entirely political, as it is in the analogous state implementation plan process of the CAA [131]; the mix of reductions from point and nonpoint sources a state may choose to meet its ambient standards is a matter for the state to legislate, negotiate, or otherwise determine. [132] As for the underlying calculations, it is reasonable that they be rationally derived from the best available data; it is unrealistic to require more. Indeed, it would be fatal.

Courts may understand. In one significant challenge to TMDL calculations, involving dioxin loadings on the Lower Columbia River, EPA's numbers were upheld over a variety of objections to the methods by which they were derived. [133] If the courts continue to respect the limits of science and its role in TMDL decisionmaking, as Congress did, and as the Lower Columbia court did, the process will move forward toward its abatement goals. If, on the other hand, courts begin to require the hypertechnical, isolated, cause-and-effect kinds of proof that are emerging from cases in hazardous waste regulation [134] and toxic torts, [135] TMDLs will never get off the ground. Science, in this area of the law, will never deliver precision.

Implementation

Implementation is of course where all public laws live or die, and environmental laws have, over time, accreted layers of overlapping responsibilities and enforcement mechanisms to ensure that, at day's end, something at least remotely like what Congress intended has happened. Section 303(d) muddies the issue because Congress plainly intended for states to implement the program and for EPA to backstop it only where the states failed to do their jobs. Two implementation issues arise. The first is the time frame within which TMDLs are to be established. The second is the mechanism by which they are to be carried out. Unfortunately, for these are critical issues to the success of the program, the language of the statute is not very helpful.

With regard to the time frame, §303(d) provides only that states shall submit their WQLSs and TMDLs to EPA "from time to time," [136] with the first submission due within six months of EPA's identification of the applicable pollutants, or June 26, 1979. [137] It is obvious that Congress presumed a certain amount of good-faith effort here, a presumption that was not entirely borne out in EPA's regulations that called for one state submission and little more, [138] or in state performance. As it turned out, this dilatory pace prompted courts to begin to impose their own deadlines, as short as five years for TMDLs on all of a state's listed waters. [139] EPA then proposed policy guidance that would require the submission of all TMDLs, from all states, within 8 to 13 years. [140] Whether even this pace can be maintained, and whether it will produce load allocations and plans of sufficient quality to be effective, are legitimate and difficult questions. Within them lie several issues of assessment and monitoring technology and of the accommodation of uncertainty. These issues pale, however, before the root question of this issue: do the resulting load allocations have to be implemented at all?

Once WQLSs and TMDLs are prepared, the language of §303(d) ends. Section 303(e) proceeds to require a "continuing planning process" (CPP) with "plans" that "include" §303(d)'s TMDLs. [141] While these sections authorize EPA to approve or disapprove a CPP on the basis, inter alia, of TMDLs, they do not authorize the Agency to implement them. The question is, at this point, has the statute run its string? Does all the work of TMDLs and their load allocations wind up as references in state plans, implemented if and as the states may wish? Or does the TMDL itself have to include the means of its own implementation in order to receive EPA's approval? EPA's authority to review and reject TMDLs [142] may succeed in securing the inclusion of those steps and commitments necessary to implement them, retaining some meaningful outcome for the process. Further, if these measures are inadequate, EPA may reject a TMDL and may then promulgate measures of its own in a federal TMDL. [143] But then what? For point sources, the Agency may ensure that those additional limitations imposed by a TMDL are actually implemented through its supervision of discharge permits under the NPDES program. [144] But for nonpoint sources, here is the rub: there are no federal controls over nonpoint sources under the CWA. [145] For these sources, the §303(d) program leads, ultimately, to a state prerogative. [146] If, as will next be discussed, it is found to cover point sources at all.

Nonpoint Sources

The big enchilada. As earlier described in Chapter 2, [147] nonpoint source pollution has become the dominant water quality problem in the United States, dwarfing all other sources by volume and, in conventional contaminants, by far the leading cause of nonattainment for rivers, lakes, and estuaries alike. It is no secret to any observer of the CWA that the primary reason for this mushrooming problem is the fact that while other sources have been abated through required controls and their enforcement, no comparable controls or enforcement have been applied to agriculture, silviculture, and the rest of the nonpoint world. [148] Enter, now, TMDLs, with the potential for specific, quantified load allocations (i.e., reductions) from nonpoint sources. The nonpoint world quakes. And reacts.

From the outset of the FACA committee, agricultural interests made their view clear that §303(d) does not apply to nonpoint sources. [149] In their reading of the Act, TMDLs are to be set after the exhaustion of emission limitations, and since emission limitations are only set for point sources, TMDLs are restricted to point sources as well. [150] Chapter 2 described the genesis of §303(d) and its language and concluded that, while the section is entirely silent as to whether it applies to only point, only to nonpoint, or to both point and nonpoint sources, the members of the House Public Works Committee, where this section was born, were well aware that nonpoint sources contributed significantly to the failure to attain water quality standards, and that the most logical reading of the process they arrived at is to read nonpoint sources as included. [151] Indeed, in both the context of that time and the present, TMDLs for point sources alone make no pollution control sense at all.

This reading of the statute is bolstered by the fact that EPA has given the statute the same reading, consistently, from the issuance of its first regulations. As early as 1975, the Agency was calling for the allocation of nonpoint source loadings within TMDLs. [152] It has continued to do so in its regulations, guidelines, and draft strategy through 1996, 20 years of consistent agency interpretation. [153] Under the U.S. Supreme Court's ruling in *Chevron, U.S.A., Inc. v. Natural Resources Defense Council*, [154] and since, [155] on deference to an agency's interpretation of its statutory mandates, this regulatory history should be dispositive. Within the FACA committee, however, EPA has recognized the existence of the opposing view. [156] The opposing view, indeed, has taken the counter-offensive.

On April 29, 1997, the U.S. Forest Service wrote EPA to protest, and reject, the application of §303(d) to nonpoint sources. [157] The section "was written with point sources in mind," it said, and EPA's approach "may not satisfy the requirements of the Act." [158] Getting to the point, the Forest Service wrote that EPA was "exposing all Federal and State agencies to additional litigation" over nonpoint source controls. [159] So much was, in fact, true; siltation from forest roads and washouts from clearcuts had eliminated trout and salmon from more than one mountain river [160] and, in the spring of 1997, wiped out quite a few human habitations as well. [161] The Forest Service, as many states, believed in the application of management practices without specific limits on pollutants. [162] As support for this argument, the Forest Service pointed to §319 [163] of the CWA, adopted in 1987 specifically to address nonpoint sources of pollution. [164] Section 319, it wrote, was and should be the exclusive remedy. [165]

The argument is essentially political. As a legal argument, it is thin. In enacting §303(d), Congress, at best, said nothing about whether nonpoint sources were in or out, and would have had to have been insane to, on the one hand, spell out the TMDL process, and on the other, exclude those nonpoint sources it recognized at the time were so much the cause of the problem. [166] In enacting the 1987 Amendments with §319, Congress likewise said nothing about TMDLs, pro or con, and whether nonpoint sources were included or excluded. [167] EPA's TMDL regulations including nonpoint sources had, by that time, been on the books for 11 years. The notion that Congress repealed a federal program without referring to it by enacting another is novel to environmental law. This argument has been considered and rejected with regard to a quite similar claim that §303(d)'s application to toxic dischargers was preempted by Congress' subsequent enactment, also in the 1987 Amendments, of a separate water quality-based program for toxins. [168] In fact, Congress has, year after year, thrown program after program into the breach against specific environmental problems, often overlapping or duplicative programs, often without thinking through how the new and the old would mesh. [169] As of 1997, for example, it had enacted no fewer than six different strategies under the CWA to abate toxic pollution. [170] All remain viable. There is rarely only one way in environmental law.

In practice, §§303(d) and 319's approaches to nonpoint source pollution are compatible and, indeed, mutually supportive. Within the statutory scheme, §319 is the carrot, funding state programs for nonpoint source abatement statewide, for all waters whether they are currently above standard or below. [171] In keeping with its broad sweep, §319's provisions are voluntary. States may choose to participate or not; participating states may choose regulatory approaches or not. [172] Section 303(d), on the other hand, addresses a narrower and more nasty job: the chronically polluted waters of the United States. For this problem zone, enter a stick: quantified pollution load allocations. The nature of the allocations and of the implementing controls remain up to the states, but states do have to come up with them. The CWA is, after all, about restoring the nation's waters. In this context, the existence of both §§303 and 319 makes sense. Or at least as much sense as the multiple programs of the CWA, the CAA, and similar pollution control laws often do.

Nonetheless, given the stakes at issue and the vehemence with which the U.S. Department of Agriculture and its nonpoint source constituents will fight quantified abatement requirements, this question is far from resolved. To say nothing of what a constituency-oriented Congress may do. At this juncture, the only safe observation from the scale of nonpoint source pollution and its effect on achieving water quality standards is that, unless TMDLs include quantified restrictions on nonpoint sources, they are worth no one's time.

But Will Anybody Follow?

The CWA is an experiment in cooperative federalism. No such experiments are easy. Section 303(d) is a holdover from an earlier day of state supremacy, with a veneer of federal supervision and control. The Congress that enacted §303(d) was equally suspicious both of state enthusiasm for the hard work of pollution control and of the water quality standards method of regulation. But it was willing to give them a shot.

The effort, over more than a decade, to bring the states' responsibilities under §303(d) into play should be a little sobering to those who champion the devolution of environmental responsibilities away from federal mandates. The states have been all in favor of the responsibility for regulating water pollution through their water quality standards, right up to the point that they had to do it. When it became time to prepare TMDLs for these waters, all of a sudden this method of regulation was, according to many states, too complex and unwieldy. Load calculations could not be made for even the most common pollutants. Load allocations could not be made for nonpoint sources. We just could not get there from here.

These difficulties surfacing—once again—in water quality standards-based regulation should also throw new light on the relative effectiveness of technology-based standards. In recent years, it has become increasingly fashionable to criticize technology-based regulation as dictatorial, innovation-stifling, wasteful, and excessive. When one, now, begins to appreciate the full scale of the water quality-based alternative—perhaps 50,000 WQLSs eligible for TMDLs at an estimated $1 million per study[173] and an order of magnitude times that amount more for implementation, with no assurance of real pollution load reductions at the far end—technology standards may begin to look like quite a bargain.

There is yet one more lesson in this story. The same effort, over more than a decade, to make the program Congress envisioned in §303(d) happen should also be informative to those who seek to alter the role of citizen groups in the implementation of the CWA and other laws. So long as EPA's responsibilities were viewed as discretionary and unreviewable, virtually nothing happened. Few WQLSs. Fewer TMDLs. On this provision of law that was vital, indeed pivotal, to the enactment of the statute as we know it today—the very passage of the 1972 Act hinged on it—Congress had in effect wasted its time. The litigation that began to effectuate §303(d) was no grand conspiracy of the environmental movement. The plaintiffs in *Scott*, the Alaska cases, and *Northwest Environmental Defense Center* were unrelated and indeed unaware of each other. But in their individual and entrepreneurial fashion, they put the law to work. The genius of American public environmental law—and the reason American laws work where the similar and often stronger-looking laws of other countries do not—is brought home again by this experience. We have a three-part government, and the American public can go to court.

But at bottom, the courts can only go so far. Indeed, under §303(d), EPA can only go so far. At some point, through leverage, funding and hard negotiation, the states are going to have to buy into the program. That was the next task for EPA.

Notes to Chapter 3

1. Pub. L. No. 92-500, 86 Stat. 816 (codified as amended in scattered sections of 33 U.S.C.).

2. For a description of this task and its surrounding litigation, see Oliver A. Houck, *The Regulation of Toxic Pollutants Under the Clean Water Act*, 21 ELR 10528, 10537-39 (Sept. 1991), and sources cited therein.

3. Jeffrey M. Gaba, *Federal Supervision of State Water Quality Standards Under the Clean Water Act*, 36 VAND. L. REV. 1167, 1189 (1983) (discussing EPA's antidegradation policy). EPA's current water quality standards policies are codified at 40 C.F.R. §§131.10, .11, and .12 (1996).

4. Gaba, *supra* note 3, at 1194-95.

5. *Id.* at 1194.

6. *Id.* at 1190.

7. 2 WILLIAM H. RODGERS JR., ENVIRONMENTAL LAW: AIR & WATER 289 n.3 (1986).

8. William F. Pedersen Jr., *Turning the Tide on Water Quality*, 15 ECOLOGY L.Q. 69, 99, 102 n.155 (1988).

9. Gaba, *supra* note 3, at 1210 (citing Mississippi Comm'n on Natural Resources v. Costle, 625 F.2d 1269, 10 ELR 20931 (5th Cir. 1980)).

10. 33 U.S.C. §1251(b), ELR STAT. FWPCA §101(b).

11. *Id.* §1313(d)(2), ELR STAT. FWPCA §303(d)(2). EPA's identification of pollutants was to be done pursuant to §304(a)(2)(D). *Id.* §1314(a)(2)(D), ELR STAT. FWPCA §304(a)(2)(D).

12. *Id.* §1313(d)(2), ELR STAT. FWPCA §303(d)(2).

13. 38 Fed. Reg. 29646 (Oct. 26, 1973).

14. Environmental Defense Fund v. Costle, 657 F.2d 275, 294-95, 11 ELR 20459, 20469-70 (D.C. Cir. 1981) (EPA did not identify salinity as a pollutant until December 28, 1978, and thus the states' duty to submit TMDL calculations did not arise until June 28, 1979; The Environmental Defense Fund's (EDF's) claim was premature since EPA did not have the occasion to approve or disapprove the state TMDL submissions before the EDF filed its motion for summary judgment.).

15. Homestake Mining Co. v. EPA, 477 F. Supp. 1279, 1288 (D.S.D. 1979) (EPA had not identified the pollutants at the time of the Cheyenne River Basin Plan's adoption; although South Dakota had not established TMDLs as required by §303(d), the court held that they were not yet required until 180 days after EPA's identification of pollutants.).

16. Preparation of Water Quality Management Basin Plans, 39 Fed. Reg. 19634 (June 3, 1974) (codified at 40 C.F.R. §130) (1996).

17. 33 U.S.C. §1256, ELR STAT. FWPCA §106; *id.* §1288, ELR STAT. FWPCA §208; *id.* §1313(e), ELR STAT. FWPCA §303(e).

18. Determination of Total Maximum Daily Loads, 39 Fed. Reg. 19641 (June 3, 1974) (codified at 40 C.F.R. §131.304(a)).

19. Prohibition of Approval of Certain Planning Processes; Withdrawal of Process Approval, 39 Fed. Reg. 19639 (June 3, 1974).

20. Natural Resources Defense Council v. Train, 396 F. Supp. 1386, 1392-93, 5 ELR 20405, 20407 (D.D.C. 1975).

21. Preparation of Water Quality Management Plans, 40 Fed. Reg. 55344 (Nov. 28, 1975) (codified at 40 C.F.R. §131(1)).

22. Plan Content, 40 Fed. Reg. 55346 (Nov. 28, 1975) (codified at 40 C.F.R. §131.11(f)(3)(ii)).

23. Plan Content, *supra* note 22, at 40 C.F.R. §131.11(g)(3).

24. Board of County Comm'rs v. Costle, No. 78-0572, slip op. (D.D.C. June 20, 1978) (cited in Total Maximum Daily Loads Under Clean Water Act, 43 Fed. Reg. 42303 (Sept. 20, 1978)).

25. Total Maximum Daily Loads Under Clean Water Act, 43 Fed. Reg. 42303.

26. Mr. Thomas Jorling was Minority Counsel to the Senate Committee on Public Works and, subsequently, EPA Assistant Administrator for Water Waste Management, 1977-1979.

27. Total Maximum Daily Loads Under the Clean Water Act, 43 Fed. Reg. 60664 (Dec. 28, 1978) [hereinafter Total Maximum Daily Loads]. What EPA may have intended by its allusion to congressional intent was the expectation that technology standards take priority over water quality standards in the implementation of the 1972 Amendments. *See* Oliver A. Houck, *TMDLs: The Resurrection of Water Quality Standards-Based Regulation Under the Clean Water Act,* 27 ELR 10329, 10337-38 (July 1997), and the referenced comments of Senator Muskie.

28. Total Maximum Daily Loads, *supra* note 27, at 60666.

29. *Id.*

30. *Id.*

31. *Id.* at 60662.

32. Scott v. City of Hammond, 530 F. Supp. 288 (N.D. Ill. 1981), *aff'd in part, rev'd in part,* 741 F.2d 992, 14 ELR 20631 (7th Cir. 1984). EPA argued that Congress did not intend that EPA establish TMDLs if the states chose not to act. To support its position, EPA pointed out several instances where the CWA explicitly requires EPA to intercede in the absence of state action; thus, by negative implication, congressional intent was to rely exclusively on the states to set the TMDL machinery in motion because under §303(d) there is no explicit CWA requirement for EPA to act in the absence of state action. The argument leads to the anomalous conclusion that

EPA intervention is called for in response to *inadequate* state performance, but not in response to *no* state performance.

33. 530 F. Supp. at 290.

34. 741 F.2d 992, 14 ELR 20631.

35. *Id.* at 996, 14 ELR at 20632.

36. *Id.* at 997, 14 ELR at 20633.

37. *Id.* at 998, 14 ELR at 20634.

38. *Id.* at 997 n.11, 14 ELR at 20633 n.11.

39. Water Quality Standards Regulation, 48 Fed. Reg. 51400 (Nov. 8, 1983) (codified at 40 C.F.R. §§35, 120, 131).

40. *Id.* at 51404.

41. State Review and Revision of Water Quality Standards, 48 Fed. Reg. 51400, 51407 (Nov. 8, 1983) (codified at 40 C.F.R. §131.20).

42. No. 86-1578PA (D. Or. complaint filed Dec. 12, 1986); *see also* Northwest Envtl. Defense Ctr. v. Thomas, No. 86-1578 BU (D. Or. consent decree filed June 3, 1987).

43. Alaska Ctr. for the Env't v. Reilly, 762 F. Supp. 1422, 21 ELR 21305 (W.D. Wash. 1991); Alaska Ctr. for the Env't v. Reilly, 796 F. Supp. 1374, 22 ELR 21204 (W.D. Wash. 1992), *aff'd sub nom.* Alaska Ctr. for the Env't v. Browner, 20 F.3d 981, 24 ELR 20702 (9th Cir. 1994).

44. 762 F. Supp. at 1425, 21 ELR at 21306.

45. *Id.* at 1428, 21 ELR at 21307.

46. 796 F. Supp. at 1379, 22 ELR at 21206 (citing Affidavit of Robert Burd at 7, Ex. 3, Defendants' Opposition to Plaintiffs' Motion to Compel).

47. 796 F. Supp. at 1379, 22 ELR at 21206.

48. No. 87 C 4196, 1991 WL 47374, at *1 (N.D. Ill. Mar. 28, 1991).

49. *Id.* at *5.

50. 843 F. Supp. 1304, 24 ELR 21006 (D. Minn. 1993).

51. *Id.* at 1308, 24 ELR at 21007.

52. *Id.*

53. *Id.* at 1314, 24 ELR at 21010.

54. *Id.* ("Although Minnesota and the EPA may not be implementing TMDLs as quickly as plaintiffs would like, the Act does not set deadlines for the development of a certain number of TMDLs. The Act instead requires the development of TMDLs 'in accordance with the priority ranking' of the WQLS list.").

55. U.S. GAO, WATER POLLUTION: MORE EPA ACTION NEEDED TO IMPROVE THE QUALITY OF HEAVILY POLLUTED WATERS, GAO REPORT TO THE CHAIR-

MAN: SUBCOMMITTEE ON REGULATION AND BUSINESS OPPORTUNITIES COMMITTEE ON SMALL BUSINESS HOUSE OF REPRESENTATIVES (Jan. 1989).

56. *Id.* at 4.

57. *Id.* at 24.

58. *Id.* at 23.

59. *Id.* at 6.

60. *Id.*

61. *Id.*

62. *Id.*

63. *Id.* at 34-36.

64. Tom Wilson, *Taking the Fear Out of TMDLs*, NONPOINT SOURCES NEWS—NOTES, Oct. 1990, at 19-21.

65. *Id.* at 19.

66. *Id.*

67. *Id.* at 20.

68. *Id.*

69. *Id.* at 20, 21.

70. The minimalist nature of EPA's implementation of §303 is reflected in a 1996 memorandum from EPA Region VIII to the state of Wyoming stating that "past decisions have allowed for 'functional equivalent TMDLs' when it is shown that actions on the part of the state met the substantive intent of the Act (reference: Sportsmen's Clubs of Texas v. Layton, No. CA 3-86-0121-R N.D. Texas)." Letter from Carol Campbell, Ecosystems Protection Programs, Region VIII, U.S. EPA, to Gary Beach, Administrator, Water Quality Division, Department of Environmental Quality, Wyoming (June 26, 1996) (on file with author). To the contrary, a review of the docket of the captioned case shows no decision, order, or other resolution on "functional equivalency," or any other substantive issue in the case. Up to June 1996, EPA Regions were still finding, if not inventing, slender reasons to avoid promulgating TMDLs.

71. U.S. EPA, PUB. NO. 440/4-91-001, GUIDANCE FOR WATER QUALITY-BASED DECISIONS: THE TMDL PROCESS (Apr. 1991).

72. Memorandum from Geoffrey H. Grubbs, Director, Assessment and Watershed Protection Division, EPA, to Water Quality Branch Chiefs, Regions I-X; Approval of [§]303(d) Lists: Promulgation Schedules/Procedures, Public Participation (Oct. 30, 1992) (on file with author).

73. U.S. EPA, NATIONAL WATER QUALITY INVENTORY, 1994 REPORT TO CONGRESS (Dec. 1995).

74. Memorandum from Robert Perciasepe, Assistant Administrator for Water, U.S. EPA, *A Healthy Watershed Strategy* (Aug. 9, 1996) (on file with author).

75. 951 F. Supp. 962, 964 (W.D. Wash. 1996) (describing procedural background of case).

76. *Id.*

77. *Id.* at 969.

78. *Id.* at 964.

79. *Id.*

80. *Id.* at 962.

81. *Id.* at 964.

82. *Id.* at 967.

83. *Id.*

84. *Id.* at 969.

85. No. 1:94-cv-2501-MHS, 1996 WL 534909, at *1 (N.D. Ga. Mar. 25, 1996).

86. *Id.* at *3.

87. *Id.*

88. *Id.*

89. *Id.* at *6.

90. *Id.*

91. *Id.* at *1.

92. *Id.* at *6.

93. Sierra Club v. Hankinson, 939 F. Supp. 872, 873 (N.D. Ga. 1996).

94. Sierra Club v. Hankinson, No. 1:94-cv-2501-MHS, 1996 WL 534914, at *1 (N.D. Ga. Aug. 30, 1996).

95. *Id.* at *2.

96. *Id.*

97. *Id.*

98. *Id.*

99. As of December 12, 1996, EPA was under separate court orders to propose TMDLs in Oregon, Alaska, and Georgia; litigation to compel WQLS lists and/or TMDLs were pending in Idaho, New York, Georgia (WQLSs), New Jersey, Pennsylvania, Delaware, West Virginia, Louisiana, New Mexico, Kansas, California (two cases), Washington, and Oregon; notices of intent to sue had been filed in Alabama, Florida, Mississippi, North Carolina, Wyoming, and Arizona. EPA, TMDL Litigation (Dec. 2, 1996) (unpublished memorandum on file with author). EPA may have overlooked its still-pending case in Texas. *See supra* note 71.

100. Memorandum from Robert Perciasepe, Assistant Administrator for Water, U.S. EPA, to Regional Administrators, EPA Regions I-X, *EPA Action on 1996 Lists, Priority Rankings and TMDL Targeting Plans Submitted by States Under [§]303(d) of the Clean Water Act* (Aug. 9, 1996).

101. Memorandum from Robert Perciasepe, Assistant Administrator for Water, U.S. EPA, to State Environmental Commissioners and Regional Administrators, *Total Maximum Daily Loads: A Key to Improving Water Quality* (Feb. 26, 1996).

102. Memorandum from Robert Perciasepe, *supra* note 100.

103. *Water Pollution: "Staged Approach" Outlined by EPA for Dealing With Listings of Polluted Waters, Setting of TMDLs*, [27 Current Developments] Env't Rep. (BNA) 925 (Aug. 23, 1996).

104. Memorandum from Robert Perciasepe, *supra* note 100.

105. *Id.*

106. Oral presentation of Geoffrey H. Grubbs, Director of EPA Water Office Assessment and Watershed Protection Division, Federal Advisory Committee Meeting on TMDLs in Galveston, Texas (Feb. 19-21, 1997).

107. Conversation with Geoffrey H. Grubbs, EPA, in Washington, D.C. (Dec. 5, 1996).

108. U.S. EPA, Draft TMDL Program Implementation Strategy (Nov. 18, 1996) [hereinafter Draft Strategy].

109. *Id.* at 3.

110. *Id.*

111. *Id.*

112. *Id.* at 10.

113. *Id.* at 12.

114. *Id.* at 8.

115. *Id.* at 16.

116. *Id.* at 18, 19. EPA identified CWA §319 (nonpoint pollution), State Revolving Funds, and Farm Bill conservation programs. For example, the 1996 Farm Bill's Environmental Quality Incentives Program provides over $2 billion available annually which, if appropriately directed, could provide major assistance in implementing TMDLs. *Id.*

117. *Id.* at 22.

118. *Id.* at 18. On the last and critical point, the Agency would "carefully consider" the "potential consequences to a pollution source in the event that implementation does not occur," such as penalties or sanctions.

119. U.S. EPA Press Release (Nov. 19, 1996) (on file with author). The committee includes four state representatives, four representatives of environmental organiza-

tions, and at least four representatives of point and nonpoint source discharges. *Id.* at 3.

120. *Id.* at 2. The only subject areas off limits to the FACA committee discussions are legislation, appropriations, and litigation. Wisely so, if the committee was to have any hope of achieving consensus. Introductory Remarks of Geoffrey H. Grubbs, Assessment and Watershed Protection Division, Federal Advisory Committee on TMDLs (Nov. 19-21, 1996).

121. *Id.*

122. 33 U.S.C. §1313(d)(1)(A), (C), ELR Stat. FWPCA §303(d)(1)(A), (C).

123. 40 C.F.R. §130.7(c)(ii) (1996) ("TMDLs shall be established for all pollutants preventing or expected to prevent attainment of water quality standards.").

124. EPA has recognized the softness of this interpretation, and has indicated its intention to revisit the question. *See* Draft Strategy, *supra* note 108, at 12 ("EPA will further explain the conditions under which a TMDL is not necessary and when a water does not need to be listed.").

125. *Id.* at 7.

126. For the difficulties in modeling the effects of nutrient loadings, see U.S. EPA, Background Paper No. 4: Science and Technology, FACA Committee Meeting (Nov. 19-21, 1996).

> [C]ertain types of water quality problems and processes are still poorly understood. For example, excessive nutrients in rivers can cause the growth of attached algae. The relationship between nutrient loading and attached algal growth is very difficult to quantify and therefore definition of an acceptable load and determination of a TMDL is problematic.

Id. at 4. These difficulties noted, the downstream effects of nutrient loadings can be enormous. Louisiana is currently experiencing an 8,000 square mile "dead zone" of anaerobic water at the mouth of the Mississippi River, due largely to nutrient runoff from farms in the Midwest, over 1,000 river miles away. Elizabeth Coleman, The Persistent Enemy: Hypoxia on Louisiana's Continental Shelf, Coast and Sea: Marine and Coastal Research in Louisiana Universities 7 (1992). More than 70% of the total nitrogen delivered to the Gulf of Mexico by the Mississippi River originates *above* the confluence of the Ohio and Mississippi. Richard Alexander et al., The Regional Transport of Point and Nonpoint Source Nitrogen to the Gulf of Mexico, EPA Gulf of Mexico Hypoxia Management Conference (Dec. 5, 1995).

127. "Such load shall be established at a level necessary to implement the applicable water quality standards with seasonal variations and a margin of safety that takes into account any lack of knowledge concerning the relationship between effluent limitations and water quality." 33 U.S.C. §1313(d)(1)(c), ELR Stat. FWPCA §303(d)(1)(c).

128. 42 U.S.C. §7409(b)(1), ELR Stat. CAA §109(b)(1); 33 U.S.C. §1317(a)(4), ELR Stat. FWPCA §307(a)(4); 42 U.S.C. §9621(d)(1), ELR Stat. CERCLA §121(d)(1); 16 U.S.C. §1536(a)(2), ELR Stat. ESA §7(a)(2); for a discussion of its "best guess" standard, see Oliver A. Houck, *The "Institutionalization of Caution" Under Section 7 of the Endangered Species Act: What Do You Do When You Don't Know?*, 12 ELR 15001 (Apr. 1982).

129. *See* Lead Indus. Ass'n v. EPA, 647 F.2d 1130, 10 ELR 20643 (D.C. Cir. 1978), *cert. denied*, 449 U.S. 1042 (1980) (affirming national ambient air quality standards for lead based on a series of conservative assumptions on risk and exposure, over a host of industry objections); Hercules, Inc. v. EPA, 598 F.2d 91, 8 ELR 20811 (D.C. Cir. 1978) (water quality standards); Environmental Defense Fund v. EPA, 598 F.2d 62, 8 ELR 20765 (D.C. Cir. 1978) (polychlorinated biphenyl standards); Ethyl Corp. v. EPA, 541 F.2d 1, 6 ELR 20267 (D.C. Cir. 1976) (lead levels in gasoline).

130. Lewis County Util. Corp. v. Washington Dep't of Ecology, No. 96-043, 1997 WL 240790 (Wash. Pollution Control Bd. Apr. 18, 1997) (challenging denial of water withdrawal permit, alleging a "lack of evidence that the amount of water requested would have a significant or measurable impact"); *see also* Statement on Behalf of Chemical Manufacturers Association, FACA Meeting (Nov. 19-21, 1996), *in* EPA, Draft Summary of Meeting One 6 (urging that no TMDL restrictions be imposed until the science of each assessment is corroborated). The degree of supporting science is clearly where the challenges to TMDLs will lie. These challenges were, of course, instrumental in emasculating water quality-based regulation under the FWPCA of 1965. *See* Houck, *supra* note 27, at 10330 n.10.

131. 42 U.S.C. §7410, ELR Stat. CAA §110; *see* William H. Rodgers Jr., *Implementation Plans: Procedure and Evaluation, in* Environmental Law 196-202 (1994).

132. Union Elec. Co. v. EPA, 427 U.S. 246, 6 ELR 20570 (1976).

133. Dioxin/Organochlorine Ctr. v. Rasmussen, 37 ERC 1845 (W.D. Wash. 1993), *aff'd sub nom.* Dioxin/Organochlorine Ctr. v. Clarke, 57 F.3d 1517, 25 ELR 21258 (9th Cir. 1995). Among the points at issue were EPA's assumptions of safe levels of exposure, and its margin of safety at 22% of total loadings.

134. United States v. Ottati & Goss, Inc., 900 F.2d 429, 20 ELR 20856 (1st Cir. 1990) (reversing Superfund cleanup decision).

135. *See* Brock v. Merrell Dow Pharmaceuticals, Inc., 874 F.2d 307 (5th Cir. 1989) (epidemiological evidence insufficient to show causation); Turpin v. Merrell Dow Pharmaceuticals, Inc., 959 F.2d 1394 (6th Cir. 1992) (animal studies evidence insufficient proof); Sorensen v. Shaklee Corp., 31 F.3d 638 (8th Cir. 1994) (ingestion of chemically treated substances insufficient evidence of causation).

136. 33 U.S.C. §1313(d)(2), ELR Stat. FWPCA §303(d)(2).

137. *See supra* note 27 and accompanying text. EPA issued its identification on December 27, 1978.

138. *See supra* note 29 and accompanying text.

139. *See* Sierra Club v. Hankinson, No. 1:94-cv-2501-MHS, 1996 WL 534909, at *1 (N.D. Ga. Mar. 25, 1996).

140. Draft Memorandum of Robert Perciasepe, Assistant Administrator for Water, U.S. EPA, *New Policies for Developing and Implementing Total Maximum Daily Loads (TMDLs)* 2 (Mar. 21, 1997).

141. 33 U.S.C. §1313(e)(1), ELR Stat. FWPCA §303(e)(1).

142. *Id.* §1313(d)(2), ELR Stat. FWPCA §303(d)(2).

143. *Id.*

144. *Id.* §1342(i), ELR Stat. FWPCA §402(i) (EPA review of NPDES permits).

145. *See* Houck, *supra* note 27, at 10342.

146. EPA, of course, holds residual leverage that could be important in influencing a state to regulate nonpoint pollution, including direct funding assistance, related point-permit review, and approval of state-delegated programs. This leverage and its limits are further explored in Chapter 4.

147. Houck, *supra* note 27, at 10342-43.

148. *Id.*, and sources cited therein.

149. Conversation with Richard Parrish, FACA committee member (Mar. 11, 1997).

150. *Id.*

151. Houck, *supra* note 27, at 10337.

152. Preparation of Water Quality Management Plans, *supra* note 21, at 55346, §131.11(f)(3) ("for each water quality segment, a total allocation for point sources of pollutants and a gross allotment for nonpoint sources of pollutants"). These gross allocations were then to lead to point source load allocations, *id.* at 55346, §131.11(g), and nonpoint controls, *id.* at 55346, §131.11(j).

153. *See* Draft Strategy, *supra* note 108, at 20.

154. 467 U.S. 837, 14 ELR 20507 (1984) (deference to EPA's somewhat fluid policy on nonattainment under the CAA).

155. *See, e.g.,* Babbitt v. Sweet Home Chapter of Communities for a Great Or., 115 S. Ct. 2407, 25 ELR 21194 (1994) (deference to U.S. Department of the Interior's interpretation of §9 of the Endangered Species Act).

156. U.S. EPA, Background Paper No. 2: Criteria for EPA Approval of State, Tribal TMDLs, FACA Committee Meeting 2 (Nov. 19-21, 1996):

> (It has been suggested that since TMDLs do not have a direct regulatory effect (except through NPDES permits), they should not be a high priority, especially in watersheds impaired mainly by nonpoint sources. On the other hand, it has been argued that nonpoint source management programs should be guided by TMDLs and load allocations.)

157. Letter of Arthur Bryant, Director, Watershed and Air Management, U.S. Forest Service, to Geoffrey H. Grubbs (Apr. 29, 1997).

158. *Id.* at 1.

159. *Id.* at 2.

160. *See* National Wildlife Fed'n v. U.S. Forest Serv., 592 F. Supp. 931, 14 ELR 20755 (D. Or. 1984) (describing destruction of salmon streams by clearcutting and resultant landslides).

161. *See* Hal Bernton, *Local Stories of Clear-cuts & Mudslides*, PORTLAND OREGONIAN, Feb. 2, 1997, *available in* 1997 WL 4139560; *see also* Jeffrey St. Clair, *U.S. Environment: Logging Practices Unleash Lethal Landslides*, INTER PRESS SERV., Jan. 6, 1997, *available in* 1997 WL 7073076.

162. Letter of Arthur Bryant, *supra* note 157.

163. 33 U.S.C. §1329, ELR STAT. FWPCA §319.

164. Letter of Arthur Bryant, *supra* note 157.

165. *Id.*

166. *See* Houck, *supra* note 27, at 10337 (discussing the House committee report on TMDLs and nonpoint source pollution).

167. *See* SENATE COMM. ON ENVIRONMENT AND PUBLIC WORKS, 100TH CONG., 2D SESS., A LEGISLATIVE HISTORY OF THE WATER QUALITY ACT OF 1987 (1987).

168. Dioxin/Organochlorine Ctr. v. Rasmussen, 37 ERC 1845, 1848 n.3 (W.D. Wash. 1993), *aff'd sub nom.* Dioxin/Organochlorine Ctr. v. Clarke, 57 F.3d 1517, 25 ELR 21258 (9th Cir. 1995).

169. For a discussion of the choice among several strategies under the CAA to control human exposure to lead, see FREDERICK R. ANDERSON ET AL., ENVIRONMENTAL PROTECTION: LAW AND POLICY 174-81 (2d ed. 1990).

170. *See* Houck, *supra* note 2 (describing CWA toxics regulation through separate programs based on human health standards, technology standards, water quality criteria, toxic water quality criteria, whole effluent testing, and biological criteria).

171. 33 U.S.C. §1329, ELR STAT. FWPCA §319; *see* Houck, *supra* note 27, at 10342.

172. Houck, *supra* note 27, at 10342.

173. EPA surveys estimate the cost of TMDL development from $4,039 to $1,023,531. U.S. EPA, TMDL DEVELOPMENT COST ESTIMATES: CASE STUDIES OF 14 TMDLS—PART II. COST ESTIMATION APPROACH (visited Oct. 20, 1999) http://www.epa.gov/owow/tmdl/part 23t.html. A representative of the Georgia Department of Natural Resources has reported TMDL development costs in that state from $75,000 to $5 million. Presentation of Alan Hallom, Georgia Department of Natural Resources, EPA Summary, FACA Committee Meeting 1 (Nov. 19-21, 1996).

Chapter 4:
A New Framework

Pieces of the Frame

The descriptions that follow are of complex events surrounding the implementation of CWA §303(d). Every lawsuit is its own private war; every initiative proposed by EPA, the FACA committee, the White House, and other agencies is underpinned by reams of paper, options, and thoughtful, at times argumentative, discussion; each state response is unique; and each TMDL relates to a hydrology all its own. The purpose of this discussion is to capture their commonality, and their places in this new armada on water pollution that is assembling around and through the use of TMDLs.

The Litigation

> While I am pleased with the progress that many States are making, we still have a long way to go before we achieve our water quality goals everywhere. I remain very concerned about the extraordinarily high rate of litigation in this program and I think it is crucial that we Federal managers, together with our State partners, take every step we can to make sure that this program is carried out effectively and quickly.
>
> —Robert Perciasepe, Assistant Administrator for Water, EPA [1]

Against a background of federal environmental programs in which litigation has played a central role, it is hard to think of any program more precipitously driven by citizen suits from absolute zero toward its statutory destiny than TMDLs. Short of some outside impetus, whatever Congress prescribed in §303(d) was going to be ignored for no more complex reasons than (1) compliance was hard and (2) ignoring seemed possible. [2]

Starting in the early 1990s, a first wave of lawsuits established that ignoring §303 was no longer possible and that continued state inaction constituted action, triggering EPA's duty to respond. [3] By January 1999, litigation had challenged compliance in more than half the states of the country, and yet more was brewing. The issues in these cases have tracked the literal requirements of the statute, raising first the failure to list state waters, then the adequacy of these lists, and then the failure to prepare TMDLs, leading to schedules for their preparation ranging from 12 [4] years to as few as 5. [5] The early violations were essentially procedural, and the courts were able to avoid the content, or lack of content, of the TMDLs themselves.

This will change. The newer cases have begun to question the substance of what is currently being proffered as TMDLs. [6] Under §303 and EPA regulations, a TMDL is to include the sum of both point source waste load allocations (WLAs) and nonpoint source LAs, plus a margin of error for uncertainty and a margin for future growth. [7] The majority of TMDLs in Louisiana, New York, and several other states—if not nearly all states—were alleged with credible specificity to be point source WLAs, plus nothing. [8] This deficiency was doubtless the result of states, EPA, and, once a case is filed, the U.S. Department of Justice throwing any information available into the breach against charges that the environmental agencies had not been doing their job. On a clear day, and away from the shadow of a lawsuit, there was no reasonable way EPA could characterize much of the states' work here as TMDLs and the courts have so held. [9] More fundamentally, however, this limited focus on WLAs resulted from the tendency of state and federal regulators to finger identifiable point sources, even beleaguered municipal waste treatment systems, rather than tackle the timber industry, fertilizer manufacturers, and the rest of the nonpoint world.

Yet more rounds of citizen suits can be expected over the contents and, then, the implementation of TMDLs. Whether TMDLs should include provision for their own implementation is a gut issue unsettled by the statute and was a live debate in the FACA committee. [10] Environmental interests see implementation as a necessary component of §303(d), which is to say mandatory. [11] Agriculture and other interests see implementation carried out through §319 planning for nonpoint sources or state water quality plans under §303(e), which is to say voluntary. [12] While these parties war over the issue of implementation at the national level, citizen suits and state practice have begun establishing the precedent. A consent decree in the state of Washington required a schedule for TMDLs to include plans for their own implementation. [13] A TMDL for the Newport Bay/San Diego Creek watershed in Orange County, California, included a detailed implementation and nutrient management plan, with provision for monitoring and review. [14] EPA's new proposed TMDL regulations capitulate and call for a TMDL plan.

The litigation will not be all from the citizen side. Industry has already mounted serious challenges to TMDLs. [15] Agriculture and timber interests have given notice that they are ready to challenge the application of TMDLs to nonpoint sources [16] and, by implication, to the inclusion of implementation and enforcement measures. [17] They have also given notice of their intent, in the name of "sound science," to challenge listings of waters and identification of sources based on anything short of dispositive evidence. [18] Responding to this or some other impetus, states have taken more conservative positions in their latest submissions to EPA on the listing of impaired waters. [19] The adequacy of information needed to list these waters, as well as the adequacy of information quantifying loadings from particular sources, is certain to be an issue in cases to come. More of an issue, perhaps, than it should be. The statute anticipates uncertainty and calls for a margin of error in its calculations [20]; as one EPA official has put it, just add the margin "and keep moving." [21] The Agency's calculations, further, should be afforded considerable judicial deference. [22] Deference, however, is tested in courts every day.

The likely role of TMDL litigation in the foreseeable future is for environmental groups to keep the process moving at a pace that is plainly uncomfortable to EPA, the states, and the regulated community [23]; for industry to challenge the basic assumptions of the program before they agree to buckle down to it; and for both environmentalists and industry to watchdog the resultant listing and TMDL decisions for those that are grossly insupportable in fact, either way. In short, the classic role of environmental litigation through the years.

Further EPA Guidance

> The increased scrutiny that we all face as we assist States in implementing the TMDL program requires that we do our best to help States develop approvable and defensible section 303(d) lists in 1998.
>
> —EPA Memorandum (August 17, 1997) [24]

Pressed by the litigation, in late 1997 EPA issued two guidance documents on the TMDL program in order to retake the initiative. The first document clarified the scope of listed waters. [25] The second set first ever schedules for the resulting LAs and requirements for their content. [26] Although couched in the language of cooperation and assistance to state agencies, each was clearly intended to move the program forward—and ahead of the courts.

□ *Listings.* The listing guidance came first, perhaps to take advantage of state biennial water quality reviews that were then in motion. Section

305(b) of the CWA requires the states to report the condition of their water quality to EPA every two years. [27] EPA regulations require state §305(b) reports by April 1 of even years. [28] Although §303(d) leaves the timing for state listings of impaired waters more open-ended (e.g., to be submitted "from time to time"), [29] since 1991, EPA guidance has called for state §303(d) lists to be submitted concurrently with §305(b) reports, which scheduled the first real show for April 1998. [30]

EPA's new listing document was a remarkable-to-read exercise in loophole closing. Generically, it opened by reiterating that states must consider "all existing and readily available" data in their listings, including information "actively solicited" from other agencies, the public, and academia [31]; the water-watching public, for its part, alerted for the first time nationally on the nature and importance of this drill, would participate actively and, in the end, help boost the identification of impaired waters to uncomfortable new highs. [32] The document also reiterated that waters could be exempted from listings as "expected to meet" water quality standards only if those expectations were to be met in the next two years, a relatively small window. [33] The heart of the document, however, was in its appendix, [34] which proceeded to list and then summarily dismiss excuses, difficulties, and objections to the listing of impaired waters as if they were complaints from someone who really didn't want to take this course in the first place. A sample of the issues follows, each of which can be introduced by the question: Do we *really* have to include . . .

> . . . waterbodies where water quality standards are in the process of being revised (read: we are busy downgrading them)? Answer: yes. The current standards are the applicable standards. [35]

> . . . waters impaired by atmospheric deposition? Yes. Controlling airborne pollution "may be difficult," but waters impaired by "all sources" should be listed. [36]

> . . . waters impaired by temperature? Yes. Ditto, and heat is a pollutant. [37]

> . . . waters impaired by unknown sources, or by an unknown pollutant? Yes and yes. The question is pollution; take your best shot at its cause. [38]

> . . . waters impaired by nonpoint sources only? Yes, without argument and "consistent with long-standing EPA policy, regulations and practice." [39]

In its listings guidance, then, EPA meant business and made sense. Polluted waters are not going to get addressed by the TMDL program—or even thought about—unless they are acknowledged in the first place. EPA's insistence on comprehensiveness was no doubt bolstered by the fact of its express statutory authority to disapprove the lists, and its capability, in the event of a state default, to do the listing job itself. [40] Although uncertain in its science and short on good monitoring data, listing would be a relatively easy task as compared to the steps to come.

☐ *TMDLs.* In its TMDL guidance, EPA faced a tougher chore in diplomacy, semantics, and, ultimately, the law. When we come to the root cause of water quality impairment in the United States—nonpoint source pollution—federal authority under §303 only goes so far, and then ends. [41] EPA's guidance would extend this authority fully in some respects, but hold other aspects in reserve.

EPA TMDL guidance had been an iterative process since 1991, when the Agency first began to take its §303 responsibilities in earnest. The Agency's April 1991 *Guidance for Water Quality-Based Decisions: The TMDL Process* remains in force and, in many ways, the most detailed prescription available for listings and LAs. [42] Subsequent directives clarified specific aspects of the program, [43] but insufficiently to stave off citizen suits and judgments that were imposing schedules and review requirements on their own. [44] The tail continued to wag the dog because the head had not taken control. In October 1997, EPA issued a memorandum to its Regional Administrators entitled *New Policies for Establishing and Implementing TMDLs,* [45] which announced two new steps for the program and, for the first time in print, its enforcement options to secure state compliance.

The first step was a process, a schedule for the development of all TMDLs by all states, and a deadline. Under preexisting guidance, the states and EPA regions had the discretion to plan for TMDLs, literally, to infinity. It was indeed the open-ended nature of the process that impelled reviewing courts to reject state and EPA proposals that extended well into the next century, and to impose tight schedules on their own. [46] EPA now announced that the April 1998 state submissions were to include not only a complete list of impaired waters and proposed TMDLs for the next 2 years, but also a "specific written agreement" between the state and EPA for the completion of *all* TMDLs within from 8 to 13 years. [47] The deadline chosen here reflected the generous end of the schedules that were emerging from ongoing litigation and consent decrees. [48] It was an inevitable compromise between the eternal need for more information and the equally pressing need to, at last, get the show on the road.

The deadline set, EPA next turned to the controversy at the heart of the process—waters polluted primarily or exclusively by nonpoint sources. Acknowledging that its current guidance was "incomplete" in this regard, the Agency stated that "[i]mplementation of load allocations for nonpoint sources in these waters is essential if we are to maintain steady progress toward clean water goals." [49] As discussed in an earlier chapter however, §303 provides no direct authority for EPA to implement LAs for nonpoint sources, [50] and members of nonpoint industries were taking the position that §303 did not reach their discharges at all. [51] On the latter issue, EPA could hang firm on its previous insistence that TMDLs include load allocations from nonpoint sources. [52] On the issue of implementation, new EPA guidance would begin by recognizing the voluntary measures of the §319 program as the "primary implementation mechanism." [53] This said, however, the goal was "to achieve TMDL load allocations" for all nonpoint sources, and "all available Federal, State and local programs and authorities" were to be used. [54] Each state, therefore, was to "describe its plan for implementing" nonpoint LAs, water segment by water segment, or by watershed, or statewide; these "implementation plans" were to be submitted as §303(e) plan revisions either "coupled with a proposed TMDL" or as part of an "equivalent" process. [55] Each plan would provide "reasonable assurances" that the LAs "will in fact be achieved." [56] What we had here was the evolution of a new thing, a TMDL-oriented plan.

Because nonpoint LAs are so central to the success of the TMDL program and, indeed, to the restoration of water quality nationwide, it is worth a moment to examine the strengths and weaknesses of EPA's approach. A first observation is that it is not really new: EPA had ostensibly required "reasonable assurances" of implementation of its WLAs and LAs since at least 1991. [57] Stated for the first time, however, was the direct application of this requirement to exclusively nonpoint waters and the additional requirement of an implementation plan. On the plan itself, however, the requirement began to melt. For a state to have the option of offering an implementation plan for "all affected waters" [58] runs a real risk of describing everything and requiring nothing. For the plan to be offered as part of a "geographic planning process" [59] or as part of state water quality management plans is also patently amorphous and runs a serious risk of continuing nonpoint source nonmanagement. As anyone who has dealt with state water quality plans knows, they are not "plans" in a dictionary sense of the word; rather, like state implementation plans under the CAA, [60] they are more a process composed of criteria, standards, and abbreviated assessments, some published and some in file drawers, an environment in which site-specific implementation measures can lose their focus, if not simply get lost. [61] On the one hand, it is hard not to sympathize with the flexibility EPA offered here, given its shortage of authority over nonpoint sources and its obvious need for a significant state buy-in. On the other hand, it is hard to have confidence in "reasonable assurances" from plans that could appear in so many different and diffuse ways.

The last and perhaps most significant aspect of the new TMDL guidance was its articulation of the tools in EPA's closet to enforce the implementation of nonpoint source TMDLs. The memorandum outlined a scenario of gradual escalation, beginning with "constructive and focused discussion" with state managers. [62] Given the position of at least some state agencies that they had no regulatory authority over nonpoint sources at all, [63] these discussions might be quite constructive, no matter how focused. The ensuing steps included

(1) requiring a state to "update" its water quality management plan,

(2) diverting "substantial grant dollars" to states that are providing genuine nonpoint LAs,

(3) initiating additional [NPDES] review of point sources "(including minors)" affecting the listed water, and

(4) denying a state "enhanced benefits status" under §319, subjecting it to more oversight on its §319 programs. [64]

One finishes this list asking, is this all? The measures offered are both weak and, in some cases, counterintuitive. Updating a water quality management plan is, at best, a hassle and a diversion from resources the state could better spend on pollution control. Diverting grant assistance to performing states fails to deliver money to the states that need it the most (i.e., the ones with the most significant nonpoint source pollution and the most concomitant resistance to nonpoint controls). Ratcheting down further on point sources, even "minor sources," who are now carrying the entire brunt of the cleanup, presents some obvious equity problems—although it also presents the prospect of their alliance in efforts toward nonpoint source management. As a practical matter, furthermore, this leverage disappears entirely for polluted waters that have few or no point sources to blame. As for denying "enhanced benefits status" to noncomplying states, this sanction may not be denying them anything to which they, as noncompliers, would be entitled anyway; at its strongest, it adds a hassle factor for nonpoint planning.

Which begs the question "could EPA do more?" The answer is clearly yes. The answer may also be that everybody already knows it, so EPA did not need to say it. The first unstated authority is EPA's ability to deny new point source permits in water quality limited (i.e., TMDL-required) waters. By long-standing EPA regulation, no new source may "cause or contribute to" the violation of water quality standards [65]; if a water segment is already in violation, any "actually detectable or measurable" contribution would seem to be prohibited. [66] If a TMDL has been prepared, the new source must demonstrate that there is a remaining LA for its discharge and that all other dischargers are on compliance schedules to meet water quality standards. [67] New sources, then, become leverage both for the preparation of TMDLs and their effective implementation. [68] Corollary authority exists for modifying permits for existing sources based on new information, such as, arguably, the fact of water quality impairment or TMDL allocations, that would have justified different permit considerations and was not available at the time of issuance. [69] This regulation would seem to enlist the leverage of all point sources, new and existing, following the new information underlying the listings of April 1998.

A third unstated authority is EPA's ability to revoke a state-delegated program for failure to develop, implement, or enforce TMDLs. [70] This leverage is both more and less than meets the eye. The track record of EPA in revoking state-delegated programs—or even threatening to revoke them—is minimal. [71] In the interests of federalism and political survival, EPA has steered a wide berth around underperforming state programs, some openly defiant of EPA requirements. [72] The threat in the case of unperformed nonpoint TMDLs is even more illusory, as it could involve EPA in permitting and land use decisions beyond its resources to administer or politically to survive. On the other hand, viewing the threat from a state perspective, EPA has competently administered many full CWA programs for years [73]; sufficiently provoked, it could revoke a delegated program and do so again. The loss of such a program to a state is more than the loss of financial or other support; it is the loss of prestige and political power, and these are high stakes to risk in a game of chicken.

This last observation is one that EPA could best leave unsaid. To mention revocation would only alienate the states whose cooperation was badly needed to make nonpoint source management a reality. In a legal culture full of "gorillas in closets" that are rarely seen, but radiate their presence nonetheless, this gorilla, too, was there.

The FACA Committee

> The Committee, however, could not agree as to whether waters impacted only by nonpoint sources should be included on the § 303(d) list.... Some Committee members... observed that.... the §303(d) listing requirement may be duplicative and unnecessary. They were also concerned that TMDLs might result in (or, in and of

themselves constitute) a mandatory water-quality based limit that
could be enforced against nonpoint sources.

—Facilitator's Report, FACA Committee [74]

In late 1996, seeing the storm on the near horizon and, indeed, breaking
around its ears, EPA formed a FACA committee to attempt to arrive at a consensus on the direction and requirements of the TMDL program. [75] Members included state water program officials, local officials, a Native American representative, agribusiness, the timber industry, point source industry,
municipal sewage plants, and environmentalists; officials of EPA, the U.S.
Natural Resources Conservation Service (U.S. Department of Agriculture
(USDA)), and the U.S. Forest Service served as ex officio members. [76] All
the players were in the room. Their meetings were open to, attended by, and
addressed by other members of the public. Their work was published, meeting by meeting and workgroup by workgroup, on the Internet. Their gradual
consensus and hardening points of difference were described, as they
evolved, in an iterative facilitator's report. [77] In all, this was a remarkably
transparent process, and, given the diversity of interests represented, it led
to a rather heartening convergence of viewpoints—up to the real point:
nonpoint source pollution controls. On this central issue, the FACA committee could only deliver part of the goods.

The final committee report contained more than 100 pages of recommendations, analysis, and appendices. In the main, the report and recommendations reinforced emerging EPA guidance, and the cross-pollination from the
FACA committee to EPA's latest memoranda was obvious even in the language used for EPA's new listing and TMDL prescriptions. [78] The committee reached considerable agreement on the need for better information, [79] for
public and "stakeholder" participation, [80] for comprehensive listings, [81] for
specificity in TMDLs, [82] for an "implementation plan," [83] for "reasonable
assurances" that the plan would be implemented, [84] and on mechanisms for
monitoring and implementation. [85] The report offered consensus suggestions
for adaptive management, [86] for "extremely difficult problems" such as atmospheric deposition and flow obstruction, [87] and even a detailed "hierarchy approach" to TMDL approval by EPA. [88] The honeymoon ended, however, at
TMDLs for nonpoint sources, and the enforcement of TMDLs generally. Simply put, nonpoint sources wanted no part of a program that would be enforced.

The disagreement took two forms. First, to timber and agriculture representatives, waters impaired primarily or entirely by nonpoint sources
should not be listed under §303(d)(1), but rather under the voluntary and in-
formational provisions of §303(d)(3) or §319 [89]; listing under §303(d)(1)
would be "duplicative" and "unnecessary." [90] As a second line of defense,
they argued that the implementation of all TMDLs should not come through

§303(d) approvals but, rather, through the approval of state water quality plans under §303(e). [91] Both arguments threaten to emasculate the statute. To deflect nonpoint TMDL planning to the information-only framework of §303(d)(3), or to the voluntary world of §319, is to ensure that it will not bear fruit in the lifetimes of anyone now living; it also contradicts a sensible reading of §303(d)(3), which seems directed to waters that currently *meet* water quality standards. [92]

The argument for implementation through §303(e) is at least facially better grounded in law, but is so clearly motivated by the fear that §303(d) requirements could be enforceable ("there were some concerns that reliance on §303(d) could lead to judicial enforcement of TMDL implementation plans in unexpected or unintended ways") [93] and by the confidence that implementation through §303(e) will not ("[t]he extent and timing of EPA review of TMDL implementation plans submitted under §303(e) is less clear [than review under §303(d)]"), [94] that this motive alone should be its undoing. Further, to function at all, approvals under §303(e) would require EPA to reinvent the same site-specific review for particular water bodies now called for under §303(d) [95]; even then, §303(e) approvals would not necessarily be based on regulatory criteria or subject to citizen suits for their timeliness or content. [96] At bottom, the unresolved issue was enforcement. The FACA committee tried hard for consensus and did not get there. It would be EPA's call. The issues left open by the FACA committee then—and through no lack of trying—were fundamental to the success of the TMDL program. If nonpoint waters were not included, along with a specific plan for cleanups, the program would be wasting everyone's time.

The Federal Family

TMDLs operate in an environment too hostile to succeed on their own. They face reluctance, to put it mildly, from point and nonpoint sources, state regulatory agencies, and state and federal land management agencies; they face serious shortages of funding; and they face a host of disincentives to conserve soil and water found in tax policies, property law, water law, and commodity support and subsidy programs. To expect desk-level, state water quality personnel to deal effectively with the timber industry, hog farmers, cattle ranchers, real estate developers, irrigation return flows, agricultural chemicals, and the rest of the nonpoint world without assistance from other state and federal agencies is to expect the impossible.

Starting in 1997, other federal programs began to rally around the TMDL approach in ways that give it at least a hope of accomplishing the job ahead. The rally was lead, or at least cheer-led, by the President, who announced a new Clean Water Action Plan focused primarily on nonpoint source pollution. It was supported by the acceleration of several other trends, including

the increased treatment of diffuse sources (e.g., animal feedlots and municipal stormwater) as point sources under the CWA, the treatment of public
lands uses (e.g., grazing and timber) as "dischargers" under the Act, and the
emergence of quasi-technology standards for nonpoint source pollution under the Coastal Zone Management Act. While each is properly the subject
of its own chapter, if not its own book, they are summarized here for purposes of assessing their impact on the TMDL program.

☐ *The Clean Water Action Plan.*

> In most cases, the development of TMDL and wasteload alloca-
> tions for specific impaired waters within the watershed will form
> the core of the Watershed Restoration Action Strategy. [97]

In November 1997, the Vice President of the United States announced a
strategy for addressing the chronic and remaining pollution of the nation's
waters, primarily from nonpoint sources. [98] From a political standpoint, the
Administration was recapturing the initiative in pollution control. Just two
years earlier, Congress had taken a very direct run at the CWA with amendments that, inter alia, would have relaxed its already soft provisions for
nonpoint source control. [99] After a highly visibly defeat on this issue, Congress had sidestepped the CWA and had gone off in search of other prey.
Equally telling, from the standpoint of an Administration that reads its public opinion polls, was that when the Clean Water Action Plan emerged six
months later, it was announced not by the Vice President but by the President of the United States. [100] Whatever collateral damage the Presidency
was suffering during this time, the announcement would focus several
agencies of the United States on nonpoint source pollution.

The plan was refreshingly frank about the problem. Although sprinkled
with success stories of waters that had been restored across the country, it
presented the "bottom line" assessment that 50% of the nation's watersheds
were polluted, including some 1,500 water bodies that did not meet water
quality standards. [101] Only 16% of U.S. watersheds had "good" water quality. [102] Turning to the causes, in a paragraph entitled *Polluted Runoff Is the
Most Important Source of Water Pollution*, the plan continued,
"[n]ationally, agriculture is the most extensive source of water pollution, affecting 70 percent of impaired rivers and streams and 49 percent of impaired lake areas." [103] Based on state identification of water pollution
sources, the plan quantified their relative contributions as follows:

Rank	Rivers	Lakes	Estuaries
1	Agriculture	Agriculture	Industrial Discharges
2	Municipal Point Sources	Unspecified Nonpoint Sources	Urban Runoff/ Storm Sewers

Rank	Rivers	Lakes	Estuaries
3	Hydrologic Modification	Atmospheric Deposition	Municipal Point Sources
4	Habitat Modification	Urban Runoff/ Storm Sewers	Upstream Sources
5	Urban Runoff/ Storm Sewers	Municipal Agriculture [104] Point Sources	

To environmentalists and, one supposes, no small number of regulated point sources, these admissions at this level of government were a breath of fresh air. To at least some nonpoint dischargers, on the other hand, the President had "declared war on the farmer." [105]

The proposed solutions would be more numerous. A first was money: an increase of more than half a billion dollars in nonpoint pollution control spending for fiscal year 1999, and an increase of over $2.3 billion over the next five years. [106] A second was a bevy of existing programs of EPA, the USDA, the U.S. Department of the Interior, the U.S. Army Corps of Engineers, the U.S. Forest Service, and the National Oceanic and Atmospheric Administration (NOAA) that would be accelerated, reinforced, and given specific numerical goals. [107] The USDA would protect miles of riparian habitat and set aside acres of erodible lands; together with the Corps' permitting program, it would achieve a net *gain* in wetlands of 100,000 acres a year. [108] While few of the announced efforts were entirely new, and some not new at all, their emphasis and goals and the coordination offered were certainly new; like President Bush's "no net loss of wetlands" initiative several years before, they held the potential for at least legitimizing the effort within the federal family.

The plan filled EPA's plate, too, with new and old helpings of regulatory work, including quasi-point source initiatives described below and the long-overdue task of developing water quality criteria for nutrients. [109] In the middle of the plate, however, was EPA's old friend "watershed management," to be effectuated by new watershed restoration action strategies. [110] This strategy would bottom—late in the plan and at a point probably reached only by the most attentive or suspicious reader—on . . . TMDLs. [111] Indeed, TMDLs would "form the core" of the strategy. A watershed approach "can be a smarter, more effective and cost-efficient way to implement TMDLs," the report went on encouragingly, creating an opportunity to "bundle" TMDLs and "strike an appropriate balance" among dischargers. [112] In this construct—and to this author, appropriately—TMDLs are not an adjunct to watershed planning; rather, they are the *basis* of watershed planning, not because they are scientifically bulletproof, comprehensive, or efficient, . . . but because they are objective, measurable, and the only approach so far that can be enforced by law.

☐ *From Nonpoint to Point Source Regulation.* The great axiom of the CWA is that point sources are strictly regulated while nonpoint sources, in the delicate phrase of one commentator, are "immune from important features of the Act" [113] such as effluent standards, permits, and enforcement (i.e., those features that have made the NPDES program work). The history of nonpoint source pollution control since 1972 is of an attempt, to date largely unsuccessful, to find replacements for these features through voluntary, local programs. The rationales offered for treating nonpoint sources separately under the Act include

(1) the alleged "number and variety of nonpoint sources";

(2) the "site-specific nature" of the pollution; and

(3) the "lack of known control technologies." [114]

On reflection, none of these reasons are terribly convincing, because

(1) we have a great number and variety of point sources as well (several hundred major industrial categories and subcategories, and more to come);

(2) each industrial discharge, too, has site-specific effects on its receiving water (effects that are irrelevant to the setting of technology-based guidelines); and

(3) the control technologies for nonpoint pollution (e.g., shelter-belts, nutrient caps, retention ponds) are anything but unknown, complex, technologically difficult, or even very costly.

In truth, we do not avoid regulating nonpoint source pollution because we are unable to figure out how to do it. Rather, we have deferred to the myth that its impacts are essentially local and of secondary importance, as we have deferred to legislatures dominated by rural constituencies unaccustomed to any regulation and ready to fight. Recently—albeit with glacial slowness—both the myth and the dominance have begun to melt, reopening the question of nonpoint source controls. One answer to the problem is simply to treat a greater number of dischargers as point sources, bringing them into the operational features of the Act.

EPA and Congress have been wrestling with the application of the NPDES program to agriculture, silviculture, and land-based pollution since the adoption of the Act in its modern form. [115] In 1973, the Agency adopted a definition of point sources that included runoff collected or channeled virtually in any way, but then proceeded to exempt discharges from all silviculture, all urban storm sewers, and all but the largest agricultural operations. [116] These exemptions were immediately challenged by a citizen suit and rejected by both the federal district and appellate courts of the District of Columbia. [117] Facing EPA arguments—similar to those noted above—that nonpoint sources were too numerous, diffuse, and difficult to regulate, these courts suggested the use of alternative permit conditions and general permits, and concluded with the inspiration that "[i]magination conjoined with determination will likely give EPA capability for practical administration. If not the remedy lies with Congress." [118]

Congress did not wait to see. Firmly held by the myth that nonpoint source pollution was a local affair, Congress amended the Act in 1977 specifically to exclude irrigated agriculture from point source regulation, [119] and in 1987 went further to exempt all agricultural stormwater discharges. [120] As a result, with the exception of concentrated animal feedlots, agricultural pollution was exempted from the Act even when it came from and through discrete collection systems. The scope of this exemption went largely unchallenged until 1994 when the Second Circuit ruled in *Concerned Area Residents for the Environment v. Southview Farm* [121] that a large dairy farm, in its entirety, was a point source under the CWA. [122] The court reasoned in the alternative that the machines that spread manure on the farm, and the drainage system conveying these wastes to navigable waters, were point sources as well. [123] This ruling contained the seeds of reclassifying a great deal of mechanized agriculture as point sources, an invitation that EPA has not yet accepted.

Instead, under the impetus of other CWA amendments in 1987, [124] EPA has proposed to develop standards for a number of diffuse sources. The most important of these proposals, from the standpoint of abating serious pollution, involve animal feeding operations (AFOs) and municipal storm sewers. Each of these programs could serve to take considerable weight off of remaining nonpoint programs and could give the TMDL approach for polluted waters the additional leverage that comes from the availability of point source-like permits and standards.

• Animal Feeding Operations and Concentrated Animal Feeding Operations.

On June 21, 1995, the eight-acre manure lagoon at Oceanview Farms in Onslow County burst through its dam. What followed was seen on news reports around the world, as 25 million gallons of excrement surged over a road, through a neighboring tobacco field and into the New River. The odoriferous tide was two feet deep and flowed for over two hours, ending up in the river, where it killed "virtually all aquatic life in the 17-mile stretch between Richlands and Jacksonville." When it was over, the New River had been the victim of a spill more than twice the size of the oil spill that followed the wreck of the Exxon Valdez.

—Analysis of the North Carolina Hog Farming Industry [125]

EPA recognizes that its existing regulatory programs related to animal waste management are not being implemented consistently and have not kept pace with evolving technologies or industry practices that have altered the type and magnitude of related adverse environmental and public health impacts.

—EPA Animal Feeding Operations Strategy [126]

As noted above, the CWA definition of point sources has included from the outset discharges from concentrated animal feeding operations (CAFOs). In 1976, EPA issued regulations for CAFOs that excluded all but industrial-sized operations: only CAFOs with more than, for example, 1,000 slaughter cattle, 2,500 hogs of more than 55 pounds apiece, or 30,000 chickens (or 100,000 chickens if a facility used "continuous overflow watering") were automatically included [127]; smaller operations would be included if they discharged directly into U.S. waters or could be shown to impair water quality on a site-specific basis. [128] In theory, the requirement was "zero discharge" based on interim storage in lagoons and land application. [129] Overflow from waste lagoons during heavy storms was exempted, as was the practice of spreading animal wastes on land. [130] This done, EPA turned to other business.

In practice, the EPA regulations were underinclusive and ineffective. Of the nearly half a million farms with confined (not pasture) feedlots in America, only 6,600 contained sufficiently high numbers of animals to require a permit; another 32,000 mid-sized operations were potentially subject to regulation depending on their method of discharge. [131] As of 1995, 20 years after EPA's CAFO regulations were promulgated, only 25% of even the largest operations had NPDES permits. [132] Meanwhile, the industry was changing toward ever greater concentration of animals on smaller landscapes. Between 1991 and 1996, hog production increased 8% while the number of facilities dropped by 20%. [133] As the size of individual operations grew, traditional methods of waste management failed; lagoons overflowed, adjacent fields rejected overloads from increased land spreading. [134] The pollution from these wastes, always recognized as oxygen-depleting, was beginning to be seen as toxic as well. [135] In 1993, an EPA workgroup recommended additional "guidance" on CAFOs [136]; a 1995 U.S. GAO report followed suit. [137] At about the same time, the manure hit the fan on the New River delta of North Carolina, and then the Chesapeake Bay, in ways that could no longer be ignored.

The breakout of pollution from the mellifluously named Oceanview Farms was not an isolated event. Coastal North Carolina, home to a hog industry so new and so vigorous that it outsold tobacco as the state's number one crop, [138] began experiencing a "devastating series" of hog spills and fish kills. [139] By that time, pigs were outnumbering people by as much as 34 to 1 in some counties and, with pigs producing from two to four times the waste per day of an average human adult, the fuel for more contamination was on hand. [140] The 1995 Oceanview disaster killed an estimated 10-125 million fish and closed 364,000 acres of commercial fishing grounds; it was accompanied by several other spills the same summer of more than a million gallons each. [141]

One summer later along the Chesapeake Bay, Maryland officials closed a 17-mile stretch of the Pocomoke River where 30,000 fish had died and fishermen and scientists had become ill from exposure to the water. [142] Shortly thereafter, officials closed another waterway with fish infected by *Pfiesteria piscicida*, the so-called cell from hell, which flourishes in high-nutrient, low-oxygen conditions. [143] These conditions led investigators to the chicken industry on Maryland's Eastern Shore which, in the Pocomoke region alone, produces more than 100 million friers a year for Perdue and other large corporations. [144] Fearing the worst from an outbreak on the Chesapeake so close to Washington, D.C.—that EPA might actually come forward with regulations—the American Farm Bureau quickly announced that it advocated "nonregulatory solutions before you let the federal gorilla out of the closet and step on these folks." [145] But the events were too stark and too well publicized [146] and, for once, EPA was not inclined to listen.

In March 1998, on the heels of the President's Clean Water Action Plan, EPA announced a Draft Animal Feeding Operation Strategy directing a new series of initiatives at the problem, [147] led by politically correct offers of assistance to states on research, monitoring, enforcement, and watershed planning. [148] The strategy then moved to the heart of the matter: expanded permitting and more comprehensive effluent guidelines. [149] Beginning with CAFOs in the most heavily impacted watersheds, EPA and the states would place all large CAFOs under permit within seven years, including facilities previously exempted as "no discharge" and treated discharge operations. [150] Adopting the flexibility suggested 20 years earlier by the D.C. Circuit, [151] these permits would include individual permits for the largest CAFOS, "watershed-specific" permits for groups of facilities in a given area, and general permits for other operations; these permits would include "appropriate conditions" for the land application of animal wastes as well. [152]

The permits would be based on new federal effluent guidelines, issued informally on "key permitting issues" by late 1998, [153] and as formal BAT and new source performance standards by December 2001. [154] The development of these standards would be a collaborative effort with the industry and the public—as effluent guideline development has become in the 1990s, but there is no mistaking the assertion of federal authority in this new strategy. And there is every reason to expect that, if and when these permits and guidelines are in place, pollution loadings will drop as dramatically as they have in every other NPDES-regulated category of the CWA.

As this comes to pass, discharges that in the aggregate contributed to an estimated 13% of the polluted rivers of the country will move, from what has largely been ad hoc water quality-based treatment, to federally pre-scribed management and technology practices. It bears remembering in all of this that EPA and the states have had, all along, the authority and duty to regulate AFOs and CAFOs individually and more strictly on the basis of water quality standards, whenever they found water quality impairment; North Carolina, furthermore, was and is considered to be a leader among the states in water pollution control. [155] Yet water quality-based controls did not happen, not in North Carolina until after a series of disasters, and not in sev-eral other states to this day. [156] All of which says something about both the ability of states to control local industry and the ability of anyone to control discharges by water quality standards. When things got serious, we turned once again to more extensive BAT.

- Stormwater.

  Using Washington DC as an example, the group found that the amount of lead in the city's runoff in 1988 (26,000 pounds) was nine times the total amount discharged from all of Virginia's facto-ries in 1987 (2,900 pounds).

  —*BNA Environment Reporter* [157]

  Sediment loadings rates from construction sites are typically 10 to 20 times that of agricultural lands, with runoff rates as high as 100 times that of agricultural lands, and typically 1,000 to 2,000 times that of forest lands.

  —EPA [158]

EPA has approached stormwater regulation with the same aware-ness-cum-trepidation that it has agriculture, and for many of the same rea-sons. The Agency faces cash-strapped municipalities without either the threat of injunction which it holds over industrial sources [159] or the leverage of funding it provides for municipal sewage treatment. [160] Stormwater rem-edies, further, while often obvious and available, smack of the kind of land use control of which no federal agency dares stand accused. On the other hand, urban runoff is major pollution, in coastal areas it is the *dominant* source of water pollution, [161] and it is discharged for the most part through pipes, drains, and other discrete conveyances (i.e., point sources under the CWA). [162]

EPA's first response was to duck, and in 1973 the Agency moved to exempt stormwater runoff sources from point source regulation as too diffuse, too impractical, too numerous, etc. [163] When this approach was invalidated, stormwater management fell into a cycle of inconclusive rulemakings, litigation, and paralysis for the next 15 years. [164] Finally, in 1987, prompted by increasing information on the volume, contamination, and outright toxicity of urban runoff, Congress stepped in. [165]

The choice before Congress was between imposing industrial-type point source standards or continuing the limbo of nonpoint source management. Its decision was to advance the NPDES approach for major sources as far as possible, leaving some flexibility for smaller municipal stormwater systems. Industrial stormwater would henceforth be regulated through NPDES permits under effluent limitation guidelines [166] and a new, hybrid, technological standard, "maximum extent practicable," which was to include "management practices, control techniques and system, design and engineering methods" and "such other provisions" as EPA found appropriate for runoff pollution control. [167] On a slower track, EPA was to develop regulations for smaller communities that "may include performance standards, guidelines, guidance, and management practice and treatment requirements, as appropriate." [168] Stormwater runoff was thus moved from the de facto nonpoint to the permit world, with the apparent expectation that it would be made subject to explicit engineering and best management practices (BMPs).

For industrial sources this expectation is more or less coming to pass. EPA's program for industrial runoff is administered through individual (best professional judgment), group (multisector), and general permits, each based on BMPs. [169] General permits (available to smaller operations) are based on site-specific BMPs submitted by the applicant, while group permits (available, as an option, to larger activities by industrial category) are based on a list of BMPs developed, through rulemaking, with each affected industry. [170] By whatever route, the end result is permits with a relatively specific set of "good housekeeping practices" ranging from required ground cover to the separate handling of construction debris.

For municipal sources, EPA has moved with more caution on a problem that by its own data is responsible, inter alia, for nearly 50% of the impairment of the nation's estuaries. [171] By statute, EPA was to address large storm systems first and, in 1990, the Agency finally promulgated its Phase 1 regulations for communities of over 100,000 inhabitants. [172] The regulations consist largely of suggested practices (e.g., street sweeping) and public education campaigns (e.g., the encouragement of reduced lawn watering), coupled with discharge and water quality monitoring. [173] Municipal runoff control mechanisms well described in the literature—such as permeable surfaces, retention ponds, and greenbelts—are nowhere in view. [174] Actual Phase 1 permits, accordingly, consist of descriptions of such ongoing municipal operations as cleaning storm drains, and such public awareness initiatives as, in the case of the city of New Orleans, the Storm Drain Stenciling Project (e.g., "Drains to Lake"), on the apparent thesis that the large slugs of toxins that characterize the "first flush" from the city streets during each rainfall are the product of individual and uninformed toxic dumpers. [175] EPA has defended the insubstantial nature of its stormwater permit for the city of New Orleans by asserting that "the single most important pollution prevention practice for [municipal] permits is public education" which will "help create the changes that need to occur in how citizens view and approach potential urban runoff pollution sources and activities." [176] For the near future, then, and whatever Congress might have meant for the application of "maximum extent practicable" control standards to large municipal stormwater sources, we have business as usual, plus education, plus monitoring.

Meanwhile, EPA has also been under a statutory requirement and court orders to expand its coverage of runoff sources under Phase 2 regulations for smaller municipal systems and construction sites. [177] Stimulated, perhaps, by the President's Clean Water Action Plan, the Agency has now proposed new Phase 2 stormwater rules that will include permitting for an estimated 3,500 more municipalities and another 100,000 construction sites per year. The key word here is "permitting" because, although the statute does not specify permits as a necessary ingredient of EPA's Phase 2 program, [178] and although states have lobbied for the adoption of "non-NPDES" state programs instead, [179] EPA has chosen to stay with a permits approach because permits are "enforceable under the CWA" and, more tellingly, "would ensure that citizens could participate through the permit issuance process as well as participate in enforcement proceedings" [180]; a more frank acknowledgement of the need for citizen suits would be hard to find. The net thus widens; it remains to be seen what will happen with the catch.

The first thing that will happen is, at least for Phase 2 permits, potentially stronger BMPs. EPA's proposals for Phase 2 put out for public discussion contain significantly more substantive criteria, such as mandatory standards for "post-construction stormwater management in new development and redevelopment" which may require "limiting growth to identified areas," "minimizing impervious area," "maintaining open space," and "structural BMPs" (e.g., retention ponds, wetland falters, and porous pavement). [181] Here, at least we are beginning to *talk* about real pollution controls.

EPA's application of water quality standards is more ambiguous. The Agency has long insisted, indeed from the start, that municipal stormwater sources comply with water quality standards. [182] The question has always been: how? Given the highly fluctuating rates and contamination levels of stormwater discharges, water quality standard-based effluent limitations would be a nightmare to develop, and the Agency turned to BMPs. [183] EPA would impose more controls only where warranted by "cost considerations and water quality effects," [184] and its current Phase 1 regulations and permits require no more. The Phase 2 proposals continue this approach, but end the story as follows: "If additional specific measures to protect water quality were imposed, they would likely be the result of an assessment based on TMDLs, or the equivalent of TMDLs, where the proper allocations would be made to all contributing sources." [185] Which returns us to TMDLs.

Eleven years after the 1987 CWA amendments calling for stormwater management under federal permit, EPA has effectively asserted sufficient jurisdiction to move stormwater pollution into the point source world through largely voluntary, largely preexisting, BMPs—plus education, plus monitoring to determine the need for more serious permit requirements in the future. TMDLs will provide additional, earlier pressure to get on with the next phase of the stormwater program. Conversely, although polluting cities may be able to fudge their discharge monitoring sufficiently to delay more serious requirements under the stormwater program, if they are discharging into impaired waters, then §303(d) assessments will bring the problem to their doors anyway, and the obligation to join industrial dischargers, municipal sewage treatment works, agricultural sources, and the rest of the TMDL bazaar.

☐ *Grazing and Timber on Public Lands.*

> Nonpoint source water pollution on the public lands of the West is a problem of significant proportions, due to the immense land area involved, the ubiquity of the pollution sources, and the vulnerability of many surface waters . . . . The western states themselves have identified grazing (a subcategory of agriculture) as the [nonpoint source] category having the greatest impacts on the quality and beneficial uses of their waters.

> —Debra L. Donahue, *The Untapped Power of Clean Water Act Section 401* [186]

> In 1975 a severe storm hit the Mapleton District. A Forest Service survey of 70 percent of the district showed 245 landslides. Of these slides, 9 percent were natural events, 14 percent were road related, and 77 percent were in clearcut units apparently unrelated to roads or landings. . . . In 1982 a Forest Service aerial photo survey showed fifty road-related and seventy-nine clearcut related landslides. These slides scoured 14.29 miles of streams.
>
> —U.S. District Court for the District of Oregon [187]

While we tend to think of the impacts of public lands grazing and timber harvest as alterations of the landscape and its wildlife populations, they have altered aquatic landscapes and aquatic life as dramatically and, in some cases, more irreversibly, through the degradation of water quality.

Cattle grazing has long been recognized as a primary source of pollution in western waters, which tend to be scarce to begin with and lack the volume to flush, mix, biodegrade, and otherwise accommodate the loads of oxygen demand and sediments input directly from livestock manure and indirectly from destabilized riparian zones. [188] There are 2 million livestock across the West today, and there have been as many as 20 million at times in this century. [189] They congregate at, on, and in any water source at hand. An adult cow produces more than 80 pounds of manure per day, nearly 16 tons per year. [190] In all bovine innocence, they trample streambanks into mudslides and pound their watering holes into so-called sacrifice areas and water gaps. [191] With the loss of vegetation comes the loss of shade, the onset of thermal pollution and serious algae bloom. [192] Overgrazing, even on lands miles distant from western watercourses, leads to accelerated runoff from periodic storms, further degrading water quality.

All of which has been documented for years. Wyoming, for example, reports sediments and nutrients, for both of which grazing is the primary source, as the number one and number two causes of water quality impairment in the state. [193] None of which has made any significant difference in western range management. To at least some western cattlemen, these concerns are a product of "ripariopsychorrhea," described as a "fictional mental disease with scatological overtones." [194] Western legislators and water quality regulators have responded in kind by allowing broad variances for grazing, logging, and similar activities or by exempting them from controls altogether. [195] Federal grazing managers, until recently, have been equally forgiving.

On the steeper slopes of national and other forests, timber harvests, almost uniformly by clearcut, have produced even more spectacular, if less ubiquitous, damage. Ironically, it was the effects of wildcat logging at the end of the last century that propelled the President and Congress toward national forest management, with the explicit purpose of protecting forest watersheds from further damage. [196] Despite the Organic Act of 1897 [197] and the more recent National Forest Management Act, [198] however, the pressure for high timber yields drove the annual cut on public lands alone from 1 billion to more than 12 billion board feet per year, [199] a harvest that could only be attained by practices that stripped the land of all trees and cover. Western mountainsides began collapsing into their streambeds. [200] Logging roads became gullies, conduits for silt and mud. With the increase in turbidity, salmon and other fisheries were eliminated from watersheds, then basins, then entire states. [201] Some runs have gone extinct, and others are perilously close to following suit. [202] For a number of below-quality rivers of the West, logging roads are the only significant man-made source of pollution. [203] On the steep slopes of the Pacific Range, clearcuts continue to cause blowouts and mudslides that take houses and small communities right into the riverbed. [204] The more chronic and long-term damaging effects to water quality, of course, come with every rain.

Forest managers have been no more willing to come to grips with these effects on water resources than have their counterparts on the public range. As with the impacts of cattle on riparian areas, these impacts are well known and admit of rather obvious remedies: stepping cattle and clearcuts back from the watercourses and adopting a baseline for native groundcover. However well known, these remedies are firmly opposed by grazing and timber companies, even when the survival of species as cherished as the salmon are at stake. [205] The strength of this opposition does not lie solely in economics, the lack of reasonable alternatives, or even the importance of these industries which contribute a surprisingly small and dwindling share to even their regional economies. Like agriculture and its image of the small farmer, timber and grazing are supported by images of Paul Bunyan and John Wayne that have dazzled legislators and intimidated regulators at all levels of government; outright violence against managers who attempt to impose environmental requirements is not unknown. [206] The Forest Service itself seems intimidated. While the agency has regulations explicitly requiring mining operations, for example, to comply with state water quality requirements, [207] one cannot find any similar regulation requiring timber operators to obey state water quality standards. [208] The imposition of this requirement on the timber industry, then, would have to come from the outside. Which is exactly what is happening.

The pieces of this puzzle are not yet fully assembled. We have legal theories, pending lawsuits, cases on administrative appeal, cases on federal circuit appeal, and Administration initiatives all contributing to a picture that could have a dramatic effect on TMDLs for western waters. One theory would extend the reasoning of *Southview Farm* [209] to consider grazing "sacrifice areas," for example, and forest logging roads as point source dischargers under the CWA. [210] While this theory percolates untested, a more modest theory emerges that even if these activities are not point sources under the Act, they are dischargers and therefore constitute activities requiring state certification under §401 that their impacts will not violate state water quality standards. [211] The §401 thesis has had a mixed reception, initially accepted in *Oregon Natural Desert Ass'n v. Thomas* [212] (involving grazing permits) then rejected on appeal and again in *Idaho Conservation League v. Casewell* [213] (involving the construction of two national forest roads). The split here centers on whether the term "discharge," in the context of §401, is itself limited to point sources and "nonpoint sources with discrete discharge points," or whether it includes other means of conveyance as well. [214] Reportedly, following the *Oregon Natural Desert* opinion, EPA began drafting regulations for grazing impacts [215] which are now on hold, pending appeal of the case to the U.S. Supreme Court. [216]

Meanwhile, a third and more direct approach has arisen under §313 of the Act, which mandates that all federal agencies "having jurisdiction over any property" or engaged in "any activity" that results or may result in "the discharge or runoff of pollutants" shall be "subject to, and comply with all . . . State . . . requirements . . . and process and sanctions respecting the control and abatement of water pollution" in the same manner as nongovernmental entities. [217] This provision has led to declarations from the Ninth Circuit in *Northwest Indian Cemetery Protective Ass'n v. Peterson* [218] and *Marble Mountain Audubon Society v. Rice* [219] that the Forest Service must comply with state water quality standards. These holdings, both involving federal timber sales, were reinforced in *Oregon Natural Resources Council v. U.S. Forest Service,* [220] which found that a citizen suit over yet another timber sale based on §313 would lie under the Administrative Procedure Act (APA), [221] even though it would not qualify under the citizen suit provision of the CWA itself. [222] A similar §313 case involving grazing impacts on a desert spring designated under the CWA as an "outstanding natural resource water," *National Wildlife Federation v. Bureau of Land Management,* [223] has led to an administrative stay of the proposed grazing, in effect a preliminary injunction, foreshadowing the likelihood of success on the merits. The power of the §313 approach is that its language is not restricted to "discharges" but includes the "runoff of pollutants" as well. Nor does it lead simply to state certification, [224] which is in many states a routine and meaningless formality. Coupled with a cause of action by citizen groups under the APA, §313 could go a long way to provide proactive and explicit scrutiny of timber and grazing impacts on water quality, independent of whatever a state chose to do under §401. [225]

Against this background—and responding both to a heightened concern for water quality and to a lessening of the stranglehold that the extractive industries have had over the public and the politics of a rapidly urbanizing West [226]—the Administration has been mounting an offensive of its own based largely on water quality impacts. In fact, this is an offensive that has been building for years in reaction to a series of "train wrecks" under the Endangered Species Act [227] and to the evolving—if still elusive—principles of ecosystem management. [228] Recognizing the importance of healthy riparian ecosystems, Secretary of the Interior Babbitt began a series of discussions on "rangeland reform," leading to the promulgation of regulations in 1995 on, inter alia, the restoration of "rangeland health." [229] The national regulations contain specific goals for vegetation and water quality which, if not met, call for "appropriate action" including reductions in livestock use [230]; among these goals are that "water quality [comply] with State water quality standards." [231] Bureau of Land Management (BLM) districts were to follow with their own more specific guidelines, which are now emerging. Guidelines for Utah are illustrative, stating that:

> BLM will apply water quality standards established by the State of Utah and the Federal Clean Water and Safe Drinking Water Acts. BLM actions and other BLM land activities will not contribute to violating those standards. As indicated by a measurement of nutrient loads, total dissolved solids, chemical constituents, fecal coliform, water temperature and other water quality parameters. [232]

On paper anyway, the BLM has joined the party.

The Forest Service has joined too, if in a different fashion. The Forest Service's first efforts were driven by the needs of endangered salmon and other aquatic and riparian species in the old growth forests of the Pacific Northwest; these efforts have led to greater "leave" areas along forest streams and the retention of native vegetation for the stated purpose of restoring water quality and aquatic populations. [233] A second movement was generated over the long-simmering issue of "below-cost" timber sales on forest lands, sales whose revenue did not come close to matching the Forest Service's costs in road construction, sale administration, and reforestation. [234] In early 1998, the incoming Forest Service Chief announced an 18-month moratorium on new road building in unroaded areas of greater than 5,000 acres, to be accompanied by a thorough review of road impacts and the generation of a new road policy. [235]

Extending this initiative, the President's Clean Water Action Plan announced that the Forest Service would "substantially increase" maintenance of its existing road system "to protect water quality," and, for the same purpose, would relocate over 2,000 miles of existing roads and "decommission or obliterate" another 5,000 miles. [236] Equally dramatically, the plan announced that EPA would be considering over the next year whether to require CWA permits for forest roads and to develop a pilot permit program. [237] In light of the direct relationship between forest roads, erosion, and water quality, and the no less direct relationship between new roads, new clearcutting, and more erosion, these new requirements have the potential to work significant improvements in upstream, western water quality—taking considerable pressure off of TMDLs.

The key phrase here for both the rangeland standards and the new forest policies is "potential." Both are under heavy fire from the timber and grazing industries and their champions in Congress [238]; neither may last long enough to be effectuated over the next several years. Even with the best of political support, moreover, it is not easy to calibrate the correlation between a given number of cattle and water quality several miles away; the most that can be said with confidence, is that more, or less, pollution will occur. For this reason, some states such as Arizona finesse these calculations altogether and substitute, for the purposes of certifying activities under §401, compliance with a rather loose and casually supervised list of best management practices (BMPs). [239] These difficulties and this solution are, of course, precursors of the drill to come for all western waters through TMDLs. Precise calibration of activities to impacts will rarely be possible. Resort to BMPs-plus-monitoring and more-BMPs-plus-more-monitoring will be inevitable, until the water improves or the political will gives out.

What the new grazing standards and forest initiatives offer to the TMDL process is a more direct route to the steps everyone knows are necessary—reducing cattle and clearcuts and stepping them back from the water. [240] They also offer, to understaffed and outgunned state water quality employees who will be on the line for TMDLs, a sharing of the political heat for these steps with federal land managers. If and as these federal initiatives are allowed to bear fruit.

☐ *Coastal Nonpoint Programs.*

> The "dead zone" in the Gulf of Mexico, an area of water containing so little oxygen that fish and shrimp cannot survive in it, has grown to 7,032 square miles this summer, the biggest it's been in the 10 years the zone has been measured. . . . The nutrients in the rivers' water [come] from a variety of sources, including fertilizer runoff from farms and lawns throughout the Mississippi River watershed, which includes much of 33 states.
>
> —New Orleans *Times Picayune* [241]

In 1990, faced with the reality that its CWA §319 nonpoint source pollution control program was not getting the job done and that coastal waters were taking the biggest hit, Congress moved to bring yet another statute into play, the Coastal Zone Management Act (CZMA). [242] As Congress noted, nonpoint sources were sending more than 100 million tons of sediments into the Great Lakes every year. [243] They were also contributing more than half of the phosphorous, chromium, copper, lead, and zinc delivered to coastal waters. [244] Nutrient loadings were in the process of creating "dead zones" from Long Island Sound to the Gulf of Mexico. [245] On the receiving end of runoff from everywhere, and with enormous values in recreation, commerce, and biological productivity at stake, the coastal waters had good reason for special protection, and an available mechanism in state coastal management programs. The result was the Coastal Zone Amendments Reauthorization Act of 1990 (CZARA) §6217. [246]

Originally enacted in 1972, the CZMA offered federal funding for voluntary state management programs, much along the lines of EPA's support for state nonpoint programs under the CWA. [247] Funding for state plans and their implementation was administered by NOAA under statutory goals (both "to develop" and "to protect" the coastal zone) [248] that were in obvious contradiction, and under requirements that were the ultimate in ambiguity and discretion (e.g., to give "full consideration to ecological, cultural, historic and aesthetic values, as well as the needs for compatible economic development"). [249] For the next 17 years, NOAA struggled to bring forth programs of varying quality from 29 coastal states, reviewing, cajoling, and occasionally criticizing state performance but never once pulling the trigger on its only weapon, the diminution of federal funding for failing to "adhere to" an approved state program. [250] What is clear from the 1990 amendments is that Congress was impressed by impacts of nonpoint source pollution on coastal resources and, at least in this regard, wanted NOAA and the states to run a tighter ship.

CZARA called on states to identify both land use sources and coastal water quality, [251] to revisit the adequacy of the reach of their coastal zone jurisdictions with regard to nonpoint sources, [252] and to develop "management measures" to "achieve and maintain applicable water quality standards under [CWA §303]." [253] Management measures were defined as "economically achievable measures" reflecting the "greatest degree of pollutant reduction achievable" through the "best available nonpoint pollution control practices, technologies, processes, siting criteria, operating methods or other alternatives." [254] As EPA and NOAA, jointly given the federal authority to implement CZARA, explained, this approach was deliberately "technology-based rather than water quality-based" (i.e., based on "technical and economic achievability, rather than on establishing cause and effect linkages between particular land use activities and particular water quality problems"). [255] Rather than quibble over water quality impacts, "states would be able to concentrate their resources on measures that experts agree will reduce pollution significantly." [256] Additional upgrade, where necessary, could be provided for "remaining coastal water quality problems." [257] This approach, of course, is a mirror image of the BAT-then-TMDL approach of the CWA, and CZARA's initial management measures were to mimic in their objectivity and rigor those of point source BATs themselves.

Leaving less to chance than it had in 1972, Congress also mandated that state coastal plans contain "enforceable policies and mechanisms" to implement the nonpoint management measures, policies, and mechanisms that [258] would have to be established under state law. State programs were to be submitted and approved within three years, or by May 1995. [259] If a state "failed to submit an approvable program," NOAA "shall withhold" both CZMA and CWA §319 funding by congressionally specified percentages, from 10 percent in the first year to 30% by 1999. [260] In the words of one enthusiastic commentator, CZARA contained "stringent enforcement requirements that mark the end of weak nonpoint source controls, at least in coastal states." [261]

Do not bet the farm on it. [262] As of spring 1998, three years past the deadline, not one coastal state had submitted an approved nonpoint program. [263] Twenty-two states had received "conditional approvals" for submissions that were inadequate in nearly every identified category. [264] Seven states had submitted nothing at all. [265] Relying on its "conditional approvals" of these submissions—a type of approval for which no provision is made in the statute and which circumvents the prescribed, statutory sanctions—NOAA has withheld no monies. [266]

Turning to the content of the state plans, not a great deal more that is encouraging meets the eye. Not for lack of technical guidance. In 1995, EPA and NOAA published a voluminous set of guidance with management measures for agriculture, forestry, transportation, and several other major coastal nonpoint sources. [267] The guidance contained commendable specificity (e.g., new development construction in urban areas), it would achieve a reduction in total suspended solids of 80% or no greater than preconstruction loadings, and postconstruction peak runoff rate and volume would equal predevelopment levels. [268] Easy enough to say, of course. But the hard part was yet to come—translating these measures into "enforceable" state plans. We may wait a long time.

A case in point is Louisiana, with perhaps the most important coastal zone in the country for commercial and recreational fisheries, and for the extent of coastal waters contaminated by fecal coliforms, nutrients, and other nonpoint pollution. Louisiana's plan is a telephone book-sized compendium of preexisting state programs and activities, proposing few new initiatives and nothing that could be characterized as "enforceable" authority. [269] Indeed, as a 1995 state summary assures its readers:

> Louisiana has taken the position that we will work to get passed a program that is as non-regulatory as possible, realizing that a minimum of enforceable policies must be identified as currently in existence, and deemed to be adequate, or new ones may need to be developed. [270]

In August 1996, EPA and NOAA replied with "draft findings and conditions" that objected to the state's refusal to propose extending its coastal zone boundary to include more upstream sources, found that the state's agricultural management measures (consisting largely of the distribution of educational materials) did "not include enforceable policies and mechanisms to insure implementation," and found "insufficient justification" for Louisiana's proposal to exclude forestry sources altogether from its coastal nonpoint program. [271] The state responded with a brief in its defense, arguing, inter alia, that upstream sources had no adverse impact on coastal water quality, nor did forestry, and that existing law provided fully adequate enforcement activity for agricultural sources. [272] A similar dialogue has begun with California. [273] Indeed, similar conversations are now occurring with at least 29 coastal states, and no one can say how they will bottom out. One can say, however, in the words of Justice Holmes, that the "hydraulic pressures" of "immediate interests" [274] are once again at work on statutory requirements, and something considerably less than technology-based, enforceable mechanisms will emerge from CZARA. What went wrong?

Whatever else went wrong, EPA and NOAA ran into more than they could handle from coastal states and their nonpoint source constituencies. As early as 1991, the Coastal States Organization was taking the position that CZARA was a "confusing piece of legislation" imposing "Draconian time frames" and, with some validity, that federal financial support would underwrite little more than "a nice slide show." [275] In 1994, the organization formally petitioned EPA and NOAA to relax their view of the "enforceability" of state coastal programs, and to accept existing state authority as sufficient. [276] As the state pressure mounted, the federal agencies issued program "clarification" in 1995. Entitled *Flexibility for State Coastal Nonpoint Programs*, it extended the time frames for state submissions, presented a "range of enforceable policies and mechanisms that could be used by states to implement their programs," and announced the policy of "conditional approvals" described above. [277]

The heat continued, however, and it came, predictably, from those same sources that have been opposing the application of TMDLs to nonpoint sources. Again by way of example, the Louisiana coastal nonpoint program record contains strong criticism from the Louisiana Forestry Association (forestry should be excluded from the state plan, reliance should be placed on voluntary practices), [278] the Roy O. Martin Lumber Company (ditto), [279] the Calcasieu Parish Cattlemen's Association (the plan should be delayed, agriculture should be exempted until specific impaired waterways are identified, a water quality approach rather than a technology-based approach should be used, and "all reference to the minimum backup enforcement recommended—the 'Bad Actor' law, or other enforcement measures—[should] be eliminated completely"), [280] the Louisiana Farm Bureau Federation, Inc. (ditto), [281] and Stream Property Management Inc. (ditto). [282] The record also contained, for some indication of the lateral influence of these interests, two separate letters with three attachments from the Chancellor of the Louisiana State University Agricultural Center advocating no change in the coastal boundary, the exclusion of forestry, a water quality-based approach limited to impaired waters, an exclusively voluntary approach to implementation, and no additional enforcement mechanisms. [283] Thoughtfully, the Chancellor copied every member of the Louisiana congressional delegation.

The same heat intensified on EPA and NOAA at the federal level. [284] In April 1997, the agencies began "discussions" with states and "other interested parties" (not further specified, but one is allowed to guess) over "significant impediments" to implementing the coastal nonpoint program. [285] These discussions pointed to the need for "additional flexibility" for the states, at which point the "parties proceeded to discuss in detail the specific aspects of the program that would require modification." [286] All of which led to a public notice (for the first time) in April 1998 that the agencies were proposing more "administrative changes" to the program. [287]

The changes are more than administrative. After citing the President's Clean Water Action Plan for the proposition that NOAA and EPA will work with states to ensure the development of plans to control polluted runoff "with appropriate state-enforceable policies and mechanisms" [288]—a reference that might lead one to think that stronger measures were to follow—the notice announced that the federal agencies were reconsidering the "level of detail" that should be required of states in linking the "implementing and enforcement agencies"—i.e., the notice went on to explain, "should states be required to establish clear criteria to determine where voluntary efforts have been unsuccessful and that enforcement actions are necessary?" [289] With the statutory concept of "enforceability" thus put up for grabs, the notice went on to announce that since CZARA set no deadline for the implementation of state programs, the agencies were considering extending the time frame for state compliance from 5 to 15 years. [290] As some indication of the distance the federal agencies had been moved here, the notice asked whether "a shorter [time frame], e.g., twelve years, is feasible." [291] The notice concluded with the observation that, as administrative guidance to the states, none of these requirements or deadlines were to be treated as regulations [292] (i.e., as binding or enforceable by the agencies or, as importantly, environmental citizen groups).

The messages here for TMDLs are both cautionary and direct. To begin with the obvious, coastal nonpoint programs are not likely to take any significant pressure off of TMDL development, even for highly impaired coastal waters. CZARA, at least in the more intransigent states—which tend also to be the more polluted states—is evolving toward a reenactment of CWA §319, based on largely voluntary BMPs and minimal enforcement. The congressional concept for CZARA of technology standards first, additional water quality-based management measures later, is eroding, under state and agribusiness pressure, toward a TMDL-like focus on impaired waters. Absent, of course, the impetus of citizen enforcement, which is to say, and with good evidence from the above scenario, largely at the will of the coastal states and their nonpoint constituencies.

Which presents the final lesson of the implementation of CZARA. When push comes to shove, the federal environmental agencies will not be able to hold their own without the offsetting influence of direct citizen involvement and at least the possibility of litigation. A statute that tells federal agencies to get tough, even if it provides explicit standards and deadlines, will not succeed unless, among other things, people can ensure that it does. This is of course the reason the TMDL story may have a different ending.

Early State Responses

> State officials this week are drafting a new uniform position on [CWA] implementation which does not commit states to any specific [time frame] for making determinations on how much pollution a waterbody can receive without exceeding water quality standards, but instead calls for schedules to reflect the availability of sound science.
>
> —*Inside EPA* (August 22, 1997) [293]

No one statement or chapter can fairly capture the range of state responses on any issue, and so it is with TMDLs. Some states, pressed early and hard by citizen suits and reviewing courts, got with the program and produced significant local results. [294] Other states moved in meaningful, if differing, and in a few cases truly innovative, ways on nonpoint source pollution, and the incorporation of these efforts into TMDLs was more administrative than revolutionary. [295] But for the great number of states, TMDLs were burdensome, new, and revolution-requiring in the demands they placed on water pollution control agencies and the unhappy constituencies they brought to the table. Agriculture and timber interests in agricultural and forest product states are accustomed to a fair measure of local gratitude and a corresponding lack of regulation; many state laws exempt agriculture and silviculture from water quality regulation altogether. [296] Many state legislatures have, further, forbidden state environmental agencies from adopting requirements more stringent than federal law, [297] which in the context of a federal nonpoint source program limited to voluntary measures means any regulations or requirements at all. In these states (i.e., in most states), TMDLs arrived on the doorstep like a litter of stray cats—with many unpleasant requirements and little money to provide for them.

Many states, perhaps a majority, would like to rid themselves of §303(d) requirements and return to the more comfortable world of §319. This was a position heard throughout the just-completed FACA process. The August 1997 meeting of the Association of State and Interstate Water Pollution Control Administrators featured a proposal to remove all deadlines from the TMDL program, in favor of "unique, non-regulatory, cost effective approaches" to deal with nonpoint source pollution. [298]

Few states took up the challenge with enthusiasm. [299] The most often heard responses from state officials to the looming tasks they face under §303(d) are "more time" and "more money." [300] On the matter of money, the Administration promised to commit major new resources to the process. [301] Whether states are willing to commit resources on their own remains to be seen [302]; it bears remembering that, under the CWA, water quality standards-based regulation was, supposedly, the states' responsibility and contribution to the shared goal of clean water. [303] On the matter of time, there is an obvious tension between the need to do TMDLs "right" and the need to get going. As described earlier, EPA called for the first comprehensive §303(d) lists of impaired waters by April 1998, and for the submission of TMDLs for all listed waters within no more than 13 years. Beyond the rhetoric, then, two useful measures of early state responses are the 1998 lists and the emerging, first-round TMDLs.

□ *Listings*. State responses to the listing deadline may not have been enthusiastic, but they produced numbers that swelled the universe of identified waters, and raised the stakes for the game to come.

As described in an earlier chapter, in late 1997 EPA put on a full-court press for its regions and the states to meet the April deadline with full and timely information. [304] By mid-May 1998, 28 states and territories had submitted final lists for EPA review, 26 were still in a stage of drafting and public review, and 2 (Idaho and Iowa) had yet to submit even a draft. [305] None of which should be construed as indications of widespread recalcitrance or insurmountable difficulty; 50% on-time compliance with federal deadlines is about par for the course in environmental law. On the other hand, there was certainly evidence of both good-faith difficulty and bad-faith recalcitrance over listing issues. Threshold problems arose over flow assumptions and wet-flow conditions. [306] Additional difficulties arose over the use of "old" data, data from federal agencies, and the sufficiency of the data itself. The agriculture industry complained of "drive by" listings and threatened to sue over the adequacy of their supporting information. [307] Environmentalists complained that while EPA guidance called on states to use "all credible data," states did little asking for outside data, and indeed invented such categories as "not credible enough" and "more data needed" to hold down the lists, and their subsequent workload. [308] At least one state indicated that it was going to reexamine (e.g., lower) the designation of stream uses that determine its water quality standards, explaining that if the uses were not "representative," the "system becomes flawed." [309]

These difficulties noted, the universe of listed waters expanded. An EPA summary of the previous state lists of 1996 found 15,598 impaired waters, identifying (collectively) 33,000 sources. [310] An agriculture representative predicted that these listings would double, [311] which may be an indication of how much confidence this industry has had in the integrity of the exercise in prior years. EPA projections before the FACA committee rose throughout the process to an estimate of 20,000. [312] The actual numbers, however, would be arbitrary and in a sense misleading because they were based on the arbitrary division of waters into stream segments for purposes of §303 reports; small streams and large rivers, small stretches and long ones, apples and oranges, all lumped together toward one large number. [313] On the other hand, the numbers did provide clear and convincing evidence that the nation's remaining water quality problems were larger than admitted, which admission, as any recovering alcoholic will testify, is the first step toward recovery.

Equally as meaningful, the 1998 lists contained first ever state schedules for the development of TMDLs for all listed waters. [314] Which brings us to the consideration, at last, of the ultimate product and purpose of the exercise, the TMDLs themselves.

□ *TMDLs.* At the end of §303(d) and the long, contentious, and difficult road that leads to its implementation are the TMDLs themselves, the actual plans that identify pollution loadings, allocate them to sources, and present mechanisms for their abatement. Good plans and their execution in fact will vindicate the faith that at least some members of Congress, led by the House of Representatives, had in enacting these water quality-based requirements in 1972. Weak or unexecuted plans will confirm the skepticism of the Senate and others that this approach to water pollution control could ever work. We know enough from the process to date that this is an expensive and time-consuming courtship of state and regulated interests, particularly nonpoint discharge industries. What we don't know yet is whether what is coming out the end of the pipe is worth the effort.

But we do have some early data. Over the past few years, and in increasing numbers as the pressure of citizen suits is felt, states have begun submitting, and EPA approving, TMDLs for listed impaired waters. In the fall of 1997, this author sent Freedom of Information Act requests to each EPA region for five TMDLs illustrating the implementation of §303 by their respective states. By April 1998, 9 of the 10 regions had forwarded TMDLs; Region 7, as of that date, had no approved TMDLs. Additional TMDL summaries were obtained from EPA. In all, 55 TMDLs were received and reviewed in order to make very basic determinations of what pollutants, discharge sources, load calculations, and reductions were contained in these documents, as well as their inclusion of such regulatory criteria as margins for safety and for future development.

Summaries of this analysis are presented in Appendix C. An explanation of categories analyzed and the terminology used is presented in the Appendix as well. In addition to this explanation, a further caveat should be noted about the collection and use of this data. First, neither this author nor his research assistants were water quality experts; the analysis is limited to understanding what the documents contained and their compliance with the stated rules of the program. In the same vein, the review took the documents at face value; if a calculation was said to have been made or if a BMP plan was said to exist, those statements were accepted as both true and sufficient. Doubtless, some of these statements would prove in fact to be truer, and more sufficient, than others.

The TMDLs reviewed reveal, and confirm, several features of the program that might have been predicted by its central conundrum: how to come to grips with nonpoint sources. These features include:

> 1. *Nonpoint sources are targets of last resort.* If at all possible, point sources will be identified as the sole source of even conventional pollution (e.g., solids and oxygen demand) and the sole instrument of cleanup. Despite EPA guidance defining TMDLs as the combination of point source WLAs and nonpoint source LAs and requiring both calculations for impaired waters, nearly 50 percent of the approved TMDLs (25 of a total of 55) did not even identify nonpoint source contributions. In effect, these documents described NPDES permit reductions, usually by municipal sewage treatment systems, that had taken place or would take place in the future.

2. *Even where identified, nonpoint source reductions will frequently not be calculated, and, where calculated, even more frequently will not be implemented through identified abatement plans.* Of the 30 TMDLs reviewed that acknowledged nonpoint contributions, 10 did not quantify these loadings, and only 13 projected actual, quantified reductions. Where projected, these reductions, further, were predicated in almost every case on unspecified BMPs contained in state nonpoint source or other documents and incorporated by reference. In only one case did it appear that nonpoint controls were going to be mandatory or enforceable.

3. *Statutory margins for safety and to accommodate future growth are honored more in the breach than the observance.* Only 20 documents contained margin of safety consideration, and only 6 made explicit provision for future growth. These conclusions, further, credit state assertions that margins of safety were provided not by allocating an increment for error but, rather, through the use of conservative estimates, assertions that might well be subject to question.

In sum, TMDLs have a long way to go before they contain the analysis or produce the results Congress intended in 1972. Taking the documents approved to date at face value, granting them the benefit of every doubt and making allowances for the fact that they are first efforts for many states and EPA regions, they provide little confidence that pollution sources are being addressed in any fashion beyond ratcheting down on NPDES permits where they are available and, where they are not, by passing the buck to unidentified and largely unenforceable nonpoint source BMPs. Congress, EPA, and citizen suits can lead this horse to water but it remains to be seen how much it is going to drink.

What We Have Framed

By the summer of 1999, the machinery was now almost in place for an all-out assault on, essentially, nonpoint source pollution through the use of ambient water quality standards. Ahead were perhaps 20,000 impaired water bodies and a gallery of pollution sources that have largely escaped meaningful state or federal controls. At hand was a pollution control system that is beguilingly simple to describe and frustratingly difficult to implement: expensive, site-specific, heavily reliant on science, equally reliant on monitoring, and almost completely reliant on the ability and political will of states and local governments to carry it out. We had been here before with water pollution, indeed for nearly two decades prior to 1972. We had been here before with air pollution, in the years following the ambient air stan-dards-based CAA, before it, too, gradually migrated toward technology standards. We did not make much progress this way on either occasion. The question was whether we would do better this time.

Notes to Chapter 4

1. *New Policies for Developing and Implementing Total Maximum Daily Loads (TMDLs)*, Draft Memorandum from Robert Perciasepe, Assistant Administrator for Water, U.S. EPA, to Regional Administrators and Regional Water Division Administrators, U.S. EPA (Mar. 21, 1997) (on file with author).

2. *See* Oliver A. Houck, *TMDLs, Are We There Yet?: The Long Road Toward Water Quality-Based Regulation Under the Clean Water Act*, 27 ELR 10391, 10392-93 (Aug. 1997) [hereinafter *TMDLs II*].

3. *See* Alaska Ctr. for Env't v. Reilly, 762 F. Supp. 1422, 1426, 21 ELR 21305, 21306 (W.D. Wash. 1991); Scott v. City of Hammond, 741 F.2d 992, 14 ELR 20631 (7th Cir. 1984).

4. American Littoral Soc'y v. U.S. EPA, No. 96-330, http://www.epa.gov/owow/tmdl/lawsuit1.html#n (D. Del. filed June 1996).

5. Sierra Club v. Hankinson, 939 F. Supp. 865, 27 ELR 20280 (N.D. Ga. 1996).

6. *See* Natural Resources Defense Council v. Fox, 909 F. Supp. 153, 26 ELR 20732 (S.D.N.Y. 1995); Kansas Natural Resources Council v. Browner, No. 95-2490-JWL (D. Kan. filed Oct. 1995); Sierra Club v. Saginaw, No. 96-0527 (N.D. La. filed Feb. 1996).

7.

> For pollutants other than heat, [WLAs/LAs and] TMDLs shall be established at levels necessary to attain and maintain the applicable narrative and numerical [water quality standards] with seasonal variations and a margin of safety which takes into account any lack of knowledge concerning the relationship between effluent limitations and water quality. Determinations of [WLAs/LAs and] TMDLs shall take into account critical conditions for stream flow, loading, and water quality parameters.

40 C.F.R. §130.7(c)(1) (1997).

8. Plaintiff's Proposed Findings of Fact and Conclusions of Law, at 11, 12, Natural Resources Defense Council v. Fox, No. 94 Civ. 8424 (S.D.N.Y. filed Oct. 31, 1997) ("The purported TMDLs adopted by New York State for 51 waterbodies were at best WLAs for point sources and did not incorporate [LAs] for non-point sources."); *see also* Declaration of Jack D. Smith, at 24, 25, Sierra Club v. Saginaw, No. 96-9527 (N.D. La. case filed Feb. 1996):

> The entire focus of Louisiana's procedure is on point source loads determined for conditions of flow and loads from nonpoint sources or background assumed but rarely encountered. Point source loads thus determined are then labelled WLAs or TMDLs. In no case are [LAs] for nonpoint sources is assumed, even where nonpoint sources are the inescapably dominating water quality determinant, no [LAs] are de-

veloped for individual nonpoint sources in the way that "WLAs" are developed for individual point sources.

9. *See infra* p. 104, *Early State Responses*, and p. 106, *TMDLs*.

10. National Wildlife Fed'n, *Saving Our Watersheds* (June 19-20, 1998) (TMDL implementation summit).

11. Telephone Conversation with Rick Parrish, FACA committee member (May 28, 1998) [hereinafter Parrish Conversation]; *see also* TMDL FEDERAL ADVISORY COMMITTEE FACILITATORS, FACA ROUGH DRAFT TMDL REPORT (Jan. 15, 1998) [hereinafter ROUGH DRAFT TMDL REPORT].

12. *See infra* text accompanying notes 89-96.

13. Consent Decree, Northwest Envtl. Advocates v. Browner, No. 91427R (W.D. Wash. Jan. 20, 1998).

14. Carolyn Whetzel, *EPA Intervenes in Load-Setting Process for California Streams Due to Local Delays*, State Env't Daily (BNA), Mar. 16, 1998, *available in* LEXIS, Envirn Library, Bnased File.

15. Dioxin/Organochlorine Ctr. v. Clarke, 57 F.3d 1517, 25 ELR 21258 (9th Cir. 1995).

16. *See TMDLs II, supra* note 2, at 10399-401.

17. *See infra* text accompanying notes 89-96.

18. *See infra* text accompanying note 307

19. *See infra* text accompanying note 309. This conservatism seems to contravene EPA regulations that require states to seek out and rely on all credible data. *See* 40 C.F.R. §130.7(b)(5) (1997).

20. 33 U.S.C. §1313(d)(1)(C), ELR STAT. FWPCA §303(d)(1)(C). The TMDL "shall be established at a level necessary to implement the applicable water quality standards with seasonal variations and a margin of safety which takes into account any lack of knowledge concerning the relationship between effluent limitations and water quality." *Id.*

21. *See TMDLs II, supra* note 2, at 10395 (quoting EPA Region X official Tom Wilson).

22. *See* Udall v. Tallman, 380 U.S. 1 (1965).

23. *See* Whetzel, *supra* note 14 ("Joe Karkowski of EPA Region IX told regional water quality officials that the agency would prefer to allow the regional and state process to continue, but terms of an agreement with the environmental group Defend the Bay dictate that the total maximum daily loads be established by April 13."). For an indication that the environmental community pressure on TMDLs will continue, see NATIONAL WILDLIFE FED'N, SAVING OUR WATERSHEDS: A FEDERAL GUIDE TO WATERSHED RESTORATION USING TMDLs (Jan. 1998).

24. *National Clarifying Guidance for 1998 State and Territory Section 303(d) Listing Decisions*, Memorandum from Robert H. Wayland III, Director of Office of

Wetlands, Oceans, and Watersheds, U.S. EPA 2 (Aug. 17, 1997) http://www.epa.
gov/owow/tmdl/lisgid.html [hereinafter Wayland Memorandum].

25. *Id.*

26. *See New Policies for Establishing and Implementing Total Maximum Daily Loads (TMDLs)*, Memorandum from Robert Perciasepe, Assistant Administrator for Water, U.S. EPA, to Regional Administrators and Regional Water Division Administrators, U.S. EPA (Aug. 8, 1997) http://www.epa.gov/owowwtr1/watershed/ratepace.html [hereinafter Perciasepe Memorandum].

27. 33 U.S.C. §1315(b)(1), ELR Stat. FWPCA §305(b)(1).

28. 40 C.F.R. §130.8(a) (1997).

29. 33 U.S.C. §1313(d), ELR Stat. FWPCA §303(d).

30. U.S. EPA, Guidance for Water Quality-Based Decisions: The TMDL Process 12 (Apr. 1991) (available from the ELR Document Service, ELR Order No. AD-3550) [hereinafter Guidance for Water Quality-Based Decisions].

31. *See* Wayland Memorandum, *supra* note 24, at 2.

32. *See infra* text accompanying notes 304-14; *see also* National Wildlife Fed'n, *supra* note 23 (TMDL monitoring handbook of National Wildlife Federation); Natural Resources Defense Council, Clean Water Network (May 1998) (component of CWA implementation project of the National Resources Defense Council).

33. Wayland Memorandum, *supra* note 24, at 6. This directive reiterates guidance from as early as 1991. *Id.*

34. *Id.* at app.

35. *Id.* at 4.

36. *Id.* at 5.

37. *Id.*

38. *Id.*

39. *Id.* at 8.

40. 33 U.S.C. §1314(*l*), ELR Stat. FWPCA §304(*l*).

41. *See TMDLs II*, *supra* note 2, at 10399. Essentially, §303(d) calls for the development of TMDLs, and for their implementation from state water quality management plans under §303(e).

42. Guidance for Water Quality-Based Decisions, *supra* note 30.

43. *See* Perciasepe Memorandum, *supra* note 26; Wayland Memorandum, *supra* note 24.

44. *See* Sierra Club v. Hankinson, 939 F. Supp. 865, 27 ELR 20280 (N.D. Ga. 1996); American Littoral Soc'y v. U.S. EPA, No. 96-489 (E.D. Pa. Apr. 9, 1997);

Defenders of Wildlife v. Browner, 888 F. Supp. 1005, 25 ELR 21582 (D. Ariz. 1995).

45. *See* Perciasepe Memorandum, *supra* note 26.

46. *See* Idaho Sportsmen's Coalition v. Browner, 951 F. Supp. 962, 27 ELR 20771 (W.D. Wash. 1996) (The court found that EPA had violated a duty under the CWA and the TMDL regulations and had acted arbitrarily and capriciously in failing to develop, with Idaho, a reasonable schedule for the establishment of TMDLs for all impaired waters. The court then directed EPA to file such a schedule by May 19, 1996, which EPA did. On September 26, 1996, the court rejected the schedule submitted by EPA and remanded to EPA with instructions to submit a new schedule within six months. On April 8, 1997, EPA submitted an eight-year schedule developed by Idaho. All parties stipulated that the schedule was reasonable.).

47. Perciasepe Memorandum, *supra* note 26, at 2, 3.

48. *See* U.S. EPA, *TMDL Litigation by State* (Apr. 10, 1998) http://www.epa.gov/owow/tmdl/lawsuit1.html (summarizing TMDL court decisions and consent decrees with implementation timetables ranging from 5 to 15 years).

49. Perciasepe Memorandum, *supra* note 26, at 4.

50. *See TMDLs II, supra* note 2, at 10401.

51. *Id.* at 10399.

52. GUIDANCE FOR WATER QUALITY-BASED DECISIONS, *supra* note 30, at 9.

53. Perciasepe Memorandum, *supra* note 26, at 4.

54. *Id.* at 5.

55. *Id.*

56. *Id.*

57. GUIDANCE FOR WATER QUALITY-BASED DECISIONS, *supra* note 30, at 15.

58. Perciasepe Memorandum, *supra* note 26, at 5.

59. *Id.*

60. 42 U.S.C. §7410(a)(1), ELR STAT. CAA §110(a)(1) (state implementation laws (SIPs)). For a thoughtful discussion of the analogy of TMDLs to SIPs, see Robert Adler, *Integrated Approaches to the Water Pollution Problem: Lessons From the Clean Air Act* (draft article on file with author).

61. LOUISIANA DEP'T OF ENVTL. QUALITY, STATE OF LOUISIANA WATER QUALITY MANAGEMENT PLAN (1987) (the plan consists of 11 "volumes" entitled: *Volume 1. Continuing Planning Process Document (CPP)*; *Volume 2. Regulations*; *Volume 3. Water Quality Standards*; *Volume 4. Basin/Segment Boundaries and Inventories*; *Volume 5. Water Quality Assessment*; *Volume 6. Nonpoint Source Assessment*; *Volume 7. Municipal Treatment Needs*; *Volume 8. Industrial Treatment*

Needs; *Volume 9. Residual Waste Treatment Needs*; *Volume 10. Wasteload Alloca-tions*; *Volume 11. Groundwater.*

62. Perciasepe Memorandum, *supra* note 26, at 6.

63. *See* U.S. EPA, *Nonpoint Source Pollution Control Program, Executive Summary* 1 (visited May 15, 1998) http://www.epa.gov/owow/NPS/elistudy/execsum.hmtl ("some states . . . have adopted explicit statutory or regulatory exemptions for agri-culture or forestry activities").

64. Perciasepe Memorandum, *supra* note 26, at 6.

65. 40 C.F.R. §122.4(i) (1997) (No permit may be issued "to a new source or a new discharger, if the discharge from its construction or operation will cause or contrib-ute to the violation of water quality standards.").

66. *See* Arkansas v. Oklahoma, 503 U.S. 91, 22 ELR 20552 (1992) (striking down a construction of the statute that absolutely prohibited new discharges into water quality limited waters, but upholding an EPA interpretation prohibiting discharges that "effected an 'actually detectable or measurable' change in water quality." Al-though applied to interstate effects in this case, the same result would seem to ob-tain for intrastate discharges. The difficulty here, of course, is in the proof of a "measurable" change, an exercise that plagues all water quality-based regulation and is susceptible to considerable manipulation through, inter alia, base-flow as-sumptions and the use of mixing zones. *See* Oliver A. Houck, *The Regulation of Toxic Pollutants Under the Clean Water Act,* 21 ELR 10528, 10544-46 (Sept. 1991). On the other hand, "any detectable contribution" is a lower burden of proof than, say, "harm"; at the least, any new source contributing pollution to a water al-ready in violation for that pollutant would seem to carry the burden to show *no* such detectable contribution, which could prove to be a high standard to meet).

67. 40 C.F.R. §122.4(i) (1997).

68. Potentially effective leverage comes from the ability of a new source to offset its loadings by trading, abating, or buying out pollution from existing sources. *See* GUIDANCE FOR WATER QUALITY-BASED DECISIONS, *supra* note 30, at 51.

69. 40 C.F.R. §122.62(a)(2) (1997):

> The Director has received new information. Permits may be modified during their terms for this cause only if the information was not avail-able at the time of permit issuance (other than revised regulations, guidance or test methods) and would have justified the application of different permit conditions at the time of issuance.

70. *Id.* §123.63(a)(5); *see also* Sierra Club v. Hankinson, 939 F. Supp. 865, 27 ELR 20280 (N.D. Ga. 1996) (citing with approval EPA's authorization under 40 C.F.R. §123.63(a)(5) to revoke a state program for failure to perform TMDLs).

71. *See* WILLIAM H. RODGERS JR., ENVIRONMENTAL LAW 367-68 (2d ed. 1994).

72. *Id.* at 368; *see also* Amendments to Requirements for Authorized State Permit Programs Under Section 402 of the Clean Water Act, 60 Fed. Reg. 14588 (Mar. 17,

1995) (EPA's response to a petition filed by the Environmental Defense Fund and the Chesapeake Bay Foundation seeking revocation of Virginia's delegated program CWA authority for failure to provide for citizen enforcement).

73. As of 1994, EPA still administered CWA NPDES programs in 10 states. U.S. EPA, NATIONAL WATER QUALITY INVENTORY: 1994 REPORT TO CONGRESS 390 (1994) [hereinafter NATIONAL WATER QUALITY INVENTORY].

74. ROUGH DRAFT TMDL REPORT, *supra* note 11, at 51-52.

75. National Advisory Council for Environmental Policy and Technology—Total Maximum Daily Load Committee; Public Meeting, 61 Fed. Reg. 54438 (Oct. 18, 1996) (notice of first FACA committee meeting).

76. TMDL FEDERAL ADVISORY COMMITTEE, FINAL REPORT app. B (May 20, 1998) (*List of Committee Members*) [hereinafter FACA REPORT].

77. *See* ROUGH DRAFT TMDL REPORT, *supra* note 11.

78. Compare for example the listing and TMDL guidance for "expected to meet waters" and "atmospheric deposition" and the development of "implementation plans," *supra* text accompanying notes 24-73, with the same in the FACA reports, ROUGH DRAFT TMDL REPORT, *supra* note 11.

79. FACA REPORT, *supra* note 76, at 10-11.

80. *Id.* at 10-14.

81. *Id.* at 53-57.

82. *Id.* at 30-34.

83. *Id.* at 36-40.

84. *Id.* at 39-40.

85. *Id.* at 43-46.

86. *Id.* at 46-52.

87. *Id.* app. G (*Outline of the Hierarchy Approach to TMDL Approval* (with examples)).

88. FACA REPORT, *supra* note 76, at 43.

89. ROUGH DRAFT TMDL REPORT, *supra* note 11, at 29-30. Section 303(d)(3) provides:

> For the specific purpose of developing information, each State shall identify all waters within its boundaries which it has not identified under paragraph (1)(A) and (1)(B) of this subsection and estimate for such waters the [TMDL] with seasonal variations and margins of safety, for those pollutants which the Administrator identifies under [§304(a)(2)] as suitable for such calculation and for thermal discharges, at a level that would assure protection and propagation of a balanced indigenous population of fish, shellfish, and wildlife.

33 U.S.C. §1313(d)(3), ELR STAT. FWPCA §303(d)(3). The nonpoint industry's viewpoint is consistent with its position that, since §303(d)(1)(A) speaks only in terms of waters impaired after the implementation of point source controls, nonpoint sources were meant to be excluded from the subsequent drill. For reasons stated in an earlier article, this author finds that argument unpersuasive. *See TMDLs II, supra* note 2, at 10399-400 and sources cited therein.

90. ROUGH DRAFT TMDL REPORT, *supra* note 11, at 52.

91. *Id.* at 52-53.

92. *See supra* note 89. A logical reading of the statute, and one that effectuates its clean water goals, is that §303(d)(1)(A) applies to *all* waters still polluted after the implementation of technological standards, and that §303(d)(3) sets up a separate process for ensuring the *maintenance* of waters that currently meet standards, similar to the prevention of significant deterioration program under the CAA.

93. ROUGH DRAFT TMDL REPORT, *supra* note 11, app. I, at 1. The intent to avoid enforcement could not be more plainly stated; in the stated point of view, *any* judicial enforcement is "unexpected" and "unintended."

94. *Id.* at 2.

95. *See* ROUGH DRAFT TMDL REPORT, *supra* note 11, app. I, at 3.

96. As the FACA final report hopefully words the enforceability of §303(e) planning, "[a]ccountability mechanisms under §303(e) could include a variety of oversight and leadership tools through which EPA generally influences state action." FACA REPORT, *supra* note 76, app. H, at H-1. These are, of course, the same oversight and leadership tools that have produced such unremarkable results under §319. *See* David Zaring, *Agriculture, Nonpoint Source Pollution, and Regulatory Control: The Clean Water Act's Bleak Present and Future*, 20 HARV. ENVTL. L. REV. 515 (1996).

97. U.S. EPA, *Clean Water Action Plan: Clean Water—The Road Ahead* 9 (visited Feb. 26, 1998) http://www.epa.gov/cleanwater/action/overview.html [hereinafter *CWAP—The Road Ahead*].

98. Clean Water Act; Vice President's Initiatives, 62 Fed. Reg. 60448 (Nov. 7, 1997).

99. H.R. 961, 104th Cong. (1995). Inter alia, the bill would have extended a voluntary approach toward nonpoint pollution over the next 20 years. *See* Oliver A. Houck, *TMDLs: The Resurrection of Water Quality Standards-Based Regulation Under the Clean Water Act*, 27 ELR 10329, 10343 (July 1997) [hereinafter *TMDLs I*].

100. *See* President William J. Clinton, Remarks Made at the Living Classroom Foundation, Baltimore, Md. (Feb. 19, 1998), *reprinted at* U.S. EPA, *Clean Water Action Plans: Restoring and Protecting America's Waters* (visited Feb. 26, 1998) http://www.epa.gov/cleanwater/presrem.html.

101. *See* U.S. EPA, *Clean Water Action Plan: Setting the Stage: Successes, Challenges, and New Directions* 8-9 (visited Feb. 26, 1998) http://www.epa.gov/cleanwater/action/c1a.html.

102. *Id.*

103. *Id.* at 10.

104. *Id.* at 11. With respect to estuarine impairment, other EPA data rank "urban runoff/storm sewers" as the primary culprit. *See infra* note 160.

105. Linda Korn Levy, Assistant Secretary, Office of Water Resources, Louisiana Department of Environmental Quality, Oral Briefing on State of Louisiana Water Pollution Control Program, at Tulane Law School, New Orleans, La. (Mar. 10, 1998).

106. *CWAP—The Road Ahead, supra* note 97.

107. For example, the Office of Surface Mining Reclamation and Enforcement in the U.S. Department of the Interior would increase by 50% its number of projects to clean up water polluted by acid mine drainage. EPA, *Clean Water Action Plan: Actions to Strengthen Core Clean Water Programs* 8 (visited Feb. 26, 1998) http/www.epa.gov/cleanwater/action/c2b.html.

108. *Id.* at 13.

109. U.S. EPA, *Clean Water Action Plan: America's Watersheds: The Key to Clean Water* 2 (visited Feb. 26, 1998) http://www.epa.gov/cleanwater/action/c3b.html.

110. *Restoring Aquatic System on a Watershed Basis, CWAP—The Road Ahead, supra* note 97, at 2.

111. *Id.* at 3.

112. *Id.*

113. 2 WILLIAM H. RODGERS JR., ENVIRONMENTAL LAW 127 (1986).

114. These oft-cited reasons are taken, inter alia, from RODGERS, *id.* at 124-27; George Gould, *Agriculture, Nonpoint Source Pollution and Federal Law*, 23 U.C. DAVIS L. REV. 461, 470-71 (1990); Daniel Mandelker, *Controlling Nonpoint Source Water Pollution: Can It Be Done?*, 65 CHI.-KENT L. REV. 479, 481-82 (1989); and EPA's position in *Natural Resources Defense Council v. Train*, 396 F. Supp. 1393, 5 ELR 20401 (D.D.C. 1975), *aff'd*, 568 F.2d 1369 (D.C. Cir. 1977).

115. *See* Gould, *supra* note 114; Zaring, *supra* note 96.

116. 40 C.F.R. §125.4(j) (1975).

117. Natural Resources Defense Council v. Train, 396 F. Supp. 1393, 5 ELR 20401 (D.D.C. 1975), *aff'd*, 568 F.2d 1369 (D.C. Cir. 1977).

118. 568 F.2d at 1383.

119. Pub. L. No. 95-217, §33(b), 91 Stat. 1577 (1977).

120. Pub. L. No. 100-4, §503, 101 Stat. 75 (1987).

121. 34 F.3d 114, 24 ELR 21480 (2d Cir. 1994), *cert. denied*, 115 S. Ct. 1793 (1995).

122. *Id.*

123. *Id.* at 118-19, 24 ELR at 21482-83.

124. 33 U.S.C. §1314(m), ELR STAT. FWPCA §304(m).

125. John Burns, *The Eight Million Little Pigs—A Cautionary Tale: Statutory and Regulatory Responses to Concentrated Hog Farming*, 31 WAKE FOREST L. REV. 851, 851 (1996).

126. U.S. EPA, DRAFT STRATEGY FOR ADDRESSING ENVIRONMENTAL AND PUBLIC HEALTH IMPACTS FROM ANIMAL FEEDING OPERATIONS 8 (Mar. 1998) [hereinafter EPA DRAFT STRATEGY].

127. 40 C.F.R. §122.23 & app. B (1997).

128. *Id.*

129. 40 C.F.R. pt. 412 (1997).

130. *Id.*

131. *See* U.S. EPA, *Compliance Assurance Implementation Plan for Concentrated Animal Feeding Operations* 2 (visited May 15, 1998) http://es.epa.gov/oeca/strategy.html.

132. *Id.*

133. OFFICE OF THE INSPECTOR GENERAL, U.S. EPA, ANIMAL WASTE DISPOSAL ISSUES, ch. 3, at 2 (Apr. 21, 1997) [hereinafter ANIMAL WASTE DISPOSAL ISSUES].

134. Burns, *supra* note 125, at 859-62.

135. *Id.* at 862 (describing toxic effects of *Pfiesteria* on humans).

136. *See* ANIMAL WASTE DISPOSAL ISSUES, *supra* note 133, at 2 (citing the *Report of the EPA/State Feedlot Working Group*).

137. U.S. GAO, ANIMAL AGRICULTURE: INFORMATION ON WASTE MANAGEMENT AND WATER QUALITY ISSUES (1995).

138. Burns, *supra* note 125, at 854.

139. *Id.* at 851.

140. Anthony E. Ludd & Bob Edwards, *It's a Dirty Business and the People Want Stricter Science Regulations, Results From Recent Surveys of Eastern North Carolina* 2 (materials presented at Louisiana Environment 1998: Law, Science and the Public Interest, Conference, Tulane University Law School, New Orleans, La., Mar. 6, 1998) (on file with author).

141. *Id.*; ANIMAL WASTE DISPOSAL ISSUES, *supra* note 133, at 1.

142. Margaret Kriz, *Pfiesteria Hysteria*, 29 NAT'L J. 1783 (1997); Margaret Kriz, *Fish and Fowl*, 30 NAT'L J. 450 (1998).

143. *Id.*

144. *Id.*; *see also* Elaine Bueschen, Pfiesteria Piscicida: *A Regional Symptom of a National Problem*, 28 ELR 10317 (June 1998) (describing recent outbreaks and state responses).

145. *Pfiesteria Hysteria, supra* note 142, at 1783.

146. As one state agency lobbyist observed, "I don't expect to see a poultry voluntary program to continue." *Fish and Fowl, supra* note 142, at 451 (quoting Robin Savage of the Association of State and Interstate Water Pollution Control Administrators).

147. EPA DRAFT STRATEGY, *supra* note 126.

148. *Id.* at 10-11.

149. *Id.* at 14, 16.

150. *Id.* at 15. It should be noted, however, that this EPA proposal only consolidates and strengthens the regulation of its previously described universe of large CAFOs. *See supra* text accompanying note 127. EPA has not (yet) proposed to expand this universe to smaller operations, although, under its regulations, it has the authority to do so on a case-by-case basis. *Supra* text accompanying note 128.

151. *See supra* note 117.

152. EPA DRAFT STRATEGY, *supra* note 126, at 15-16.

153. *Id.* at 15.

154. *Id.* at 16.

155. *Hog Waste Spills Result in Regulatory Changes in North Carolina, in* ANIMAL WASTE DISPOSAL ISSUES, *supra* note 133, ch. 2, at 1.

156. *What Can EPA Do?, in* ANIMAL WASTE DISPOSAL ISSUES, *supra* note 133, ch. 3, at 1.

157. *See NRDC Offers Solutions to "Poison Runoff," Calls It Leading Source of Water Pollution*, [20 Current Developments] Env't Rep. (BNA) 569 (July 21, 1989); *see also Nonpoint Sources Found by INFORM to Be Major Contributors of Toxics to Hudson River*, [18 Current Developments] Env't Rep. (BNA) 1263 (Aug. 28, 1987).

158. 55 Fed. Reg. 47990, 47992 (Nov. 16, 1990).

159. EPA's enforcement leverage begins, of course, with monetary fines, which, in the context of municipalities, is uncertain leverage even in the context of underperforming municipal sewage treatment systems. *See Air and Water, in* 2 RODGERS, *supra* note 113, at 605-09. Admittedly, on rare occasions, EPA may use the prospect of serious fines to leverage improved municipal performance. *See* Bill Voelker, *S&WB, U.S. Make a Deal: Agency to Clean Drainage to Lake*, TIMES PICAYUNE (New Orleans), Apr. 9, 1998, at 1 (describing consent decree requiring $200 million cleanup of New Orleans municipal runoff).

160. The federal government has spent more than $54 billion on municipal public sewage treatment plants since 1972. NATIONAL WATER QUALITY INVENTORY, *supra* note 73, at 179.

161. EPA and state water quality officials ascribe 46% of estuarine impaired waters to "urban runoff/storm sewers." *Id.* at ES-25.

162. *See* 55 Fed. Reg. at 47991 ("From a legal standpoint, however, most urban runoff is discharged through conveyances such as separate storm sewers or other conveyances which are point sources under the CWA."). Whether, before the 1987 CWA amendments, these point sources discharged a "pollutant" within the meaning of the CWA was an interesting question. *See* National Wildlife Fed'n v. Gorsuch, 693 F.2d 156, 13 ELR 20015 (D.C. Cir. 1982). Since 1987, Congress has explicitly called for their regulation under the NPDES program. 33 U.S.C. §1342(p), ELR STAT. FWPCA §402(p).

163. *See* 38 Fed. Reg. 1350 (May 22, 1973).

164. For a summary of these developments, see ROBERT ADLER ET AL., THE CLEAN WATER ACT 20 YEARS LATER 152-53 (1993), and sources cited therein.

165. 33 U.S.C. §1342(p), ELR STAT. FWPCA §402(p).

166. *Id.* §1342(p)(3)(A), ELR STAT. FWPCA §402(p)(3)(A).

167. *Id.* §1342(p)(1) & (2), ELR STAT. FWPCA §402(p)(1) & (2) (requiring regulation of municipal sources serving a population of 100,000 or more); *id.* §1342(p)(3)(B), ELR STAT. FWPCA §402(p)(3)(B) ("maximum extent practicable" standard).

168. *Id.* §1342(p)(6), ELR STAT. FWPCA §402(p)(6).

169. 40 C.F.R. §122.26(c)(1). *See generally* Brian Weeks, *Trends in Regulation of Stormwater and Nonpoint Source Pollution*, 25 ELR 10300 (June 1995).

170. *See* 40 C.F.R. §122.26(b)(14) (1998) (categorical permits are available to 11 classes of industry, including manufacturing, mining, utilities, landfills, transportation, and construction disturbing more than five acres of land). EPA's exception for light industry and small construction was invalidated in National Resources Defense Council v. U.S. EPA, 966 F.2d 1292, 22 ELR 20950 (9th Cir. 1992), leading to new proposals. *See infra* text accompanying note 175.

171. *See supra* note 161.

172. 55 Fed. Reg. 47990 (Nov. 16, 1990).

173. 40 C.F.R. §122.26 (1998).

174. *See* OLIVER A. HOUCK ET AL., TO RESTORE LAKE PONTCHARTRAIN 82-93 (Greater New Orleans Expressway Comm'n 1989) and sources cited therein (describing urban stormwater control mechanisms).

175. *See* U.S. EPA, Authorization to Discharge Under the National Pollution Discharge Elimination System, Sewerage and Water Board of New Orleans et al.,

NPDES LA 5000301, at 5-27 (Mar. 1, 1997) (on file with author). Within a year, the stencils have largely washed away. Author's personal observation.

176. Letter of Jack V. Ferguson, Chief, NPDES Permits Branch, Region VI, U.S. EPA, to Robert R. Kuehn, Director, Tulane Environmental Law Clinic, encl. at 1 (Feb. 11, 1997) (on file with author).

177. *See* National Resources Defense Council v. U.S. EPA, 966 F.2d 1292, 22 ELR 20950 (9th Cir. 1992). Regulations in 1995 proposed to include virtually all remaining sources over the next six years. At the same time, EPA began consulting with a Stormwater Phase II subcommittee of a separate FACA committee addressing urban, wet-water flows. 60 Fed. Reg. 21189 (May 1, 1995); *see also* U.S. EPA, NPDES STORM WATER PHASE II FACT SHEET 6 (Jan. 1998) [hereinafter NPDES FACT SHEET]. As of April 1998, EPA had issued 25 notices of meetings of this FACA committee and its subcommittees. Westlaw search (May 1998). No final FACA report had issued.

178. NPDES FACT SHEET, *supra* note 177, at 3.

179. 33 U.S.C. §1342(p)(6), ELR STAT. FWPCA §402(p)(6).

180. NPDES FACT SHEET, *supra* note 177, at 9.

181. *Id.* at 20. It seems anomalous that EPA is proposing far more prescriptive regulations for smaller municipal sources than for larger ones; the Agency's rationale is that its regulation of smaller municipal sources is a one-shot affair with little subsequent monitoring, while its regulation of larger sources will be iterative and progressive. *Id.* at 2-4. Perhaps so. And perhaps the Agency is simply reluctant to face down large municipalities without hard water quality impact data.

182. *Id.* at 2-4.

183. *See* 61 Fed. Reg. 43761 (Aug. 26, 1996); *see also* U.S. EPA, Questions and Answers Regarding Implementation of an Interim Permitting Approach for Water Quality-Based Effluent Limitations in Storm Water Permits, 61 Fed. Reg. 57425 (Nov. 6, 1996). Municipalities have also questioned the fairness of blaming them for water quality violations if the receiving waters are already contaminated beyond state standards. Telephone Conversation with Peter Lehrer, Natural Resources Defense Council (June 12, 1998) (Mr. Lehrer is a member of the stormwater FACA committee, *see supra* note 177). Of course, this problem confronts the application of water quality standards to *all* point sources, and the CWA's solution is to require them to abate their pollution emissions collectively, through TMDLs.

184. *See* 60 Fed. Reg. 17950, 17952 (Apr. 7, 1995) (describing the President's 1994 Clean Water Initiative as "clarifying that the Maximum Extent Practicable Standard should be applied in a site specific, flexible manner taking into account use considerations as well as water quality effects").

185. 63 Fed. Reg. 1595 (Jan. 9, 1988).

186. *See* Debra L. Donahue, *The Untapped Power of Clean Water Act Section 401*, ECOLOGY L.Q. 201, 278-79 (1996).

187. National Wildlife Fed'n v. U.S. Forest Serv., 592 F. Supp. 931, 14 ELR 20755 (D. Or. 1984).

188. *See* Donohue, *supra* note 186; *see also* Richard H. Braun, *Emerging Limits on Federal Land Management Discretion: Livestock, Riparian Ecosystems and Clean Water Law*, 17 ENVTL. L. 43 (1986). Braun describes, inter alia, EPA prescriptions for livestock grazing BMPs as a component of state nonpoint source programs. *Id.* at 72. These prescriptions, of course, fall, as all EPA nonpoint source regulations, on the voluntary side of state implementation.

189. *See* Ed Marston, *The Old West Is Going Under*, HIGH COUNTRY NEWS, Apr. 27, 1998, at 1.

190. *See* Larry C. Frarey & Staci J. Pratt, *Environmental Regulation of Livestock Production Operations*, NAT. RESOURCES & ENV'T, Winter 1995, at 8 ("An average 1,000 pound milk cow produces approximately eighty-two pounds of wet manure per day—twenty times that of an adult human. Thus, the 225,000 cows on 275 dairies in Tulare County, California, produce over 3.4 million tons of wet manure each year.").

191. *See* Susan E. Schell, *The Uncertain Future of Clean Water Act Agricultural Pollution Exemptions After* Concerned Area Residents for the Env't v. South View Farm, 31 LAND & WATER L. REV. 113, 127 n.111 (1995).

192. *See* Braun, *supra* note 188, at 44-49.

193. *See* Donahue, *supra* note 186, at 279-80.

194. *See* Braun, *supra* note 188, at 50 n.16 (comments ascribed to the Idaho Cattle Association).

195. *See* Jeffrey W. Styron, *Regulation of Nonpoint Sources of Water Pollution on Public Lands*, 41 NAVAL L. REV. 97, 112 (1993) ("Some states apparently except logging, grazing and other nonpoint sources of pollution from complying with water quality criteria, while other states provide liberal guidelines for allowing temporary variances or modifications for nonpoint source activities." (citations omitted)).

196. The Organic Administrative Act of 1897 reads, "No national forest shall be established, except to improve and protect the forest within the boundaries, or for the purpose of securing favorable conditions of water flows, and to furnish a continuous supply of timber to the United States . . . ." 16 U.S.C. §475 (1994).

197. *Id.*

198. National Forest Management Act of 1976, Pub. L. No. 94-588, 90 Stat. 2949.

199. CHARLES WILKINSON, CROSSING THE NEXT MERIDIAN: LAND, WATER AND THE FUTURE OF THE WEST 136-37 (1992).

200. National Wildlife Fed'n v. U.S. Forest Serv., 592 F. Supp. 931, 14 ELR 20755 (D. Or. 1984).

201. Of the 400 known stocks of Pacific salmon, 214 were identified as endangered by the early 1990s; 106 were extinct. Murray D. Feldman, *National Forest Management Under the Endangered Species Act*, NAT. RESOURCES & ENV'T, Winter 1995, at 32, 34.

202. *Id.*

203. *See* IDAHO DIVISION OF ENVIRONMENTAL QUALITY TOTAL MAXIMUM DAILY LOAD (TMDL) PROVISIONS, PROBLEM ASSESSMENT: SOUTH FORK SALMON RIVER AND WATERSHED 5 (1991).

204. *See* Jeffrey St. Clair, *U.S. Environment: Logging Practices Unleash Lethal Landslides*, INTER PRESS SERV., Jan. 6, 1997, at 115, *available in* 1997 WL 7073076 ("In the [third week of November 1996] Oregon rains, landslides killed eight people. And in all but one of the cases, the slides occurred in sites that had been clear cut in the last 10 years by timber giants.").

205. *See* WILKINSON, *supra* note 199, at 136-37.

206. *See Bomb Rips Building in Nevada*, TIMES PICAYUNE (New Orleans), Nov. 1, 1993, at A5 (describing a bomb explosion at Bureau of Land Management (BLM) offices); *Pipe Bomber Targets Forest Service Region*, LAND LETTER, Sept. 1, 1995, at 6 (bomb attack at Forest Service employee's home). Violence against environmentalists is also not unknown. *See* Tony Davis, *A Struggle for the Last Grass*, HIGH COUNTRY NEWS, May 2, 1994, at 1.

207. 36 C.F.R. §228(b) (1997).

208. The closest such requirements in the Forest Service's timber regulations appear in 33 C.F.R. §219.13 (1997), but provide no quantitative measures nor do they reference state water quality standards.

209. *See* Schell, *supra* note 191, at 126-30.

210. CWA §401 requires in pertinent part:

> Any applicant for a Federal license or permit to conduct any activity including, but not limited to, the construction or operation of facilities, which may result in any discharge into the navigable waters, shall provide the licensing or permitting agency a certification from the State in which the discharge originates or will originate . . . that any such discharge will comply with the applicable provisions of [CWA §§301, 302, 303, 306, and 307].

33 U.S.C. §1341, ELR STAT. FWPCA §401.

211. *See* Oregon Natural Desert Ass'n v. Thomas, 940 F. Supp. 1534, 27 ELR 20221 (D. Or. 1996) (appeal pending); *see also* Paul Larmer, *Judge Sends Message to Cows*, HIGH COUNTRY NEWS, Oct. 29, 1996, at 4 (quoting chief counsel for the Oregon Farm Bureau who acknowledged that "it doesn't take much of a leap to realize that this could be applied to BLM lands, and to activities such as timber harvesting . . . .").

212. 940 F. Supp. 1534, 27 ELR 20221 (D. Or. 1996), *rev'd sub nom.* Oregon Natural Desert Ass'n v. Dombeck, 151 F.3d 945, 28 ELR 21471 (9th Cir. 1998).

213. No. CV 95-394-S-MHW, 1996 WL 938215 (D. Idaho Aug. 12, 1996).

214. *See Oregon Natural Desert Ass'n,* 940 F. Supp. at 1539, 27 ELR at 20222.

215. *See EPA Drafts Regulations for Federal Nonpoint Source Activities,* INSIDE EPA, Feb. 28, 1997, at 20.

216. *See* Captain DeRoma, *Has EPA Deserted Oregon Natural Desert?,* ARMY LAW., July 1997, at 43.

217. 33 U.S.C. §1323, ELR STAT. FWPCA §313.

218. 565 F. Supp. 586, 13 ELR 20793 (N.D. Cal. 1983), *aff'd in part, vacated in part,* 764 F.2d 581, 15 ELR 20682 (9th Cir. 1985), *on reh'g,* 795 F.2d 688, 17 ELR 20021 (9th Cir. 1986), *rev'd & remanded sub nom.* Lyng v. Northwest Indian Cemetery Protective Ass'n, 485 U.S. 439, 18 ELR 21043 (U.S. 1988).

219. 914 F.2d 179, 21 ELR 20023 (9th Cir. 1990).

220. 834 F.2d 842, 18 ELR 20450 (9th Cir. 1987).

221. 5 U.S.C. §§701-706, *available in* ELR STAT. ADMIN. PROC.

222. *See* 834 F.2d at 849, 18 ELR at 20454 (holding that a citizen suit under CWA §505 would not lie because the violation was not of an "effluent limitation.").

223. No. EA A2-026-92-24 (Dep't of the Interior, Interior Board of Land Appeals, Nov. 18, 1996) (on file with author).

224. Telephone Communication with Thomas Lustig (Apr. 3, 1998) (Mr. Lustig is lead counsel in *National Wildlife Fed'n,* No. EA A2-026-92-24).

225. On the other hand, the language of §313 could be read to require only that federal agencies comply with state standards to the extent that state agencies and private parties do—raising the question whether, if a state imposes no water quality requirements on these activities, this section requires more.

226. For a glimpse of these changing dynamics, see Dustin Solberg, *Timber Town Opts for Water Over Logs,* HIGH COUNTRY NEWS, Apr. 27, 1998 at 10.

227. 16 U.S.C. §§1531-1544, ELR STAT. ESA §§2-18. For the initiative of the Secretary of the Interior to get ahead of Endangered Species Act "train wrecks," see Bruce Babbitt, *The Endangered Species Act and Takings: A Call for Innovation With the Terms of the Act,* 24 ENVTL. L. 355, 364 (1994).

228. For a description of several administrative "ecosystem management" initiatives, see Oliver A. Houck, *On the Law of Biodiversity and Ecosystem Management,* 81 MINN. L. REV. 869 (1997).

229. 43 C.F.R. §4180.1 (1995).

230. *Id.*

231. *Id.* §4180.1(c).

232. *See* BUREAU OF LAND MANAGEMENT, COMPARISON OF UTAH STANDARDS AND GUIDELINES WITH THE MINIMUM ROLLBACKS CONTAINED IN THE PREFERRED ALTERNATIVE FOR THE RANGELAND REFORM 1994 EIS 1-1, para. 2 (undated) (on file with author).

233. *See* U.S. DEP'T OF AGRICULTURE & U.S. DEP'T OF THE INTERIOR, ENVIRONMENT ASSESSMENT FOR THE IMPLEMENTATION OF INTERIM STRATEGIES FOR MANAGING ANACHRONOUS FISH-PRODUCING WATERSHEDS IN EASTERN OREGON AND WASHINGTON, IDAHO AND PORTIONS OF NORTHERN CALIFORNIA (Mar. 1994); Pacific Rivers Council v. Robertson, 854 F. Supp. 713 (D. Or. 1993), *aff'd in part, rev'd in part sub nom.* Pacific Rivers Council v. Thomas, 30 F.3d 1050, 24 ELR 21367 (9th Cir. 1994) (describing salmon-based forest planning).

234. This issue has been brewing since at least 1985. *See New Forest Service Management Scheme Proposed by Conservation Advocates*, LAND LETTER, Aug. 14, 1985, at 1.

235. *See* Todd Wilkinson, *Forest Service Seeks a New (Roadless) Road to the Future*, HIGH COUNTRY NEWS, Apr. 27, 1998, at 8; *see also Enhance Natural Resources Stewardship, CWAP—The Road Ahead*, *supra* note 106, at 5.

236. *Enhance Natural Resources Stewardship, CWAP—The Road Ahead*, *supra* note 106, at 5.

237. *Id.*

238. *See* Wilkinson, *supra* note 235 (identifying "powerful opponents" in Congress as including congressional committee chairs Rep. Helen Chenoweth (R-Idaho), Sen. Frank Murkowski (R-Alaska), Sen. Larry Craig (R-Idaho), and Rep. Don Young (R-Alaska)).

239. ARIZ. REV. STAT. ANN. §49-202.01 (1988).

240. As one commentator has observed:

> Federal agencies can accomplish a great deal toward the goal of reduction of nonpoint source pollution if they are willing to diligently develop the best BMPs for a given area during the operations phase. The biggest piece of the regulations puzzle that is missing at present is the lack of federal enforcement in monitoring the effectiveness of BMPs on public lands.

Styron, *supra* note 195, at 113.

241. Mark Schlefstein, *"Dead Zone" in Gulf Biggest in Decade*, TIMES PICAYUNE (New Orleans), July 28, 1995 at B-12.

242. 16 U.S.C. §§1451-1465, ELR STAT. CZMA §§302-319.

243. H. REP. No. 101-535, at 9 (1990).

244. *Id.*

245. *See* Carol Kaesuk Yoon, *A "Dead Zone" Grows in the Gulf of Mexico*, N.Y. TIMES, Jan. 20, 1998 at B-1.

246. 16 U.S.C. §1455b, *available in* ELR STAT. CZMA.

247. For a description of the CZMA and its implementation, *see* Oliver A. Houck & Michael Rolland, *Federalism in Wetlands Regulation: A Consideration of Delegation of Clean Water Act Section 404 and Related Programs to the States*, 54 MD. L. REV. 1242, 1294-99 (1995).

248. 16 U.S.C. §1452(1), ELR STAT. CZMA §303(1).

249. *Id.* §1452(2), ELR STAT. CZMA §303(2).

250. *See* Houck & Rolland, *supra* note 247, at 1297-98.

251. 16 U.S.C. §1455b(b)(1) & (2), *available in* ELR STAT. CZMA.

252. *Id.* §1455b(b)(7), *available in* ELR STAT. CZMA.

253. *Id.* §1455b(b)(3), *available in* ELR STAT. CZMA.

254. *Id.* §1455b(g)(5), *available in* ELR STAT. CZMA.

255. U.S. Department of Commerce & U.S. EPA, Coastal Nonpoint Pollution State Program Guidance Documents, 58 Fed. Reg. 5182, 5184 (Jan. 19, 1993).

256. *Id.*

257. *Id.*

258. 16 U.S.C. §1455(d)(16), ELR STAT. CZMA §306(16).

259. *Id.* §1455b(a)(1), *available in* ELR STAT. CZMA (30 months for state submission); *id.* §1455b(c)(1), *available in* ELR STAT. CZMA (six months for review and approval).

260. *Id.* §1455b(c)(3), *available in* ELR STAT. CZMA.

261. Clare F. Saperstein, *State Solutions to Nonpoint Source Pollution: Implementation and Enforcement of the 1990 Coastal Zone Amendments Reauthorization Act Section 6217*, 73 B.U. L. REV. 889, 890 (1995).

262. *See* U.S. Dep't of Commerce & U.S. EPA, Availability of Proposed Administrative Changes to Coastal Nonpoint Pollution Programs Guidance, 63 Fed. Reg. 12078 (Mar. 12, 1998) [hereinafter Availability of Proposed Administrative Changes].

263. *Id.* at 12078.

264. *Id.*

265. *Id.*

266. Telephone Conversation with Stuart S. Tuller, Office of Water, U.S. EPA (Feb. 25, 1998) [hereinafter Tuller Telephone Conversation].

267. U.S. EPA, GUIDANCE SPECIFYING MANAGEMENT MEASURES FOR SOURCES OF NONPOINT POLLUTION IN COASTAL WATERS (Jan. 1993) (a bible of data on and prescriptions for nonpoint sources running over 1,000 pages, separate chapters ad-

dress agricultural, forestry, urban, marina and recreation, and hydro modification sources; wetlands systems; and monitoring).

268. *Id.* at 4-12.

269. *See* COASTAL MANAGEMENT DIV., LOUISIANA DEP'T OF NATURAL RESOURCES & OFFICE OF WATER RESOURCES, LOUISIANA DEP'T OF ENVTL. QUALITY, LOUISIANA'S COASTAL NONPOINT POLLUTION CONTROL PROGRAM (Oct. 1995) [hereinafter LOUISIANA'S COASTAL NONPOINT POLLUTION CONTROL PROGRAM]. The document does reveal rather significant gaps in statutory enforcement authority over, for example, agricultural "erosion and sediment control," "grazing," and "nutrient management" and forestry "pre-harvest planning," "road management," "timber harvesting," and "revegetation in distributed areas." *Id.* at I-5. Which raises the question: what's left?

270. COASTAL MANAGEMENT DIV., LOUISIANA DEP'T OF NATURAL RESOURCES & OFFICE OF WATER RESOURCES, LOUISIANA DEP'T OF ENVTL. QUALITY, SUMMARY: LOUISIANA COASTAL NONPOINT POLLUTION CONTROL PROGRAM 10/10/95 (on file with author).

271. Letter of Joseph A. Utravitan, Acting Chief, Coastal Programs Division, Office of Ocean and Coastal Resource Management, NOAA, to Terry Howie, Director, Coastal Management, Louisiana Department of Natural Resources, and Glenda Levy, Administrator, Office of Water Resources, Louisiana Department of Environmental Quality (Aug. 22, 1997), and attachment COASTAL MANAGEMENT DIV., LOUISIANA DEP'T OF NATURAL RESOURCES & OFFICE OF WATER RESOURCES, LOUISIANA DEP'T OF ENVTL. QUALITY, LOUISIANA COASTAL NONPOINT PROGRAM FINDINGS AND CONDITIONS, DRAFT FINAL 8/5/96.

272. COASTAL MANAGEMENT DIV., LOUISIANA DEP'T OF NATURAL RESOURCES & OFFICE OF WATER RESOURCES, LOUISIANA DEP'T OF ENVTL. QUALITY, LOUISIANA COASTAL NONPOINT POLLUTION CONTROL PROGRAM, COMMENTS IN REPLY TO DRAFT FINDINGS AND CONDITIONS, DRAFT FINAL 8/5/96 (on file with author).

273. *See* U.S. EPA, *California Nonpoint Source Program, Final Draft California Coastal Nonpoint Program Findings and Conditions* (visited May 15, 1998) http://www.epa.gov/region09/water/nonpoint/cal/finaldraft.html.

274. Northern Sec. Co. v. United States, 193 U.S. 197, 400-01 (1904) (Holmes, J., dissenting) ("These immediate interests exercise a kind of hydraulic pressure which makes what previously was clear seem doubtful, and before which even well settled principles of law will bend.").

275. *See Comment Period for Nonpoint Source Guidance Extended as Industry, States Question Feasibility*, [22 Current Developments] Env't Rep. (BNA) 1795 (Nov. 22, 1991).

276. *See* Letter of H. Wayne Beam, Chairman, Coastal States Organization, to Carol M. Browner, Administrator, U.S. EPA, and Dr. James Baker, Undersecretary of Commerce, U.S. Department of Commerce (Dec. 5, 1994) (cited in Saperstein, *supra* note 261, at 921 n.117).

277. *See* Availability of Proposed Administrative Changes, *supra* note 262 (describing a January 6, 1995, letter and the March 16, 1995, document).

278. *Written Testimony Received at Public Meetings*, 2 LOUISIANA'S COASTAL NONPOINT POLLUTION CONTROL PROGRAM, *supra* note 269, §G.

279. *Id.*

280. *Written Comments Received After Public Meetings*, 2 LOUISIANA'S COASTAL NONPOINT POLLUTION CONTROL PROGRAM, *supra* note 269, §H.

281. *Id.*

282. *Id.*

283. *Id.*

284. *See* Tuller Telephone Conversation, *supra* note 266.

285. Availability of Proposed Administrative Changes, *supra* note 262.

286. *Id.*

287. *Id.*

288. *Id.* at 12079.

289. *Id.*

290. *Id.*

291. *Id.*

292. The closed-door nature of this guidance continues; in April 1998, EPA and NOAA scheduled a "workshop" with coastal states, and undisclosed "other partners," to discuss the implementation of the program and of this notice; at the request of the states who wanted to be able to "shoot from the hip without broadcasting to the world," members of the public were not allowed to attend. Tuller Telephone Conversation, *supra* note 266. The contrast between this process and that of the open, FACA meetings on the TMDL program is striking.

293. *States Drafting New Position on Key Clean Water Act Program*, INSIDE EPA, Aug. 22, 1997, at 3 (describing meeting of Association of State and Interstate Water Pollution Administration, August 1997).

294. Oregon, an early subject of TMDL litigation, has turned out to be a strong proponent of the TMDL program. *See States Lack Resources Needed to Implement TMDL Strategy, EPA Told*, Daily Env't Rep. (BNA), May 12, 1997, at A-8 (describing Oregon support for EPA requirements). For a description of TMDLs catching up with nutrient loadings into Long Island Sound, see Ann Powers, *Reducing Nitrogen Pollution on Long Island Sound: Is There a Place for Pollutant Trading?*, 23 COLUM. J. ENVTL. L. 137 (1998). For a website listing of other state TMDL programs, see http://www.epa.gov/owow/tmdl/links.html (Maryland, Montana, Oregon, South Dakota, and Washington).

295. For a comprehensive and current summary of state nonpoint programs, see U.S. EPA, *Nonpoint Source Pollution Control Program* (visited May 15, 1998)

http://www.epa.gov/owow/NPS/elistudy/ [hereinafter *Nonpoint Source Pollu-tion Control Program*]; see also U.S. EPA, *Section 319 Nonpoint Source Success Stories*, No. 841-S-94-004 (visited May 15, 1998) http://www.epa.gov/owow/NPS/sec319.html/. For a comprehensive state approach, see North Carolina Div. of Water Quality, Draft Plan, Neuse River Nutrient Sensitive Waters (NSW) Management Strategy (July 12, 1996) (unpublished, on file with author). For an indication that state programs are not so substantive, however, see the following description: "Virginia continues to develop watershed projects that combine educational programs and demonstrations, technical assis-tance, financial assistance and water quality monitoring . . . . Over 600 stu-dents participated in an educational program for all local schools, which included t-shirts and logo and poster contests." http://www.epa.gov/owow/cgi-bin/imagemap/owow-usa?433,203. The narrative continues by describing a "pilot total maximum daily load program," which turns out to be a study leading to the following remarkable conclusion: "although more research is required, the completed project shows a correlation between land use changes and change in wa-ter quality." *Id.* It sounds like money well spent.

296. *See supra* note 63.

297. *See State "No More Stringent" Laws, in Nonpoint Source Pollution Control Program, supra* note 295, app.

298. *States Drafting New Position on Key Clean Water Act Program, supra* note 293.

299. For a recent assessment of state TMDL compliance, see NATIONAL WILDLIFE FED'N, POLLUTION PARALYSIS: STATE INACTION PUTS WATERS AT RISK (Oct. 9, 1997). Comparing the performance of 53 states and territories in TMDL lists and plans, the report ranks no programs as "good," 17 as "weak," 16 as "poor," and 20 as "failing." *Id.* at 17.

300. *See States Lack Resources Needed to Implement TMDL Strategy, EPA Told, supra* note 294, at A-8 (describing state concerns with funding and timing for example:

> Bruce Anderson, an official with the Hawaii Department of Health, said in an April 14 letter, "in a period of declining state budgets, public demand for no new taxes, and resistance to regulation, we do not ex-pect to obtain sufficient funding to establish scientifically-defensible numeric targets for polluted runoff control."

see also Western Governors' Forum Outlines States' TMDL Strategies; More Money Needed, Daily Env't Rep. (BNA), Oct. 2, 1997, at A-7 ("Let's get more money from EPA now," said Dennis Hemmer, director of the Wyoming Depart-ment of Environmental Quality. Hemmer said he appreciated the opportunity to ex-change information with other states on implementing TMDLs, but he said the main issue common to all states is "wanting more money.").

301. *See supra* text accompanying note 106.

302. *See States Lack Resources Needed to Implement TMDL Strategy, EPA Told,* *supra* note 294, at A-8 (comment of Hawaii official); *see also supra* note 300.

303. *See* 33 U.S.C. §1251(b), ELR Stat. FWPCA §101(b) (recognizing the "primary responsibilities and rights of states" to abate water pollution); *see also TMDLs I, supra* note 99.

304. *TMDLs II, supra* note 2, at 10397.

305. U.S. EPA, *Status of 1998 Section 303(d) Lists 5/15/98* (visited May 15, 1998) http://www.epa.gov/owow/tmdl/tmdlmap.htm.

306. *See* Rough Draft TMDL Report, *supra* note 11, at 10-11.

307. *See* Susan Bruninga, *Time Allowed for States to Do TMDLs Too Little for Adequate Job, Group Told,* Daily Env't Rep. (BNA), Mar. 10, 1998, at A-8.

308. E-mail Communication from Nina Bell, Northwest Environmental Advocates, to Ray Gorning (Mar. 10, 1998) (on file with author).

309. *See* Bruninga, *supra* note 307 (the referenced state is Kansas). Not to be outdone in any race-to-the-bottom, Louisiana has recently relaxed its water quality standards for fecal coliforms, limiting the application of strict criteria to summer months on the stated (and amazing) rationale that primary contact recreation does not occur in Louisiana at other times of the year. Jennifer Anderson, *Water Quality,* La. Envtl. Compliance Update, May 1998, at 5.

310. *See* Bruninga, *supra* note 307. Of these 33,000 cases of impairment, 1,000 were identified as impaired by pesticides. *Id.*

311. *Id.*

312. Parrish Conversation, *supra* note 11. As of May 1998, EPA was projecting a new total of 22,851 waters which, if borne out, would represent a 50% increase over 1996. U.S. EPA, Summary Status of 1998 §303(d) Lists May 29, 1998 [hereinafter Summary Status] (on file with author).

313. The lack of comparability may be illustrated by projected listings in the state of Washington at 4,400 and in the state of Louisiana—an equally wet and agricultural state—at a mere 176. Summary Status, *supra* note 312.

314. *See supra* text accompanying note 47. As of late May 1998, EPA had received the required TMDL schedules from 40 states; 33 states projected TMDL completion within the prescribed 13-year term, while 7 projected taking from 14 to 22 years. These disparities may well reflect relative difficulties in the task among the various states; they most certainly as well reflect differences in commitment to the TMDL process.

Chapter 5:
Toward the Final Frontier

Reviewing the Bidding

W̶e had problems with science:

> We are recognizing for the first time that there is not a readily defin-
> able linear relationship between given effluent discharges and the
> quality of the receiving waters.

> —Sen. Howard Baker (R-Tenn.), Sponsor,
> FWPCA Amendments of 1972 (CWA) [1]

And we had problems with political will:

> We have heard that from the Chamber of Commerce from the very
> beginning. "Don't pass any Federal law; just let us keep it at home
> in the State." So consequently, we didn't get anything done. We left
> it to the States, year after year, and we didn't get a single thing but a
> bunch of nursery rhymes as to the Constitution, and we didn't get
> any clean water until the Federal Government insisted upon it and
> made some dollars available to the state for that use.

> —Rep. Robert Jones (D-Ala.), Chair,
> House Public Works Committee [2]

We have been here before. As we return once more to an ambient standards-based program for restoring the nation's water quality, it is useful to
remember just how thoroughly our earlier efforts to execute such a program
failed, and why.

The story began in 1948, when the federal government entered the field
of pollution abatement with a water program emphasizing the primary role
of the states and reserving to the U.S. Surgeon General the authority to, after
lengthy administrative proceedings, sue to abate discharges. [3] Seventeen
years later, with only a few states having adopted measurable indicators of

water quality and little enforcement action, [4] Congress passed the Water Quality Act of 1965 (WQA). [5] The high watermark of ambient-based water pollution control, the WQA required states to adopt water quality standards and to take the lead on their implementation; the federal role remained limited to providing funding (always popular) and technical assistance (sometimes popular) and, where interstate waters were involved, to calling an "abatement conference" of states and responsible parties. [6] These programs were supplemented by the authorization of several river basin commissions with the mission of managing water resources comprehensively in specific regions of the country. [7]

The WQA and its contemporaries were monuments of faith in the commitment of state and local governments to secure clean water in the face of powerful local interests; in the ability of science to predict aquatic impacts and to trace observed impacts to their sources; and in the practicality of treating water pollution through comprehensive, regional planning. They were enacted in a day when pollution was still viewed as a local affair with regional overtones (many states resisted even the minimal federal role under the WQA) [8] and when America had yet to meet the intransigence of historically unregulated dischargers, of complex ecosystems, of persistent pollutants, and of impacts too remote, too far downstream, to concern the people responsible for abating them. In this happy world, the attainment of water quality standards was to be a cooperative venture among dischargers and local authorities (which did not even perceive themselves as regulators). [9] The WQA's water quality standards themselves were viewed as goals and guidance for the ensuing discussions, not as enforceable or enforcement tools. [10]

Unfortunately, the world, had it ever worked this way, was going in another direction, and virtually nothing in the WQA came to pass. By 1970, only half of the states had adopted even the most rudimentary water quality standards, and the difficulties of compliance had proven to be paralyzing. [11] For its part, between 1948 and 1970, the federal government had brought only one enforcement action, against one discharger. [12] The river basin commissions were busy promoting projects of water engineering and lacked the authority to do anything about water pollution even had they cared about it. [13] Water pollution itself, meanwhile, was booming; most municipal waste was still without basic, primary treatment, and more than 300,000 industrial facilities were discharging 22 billion gallons of wastewater per year, less than one-third with any form of treatment at all. [14] All of which would be ancient history but for the reasons that underlay this failure, and remain with us today.

In actual practice, the scope and rigor of state water quality standards were heavily influenced by local dischargers, creating inequalities within states and sending some states (primarily in the South) into a classic race to the bottom. [15] The requirements of monitoring these waters—to determine which were in violation of what standards and when—was beyond the existing capacity of government at any level. The science to predict the results of new or existing discharges, even for specific point sources, was similarly out of reach, and that necessary to attribute specific water quality violations to particular sources was beyond the realm of proof. These conclusions became apparent to commentators, to courts, and, finally, to Congress itself. A few illustrative statements, from many, bear repeating.

On setting water quality standards:

> Due to the pressures of powerful economic interests, the States do not establish meaningful quality levels and create water "zones"—some good, mostly bad.
>
> —Rep. Charles Vanik (D-Ohio) [16]

On the consequent race to the bottom:

> One of the most critical problems in legislating water pollution controls is that the standards will be so haphazard that . . . industries [will move] from State to State in search of less strict pollution standards.
>
> —Rep. Michael Harrington (D-Mass.) [17]

On the underlying science:

> State and Federal governments will continue to founder on the staggering complexity of this control system, which requires working mathematically back from the permitted pollution levels in a waterway to the effluent limitations at the point source needed to achieve them.
>
> —Reps. Bella Abuzug (D-N.Y.) and
> Charles Rangel (D-N.Y.) [18]

On the influence of politics:

> These [legislators] are all men of good intentions, but they get beat over the head by powerful interests back home. I won't mention any names, but say somebody is from South Carolina or Georgia, and the Georgia Power Co. gets after them . . . . You can't find any finer men, or men of more integrity. But you can only go so far.
>
> —Rep. John Blatnik (D-Minn.), Chair,
> House Public Works Committee [19]

None of which history restrained in the least the states, local water districts, and industrial dischargers from making the strongest possible plea, during the tumultuous sessions leading to the FWPCA Amendments of

1972, for retaining the water quality standards program as the primary engine of national water pollution control. [20] State and local agencies were said to be in a far better position to know the numerous "local and natural variables" for pollution control (Gov. Nelson Rockefeller (R-N.Y.)) [21]; states had, likewise, the necessary "knowledge, experience and expertise" (National Governors' Conference) [22]; states had "predictive mathematical models" for "the development of water quality implementation plans" (Pennsylvania Department of Environmental Protection and Regulation). [23]

At bottom, however, this was a turf war. Governor after governor spoke to protest a "federal takeover," [24] a "subterfuge to encroach upon the constitutional authority" [25] of the states. Although couched in language of "expertise," to the states and their supporters in the House of Representatives (and in the American Petroleum Institute and the U.S. Chamber of Commerce) the issue was not so much clean water as it was retaining the clout to make decisions that affected state and local development. And it has so remained. Virtually every year since 1972, state agencies and their trade organizations have proposed returning the CWA to a water quality standards-based program as a matter of state sovereignty, albeit to a program that would be relaxed at the same time to eliminate "unrealistic" and "rigid" federal numerical standards as well, and afford greater "flexibility" for water quality permitting. [26] We can *do* water quality standards-based regulation, the states have maintained; just let us.

The great irony of the CWA, of course, is that back in 1972, it gave the states exactly the authority they were seeking, through §303(d). At the insistence of the states, and over the strong (indeed, barely respectful) objections of the Senate, the House of Representatives wrote, advocated, and had inserted into the Senate bill a provision that retained the traditional state water quality standards of the WQA and added those steps for their implementation that we now know as TMDLs. The process did little more than codify what the states represented that they were doing with water quality standards: identifying polluted waters, [27] targeting them for cleanup, [28] and developing total maximum pollution loads. [29] Except in one regard. Section 303(d) made the process mandatory.

Mandatory or not, a second great irony of the CWA is that, as the Senate might have predicted, the states did even less to implement §303(d) than they had to implement the WQA. [30] Nor did EPA do more. [31] To be sure, EPA's emphasis, and therefore that of the states, was on the implementation of a point source permit program and on massive funding for municipal treatment systems, but the fact remains that the residual authority was there in the law for states to do more—to do exactly what they said they were good at and wanted to do—and they did no such thing.

It is equally useful to recapitulate what states and EPA were doing all this time, for more than 20 years, beyond the industry and municipal point source worlds. They were "waste treatment planning" under §201. [32] They were statewide "water quality management planning" under §§106 [33] and 303(e). [34] They were "areawide regional planning" under §208, [35] and "basin planning" under §209. [36] They were then "nonpoint source planning" under §319. [37] And in more recent years, they were "watershed planning" under all of these authorities, [38] looking for the magic bullet that would translate abatement measures from paper to practice, and it never materialized. Not for want of encouraging regulations. Not for want of funding. Basically, for want of a bottom line. [39]

When the storm finally broke in the mid-1990s, it was brought on by citizen suits that penetrated EPA's line of defense that it had no enforceable duty to act under §303(d). [40] These suits sent the Agency and the states into a flurry of activity featuring new §303(d) guidance, a FACA committee, new state lists of impaired waters, and the first glimmers of actual TMDLs. In 1998, the Administration proposed a series of funding and technological assistance initiatives in its Clean Water Action Plan and began steps to bring large-scale, lightly regulated pollution sources—primarily municipal stormwater and concentrated animal feeding operations—under tighter controls. [41] To its credit, the plan forthrightly identified nonpoint source pollution as the leading cause, by an overwhelming margin, of water quality impairment in this country, and ordered several related federal agencies, most importantly the USDA, to take remedial steps on their own and to work with EPA to address the problem. [42] The primary engine of the Clean Water Action Plan for nonpoint source pollution, however, beyond the lubricants of funding and interagency cooperation, was the emerging program under §303(d). [43]

In August 1999, EPA proposed new regulations for the implementation of §303(d). [44] These regulations promise to be as contentious as any in environmental law and, with others also in the works, will raise many of the unresolved issues that have surrounded water pollution control since 1948. Two issues stand head and shoulders above the crowd, however. The first is whether §303(d) covers nonpoint source pollution at all, [45] and agribusiness interests (supported by the U.S. Forest Service) have filed litigation asserting the contrary. [46] The second is whether a TMDL is simply an arithmetic calculation that states are then free to incorporate in subsequent "planning," or whether the TMDL is itself both a calculation and a plan. [47] The final outcome of these issues will be huge, indeed dispositive, on the effect of §303(d) and its contribution to the CWA. If nonpoint sources are held to be beyond the mandatory provisions of this section, they will be relegated to the essentially ineffectual planning exercises that have ·characterized the last 25 years in nonpoint source control. And if TMDLs, even if they include nonpoint sources, are deferred to the never-never land of state water quality management planning, they will disappear down the same sinkhole with hardly a trace behind.

Which brings us to the major issue of today. If the CWA is going to move forward on its last great frontier, nonpoint source pollution, through the vehicle of TMDLs, is there any reason to think that an ambient water quality-based approach will work any better this time than it has in the past? This approach failed in the 1950s and 1960s for basically the same reasons that it went dormant in the 1970s and 1980s and is proving so difficult to effectuate today. We are short on science. And we are very short on political will.

TMDLs and the Limits of Science

> The source [a Los Angeles municipal sewer agency] argues that there is "no good linkage" between the use of generally accepted control measures and an impact on water quality improvements. "There's no point in setting limits if you don't know whether they'll achieve the desired result."
>
> *—Inside EPA Weekly Report* [48]

> The problem, says an [agriculture] industry source is that the information used to create state assessments and impaired waters lists is often out of date and speculatory [sic] because states do not have the resources to monitor all water bodies.
>
> *—Inside EPA Weekly Report* [49]

Pollution control systems based on ambient standards have always relied more on science than science can deliver. They are looking for numbers, thresholds, and fixed limits. They require proof of causes and effects that, arguably, come from other causes and have other effects, and pinning the tail on the right donkey has plagued air, water, and toxics programs from their inception, just as it has severely limited private causes of action for damages from widespread environmental harm. [50] Indeed, it was the limitations of this type of proof that gave rise to public environmental regulatory programs in the first place. [51] As in the early versions of the CWA, however, the science of these programs foundered every step of the way, from accurate assessment of existing conditions, to accurate predication of the effects of particular emissions, to the establishment of limits, to the proof of causation when ambient standards were violated. It was these difficulties, of course, that finally prompted Congress to shift direction in the FWPCA Amendments of 1972.

The requirements of science also make ambient-based systems far more resource-intensive than their proponents are willing to acknowledge. Working systems require constant and large infusions of money for training, monitoring, modeling, site assessments, surveillance, and enforcement. Precisely because "one size does not fit all"—as states and industry are quick to claim—every size, every water body, is a separate control system and one that is always, further, subject to change. Whatever data it produces, moreover, science is never satisfied. Scientists are not trained to be satisfied, or to project their opinions, or to predict; they are trained to question even the most obvious conclusion until all reasonable hypotheses have been disproved. And if the scientists are not satisfied—if they are not conclusive in their data and results—the regulated community will never be satisfied and will have a ready reason to resist abatement costs. Ambient-based regulation is truly a system that never rests, and that never stops asking for money.

These monies have never been on hand. They were certainly not available in 1972, and whatever models and expertise and monitoring systems were then in place slowly atrophied as the point source requirements of the CWA required other talents, and as the planning exercises were, sequentially, embraced and rejected as a waste of time. A 1977 study of wastewater treatment concluded that water quality planning was "filled with assumptions, guess work and over simplifications" because "planners don't know nearly enough about water and the way it responds to waste loads." [52] In 1984, EPA conducted an in-house assessment, *State Needs for Technical Assistance in NPDES Permitting*, that focused on water quality-based permitting. [53] Among its more than 30 separate findings:

> States often lack data on the water quality of a given site that they need for water quality impact analysis or modeling. [54]

> States often lack data necessary to determine the design discharge of the receiving water, especially for small streams. [55]
> In general, states lack knowledge of how to do realistic modeling of a pollutant's concentration and fate in a water body. [56]

> States need water quality models for a variety of geographic situations, especially for estuaries. [57]

Three years later, an Office of Technology Assessment study concluded:

> Only limited data are available on ambient pollutant concentrations in receiving waters, variability in these concentrations, and the fate of these pollutants and their impacts on indigenous organisms. In

addition, our ability to monitor water quality in relation to potential
environmental or human impacts is relatively primitive. [58]

Despite occasional EPA assertions, and repeated state assertions, to the
contrary, [59] these conditions have not much changed. In 1993, a U.S. Geological Survey official reported that basic data were lacking on such fundamental questions as, "[w]hat are the relative impacts of pollutants discharged from point and nonpoint sources?" [60] Current water quality monitoring failed to provide "consistent data for tracking trends," he continued,
and differences in sampling and reporting methods "prevented data com-
parisons between states." [61] The 1998 FACA committee on TMDLs noted
that, even at this late date, only 19% of the nation's waters were monitored
for pollution, [62] and that the states were in need of every manner of technical
assistance from monitoring to assessment to enforcement in order to meet
the demands of §303(d). [63] A 1999 report issued by current and former EPA
and state environmental agency employees concluded that even the monitoring currently undertaken of state waters is highly variable in both water
bodies assessed and methods of assessment, virtually unsupervised by EPA,
and a "game" of "politics, bureaucratic inertia and bad science" leading to
"erroneous and manipulated sets of water quality data." [64] A 1999 GAO
study concluded that even the current EPA watershed models, costing
$25,000 per study, are insufficient to calculate the effects of pollution load-
ings and the costs of their control. [65] More adequate but largely untested
models of the U.S. Geological Survey are available at $750,000. [66] Conser-
vatively estimating 100 watersheds per state, the bill for their assessment
alone could reach $4 billion.

The states and TMDL-implicated communities, meanwhile, are alert to
these weaknesses in monitoring and assessment and have already signaled
their willingness to exploit them. The first counterattack has come on the required biennial submissions of polluted waters under §303(d). [67] Opposing
listings as based on inadequate science ("drive-by listings," [68] in the words
of one agriculture industry attorney—a characterization that in some cases
may not be far from the truth), farm and other nonpoint interests have persuaded states to reduce their submissions on impaired waters to the absolutely proven, with significant results. Incongruous as it may seem in the
face of new EPA listing criteria designed to be all-inclusive, to err on the
side of listing, and to facilitate the use of "all relevant data," [69] many states
have actually cut their §303(d) lists in half since 1996, relegating hundreds
of waters to such categories as "further study," "insufficient information,"
and only "moderately impaired." [70] The state of Wyoming, for example, reduced its list of over 400 waters to 61 identified as polluted and 315 as needing "further monitoring." [71] Perhaps coincidentally—but only per-

haps—275 of the 315 waters deferred for "further monitoring" were contaminated by nonpoint sources, primarily cattle grazing. [72]

EPA, for its part, has tried to be conservative in accepting these new state §303(d) submissions, rejecting several out of hand [73] and inventing, on its own, a new CAA-like "partial approval" for several others. [74] Industry sources, on the other hand, have bridled at the closeness of EPA's review, characterizing EPA's replacement of Virginia's list as "arbitrary" and "ill-defined" [75]—the language of litigation. In Wyoming, a jurisdiction not nationally noted for its concern over "sound science," a rather targeted piece of legislation is pending to require the application of "credible data" in determining "a water body's attainment of designated uses." [76] At the same time, Governor Geringer of Wyoming was testifying before Congress that the science behind its listings of polluted waters for the past decade or so was *never there in the first place*, explaining:

> We are just finishing a correction of inaccurate classification of streams in Wyoming that resulted from another EPA approach. A few years ago, the authority for states to receive federal money for watershed work required that we declare that a waterbody was functionally impaired—regardless of its actual condition. That misunderstood incentive caused many steams to be mislabeled as impaired. As a result Wyoming was able to draw down 319 money. [77]

In short, the Devil made them do it. The work of the Devil or not, what is clear is that for years, indeed decades, the states and nonpoint industries were content with submissions that, now that they are likely to trigger compliance requirements, will be put to the bitter proof. The bill for this proof has yet to be presented, much less paid.

This said, identifying polluted waters is, from the point of view of the science involved, the easy step. The next is to identify the causes of impairment and to allocate their loads. Here is where lines get drawn deep in the sand, and among the first to draw them are the municipal sewer systems which have the not unrealistic fear that—given the states' historic reluctance to impose serious abatement measures on nonpoint polluters—municipal systems are likely to take the hit. [78] This anxiety has produced a remarkable document from the Association of Metropolitan Sewerage Agencies (AMSA), a self-styled "survival guide" for wastewater agencies entitled *Evaluating TMDLs: Protecting the Rights of POTWs*. [79] It is a guide with a purpose; as the Executive Director of AMSA explains, "We're developing guidelines to lead our members through the TMDL process and to show them when they can challenge the state in court." [80]

After declaring its member agencies to be the "foremost environmental practitioners" in the country, [81] the AMSA survival guide proceeds as a litigator's cookbook to identify, seriatim, methods of limiting or avoiding responsibility altogether under §303(d). Sewer agencies may begin by challenging listings on the basis of "sufficient reliable scientific data." [82] Or they may advocate that waters, particularly those that are contaminated from nonpoint sources, be listed under "other," nonmandatory sections of the CWA. [83] Beyond listings, the guide points out opportunities for municipal agencies to lower the applicable water quality standards by "redefining" a designated use (from primary to secondary contact recreation, for example), [84] by declaring an existing use "unattainable," [85] by proposing separate "site-specific criteria" in their discharge zones, [86] or by proposing to remove the water from listing altogether. [87] As for incorporating the TMDLs into municipal system permits, the guide offers "several strategies" for protecting publicly owned treatment works (POTWs) from "unwarranted, unnecessarily stringent" limitations such as variances, exceptions, and appeals. [88] The document concludes, without even a hint of intended irony, that "AMSA is proud to offer this indispensable TMDL evaluation manual" as a "service to all who are concerned with making genuine progress in improving our environment." [89]

EPA, of course, has seen its problem with the science of water quality management coming for a very long time. It issued an ever lengthening series of technical bulletins on water quality throughout the 1970s and 1980s, and in this decade has stepped up the pace with elaborate training opportunities, most recently a "watershed academy" featuring 23 separate courses beginning with "Watersheds 101" [90] and a web of assessment systems entitled "BASINS," [91] featuring national databases, assessment tools (called "TARGET" and "ASSESS"), local data inputs, water quality models (e.g., "QUAL2E"), and "post processing output tools for interpreting model results." [92] The chances are that the very complexity of these models and the predictions will incline reviewing courts to defer to agency conclusions, state or federal, as they have for the most part for similar modeling under the CAA [93] and for similar (and even more expensive) ambient impact-based cleanup decisions under Superfund. [94] As they should. Public environmental law, unlike private tort law, is precautionary, and that precaution requires taking science beyond the dispositive to the reasonable, farther than it may wish to go. [95]

EPA has seen a more fundamental problem coming as well with water quality management, and one it has been avoiding for decades: the adequacy of the water quality standards regulations themselves. The issue has now been dragged to its door by the TMDL litigation, and by the efforts in every state and EPA region to, at long last, begin to relate water quality impacts to sources in a comprehensive way. Commentators, courts, and others have long known and described problems inherent within the existing WQS program, [96] including a high degree of variability in state water quality criteria (based, inter alia, on assumptions of risk varying by as much as 10,000 times), [97] equally varying application factors (e.g., flow assumptions), [98] mixing zones, [99] site-specific water quality criteria, [100] downgrading uses, [101] degrading waters within uses, [102] and the absence of certain critical standards (e.g., sediments and nutrients) [103]—all of which provide considerable leeway for states to tilt their playing fields toward their immediate development interests and to avoid coming to grips with the consequences of polluted waters. [104] EPA has had chronic difficulty over the years leveraging unwilling state programs into more adequate criteria, [105] antidegradation provisions, [106] protections for outstanding natural resource waters, [107] and citizen participation. [108] None of which really mattered before, but the stakes are about to rise.

EPA now finds itself with its TMDL program in the position of a home renovator who, having furbished an elegant new structure, needs to deal with the foundation. The situation is even more dicey because states and their industry supporters have been complaining for years that the existing WQS regulations are, conversely, too rigid and inflexible, insensitive to cost-benefit analysis and insufficiently responsive to local conditions. [109] While this perspective and rhetoric have been around since at least the WQA, they led a strong and nearly successful attack on the federal program in 1982 during the Reagan Administration, [110] another in 1996 with the Contract With America Congress, [111] and are now ready to use this opportunity to try again. On July 7, 1998, EPA opened up the whole ball of wax with an advance notice of proposed rulemaking, [112] inviting comment on every aspect of its water quality standards program, including use designations, attainability, downgrading, aquatic criteria, antidegradation, mixing zones, and application factors. [113] This rulemaking will be a donnybrook among environmental interests, states, and the discharge industries, reminiscent of the legislative arguments that have marked the CWA over the years, and no more likely to put them to rest. [114]

At the same time, EPA is pushing science to new limits for the development of criteria most relevant to nonpoint source pollution. It is on a two-year schedule for the development of "region-specific," "waterbody type" technical guidance on state criteria for nitrogen and phosphorous, the two largest culprits in the nonpoint lineup. [115] It has announced plans to develop bacterial criteria for water recreation, biocriteria for wildlife, and criteria for excessive sediments and flow alteration [116]—each certain to send another set of users and dischargers (e.g., POTWs and irrigators) up the wall. [117]

We have now slid back into the maw of a program that Congress all but rejected in 1972 for, among other things, its uncertain science and elaborate indirection. The program was retained because states and industry lobbied to retain it with claims that they had this technology on hand and could do this drill, claims that they have repeated to Congress nearly every year since. In the light of the obvious shortcomings of this technology and the equally obvious shortage of resources devoted to it, these claims must seem odd, until one realizes that they are not made in the abstract but as arguments to reassert state primacy over water pollution control. Pollution control is turf control, and this is where the success of the TMDL program is most in doubt. With enough commitment of resources—and it will take another order of magnitude beyond anything yet committed under the Act—adequate science to deal with the aquatic impacts of nonpoint sources is within the realm of the possible. Adequate political will is a different story.

TMDLs and the Limits of Will

> Georgia has failed for over sixteen years to comply with the Clean Water Act's requirement that states identify total maximum daily loads of pollutants in waters that do not attain applicable standards. At its current pace, Georgia will take more than one hundred years to comply with the Clean Water Act.
>
> —*Sierra Club v. Hankinson* [118]

> As the curtain opens, a reluctant Data is trying to hide from view behind a wall of cubicles decorated with diplomas and accredited certifications. When finally forced into view by the Environmental Plaintiffs Attorneys Precision Marching Briefcase Brigade (who execute carefully coordinated maneuvers to block the exits while somehow avoiding tripping over the sprawling forms of Agency Staffers), Data reveals his secret: Mother never did abuse the victims . . . it was Humans. The Agency Staffers, Politicians, Federal and State Land Managers and Private Property Owners all deny that it was them.
>
> —Member, Western Governors'
> Association TMDL Workshop [119]

We may start with an obvious question: Where *were* the TMDLs? Granted, the states and the federal government were pursuing other CWA agendas in the early years of the Act. Given the penchant of at least some states for a water quality approach, however, and explicit provisions for that approach in §303(d), even stranger than the states' continuing assertion that they *could* do this drill was the fact that they did *not* do it—for more than 25 years.

Perhaps some states were defeated by the science and monitoring required, but *all* states? Certainly every state had adequate data on at least a few of its waterways and, as certainly every state was aware, many of these waterways were highly degraded. Indeed, for years they had been reporting these waters as degraded under the nonaction-forcing provisions of §305(b). [120]

Perhaps TMDLs were deflected by the absence of state laws supporting those measures that TMDLs would impose, particularly on forestry and agriculture. Legislation in some states does in fact place these sources on a pedestal beyond the reach of environmental controls—in itself a statement about state commitment to clean water. [121] But as a recent Environmental Law Institute study documents, many other states do not, and all states retain the residual authority in their water quality programs to move on some nonpoint sources, and in some states, on all sources. [122]

Perhaps the states were daunted by the apparent lack of ready abatement measures to incorporate into TMDL measures which could have appeared too ill defined, inchoate, or expensive. But the truth of TMDLs is that the remedial measures are usually obvious. And low-tech. And cheap. [123] Imagine what it might take to reduce fertilizer runoff from a corn field, and streamside setbacks come to mind. For other crops and animal husbandry we have such options as winter cover, retention ponds, shelterbelts, and caps on fertilizers in amounts that the soil will retain and the crops will use. Many farms practice these measures as a matter of sound economics and conservation. EPA has published an entire book on these measures, quite contemporary and detailed. [124] And they work. In the state of Florida, years of struggle, litigation, legislation, and compromise recently yielded an agreement to reverse the trend of deterioration of water quality in Everglades National Park by, inter alia, restricting the use of fertilizers in the adjacent agricultural areas: [125] fertilizers would be applied in specific amounts and in specific ways. Within a year, with the sugar crop still flourishing, nutrient loading from the agricultural areas dropped 40%. [126] These remedies are not rocket science. Compared to the technology and investments required of point source industries, they are simple, practical, and at hand.

And so, we run out of excuses. TMDLs did not vaporize from the restrictions of science or technology or state law. They vaporized on the will to do a very hard thing, to make demands on large, local industries without the backing of explicit federal standards and permits and the threat of federal enforcement. No state employee in his or her right mind would volunteer to take on the Florida sugar industry. Even the subsidy-eliminating national farm bill of 1996 tried that and failed. [127] No Idaho water quality official rises in the morning eagerly anticipating a confrontation with Boise Cascade over logging roads. The cattle industry is no easier a customer in, say, Catron County, New Mexico, where "custom and culture" ordinances have attempted to outlaw all federal environmental requirements, [128] or in Nevada where federal land management offices are occasionally bombed. [129] We are all human, and the path of least resistance toward nonpoint sources for the life of the CWA has been the happy land of planning, for which there was a steady (if thin) stream of federal funding and nothing was enforceable: a states-rights dream.

Until the TMDL litigation shattered the dream. The state and industry reactions that followed have shown the classic symptoms of psychological trauma from shock to denial, anger, and grief. It is too soon to know whether we will get to Stage Five, reconciliation, and the point where states will take hold of this exercise, make it their own, and implement it with effective, enforceable plans. The early returns are at best mixed.

On the bright side, the state of Missouri is reported to have put $1.8 million into its state budget to fund additional water pollution control staff. [130] New York claims to have put $14.2 million over the past five years toward nonpoint source management. [131] Additional TMDL funding has been reported in Virginia [132] and—to illustrate just how far this issue travels—even Louisiana. [133] Oregon has authorized its Department of Agriculture to implement and enforce TMDLs on private agricultural lands. [134] Tennessee is said to be restricting, and even denying, new permits for impaired waters, pending the development of TMDLs. [135] Connecticut, taking a broader tack, is proposing a "statewide TMDL" for total nitrogen, assigning waste load allocations first to watersheds and then to individual sources. [136] A multiple-source, multiple-state TMDL is brewing for Long Island Sound. [137] North Carolina took on its hog farmers, imposed a moratorium and subsequently pollution control requirements, and survived. [138] It can be done.

These bright spots noted, they are not the norm. Some states remain in denial. Faced with the enormity of the Midwest's contribution to the Gulf of Mexico's dead zone, the President of the Iowa Corn Growers Association, still in Stage Two, contended, "It doesn't jive. Two and two isn't making four. . . . Agriculture is being hung with the blame and we don't think it can be substantiated." [139] West Virginia has reportedly allocated no monies toward TMDLs and defaulted the process to EPA. [140] Nebraska has stated that it has sufficient resources to complete no more than one TMDL per year. [141] Kansas has reportedly backed off monitoring for suspended solids and diluted its water quality criteria for chlorides, in anticipation of having otherwise to develop TMDLs. [142] North California TMDLs, conceptually sound, have apparently languished somewhere between proposal and approval [143]; California, meanwhile, has come up with the concept of "technical TMDLs"—load allocations-minus-implementation plans—that in the words of a state research agency "almost guarantees that it will be many years before California sees TMDLs implemented, especially for nonpoint sources." [144] TMDL-limiting legislation is pending in at least California, [145] Washington, [146] and Wyoming. [147] The California Farm Bureau Federation has filed suit challenging California's TMDL program. [148] The Wyoming Association of Conservation Districts has filed suit to enjoin the entire federal Clean Water Action Plan, [149] for which TMDLs are the operative component. [150] The American Farm Bureau Federation and National Pork Producers Council have fired a preemptive shot against EPA's upcoming national regulations for the TMDL program. [151] Beyond the rhetoric, the most recent state §303(d) lists of impaired waters reflected a marked tendency to minimize water quality problems and deflect data to the contrary, limiting the scope of work to come. [152] And, as an early review of the TMDLs themselves showed, they are no bargain. They contain little quantification of pollution loadings, less identification of nonpoint sources, and a near-total avoidance of implementation measures. [153]

The news is not a great deal more encouraging on the political front, where in August 1998 the National Governors' Association proposed a substitute for TMDLs based on state programs that EPA would be compelled to approve unless the Agency found "no reasonable likelihood" of the attainment of water quality standards within the next 15 years. [154] If such a state plan were approved, particularized plans for sources or watersheds would be beyond federal review or approval. [155] The proposals were so bald that they drew a response from EPA's Office of Water to the effect that they would "dramatically weaken" the federal water program, [156] but one suspects that this observation was not news to the governors. Indeed, one could guess it was precisely their intent. In December 1998, the governors met again, this time in Washington, D.C., to discuss TMDL strategy with state water administrators; EPA was not even invited to attend. [157]

In February 1999, the governors took their case to Congress, where they met a warm reception as warriors "on the front line of the clean water battlefield." [158] In the coded language of Capitol Hill, the chair of the House Subcommittee on Water Resources and Environment predicted that the CWA's success would depend, inter alia, on identifying "appropriate state and federal roles" and "improving upon the current TMDL . . . program." [159] Translation: reduced federal oversight and less demanding TMDLs. The Governor of Maryland testified in favor of "holistic community-based watershed plans" designed to meet water quality standards; EPA's role would be limited to approving "overall" state programs. [160] The Governor of New York echoed the same and advocated in the same breath "stronger, clearer agricultural exemption language in the point source permitting language of the Act," [161] thereby eliminating any regulatory control over the primary industry and primary source of nonpoint pollution in the country. Wyoming followed suit. [162]

The reception has been equally chilly for EPA's regulatory initiatives on concentrated animal feeding operations (CAFOs), which have been the subject of several "listening sessions" around the country. [163] What EPA has heard—be it for hogs, chickens, or cows—are arguments for voluntary controls, educational programs, and funding [164]—the essence, of course, of the current nonpoint source and watershed planning programs. Even holding the potential hammer of point source regulation over these sources, EPA is not finding it easy to come to grips with entities that have remained outside the operable features of the CWA for such a long time.

EPA's response has been money, and time. The Agency has funded the pork industry to develop consensus over upcoming CAFO controls. [165] It has similarly funded the Western Governors' Association to provide a forum, indeed several forums, for discussing implementation of §303(d). [166] Anyone familiar with western natural resource policy knows that the western states are a tough act, and any effort co-chaired by the Governor of Wyoming is not going to bring environmental protection immediately to mind, but EPA and the western states have started a process similar to the TMDL federal advisory committee two years before, [167] and the agenda at least, if not the perspective, is focused, like the FACA, on practical issues in implementing TMDLs. [168] They may actually find answers short of emasculating the law. [169] The FACA committee did. And the more that people talk about actually doing TMDLs instead of how *not* to do them, the farther along toward reconciliation we proceed.

What remains, of course, is the question whether states will develop actual TMDLs that limit nonpoint source discharges in reasonable but verifiable and enforceable ways. EPA can only go so far before the law ends, [170] a proposition well known to opposing states and industry, and indeed relied on by them. As one state representative observed this past December, the Agency "can not [sic] do more [on nonpoint source pollution] without changing the Clean Water Act" and as a result is "left with a difficult dilemma": it needs to "obtain more authority over nonpoint sources by changing the law," but opening up the law could mean "losses on issues such as wetlands permitting," [171] long the target of industry and at least some wetlands-rich states. If such were one's objective, one would stonewall the TMDL program to the bitter end. For its part, EPA, supported by a few underused legal decisions characterizing agricultural and other unregulated operations as point sources, [172] has weapons in reserve as well, [173] but its experience in trying to regulate well-identified and highly polluting CAFOs shows how problematical this authority may be. As with many issues of federalism in environmental law, this is a large game of "chicken" in which neither side can afford to lose all.

As we come into the endgame of EPA's new regulatory framework for TMDLs and its many efforts to jawbone, woo, cajole, and near-bribe the states and user groups toward getting with the program, it will all come down to the will of a majority of states to do hard things that they have never been willing to do before, that will alienate powerful constituencies, and that will require in some cases changing state laws through legislatures long captured by forest, farm, and construction industries and in no mood to change. Against these odds, TMDLs are not fertile soil for those prophets of a "New Environmentalism" that go "Beyond Regulation" to a happy world of stakeholder consensus and cooperation. [174] Ambient-based water quality management has tested this utopia many times before, indeed continuously through one program or another since the 1960s, without measurable cooperation, consensus, or result. The reason TMDLs have emerged as the force they are, bringing poultry and other industries to offers of "voluntary" abatement, jolting the national governors, convening the western governors forums, stimulating honest, on-the-ground review of what condition our waters are actually in, and extracting new revenue measures for nonpoint source abatement from states with no appetite for expenditures and with little more for environmental protection, is that TMDLs are different from voluntary, consensus-based exercises. They require more.

Notes to Chapter 5

1. 117 CONG. REC. 38809 (1971).

2. *Water Pollution Control Legislation—1971: Hearings on H.R. 11896, H.R. 11895 Before the House Comm. on Public Works*, 92d Cong. 273 (1971) [hereinafter *1971 Water Pollution Control Legislation Hearings*] (statement of Mr. Jones during testimony by James Krieger, Chairman, Water and Power Committee, Los Angeles Chamber of Commerce).

3. *See generally* Water Pollution Control Act of 1948, Pub. L. No. 80-845, 62 Stat. 1155 (codified as amended at 33 U.S.C. §§1251-1387, ELR STAT. FWPCA §§101-607). For a description of the Act, see Frank J. Barry, *The Evolution of the Enforcement Provisions of the Federal Water Pollution Control Act: A Study in the Difficulty in Developing Effective Legislation*, 68 MICH. L. REV. 1103, 1105-07 (1970).

4. William H. Hines, *Nor Any Drop to Drink: Public Regulations of Water Quality Part III: The Federal Effort*, 52 IOWA L. REV. 799, 800 (1967) ("The history of state control of pollution does not support optimism toward the [state] control agency's development of rigorous standards.").

5. Pub. L. No. 89-234, 79 Stat. 903 (codified as amended at 33 U.S.C. §§1251-1387, ELR STAT. FWPCA §§101-607).

6. *See* Hines, *supra* note 4.

7. William H. Hines, *Nor Any Drop to Drink: Public Regulations of Water Quality Part II: Interstate Arrangements for Pollution Control*, 52 IOWA L. REV. 432, 432-33 (1966).

8. Hines, *supra* note 4, at 800-01.

9. *See* 2 WILLIAM H. RODGERS JR., ENVIRONMENTAL LAW 247 (1986).

10. *See* S. REP. NO. 89-10, at 9-10 (1965) (accompanying the WQA):

> Water quality standards are not designed for use primarily as an enforcement device; they are intended to provide the Secretary and State and local agencies with additional tools for objective and clear public policy statements on the use or uses to which specified segments of interstate waters may be put. Their principal objective is the orderly development and improvement of our water resources without the necessity of adversary proceedings which inevitably develop in enforcement cases.

11. S. REP. NO. 92-414 (1972), *reprinted in* 1972 U.S.C.C.A.N. 3671.

12. Weyerhaeuser Co. v. Costle, 590 F.2d 1011, 1042 n.45, 9 ELR 20284, 20297 n.45 (D.C. Cir. 1978) (citing DAVID ZWICK, WATER WASTELAND (1971); Patrick A. Parenteau & Nancy Tauman, *The Effluent Limitations Controversy*, 6 ECOLOGY L.Q. 1, 8-12 (1976)).

13. Hines, *supra* note 7, at 433. In the words of one observer: "The river basin plan is good river management, but not logical politically." *Id.* at 433 n.2 (quoting FRANK GRAHAM, DISASTER BY DEFAULT 217 (1966)). The author goes on to describe water basin planning under the 1966 Clean Rivers Restoration Act as "singularly unproductive of regional water pollution control efforts." *Id.* at 456.

14. William H. Rodgers Jr., *Industrial Water Pollution and the Refuge Act: A Second Chance for Water Quality*, 119 U. PA. L. REV. 761, 764-65 (1971).

15. These difficulties and those described subsequently are discussed, inter alia, in WILLIAM H. RODGERS JR., ENVIRONMENTAL LAW (2d ed. 1994). For a further discussion of the practical difficulties in this approach and the race to the bottom in southern states over standards for dioxins, see also Oliver A. Houck, *The Regulation of Toxic Pollutants Under the Clean Water Act*, 21 ELR 10528, 10532 (Sept. 1991).

16. H. REP. NO. 92-911, at 396 (1972), *reprinted in* ENVIRONMENTAL POLICY DIV., CONGRESSIONAL RESEARCH SERV., LIBRARY OF CONGRESS, A LEGISLATIVE HISTORY OF THE WATER POLLUTION CONTROL ACT AMENDMENTS OF 1972, at 494 (1973); *id.* at 517.

17. *Id.* at 517.

18. *Id.* at 865; *see also* S. REP. NO. 92-414 (1972), *reprinted in* 1972 U.S.C.C.A.N. 3675 (statement of the Senate conferees):

> Water quality standards, in addition to their deficiencies in relying on the assimilative capacity of receiving waters, often cannot be translated into effluent limitations—defendable in court tests, because of the imprecision of models for water quality and the effects of effluents in most waters.

19. HARVEY LIEBERT, FEDERALISM & CLEAN WATERS 59 (1975) (quoting Janice Heard, *Environment Report: Water Pollution Proposals to Test Blatnik's Strength as Public Works Chairman*, 3 NAT'L J. 1719 (1971)); *see also* GRAHAM *supra* note 13, at 24-25; William H. Hines, *Nor Any Drop to Drink: Public Regulations of Water Quality Part I: State Pollution Control Programs*, 52 IOWA L. REV. 186, 205 n.96 (1966) (quoting the Assistant Secretary of the U.S. Department of Health, Education, and Welfare):

> Part of your problem, speaking very frankly, is that the polluters in a given state are likely to be your communities and cities which belong to your political party and my political party. It gets a little embarrassing to move against your fellow partisans and embarrass them publicly or force them to float a bond issue or increase taxes.
>
> Secondly, in many instances your big polluters are your big employers, big industries. And at a time when the states are involved, as they have been and will continue to be, in very keen competition for industry, for jobs, it is certainly an extremely difficult job for a state governor or legislature to face up to some of the biggest employers in the state and say "you must do this."

Little changed over the next 30 years. In 1995, the incoming Governor of Louisiana took out an advertisement in the *Wall Street Journal* depicting a man bent over backwards, and captioned "What has Louisiana done for business lately?" *See* Suz Redfern, *DED Goes Big Time With Tort Reform Ad*, GREATER BATON ROUGE BUS. REP., Sept. 17-30, 1996, at 52. The advertisement touts changes in Louisiana law limiting the liability of businesses for environmental, product, and workplace injury.

20. This history is discussed at length in Oliver A. Houck, *TMDLs: The Resurrection of Water Quality Standards-Based Regulation Under the Clean Water Act*, 27 ELR 10329 (July 1997) [hereinafter *TMDLs I*].

21. *1971 Water Pollution Control Legislation Hearings*, *supra* note 2, at 667 (statement of Nelson A. Rockefeller, Governor of New York).

22. *Id.* at 520.

23. *Id.* at 995 (statement of Wesley E. Gilbertson, Deputy Secretary for Environmental Protection and Regulation, Pennsylvania Department of Environmental Resources).

24. *Id.* at 52 (letter of J. James Exon, Governor of Nebraska).

25. *Id.*

26. *See TMDLs I*, *supra* note 20, at 10338-39 (citing *Eidsness Says Administration Favors Water Quality-Based Pollutant Controls*, [13 Current Developments] Env't Rep. (BNA) 805 (Oct. 15, 1982), and *Hernandez Says EPA Seeks to Return Management of Water Programs to States*, [13 Current Developments] Env't Rep. (BNA) 850 (Oct. 22, 1982)).

27. "Each State shall identify those waters within its boundaries for which the effluent limitations required by section 1311(b)(1)(A) and section 1313(b)(1)(B) of this title are not stringent enough to implement any water quality standard applicable to such waters." 33 U.S.C. §1313(d)(1)(A), ELR STAT. FWPCA §303(d)(1)(A).

28. "The State shall establish a priority ranking for such waters, taking into account the severity of the pollution and the use to be made of such waters." *Id.*

29. "Each State shall establish for the waters identified in paragraph (1)(A) of this subsection, and in accordance with the priority ranking, the total maximum daily load, for those pollutants which the Administrator identifies under Section 1314(a)(2) of this title as suitable for such calculation." *Id.* §1313(d)(1)(C), ELR STAT. FWPCA §303(d)(1)(C).

30. For a discussion of state and federal implementation of §303(d), see Oliver A. Houck, TMDLs, *Are We There Yet?: The Long Road Toward Water Quality-Based Regulation Under the Clean Water Act*, 27 ELR 10391 (Aug. 1997) [hereinafter *TMDLs II*]

31. *Id.*

32. 33 U.S.C. §1281(c), ELR STAT. FWPCA §201(c). Section 201(c) provides for "waste treatment management plans" on an "areawide basis" providing "control or

treatment for all point and non-point sources of pollution." For a general discussion of CWA planning programs, see RODGERS, *supra* note 15, at 23-27.

33. 33 U.S.C. §1256(a), ELR STAT. FWPCA §106(a). Section 106(a) provides for "grants to States and to interstate agencies to assist them in administering programs for the prevention, reduction, and elimination of pollution, including enforcement directly or through appropriate state law enforcement officers or agencies."

34. *Id.* §1313(e), ELR STAT. FWPCA §303(e). Section 303(e) provides that "each State shall have a continuing planning process." The section further provides that "the Administrator shall from time to time review each State's approved planning process for the purpose of insuring that such planning process is at all times consistent with [the CWA]."

35. *Id.* §1288, ELR STAT. FWPCA §208. Section 208 provides for the "development and implementation of areawide waste treatment management plans."

36. *Id.* §1289, ELR STAT. FWPCA §209. Section 209 supports planning for "all basins in the United States."

37. *Id.* §1329, ELR STAT. FWPCA §319. Section 319 provides funding for state nonpoint source management programs.

38. The current EPA watershed approach framework is outlined at the EPA website http://www.epa.gov/OWOW/watershed/framework.html (visited May 20, 1999). For a discussion of the current resurgence of the watershed approach, see Robert W. Adler, *Addressing Barriers to Watershed Protection*, 25 ENVTL. L. 973, 977-79 (1995).

39. In the words of one commentator, "[p]lanning has become less the strategy for cleanup it was intended to be, and more an institutional truce between the cleaners." 2 RODGERS, *supra* note at 9, at 318.

40. *See TMDLs II, supra* note 30, at 10395-96.

41. *See* U.S. EPA & U.S. DEP'T OF AGRIC., CLEAN WATER ACTION PLAN: RESTORING AND PROTECTING AMERICA'S WATERS, EPA 840-R-98-001, at 54-65 (Feb. 1998) [hereinafter CWAP].

42. *See Oliver A. Houck, TMDLs III: A New Framework for the Clean Water Act's Ambient Standards Program*, 28 ELR 10415, 10424 (Aug. 1998) [hereinafter *TMDLs III*].

43. TMDLs would "form the core" of the clean water strategy. CWAP, *supra* note 41, at 79.

44. Proposed Revisions to the Water Quality Planning and Management Regulation, 64 Fed. Reg. 46012 (1999) (to be codified at 40 C.F.R. pt. 130) (proposed Aug. 23, 1999) and Revisions to the National Pollution Discharge Elimination System Program and Federal Antidegradation Policy in Support of Revisions to the Water Quality Planning and Management Regulation, 64 Fed. Reg. 46058 (to be codified at 40 C.F.R. pt. 122 et al.) (proposed Aug. 23, 1999).

45. *See TMDLs III, supra* note 42, at 10421-22.

46. *See* Letter from Arthur Bryant, Director, Watershed and Air Management, U.S. Forest Service, to Geoffrey H. Grubbs (Apr. 29, 1997) (described in *TMDLs II, supra* note 30, at 10400) (Forest Service challenge to nonpoint coverage); *Litigation May Resolve Federal Dispute Over Runoff Controls*, INSIDE EPA WKLY. REP., Jan. 29, 1999, at 18 (discussing recently filed lawsuit by the Missouri Soybean Association).

47. *See TMDLs III, supra* note 42, at 10422. This issue, in turn, has two facets. The first is whether a TMDL must include source controls; to date, EPA has resolved this question by requiring "reasonable assurance" that TMDL measures will be implemented and effective. *Id.* The second is whether outside parties (i.e., citizen groups) will be able to review both the approval of the plan and its implementation under §303(d), and it is this prospect that has been so anathema to nonpoint industry. *Id.* at 10421 & n.93.

48. *Sewerage Officials Protest EPA Settlement*, INSIDE EPA WKLY. REP., Feb. 5, 1999, at 8.

49. *Feedlot Strategy Could Boost Permitting Over Voluntary Action*, INSIDE EPA WKLY. REP., Nov. 20, 1998, at 9.

50. For a discussion of the difficulties in proof arising from private damage actions, see Brock v. Merrell Dow Pharm., Inc., 874 F.2d 307 (5th Cir. 1989) (epidemiological evidence insufficient to show causation); Turpin v. Merrell Dow Pharm., Inc., 959 F.2d 1394 (6th Cir. 1992) (animal studies evidence insufficient proof); Sorensen v. Shaklee Corp., 31 F.3d 638 (8th Cir. 1994) (ingestion of chemically treated substances insufficient evidence of causation); *see also* JONATHAN HARR, A CIVIL ACTION (1995) (difficulties in proving causation from toxic release).

51. *See* ROBERT V. PERCIVAL ET AL., ENVIRONMENTAL REGULATION LAW, SCIENCE AND POLICY, ch. 2.A (2d ed. 1996) (inadequacies of the common law are crucial to understanding the rapid growth of public law).

52. JEROME HOROWITZ & LAWRENCE BAZEL, AN ANALYSIS OF PLANNING FOR ADVANCED WASTEWATER TREATMENT 23 (1977) (cited in Lawrence Bazel, *Water Quality Standards Maximum Loads and the Clean Water Act: The Need for Judicial Enforcement*, 34 HASTINGS L.J. 1245 (1983).

53. U.S. EPA, PROGRAM EVALUATION, OFFICE OF WATER QUALITY, ASSESSMENT OF STATE NEEDS FOR TECHNICAL ASSISTANCE IN NPDES PERMITTING (Apr. 25, 1984).

54. *Id.* at III-12.

55. *Id.*

56. *Id.* at III-9.

57. *Id.* at III-11.

58. OFFICE OF TECHNOLOGY ASSESSMENT, WASTES IN MARINE ENVIRONMENT 206 (Apr. 1987). The report also noted:

First, it is questionable whether EPA has sufficient resources to continue to develop and update the Federal water quality criteria, or to evaluate water quality standards that are developed by States. Moreover, a large increase in compliance monitoring and enforcement burdens would also be anticipated.

Id.

59. For a statement more based on hope than reality, the EPA Assistant Administrator for Water testified in 1986 that:

Before the 1972 law, you'd get into these long, long debates with dischargers who would say "No, let me prove to you that this isn't a problem." So I guess my feeling is that having established a very strong nationwide enforcement structure, we have got a tool that will allow us not to get lost in endless scientific debates.

Secondly, we've learned something in the last 20 years. Our monitoring technology is much better than it was 20 years ago.... So we've got a lot of information we didn't have 20 years ago. So the combination of the much better information and much better permitting and enforcement base means that I think we have a chance we didn't have then.

Id. at 4 (quoting Rebecca Hanmer). For repeated state assertions of their technological capacity to conduct water quality-based permitting, see *TMDLs I, supra* note 20, at 10332-33.

60. *Congress Lacks Conclusive Data Needed to Assess Water Act, Hydrologist Says*, [23 Current Developments] Env't Rep. (BNA) 3235 (Apr. 30, 1993).

61. *Id.*

62. *See* TMDL FEDERAL ADVISORY COMMITTEE ACT COMMITTEE, FINAL REPORT 3 (May 20, 1998).

63. *See id.* at 70-72.

64. PUBLIC EMPLOYEES FOR ENVIRONMENTAL RESPONSIBILITY, MURKY WATERS, OFFICIAL WATER QUALITY REPORTS ARE ALL WET: AN INSIDE LOOK AT EPA'S IMPLEMENTATION OF THE CLEAN WATER ACT 2, 3 (1999). To be noted, however, this report treats §305(b) assessments of *all* state waters, and not the more particular assessments supporting §303(d) TMDLs; indeed, one complaint of the report is that the TMDL program was eclipsing reporting under §305(b). *Id.* at 47.

65. U.S. GAO, *Water Quality: Federal Role in Addressing and Contributing to Nonpoint Source Pollution*, GAO/RCED-99-45, ch. 0:3 (Feb. 26, 1999) http://www.frwebgate.access.gpo.gov.cg [hereinafter GAO Report].

66. *Id.* ch. 0:4.2.

67. Under 40 C.F.R. §130.8(a) (1997), states are to submit §303(d) lists to EPA every two years, along with other reporting under §315(b).

68. *See* Susan Bruninga, *Time Allowed for States to Do TMDLs Too Little for Adequate Job, Group Told*, Daily Env't Rep. (BNA), Mar. 10, 1998, at A-8.

69. EPA issued two guidance documents on the TMDL program. *See* National Clarifying Guidance for 1998 State and Territory Section 303(d) Listing Decisions, Memorandum from Robert H. Wayland III, Director of Office of Wetlands, Oceans and Watershed, U.S. EPA 2 (Aug. 17, 1997) http://www.epa.gov/owow/tmdl/lisgid.html. These criteria are described in *TMDLs III, supra* note 42, at 10418.

70. *E.g.*, Missouri Department of Natural Resources, Recommended 303(d) Waters (Sept. 23, 1998) (on file with author) (describing three categories of impaired waters, including a category for "runoff" for which "data is older or of lesser quality than those formally listed").

71. E-mail Communication from Raymond V. Corning, Member of the Wyoming Department of Environmental Quality TMDL Work Group, to Wyoming, Department of Environmental Quality TMDL Work Group (Aug. 15, 1998) [hereinafter Corning E-mail] (on file with author).

72. *Id.*

73. *See, e.g.*, *U.S. EPA Proposes Additions to Virginia's 1998 Impaired-Waters List*, Water Env't Fed'n Rep., Dec. 30, 1998; *U.S. EPA Challenges Latest Iowa TMDL List* (Apr. 30, 1999) http://www.wef.org/docs/wefreporter/archive/1999/wefreporter.html; for a discussion of partial approvals under the CAA, see, e.g., Rodgers, *supra* note 15, at 200-02.

74. *See* Office of Water, U.S. EPA, *Total Maximum Daily Load (TMDL) Program* (visited Mar. 30, 1999) http://www.epa.gov/owow/tmdl/tmdlmap.htm (indicating five state programs as partially approved).

75. *Industry Argues Lawsuits Are Preventing Cleanup of "Impaired Waters,"* Inside EPA Wkly. Rep., Nov. 27, 1998, at 10.

76. S. 319-27, 55th Legis. Sess. (Wyo. 1999).

77. *Hearing on Governors' Perspectives on the Clean Water Act Before the Subcomm. on Water Resources and Env't of the House Comm. on Transportation and Infrastructure*, 106 Cong. 4 (1999) [hereinafter *Hearing on Governors' Perspectives*] (statement of Jim Geringer, Governor of Wyoming).

78. *Treatment Works Urged to Sue States to Force Pollution Control*, [29 Current Developments] Env't Rep. (BNA) 1552 (Dec. 4, 1998) ("The fear among many regulated entities, such as [publicly owned treatment works (POTWs)], is that the TMDL program still will not contain enforceable mechanisms for nonpoint sources. They worry that the burden to achieve the next level of improved water quality will fall on them rather than on the nonpoint sources.").

79. *See* AMSA, *Evaluating TMDLs . . . Protecting the Rights of POTWs* (visited May 20, 1999) http://www.amsa-cleanwater.org/tmdl/tmdl.htm.

80. *Id.*

81. *Id.*

82. *Id.*

83. As stated in its introduction, "it will advocate the strongest legal, scientific and policy arguments available to POTWs to protect their rights under these programs." *Id.* at Introduction.

84. *Id.*

85. *Id.* at Executive Summary: POTW's Stake in the TMDL Process.

86. *Id.* at Executive Summary: Evaluating TMDLs.

87. *Id.*

88. *Id.*

89. *Id.* at Executive Summary: Conclusion. In January 1999, southern California municipal sewer districts brought suit to overturn a TMDL settlement for ocean waters and more than 130 streams' watersheds in Los Angeles and Ventura counties; the gauntlets are going down. *See* Betty Streisand, *A New Day at the Beach: A Landmark Deal May Finally Force a Cleanup of Southern California's Dirty Waterways,* U.S. News & World Rep. (Feb. 1, 1999) http://www.usnews.com/usnews/issue//990201/1cali.htm.

90. *See* Office of Water, U.S. EPA, *Watershed Training Opportunities* (Feb. 1998) http://www.epa.gov/owow/watershed/wacadamywtopps.html.

91. *See* Office of Water, U.S. EPA, *Basins 2.0: A Powerful Tool for Managing Watersheds* (visited Mar. 30, 1999) http://www.epa.gov/ost/basins/basinsv2.html.

92. *Id.*

93. *See* Frederick R. Anderson et al., Environmental Protection Law and Policy 248 (2d ed. 1990) (courts have generally deferred to EPA's selection of modeling techniques).

94. *See* United States v. Northeastern Pharm. & Chem. Co., 810 F.2d 726, 17 ELR 20603 (8th Cir. 1986); *see also* U.S. EPA v. TMG Enter., 979 F. Supp. 110 (W.D. Ky. 1997).

95. For judicial approval of this precautionary approach, see Ethyl Corp. v. U.S. EPA, 541 F.2d 1, 6 ELR 20267 (D.C. Cir. 1976) (lead levels in gasoline); Environmental Defense Fund v. U.S. EPA, 598 F.2d 62, 8 ELR 20765 (D.C. Cir. 1978) (polychlorinated biphenyl standards); Hercules, Inc. v. U.S. EPA, 598 F.2d 91, 8 ELR 20811 (D.C. Cir. 1978) (water quality standards); for a description of a recent decision upholding a TMDL based on less-than-dispositive science, see Rick Steelhammer, *Appeals Board Upholds Blackwater Waste Limit,* Charleston Gazette (W. Va.), Mar. 31, 1999, *available in* 1999 WL 6719305.

96. *See* 2 Rodgers, *supra* note 9, at 288-89; *see also generally* Houck, *supra* note 15, at 10531-32. One recent commentator on an EPA water quality standards rulemaking has observed:

We believe that there is already too much flexibility in the WQS program. For example, state mixing zones violate federal guidelines (like Montana's 6-mile long mixing zone), and allow the elimination of uses and the lowering of water quality in direct contradiction of antidegradation policies; state antidegradation policies in New Hampshire and elsewhere consider "insignificant" the elimination of as much as 25% of the assimilative capacity of high quality waters; some states use site specific water quality criteria to justify the dumping of metals (in places like Baltimore Harbor) that exceed state and federal standards; [polychlorinated biphenyls] are allowed to be discharged into Massachusetts Bay despite sediments that already violate state standards; the poultry industry is allowed to degrade high quality waters and fisheries in Oklahoma and elsewhere; and variances are granted to authorize "temporary" activities (such as the construction of ski areas in Vermont) that permanently alter streams and impair water quality.

Comments of Center for Maine Conservation on Advance Notice of Proposed Rulemaking (Jan. 4, 1999); *see infra* note 103.

97. *See* Houck, *supra* note 15, at 10551 (comparing dioxin standards for Minnesota with standards in Alabama, Georgia, Maryland, and Virginia).

98. *Id.* at 10546 (comparing critical low flow calculations in Louisiana, based on lowest flow recorded, with those in Virginia, based on average lows over time).

99. U.S. EPA, TECHNICAL SUPPORT DOCUMENT FOR WATER QUALITY-BASED TOXICS CONTROL (Sept. 1985) (with table of "state-by-state mixing zone dimensions" showing calculations varying from one-fourth to three-fourths of the cross-sections of the receiving waters, and from 10 to 33% of this volume); Houck, *supra* note 15, at 10545.

100. *See* Andrea Foster, *Prodding EPA to Step Over States*, CHEMICAL WK., Oct. 14, 1998, at 74 ("Industry is hoping that EPA will provide flexibility for states to set water quality standards for watersheds on a case-by-case basis, using cost-benefit analysis to choose appropriate remedies."). Industry's expectations for weaker standards from such a process could not be more apparent.

101. Under these regulations, a state may lower its water quality standard (e.g., from primary to secondary contact recreation) when a state can demonstrate six limited circumstances, for example, when natural concentrations prevent attaining the original standard. 40 C.F.R. §131.10(g)(1) (1998).

102. Under these regulations, a state may permit a reduction of water quality within its water quality standard (e.g., from 6 micrograms per liter (μg/l) to 5 μg/l of dissolved oxygen) when "necessary to accommodate important economic or social development." *Id.* §131.12(a)(2).

103. Office of Water, U.S. EPA, *Water Quality Criteria and Standards Plan—Priorities for the Future* (Apr. 1998) http://www.epa.gov/OSTg/standards/plansfs.html [hereinafter *Priorities for the Future*] (identifying the development of nutrient and

sediment criteria as "priority areas"). As one EPA official has observed, "[i]f you don't have a standard out there how do you know how much is enough?" Tripp Baltz, *Numeric Target Ranges Important Part of Agency's Natural Nutrient Strategy,* [29 Current Developments] Env't Rep. (BNA) 610 (July 17, 1998).

104. An example from Virginia: setting a dioxin standard 100 times less protective than recommended by EPA (and 10,000 times less protective than that of Minnesota), the Executive Director of the Virginia Water Board instructed his colleagues: "It is your responsibility to find the answer of what is environmentally safe and to set a standard to regulate what is environmentally safe; yet at the same time, you have a responsibility not to go beyond what is achievable and responsible from a socio-economic standpoint." Comments of Richard N. Burton to the Virginia State Water Control Board Re: Dioxin Water Quality Standards (May 14, 1990), Attachment to Environmental Defense Fund v. Virginia State Water Control Bd., No. HA-731-3 (Va. Cir. Ct. Richmond). It was, of course, the fact and the continuing prospect of just such "tilting" that induced Congress to impose national standards in the 1972 CWA.

105. *E.g.,* Mississippi Comm'n on Natural Resources v. Costle 625 F.2d 1269, 10 ELR 20931 (5th Cir. 1980) (dissolved oxygen); *see also IG Calls for Region III to Step Up Oversight of State Water Quality Programs,* INSIDE EPA WKLY. REP., Apr. 9, 1999, at 111 ("States are supposed to conduct triennial reviews of their programs and make updates to their standards. But as of 1998, Maryland, Delaware, [the] District of Columbia, Pennsylvania and Virginia were all between 1-5 years late in their triennial review"). Extrapolating from Region III to all 10 EPA regions, there appears to be a considerable oversight problem here.

106. *See, e.g.,* Fowl River Protection Ass'n v. Board of Water & Sewer Comm'n, 572 So. 2d 446 (Ala. 1990); Rivers Unltd. V. Schregardus, 685 N.E.2d 603 (Ohio Ct. C.P. 1997).

107. *See* Erin P. Billings, *EPA Tells Montana to Clean Up Water Laws,* BILLINGS GAZETTE, Jan. 7, 1999, *available in* 1999 WL 11717496 (describing EPA's rejection of Montana water quality standards for, among other shortcomings, failure to protect high quality waters).

108. *See* 60 Fed. Reg. 14588 (Mar. 17, 1995) (citing cases from Virginia).

109. *See TMDLs I, supra* note 20, at 10344.

110. *Id.* at 10339.

111. *Id.* at 10343.

112. Advance Notice of Proposed Rulemaking on Water Quality Standards Regulations, 63 Fed. Reg. 36742-806 (July 7, 1998).

113. *Id.*

114. *See State Officials Urge EPA Not to Undertake Comprehensive Revision of Water Regulation,* [27 Current Developments] Env't Rep. (BNA) 2073 (Feb. 14, 1997) (quoting the President of the Association of State and Interstate Water Pollu-

tion Control Administrators as "vehemently" disagreeing with national standards for mixing zones and antidegradation of water bodies); *id.* at 2074.

115. *Development of Nutrient Criteria Guidance for All Regions to Be Accelerated, EPA Says,* [29 Current Developments] Env't Rep. (BNA) 609 (July 17, 1998) ("The strategy calls for nutrient criteria guidance that is region specific; waterbody-type technical guidance that includes sections on over enrichment indicators, sampling and analytical techniques, and management methods; state and tribal adoption of nutrient criteria and standards; establishment of nutrient teams composed of state and federal officials to manage nutrient criteria projects; and a system to manage and evaluate the program.").

116. *See Priorities for the Future, supra* note 103.

117. Reacting to EPA's proposal to address phosphorous in its nutrient management strategy, the American Farm Bureau Federation responds:

> "Too little is known about phosphorus and how it affects water quality," Watkins said. "Other variables that figure into the equation," she said, "include soil type, the amount of phosphorus already in the soil, the amount of phosphorus taken in by plants and crops as food, and current management practices. You can't just jump into a phosphorus standard without knowing how it works," she said.

USDA Proposal to Include Phosphorus in Nutrient Plans Concerns Farm Group, 29 Env't Rep. (BNA) 610 (July 17, 1998) (quoting Rosemarie Watkins, Director of Governmental Relations for the American Farm Bureau Federation).

118. 939 F. Supp. 865, 866, 867, 27 ELR 20280, 20280-81 (N.D. Ga. Mar. 25, 1996); *see also* Alaska Ctr. for the Env't v. Reilly, 762 F. Supp. 1422, 1425, 21 ELR 21305, 21306 (W.D. Wash. 1991) ("The state's 1990 305(b) Report notes that TMDLs have 'not been attempted' and makes no promise to 'attempt' them.").

119. Mark Solomon, The Four Steps of Clean Water Act Denial, A Play in Four Acts (Jan. 25, 1999), *attached to* E-mail Communication from Kathy Nemsick, Natural Resources Defense Council, to Oliver Houck (Jan. 25, 1999) (on file with author). Mr. Solomon, formerly of the Lands Council, has been a participant in the Western Governors' Association workshop on TMDLs. *See infra* text accompanying notes 165-69. The play ends with "Act Four: Pay Me!," described as:

> The final Act opens with a chorus of the Agency Staffers, Politicians, Federal and State Land Managers and Private Property Owners singing a rousing rendition of "Pay Me!" in which the lead voice of the Private Property Owners tearfully claims that if only he had enough money he would be able to stop beating his Mother. In a second verse performed in a round by the Agency Staffers, Politicians, and Federal and State Lands Managers, Nation's Waters is assured that if they had enough money to find a new Data, they could show Nation's Waters that despite her flowing wounds she really had nothing to complain about.

120. *See TMDLs III, supra* note 42, at 10418.

121. For a discussion of state-law limitations on nonpoint source controls, see *TMDLs II, supra* note 30, at 10400.

122. ENVIRONMENTAL LAW INST., ENFORCEABLE STATE MECHANISMS FOR THE CONTROL OF NONPOINT SOURCE WATER POLLUTION (1997); for an additional discussion of these authorities, see MARC RIBAUDO & DANETTE WOO, U.S. DEP'T OF AGRIC., SUMMARY OF STATE WATER QUALITY LAWS AFFECTING AGRICULTURE (undated). Pennsylvania, for example, has required nutrient management programs for virtually all agricultural operations. *See* Pamela S. Clarke & Stacey M. Cronk, *The Pennsylvania Nutrient Management Act: Pennsylvania Helps to "Save the Bay" Through Nonpoint Source Pollution Management,* 6 VILL. ENVTL. L.J. 319 (1995).

123. The major expenses in nonpoint source pollution arise from compensating farmers and other nonpoint sources for land use practices that will reduce runoff and protect downstream uses. Although these costs can be considerable, *see* Andrew Revkin, *U.S. to Pay Farmers to Shoo Cows Off City's Watershed,* N.Y. TIMES, Aug. 26, 1998, at B3 (describing a "$10.4 million program to pay farms to stop growing crops and grazing cattle along streams feeding the city's upstate reservoirs . . ."; farms will receive a yearly fee of $100 to $150 per acre), they are far less expensive than additional technological controls on point sources. (New York City has reportedly spent $600 million to date on technology to protect its own water supply. *Id.*) These payments are also anomalous in the Clean Water Act and other pollution control programs in compensating dischargers for abating pollution. At some point, they become ridiculous. *See* Defenders of Wildlife, *Grazing Losses Mount in Idaho* (May 5, 1999) http://www.defenders.org/gline872.html (describing federal expenditure of $100,000 to protect streams on three grazing allotments priced at $10,000 per year).

124. OFFICE OF WATER, U.S. EPA, GUIDANCE SPECIFYING MANAGEMENT MEASURES FOR SOURCES OF NONPOINT POLLUTION IN COASTAL WATERS (Jan. 1993) (available from the ELR Document Service, ELR Order No. AD-78).

125. *See* Everglades Forever Act, Fla. S. 373.4592(d)-(e) (1999).

126. Telephone Conversation with Tom Ankersen, Director, Conservation Law Clinic, University of Florida College of Law (May 23, 1999); for a discussion of the Nutrient Removal Project, see Thomas Ankersen, *Ecosystem Management and the Everglades: A Legal and Institutional Analysis,* 2 FLA. ST. U. J. LAND USE & ENVTL. L. 496 (1996).

127. *See* Curt Anderson, *House Rejects Pleas to End Aid to Agriculture,* TIMES PICAYUNE (New Orleans), July 25, 1997, at A3; *see also House Republicans Question Increase in Interior Spending, Everglades Sugar Tax,* 27 Env't Rep. (BNA) 2209 (Mar. 7, 1997) (rejecting a state tax on sugar intended to support restoration of the Everglades); for a description of the sugar subsidy, the equivalent of $1.4 billion annually, see U.S. GAO, SUGAR PROGRAM UNDER CHANGING CONDITIONS 4, 5 (Apr. 16, 1993).

128. Anna P. Miller, *The Western Front Revisited,* 26 URB. LAW. 845 (1999).

129. *See* Associated Press, *Bomb Rips Building in Nevada*, TIMES PICAYUNE (New Orleans), Nov. 1, 1993, at A5.

130. E-mail Communication from Ken Midkiff, Sierra Club, to Oliver Houck (Mar. 31, 1999) (on file with author).

131. *Hearing on Governors' Perspectives, supra* note 77, at 3 (statement of George E. Pataki, Governor of New York) (on file with author).

132. E-mail Communication from Rick Parrish, Southern Environmental Law Center, to Oliver Houck (Apr. 8, 1999) (on file with author).

133. *See* LA. REV. STAT. ANN. §30:2089 (West 1997). The Louisiana bill enacted fees on discharges to provide for further development of TMDLs.

134. *See* OR. REV. STAT. §568.909 (1998).

135. *See supra* note 124; for a discussion of this seldom-used authority—indeed, requirement—see *TMDLs III, supra* note 42, at 10420.

136. E-mail Communication from Dave Gault, L1 Soundkeeper Fund, to Jodi Theut (Apr. 2, 1999) (on file with author).

137. *See A Total Maximum Daily Load (TMDL) for Long Island Sound: Charting a Course to Clean Water* (visited June 18, 1999) http://www.soundkeeper.org/tmdl/.

138. For a description of the impacts of hog farming and a chronology of regulatory measures taken by North Carolina, see Environmental Defense Fund, *Hog Factories And Government Regulation: The Strait Poop* (visited June 4, 1999) http://www.hogwatch.org/getthefacts/factsheets/regs.html.

139. *Iowa Farms Hear About Gulf Hypoxia*, GULFWATCH, May/June 1996, at 1.

140. E-mail Communication from Margaret James West, Virginia Rivers Coalition, to Rick Parrish, Southern Environmental Law Center (Apr. 1, 1999) (on file with author).

141. E-mail Communication from Duane Hovorka, Nebraska Wildlife Federation, to Oliver Houck (Mar. 31, 1999) (on file with author).

142. E-mail Communication from Charles Benjamin, Legislative Coordinator, Kansas Natural Resource Council, to Oliver Houck (Mar. 30, 1999) (on file with author).

143. E-mail Communication from Joseph Brecher, attorney, to Oliver Houck (Mar. 31, 1999) (on file with author). Mr. Brecher is currently representing California environmental organizations in TMDL litigation.

144. JENNIFER RUFFOLO, CALIFORNIA RESEARCH BUREAU, TMDLs: THE REVOLUTION IN WATER QUALITY REGULATION 25 (Apr. 1999).

145. *See* California Clean Waters Program Draft TMDL Bill—Version I (Mar. 4, 1999) (on file with author).

146. *See* HB 2171 (1998) (on file with author); *see also Hearing on HB 2171 Before the House Comm. on Agriculture and Ecology* (Feb. 25, 1999) (statement of Nina Bell, Executive Director, Northwest Environmental Advocates).

147. *See supra* note 76; *see also* E-mail Communication from Dan Helig, Wyoming Outdoor Council, to Oliver Houck (Mar. 31, 1999) (on file with author).

148. E-mail Communication from Alan Levine, Coast Action Group, to Kathy Nemsick (July 26, 1999) (on file with author). Co-plaintiffs in the suit are the Mendocino County Farm Bureau and the American Farm Bureau Federation. *see also* Vicki Monks, *Farm Bureau vs. Nature*, DEFENDERS, Fall 1998, at 16.

> The American Farm Bureau Federation (AFBF) boasts 4.7 million members in all 50 states. However, the bulk of these members are not farmers, as only about 1 million full-time farmers reside in the United States. Most members join to get cheap insurance from AFBF-affiliated companies. Dues from these members, as well as income from a wide array of AFBF businesses, such as co-ops, garner millions of dollars yearly for tax-exempt AFBF's 2,800 state and county affiliates.

149. E-mail Communication from Dan Helig, Wyoming Outdoor Council, to Oliver Houck (Mar. 31, 1999) (on file with author). The Clean Water Action Plan is described in *TMDLs III, supra* note 42, at 10426.

150. *See TMDLs III, supra* note 42, at 10423.

151. American Farm Bureau Fed'n & National Pork Producers Council, Advance Comments on TMDL Rulemaking (Aug. 25, 1998) (on file with author). The comments challenge, inter alia, the application of TMDLs to nonpoint sources and the requirement for an implementing plan.

152. *See TMDLs III, supra* note 42, at 10422.

153. *See id.* at 10436-37, 10439-43 (appendix individually examining 55 TMDLs from 22 states).

154. *See* Susan Bruninga, *Governors' Resolutions Seek Stronger Role in Water Programs,* [29 Current Developments] Env't Rep. (BNA) 739-40 (Aug. 7, 1998).

155. *Id.* at 740.

156. *See* Letter from Office of Water, U.S. EPA, to Thomas Curtis, Director, Natural Resources Group, National Governors' Association Hall of States (July 23, 1998).

157. *See Nonpoint Sources: Faulting EPA-USDA Livestock Strategy, States Say Their Programs Already Work,* 29 Env't Rep. (BNA) 1757, 1758 (Jan. 8, 1999).

158. *See Hearing on Governors' Perspectives, supra* note 77, at 1 (statement of Sherwood L. Boehlert, Chairman, Subcommittee on Water Resources and Environment) (on file with author).

159. *See id.*

160. *Hearing on Governors' Perspectives, supra* note 77, at 5 (statement of Parris Glendening, Governor of Maryland) (on file with author).

161. *See id.* (statement of George E. Pataki, Governor of New York) (on file with author).

162. *See* Corning E-mail, *supra* note 71, at 3.

163. Tripp Baltz, *Ranchers and Farmers in the West Sound Off on Pollution Control Strategy,* [29 Current Developments] Env't Rep. (BNA) 1646 (Dec. 18, 1998).

164. *Id.* ("Rice [Executive Vice President of the Colorado Farm Bureau] and others urged representations of EPA not to change to 'voluntary' nature of the draft strategy."); *see also Farmers Seek USDA, EPA Funds for Proposed Animal Feeding Strategy,* [29 Current Developments] Env't Rep. (BNA) 1553, 1557 (Dec. 4, 1998 ("Agricultural interests applauded the voluntary aspects of the program but expressed some concerns about the scope of the regulatory side of the plan.").

165. *See* Susan Bruninga, *Clean Water Group Gets Federal Grant for Technical Assistance to Pork Producers,* [29 Current Developments] Env't Rep. (BNA) 1396 (Nov. 13, 1998) ("Most of the grant will go to a project to provide technical assistance to large-scale pork producers who have been targeted as sources of treatment pollution in areas such as Eastern North Carolina.").

166. *See* Western Governors' Ass'n, *Workshop Summary: Western Watershed/TMDL Nonpoint Issues* (Mar. 1999), *at* http://www.westgov. org/wga/publicat/vegasdoc.htm.

167. For a discussion of the FACA committee process and report, see *TMDLs III, supra* note 42, at 10421-23.

168. Panel topics for the January meeting in Las Vegas included *Sound Science in State Watershed/TMDL Planning (Federal Perspectives), Sound Science in State Watershed/TMDL Planning (State Perspectives),* and *Managing the TMDL Listing Process.* The Western Governors' Association met again in March in Portland, Oregon, for a panel discussion entitled *Intra-State Coordination of TMDL Development and Implementation: A Case Study* http://www.westgov. org/wga/publicat/vegasdoc.htm.

169. They may, on the other hand, simply emphasize and confirm the inadequacies in existing state water quality programs that will make TMDLs all the more time-consuming, data-consuming, expensive, and limited in scope and effect; a review of the panel outlines is not reassuring in this regard. *See id.*

170. *See TMDLs III, supra* note 42, at 10424.

171. *Industry Says EPA Will Need CWA Reauthorization to Address Runoff,* INSIDE EPA WKLY. REP., Dec. 11, 1998, at 1, 2.

172. *See* Concerned Area Residents for the Env't v. Southview Farms, 34 F.3d 114, 24 ELR 21480 (2d Cir. 1994) (dairy farm operations as point sources); *see also* Community Ass'n for Restoration of the Env't v. Henry Bostona Dairy, No.

CY98-3011.EFS, slip op. (E.D. Wash. May 17, 1999) (land application of CAFO wastes subject to CWA permits).

173. *See TMDLs III, supra* note 42, at 10425-26; *see also Court Upholds TRI Listing of Nitrates, Defers to EPA on Chronic Health Effects*, 29 Env't Rep. (BNA) 1397 (Nov. 13, 1998). *But see* Fertilizer Inst. v. Browner, No. 98-1067 (GK), slip op. (D.D.C. Apr. 15, 1999) (rejecting Toxics Release Inventory listing of phosphoric acid).

174. *See* Dan Esty, *Revitalizing Environmental Federalism*, 95 MICH. L. REV. 570 (1996); J.B. Ruhl, *Thinking of Environmental Law as a Complex Adaptive System: How to Clean Up the Environment by Making a Mess of Environmental Law*, 34 HOUS. L. REV. 933 (1997); Karl Hausker, *Reinventing Environmental Regulation: The Only Path to a Sustainable Future*, 29 ELR 10148 (Mar. 1999); for a critique of this same enthusiasm for "post regulatory" programs, see Rena I. Steinzor, *Reinventing Environmental Regulation Through the Government Performance and Results Act: Are the States Ready for Devolution?*, 29 ELR 10074 (Feb. 1999). Of course, the interest in new wave environmentalism has been with us for decades under different labels, among them "New Federalism." For a dated but still valid analysis of this wave and the serious questions of state commitment to pollution control and the inability to do so at the local level, see COMMITTEE ON ENV'T & PUBLIC WORKS, U.S. SENATE, FEDERAL-STATE RELATIONS IN TRANSITION: IMPLICATIONS FOR ENVIRONMENTAL POLICY, S. REP. NO. 97-7 (1982).

Chapter 6:
The TMDL Program to Come: Aftershock and Prelude

EPA is in the process of redesigning the CWA's TMDL program.[1] Section 303 of the Act requires states and, if necessary, EPA to: (1) identify waters that do not meet water quality standards; (2) establish the TMDLs for pollutants discharged into these waters that will achieve these standards; and (3) incorporate these loads into state planning.[2] These are of course the classic steps of ambient-based water quality management.

Ambient-based management has not worked well in any media—air, water, or waste.[3] It requires enormous amounts of data. It requires analysis that is rarely definitive and nearly always litigable. It launches a process that never ends. These same factors plagued the CWA's predecessors and the similarly constructed Clean Air Act (CAA). They have prolonged and frustrated decisions under federal pesticide, toxic substances, safe drinking water, hazardous waste, and Superfund laws as well. EPA's task with TMDLs is not an easy one, then, under the best of circumstances.

The circumstances of TMDLs are not ideal. The Agency has a skimpy statute to work with, and the Clinton Administration's efforts to flesh it out met with a firestorm of opposition. EPA now faces states on red alert for anything that sounds like a federal environmental requirement, and is well below baseline in their ability to staff, finance, maintain, or enforce a program of this complexity. It also faces powerful resistance from major industries that have, to date, enjoyed virtual immunity from the CWA, and from their allies in the U.S. Congress and the current Administration.[4] In January 2002, the Office of Management and Budget, after private meetings with industry, placed TMDLs on a short list of "outdated or outmoded" rules.[5] It did not need to. The old rules were already dead, and EPA had given sufficient notice that the program would be changed.

This Chapter attempts to summarize the events leading to the adoption of final TMDL rules in the year 2000, and recent studies, agency initiatives, and litigation that will affect the new program to come. It concludes with an assessment of the program now forming, and with recommendations that would assist such a program in reaching the CWA's clean water goal.

The Showdown

The year 2000 saw a dramatic showdown between Congress and the executive branch over TMDLs. In retrospect, it was unavoidable. The Agency, which was trying to build a carrot-and-stick program, ran into constituencies implacable in their opposition to sticks, too powerful to need to compromise, and with ready access to Capitol Hill. What ensued was a high-stakes clash of power in which EPA won the battle but its opposition, strongly backed by Congress, won the war.

The showdown concerned EPA's first ever, comprehensive regulations for the TMDL program.[6] The Agency and the states had been operating under skeletal regulations originating in 1978 that repeated requirements of the statute but provided little additional guidance.[7] As written earlier, the stage was set for underperformance, and underperformance happened.[8]

Shocked into motion by citizen suits in the early 1990s, EPA struggled to get ahead of district court mandates with a flurry of TMDL guidance to the states that fleshed out preliminary requirements for impaired water listings and for the contents and schedules for TMDLs themselves.[9] At the same time EPA convened a Federal Advisory Committee Act (FACA) committee with representation from state water agencies, agribusiness, timber, industrial point sources, municipal sources, environmentalists, Native Americans, academics, and, ex officio, EPA and the U.S. Department of Agriculture (USDA). Its mission was to forge a consensus on program regulations.[10]

Consensus was not in the cards. At bottom, the timber and agriculture industries were not going to accept that CWA §303(d) covered nonpoint sources or that, if it did, it required implementation plans. To these industries, the CWA's only lawful vehicle to abate their discharges was the voluntary, grant-in-aid program under §319. TMDLs smacked of first ever regulation, a causa belli.[11] A Farm Bureau Federation representative wrote that the program had been "hijacked by a vast national bureaucracy of parasites."[12] An article in the fall 1999 issue of *Range Magazine* called TMDLs and the Administration's supporting Clean Water Action Plan "perhaps the most anti-agricultural document ever produced in Washington, DC."[13] Before EPA had even proposed regulations the hype was reaching best available technology (BAT) levels for the English language.

EPA, for its part, could not let the issue slide. Environmental lawsuits were setting its agenda, case by case, state by state, with differing and at times highly demanding schedules for impaired waters listings and TMDLs.[14] The Agency and the states were making decisions on the basis of guidance memoranda[15] that had never been subjected to notice-and-comment rulemaking under the Administrative Procedure Act (APA)[16] and that carried no force of law.

In July 1999, EPA proposed draft, comprehensive regulations for the TMDL program[17] and launched a series of meetings, briefing sessions, and telethons in an attempt to calm the waters. To no avail. Most states and affected industries remained adamantly opposed. It is likely that in the tenor of the times—anti-government sentiment at a high fever and anti-Clinton sentiment in Congress even higher—no regulatory effort would have met a different reception. At which point EPA's choices were to drop nonpoint sources and implementation plans from the program or face the consequences. Drop them it would not do. Instead, the Agency softened other aspects of its proposal, clarified that TMDL implementation plans could be satisfied through "voluntary means and education," lengthened the deadlines for TMDL submissions, and hoped for the best.[18]

The rulemaking took a year. More than 34,000 comments were received, which, even discounting mass-mailings from industry trade associations, indicated no small controversy.[19] At the same time, with little confidence in the administrative process, states and nonpoint industries turned up the heat and took their case to Congress.[20] They were warmly received. Congressional committees held field hearings stocked with farmers and small woodlot owners afraid, in some cases told, that EPA was going to require permits for the use of their land.[21] Committees held hearings on Capitol Hill in which their mistrust of EPA was so marked that one took the unprecedented step of insisting that Agency witnesses provide their testimony under oath.[22] Committee members accused EPA of "secret meetings" with environmentalists.[23] Learning that an Undersecretary of Agriculture had cooperated with EPA in developing a timetable for nonpoint source TMDLs, a representative from Arkansas inserted a budget rider in the agriculture appropriations bill removing the Undersecretary from authority in the matter.[24] The legislation passed.[25]

By April 2000, battered by the House and Senate, EPA began adding concessions to its most vocal opponents. It would drop its proposal to include "threatened waters" in TMDLs, despite its belief that attending to these waters early would save time and money later on.[26] It would drop a requirement that gave waters used for human consumption and for endangered species priority attention, despite its belief that these priorities were required by law.[27] It would drop a process allowing the public to petition for review of TMDL decisions, despite its belief that administrative review was preferable to litigation.[28] It would promise flat out that forestry practices would not be subject to national pollutant discharge elimination system (NPDES) permitting "under any circumstances."[29] And at seven congressional hearings, as if the white flag on these issues were not fully visible, the Agency stressed that it was trying to enhance flexibility and leave TMDL implementation to the states.[30]

Too much flexibility, for some parties. Following publication of the proposed rules in 1999 and continuing into the early months of 2000, several environmental groups, including lead TMDL litigating groups, became disenchanted with EPA's concessions. They saw in the proposals a recipe for endless delay, well beyond the deadlines they were establishing through citizen suits.[31] They also saw little assurance in implementation programs based on voluntary measures and education. On another side, however, were environmental groups that, having litigated over lists and TMDL schedules, were now engaged in their states on implementation issues. In their view, without regulations setting implementation standards, the rest of the TMDL process—listings, schedules of submissions etc.—even on accelerated schedules, led to no productive end. The environmental community split, some seeing the doughnut, others the hole.[32]

In May 2000, the split broke open when six national environmental organizations wrote the EPA Administrator calling on her to scrap the regulations and go back to the drawing board.[33] The letter could not have caught the Agency at a more vulnerable moment. Already under attack from the states, industry, and Congress, EPA was left without a single, unified constituency, while its opponents gained the argument that here was a rule that nobody liked.[34] Such an argument is persuasive in Congress; if nobody likes it, there are no political consequences to ditching the rule. Months later, seeing the entire program under vigorous attack on Capitol Hill, several of the dissenting groups switched sides to support the rule, but the political damage had been done. With the exception of a few environmental groups, a few of the more progressive states, e.g., California, Maryland, and Vermont,[35] and the Association of Metropolitan Sewerage Agencies (who saw TMDLs for nonpoint sources as a way to begin to share the burden of cleaning up impaired waters that otherwise fell largely on their shoulders),[36] EPA was on its own.

In full cry now, Congress hosted a competition of bills seeking to derail EPA's regulations. The lead vehicle, Senate Bill 2417, labeled with no apparent irony the "Water Pollution Program Enhancements Act of 2000," characterized the regulations as "hasty," "unscientific," "one-size-fits-all," and "unlikely to improve water quality."[37] It would put the EPA program on hold pending studies on its supporting science and on the effectiveness of alternative, voluntary programs and their costs.[38] Other bills would simply repeal the TMDL rules in full or exempt particular industries, e.g., forestry, from their scope.[39]

Meanwhile, the Administration, convinced that it could not persuade Congress that its process over the previous three years had been anything but hasty, that its regulations were reasonable, and that an approach preserving state authority to determine where, what, and how pollution would be abated was hardly "one-size-fits-all,"[40] began a race to beat the clock. Passing whatever bill Congress chose would take time. EPA accelerated its regulations review.

Outraged, now, by what appeared to be a stiff-arm of its concerns and an end-run on its authority, Congress looked for another vehicle to block the Administration. They found it in the Fiscal Year (FY) 2001 Military Constructions/FY 2000 Urgent Supplemental Appropriations Bill, an obscure funding measure that in neither House contained any mention of TMDLs.[41] Overnight and without notice, Congress tacked on a provision that no funds would be used in FY 2000 or 2001 to "make a final determination on or implement any new rule relative" to EPA's regulations.[42] It further mandated a study of the program by the National Academy of Sciences (NAS) to determine the adequacy of the scientific basis for the TMDL program.[43] Among other things, the study would delay the program; even better, the study might derail it.

As appropriations for expenditures that were unavoidable and in some cases already expended, the supplemental appropriations bill was must-sign legislation.[44] It was also, in a decade marked by environmental-legislation-by-appropriations-rider, a high watermark for this political art.[45] President William J. Clinton appeared check-mated; in order to cover, inter alia, monies spent for hurricane relief in Nicaragua, he would have to sign away the TMDL rule. A small window of opportunity remained, however, a gap of several days before which, with or without the president's signature, the bill would become law.[46] The EPA Administrator signed off on the regulations on July 11.[47] The final rule was published on July 13.[48] The same day, the last available, President Clinton signed the appropriations bill[49] prohibiting half of what his Administration had just done.

In the final regulations, EPA acknowledged the appropriations rider by delaying their effect until October 31, 2001, or until the expiration of the rider, whichever came first. As a practical matter, with a ban on funding program implementation, it would be delayed until whichever came second. In the meantime, EPA's skeletal regulations from the 1980s and subsequent guidance would remain in effect. The program would continue under the old rules. Environmentalists left the field bloodied but relieved that the TMDL program had not been repealed. The agriculture and timber industries left triumphant but insecure in their victory. The threat of TMDL-imposed requirements on nonpoint sources had been parried but it had not been eliminated.

The Aftermath

On the heels of the TMDL showdown came the national presidential elections, and, when the dust finally settled, a new philosophy toward environmental protection. EPA Administrator Christine Todd Whitman was a governor from a state with a proven, if not unmixed, capability and record in pollution control,[50] one of the more successful examples of federalism in a country where federalism can also simply mean the abandonment of national goals.[51] While TMDL issues continued to play out in the courts and percolated below the surface of a still-suspicious Congress, the lead action, although not all of the action, rebounded to EPA. We are a year away from a new TMDL program. From EPA's recent initiatives and statements, however, the contours of the new program are evident. The sections that follow attempt to summarize what is happening and likely to happen over the next year—the critical period in which the program jells.

Sobering News

If the flap over EPA's regulations produced no final resolution, it stimulated four studies on the underpinnings of the TMDL program. One was a state-of-readiness survey by the U.S. General Accounting Office (GAO) assessing the capabilities of water regulatory agencies to assess and manage water quality. In a second, previously mentioned study, the NAS would ascertain the state of the science supporting TMDL decisionmaking. A third study by EPA would project the total short- and long-term costs of the TMDL program. A fourth, by EPA's Inspector General, audited state water program enforcement. Taken individually, they provide answers to the questions asked. Taken together, they raise a larger question that is far more difficult to answer: will this dog really hunt?

☐ *State Capacity.* As described in an earlier discussion of TMDLs, ambient-based water quality management has always been severely challenged by its demands for current, continuous, and definitive data.[52] The information needed to support water quality criteria, to identify polluted waters, to determine the causal pollutants, to identify the sources of these pollutants, to sift out background, natural, atmospheric, and other exogenous sources, to quantify these loadings, and to apportion load reductions among these sources, all in ways that are defensible in a court of law (since any significant restrictions will be challenged), was a primary reason Congress abandoned ambient-based management in 1972 and turned to BAT.[53]

In the years that followed, the picture did not improve. A 1984 EPA survey of state water quality management needs identified more than 30 "difficulties" in state capacity, including: "lack of knowledge of how to do realistic modeling of a pollutant's concentration and fate in a water body"; "lack [of] data on the water quality of a given site"; and "lack [of] data necessary to determine the design discharge of the receiving water."[54] A 1987 Office of Technology Assessment report found that "[o]nly limited data are available on ambient pollutant concentrations in receiving waters, variability in these concentrations, and the fate of these pollutants and their impacts on indigenous organisms," and that "our ability to monitor water quality in relation to potential environmental or human impacts is relatively primitive."[55] A 1993 GAO report found that even the U.S. Geological Survey faced "formidable data management challenges" in assessing natural water quality because, inter alia, efforts to collect, analyze, and store data were so costly and labor intensive.[56] A 1999 report issued by former EPA and state agency employees called state monitoring and assessment "variable," "manipulated," and "erroneous"; a game of "politics, bureaucratic inertia and bad science."[57] Reports on the similar CAA program have consistently found the same.[58]

Which brings us to today. In March 2000, the GAO released its study of the adequacy of the information underlying the evaluation of national water quality and pollution control strategies.[59] Because the federal CWA program relies on state assessments, the report focused on state capabilities, surveying all 50 states and probing the programs of 4 representative states in more detail.[60] In sum, the GAO found wide inconsistency and incomplete information on existing water quality, the foundation information for everything that is supposed to follow.[61]

According to the GAO, as of the year 2000, a majority of the nation's waters remain, in practice, unmonitored and unassessed, even by the most primitive of indicators. Assessment levels range from 72% for estuaries, to 40% for lakes, ponds, and reservoirs, to 19% for rivers and streams, and to 6% for oceans shoreline waters.[62] The numbers are worse than they look. Only one-half of the 19% of assessments for rivers and streams was performed by actual monitoring; the other one-half by estimates, extrapolations, and unspecified "other means."[63] Further, the monitoring may be infrequent, e.g., monthly or, for pesticides, annually, for only a few contaminants, e.g., oxygen levels, solids, and bacteria, and not representative of more serious pollution.[64]

The states themselves were equally pessimistic about their data-readiness. Only 6 states reported sufficient information to "fully assess" state waters, and only 18 reported sufficient information even to identify waters as polluted for TMDL listings.[65] Moving on down the TMDL program requirements, while 40 states reported confidence in their ability to identify point sources of pollution (not that hard a trick, given that point source loadings are characterized in each NPDES permit), only 3 reported confidence in their ability to identify nonpoint sources, the sources primarily at issue in the TMDL program.[66] Similarly, while 29 states felt that they had sufficient data to develop point source TMDLs, only 3 had data sufficient to develop nonpoint source TMDLs.[67] In other words, for the type of pollution for which TMDLs are most important—that from crops, cattle, clearcutting, roadbuilding, and suburban and urban construction—only 3 states of 50 have enough data, or will admit to having enough data, to act.

This lack of basic information—historic, present, and incontrovertible—has always placed state water quality regulators in a tactical bind. On the one hand, the facts speak for themselves. On the other hand, state water quality agencies have fought tenaciously since the 1960s for the primary responsibility to manage the nation's waters.[68] Ambient-based programs give them the power to determine water use categories, a threshold and essentially political decision that allows low water quality in states with little inclination to face pollution dischargers.[69] It is easier to declare the use of a somewhat polluted river to be "secondary contact recreation," e.g., boating, than to be "primary contact recreation," e.g., swimming, and then have to clean it up.[70] States have additional leeway under ambient management programs to allocate pollution cleanup-responsibilities among dischargers, a leeway that carries its own, obvious political clout. In effect, the CWA's NPDES program robbed states of both authorities.[71] It further starved technocracies of state water engineers, private consultant firms, and water research institutions of federal and state funding for data collection, modeling, and analysis, chores that—in a program based on ambient impacts and constant adjustments to those impacts—never end. Authority and funding are strong motivators, and it has been no surprise to see states consistently assert before Congress complete confidence in their ability to manage ambient-based programs and at the same time assert poverty when it comes to the tools—raw data, trained personnel, assessment techniques, and modeling—needed to make them work.[72]

Over time, wearied of technology-standard battles, EPA has joined the state chorus. In 1987, with amendments to the CWA launching new ambient-based programs for toxic dischargers and inaugurating the §319 nonpoint source program, EPA's Assistant Administrator for Water would testify to Congress:

> Before the 1972 law, you'd get into these long, long debates with dischargers who would say[:] "No let me prove to you this isn't a problem." [W]e've learned something in the past 20 years. Our monitoring technology is much better than it was 20 years ago. So the combination of the much better information and the much better permitting and enforcement base means that I think we have a chance we didn't have then.[73]

Whether this testimony was actually believed, wishful thinking, or simply expedient in an era when EPA was looking to shed environmental responsibility to the states, time would show otherwise.

In October 2001, notwithstanding the GAO's findings, EPA would pronounce:

> In recent years, EPA and the States have made great strides in implementing the existing [§]303(d) program to list impaired waters and develop and implement TMDLs. States have substantially improved their TMDL programs while the Agency has provided the States with significant increases in technical and financial support to expand and strengthen all elements of their programs.[74]

There is something about the phrase "making great strides" that, like the phrase "full and frank discussion" in the field of diplomacy, seems to confirm that the goal, if attainable at all, is still a long way away.

☐ *Supporting Science.* As noted earlier, in July 2000, Congress not only deferred the regulatory program until further notice but mandated a study by the NAS as well. The requested points of study were the sufficiency of knowledge about point and nonpoint sources and the state of monitoring and modeling needed to predict pollution loadings and develop TMDLs.[75] The study began in January 2001, and was due in June—tall orders for a short amount of time.[76] In effect, the report would be written by a few individuals, and, as it happened, ones with strong, preexisting points of view on the TMDL program.

On one level, the NAS report is an affirmation of the TMDL program. The message on the adequacy of the supporting science was blunt: the science is there, its uncertainty can be reduced, and uncertainties that remain should not be used as an excuse for delay or inaction.[77] In words that echo those of water quality administrators in the 1960s and EPA's Assistant Administrator for Water in the 1980s, the committee reported that "the data and science have progressed sufficiently over the past 35 years to support the nation's return to ambient-based water quality management."[78] These messages may not have been welcome news to those in Congress who saw "bad science" as a reason to oppose EPA's TMDL regulations.[79] They seem to have been as unwelcome to—or unread by—EPA, which quickly used the National Research Council (NRC) report as a reason to suspend its regulations into the year 2003.[80]

Buried not very deeply in the report, however, were three additional themes that cast a longer shadow over the program. The first relates to the technology and personnel demands of adequate ambient-based management. The science might be there in theory, but in practice it certainly was not, either in models, data collection, training, or state capacity.[81] Further, the committee added two technology demands that threaten to push the current state-of-unreadiness over the edge. One was an insistence on greatly increased monitoring in order to produce a sufficient number of current and statistically accurate samples that would, in turn, reduce uncertainty and inconsistency in decisionmaking and provide a basis for "adaptive management," i.e., management responding to changed and changing conditions.[82] Criticizing EPA and state reliance on static and insufficiently comprehensive monitoring,[83] good science would require increased and constantly maintained data collection. At which point, given an already taxed system producing minimal data on only 19% of the nation's waterways, we may be at the limits of funding and political will.

The other high-tech demand came with the committee's support for biological monitoring and biological criteria.[84] As a theoretical matter, few could contest that the living environment of an aquatic system is a more complete measure of its health than are numerical, chemical criteria; the real thing is always better than a partial surrogate.[85] As a practical matter, however, biological monitoring is infinitely more complex in what is getting monitored and how impacts are measured, e.g., the number of minnow per one-quarter mile and their relative states of health, than the use of chemical or physical parameters, e.g., 0.04 micrograms/liter of oxygen, 0.10 parts per million of dissolved solids. Recognizing this fact, the report recommends the use of both chemical and biological monitors in order to assure scientific accuracy.[86] At this point we may have crossed the limits of funding and political will.

A second theme of the report, indeed the central theme to those who chaired and wrote it, was the recommendation that the TMDL process approach the identification of impaired waters in two stages, a preliminary stage of eligible waters and a second stage of formal listing.[87] The data requirements for eligible waters would be broad and permissive, including water quality data from several years back and additional data such as fish kills or fish advisories (for public health purposes).[88] No legal consequences would flow from this preliminary list, however, other than additional monitoring. For the formal listing a rigorous set of continuous data would be required proving water quality impairment to a 90% confidence level.[89] The advantage of a two-tiered listing process would be final listings that are more resistant to litigation, more persuasive to pollution dischargers, and more focused on badly polluted waterways. The minus would be the potential for a limbo of eligible-but-unproven waters—a phenomenon already witnessed in the CAA and Endangered Species Act—that escape attention or treatment.[90]

The report cast a third shadow over the TMDL program by recommending, repeatedly, that states redetermine their water standards and uses for each impaired water body before TMDLs are performed.[91] It explained:

> [I]t does *not* follow that a water body lacking integrity [, e.g., polluted,] is impaired or that restoring biological integrity is either possible or desirable. A water body that is described as lacking "biological integrity" should not be assumed to be in a less-than-desirable state.[92]

What we have here is an open invitation to lower environmental protection. Were the invitation overlooked, a sidebar in the report entitled, "Six Reasons for Changing Water Quality Standards"[93] provides a recipe for dropping a designation from, say, primary contact recreation to secondary contact recreation when utilities, the sugar industry, or pulp and paper manufacturers dig in their heels.

The report concludes that, "the scientific foundation for adaptive implementation must rely on state initiative and leadership."[94] "Today," it notes with no approval, "EPA retains an extensive oversight" of the TMDL program[95]; instead, the report's approach will "require increased state assumption of responsibility for individual TMDLs, with EPA oversight focused at the program level instead of on each individual water segment."[96] One does not have to be a proponent nor an opponent of devolution to recognize that at this point the report is not treating the adequacy of science to support the TMDL program. It is taking sides in a political debate over federalism.

In the final analysis, reports are written by people. Under normal circumstances, NAS reports are written over several years, by scientists with little financial or political connection to the issues before them, and with a balance of points of view.[97] As the NRC staff director of this report has complained, however, this one was otherwise, a rush job with little time for panel building or, for that matter, report writing.[98] The result was a small group with an attitude. The panel chair, a witness for the Florida Pulp and Paper Association in hearings on the above-mentioned Florida rules who is also reported as having accused EPA of "heavy handed 'intrusion'" in North Carolina TMDLs, has stated that he "jumped at it [the chairmanship], because it was a great opportunity to make some of the arguments I've been making"; he is also quoted as referring to two subsequent TMDL-related consultant contracts as "an opportunity to push my agenda."[99] Florida had its own representative on the committee as well, who happened to write the section endorsing Florida's two-tiered program, a "great job on the committee" according to his state agency supervisors.[100] The report's principal author[101] had, just two months before the committee geared up, published an article through the Cato Institute entitled *The Trouble With Implementing TMDLs*[102]—a title remarkably similar to that of the final chapter of the NRC report[103]—expressing the fear that EPA would turn the TMDL program into a NPDES-like permit system.[104] Such an extension would be "costly, contentious, environmentally suspect, and often inequitable."[105] Warming to a close, he concluded: "Congress should explicitly affirm that the ends of the Act are to secure ambient water quality goals, not to eliminate all discharge."[106] Thus concluded the NRC report as well.[107] Congress, of course, decided otherwise in the CWA of 1972,[108] but the argument lingers on.

At bottom, a small group of industry consultants, state agency representatives, and water quality engineers have affirmed their faith in an ambient-based water quality program. In response to Congress' question, they found that TMDLs are supportable by science—lots more of it. Which leads to the next question: costs.

□ *Costs of the TMDL Program.* As it put EPA's final TMDL regulations on hold in July 2000, Congress also directed EPA to study the total costs of implementing such a program.[109] In December 2000, EPA announced the study and published a call for information in the *Federal Register.*[110] Fewer than one-half of the states submitted data, the majority on listing and load allocation costs, which was about as far as most states had progressed.[111] Based on these data and the contributions from industry and other participants in a few (very costly) TMDLs, EPA took its best shot and published a draft report for public comment in August 2001.[112] The comment period closed at the end of 2001,[113] and a final report is expected in the spring of 2002. While the final version is not available, its basic content, like that of the TMDL program itself, is visible.

The scope of the work was defined by the 1998 state lists of impaired waters under CWA §303(d), the last of such submissions. About one-third of the nation's waters were polluted, including 300,000 miles of rivers and shoreline and 5 million acres of lakes.[114] After 28 years of pollution control efforts under the CWA of 1972 and another 20 years of previous federal assistance programs, nearly 22,000 water bodies were identified as not meet-

ing state water quality standards.[115] These waters would require an anticipated 36,000 TMDLs.[116]

Turning to the sources of pollution, state data identified less than 5% of
impairment from point sources only and about 25% from a combination of
point and nonpoint sources.[117] Nonpoint sources were the exclusive sources
of pollution for 50% of the listed waters, with the remaining waters polluted
by combinations of nonpoint and "other" sources.[118] The leading source of
impairment was agriculture at 24.6%, with another 11.4% attributed to
unspecified "nonpoint" causes.[119] The three leading pollutants were ag-
riculture-driven: sediments, pathogens, and nutrients.[120] In overview
and subject to regional exceptions, e.g., forestry in the northern Rockies
and acid mine drainage in the Appalachians, the task at hand would be
more than 20,000 TMDLs for nonpoint sources, primarily for agricultural runoff.

EPA estimated the costs for impaired water listings, for TMDL load calculations, and for implementation in two stages: state costs in TMDL development, and source costs in their implementation. The state costs, more easily calculated, were found to be between $63 and $69 million per year nationwide, which amounts to approximately $1 billion over the next 10 to 15
years to get the job done.[121] Another $17 million a year would be needed for
additional water quality monitoring required by the program.[122] While
many knowledgeable commenters will have their crack at these estimates,
the assumption that the anticipated load of TMDLs can be handled for a little over $1 million a year per state seems optimistic, and the assumption that
only an additional $300,000 or so per state would meet the levels of moni-
toring and data called for in the NRC study seems optimistic as well.

EPA approached source implementation costs under three "scenarios."[123]
The first, obviously disfavored and something of a stalking-horse for the
two that followed, was described as the "least flexible TMDL program"
model and based on requiring—either through NPDES permits or by aggressive "inducement" under CWA §319 and other funding programs—all
point and nonpoint sources to abate their discharges by the "next treatment
step."[124] The second scenario, the "moderately cost-effective" model,
would more finely calculate the reductions to be achieved by the "next
treatment steps" and allocate them in a way that "let off" some or many
dischargers and did not "overshoot" the water quality goal.[125] The third
and favored approach, labeled "more cost-effective," played with the second scenario to assign reductions to sources that have low reduction costs
either through targeted allocations or by emissions trading.[126]

Under EPA's more cost-effective scenario, TMDL implementation was
estimated to cost $900 million to $3.2 billion per year.[127] Under the
disfavored least flexible scenario, annual costs would range between $1.9

and $4.3 billion per year.[128] Two noteworthy facts appear from the data. The first is that under all scenarios, both point and nonpoint sources took approximately equal cost hits, although nonpoint sources were the overwhelming sources of pollution; i.e., point sources, already regulated, present marginal cost savings compared to agriculture and other sources that have been heretofore requirement-free. The second fact is that even with the most optimistic, cost-minimizing, market-oriented trading imaginable, the high-end projections for the best and worst scenarios were at $3.2 and $4.3 billion, respectively, which is not all that far apart. In other words, you can save money by trading, up to a point, but it is no panacea.

As this Article is being written, EPA is closing its comment period on the cost analysis, but the comment it has received from all sides indicates that the estimates are low. A joint coalition of industrial dischargers and municipal wastewater treatment facilities calling itself the "Federal Water Quality Coalition" criticized several assumptions relative to costs to its members,[129] as has the American Forest and Paper Association, which feared that "likely administrative and political pressures" would require "a much broader application of the TMDL program" to forest industries.[130] The American Farm Bureau took issue with the best management practices that EPA defined as "cost-effective reductions."[131] A conservative think tank offered annual cost ranges of $2.5 to $5.26 billion.[132] Even an environmental representative stated: "I think they have undershot their numbers somewhat."[133]

The commentators probably have undershot the numbers, but so what? No one familiar with the soaring costs of a public works project or a home improvement contract can be surprised by undershooting. On the other hand, with a little more experience and a little less resistance from the states and industry, the numbers could come way down. The first can openers are always the most expensive.

In the final analysis, what is striking about cost estimates for the TMDL program is not the extent to which they differ but rather their common ground. Cost estimates for implementation of the CAA Amendments of 1990 were at odds by a factor of 10. If, all told, TMDL cost estimates come in at somewhere between $25 to $50 billion over 15 years, that is a pretty strong concurrence for a large federal program. Whether Congress is willing to fund such an exercise over the long haul is something very different. In May 2001, the chairman of the NRC' study was testifying on Capitol Hill against a proposed $30 million cut in the Geological Survey's toxic substances hydrology and water quality assessment programs,[134] which provide a starting point for ambient water quality management. Congress may or may not listen, and it can always listen differently from year to year. Ambient-based programs from start to finish are a very expensive way to go.

☐ *State Enforcement.* Effective, state-based ambient water quality programs depend at the front end on raw data and, at the far end (following use designation, standard-setting, monitoring, modeling, impact analysis, load reduction negotiations, trading, permitting, reporting, and inspections) on enforcement. Under the CWA, 44 states have assumed enforcement authority along with all other aspects of delegated programs,[135] with EPA financial assistance and oversight. In practice, with the exception of significant violations or citizen suits, most water program enforcement begins and ends with the states. Here, too, comes the question of whether state institutions are up to the job.

The question is not new. For the past 20 years, reports by the GAO, the EPA Inspector General, academics, and the press have assessed state environmental law enforcement programs and concluded that they lacked adequate monitoring of regulated entities, failed to act in a timely fashion when violations were noted, imposed minor and ineffective sanctions, failed to recover the economic benefit gained from noncompliance, and varied widely from state to state.[136] The CWA audits have been particularly damning. During 1992-1994, for example, 18 to 27% of all major CWA-regulated facilities were in significant noncompliance.[137] From October 1998 to January 2000, 26% of major facilities were in significant violation, 159 of them in significant violation throughout the entire 15-month period.[138]

Neither is the question one of personnel. There is no reason to believe that were federal and state enforcement personnel to replace each other, enforcement results would differ. The problems reflect a chronic shortage of resources, made more significant as states assume increasing responsibility for environmental programs.[139] They also reflect inconsistency in federal oversight from administration to administration, from EPA region to region, and from the ambiguity in knowing when to intervene.[140] They also reflect differences in the philosophy of compliance—carrots or sticks—that pervade all environmental law.[141] And at bottom they reflect the gut-level difference in opinion over the importance of environmental protection so notable between, say, states of the northern tier and the deep South. Unfortunately, the facts underlying the U.S. Supreme Court's recent CWA standing decision in *Friends of the Earth, Inc. v. Laidlaw Environmental Services (TOC), Inc.*[142]—a state enforcement order drawn up by the violating discharger itself and imposing sub-minimal sanctions for the violations—was no anomaly. State enforcement actions are characterized by concessions to dischargers,[143] and a tougher line risks political consequences. The Louisiana Secretary of Environmental Quality was dismissed by the governor for bringing an enforcement action against a hazardous waste incinerator.[144]

Enforcement is hard, state agencies are human, and they are very close to the heat.[145]

In 2001, EPA's Office of the Inspector General conducted another audit of state CWA enforcement programs to determine whether they adequately "protect the environment and human health."[146] The published results concluded in polite language, e.g., state enforcers "could be much more effective in deterring noncompliance,"[147] that the states were wanting in every aspect of enforcement from identifying violators, to taking enforcement actions, to the assessment of penalties and fines.[148] More particular shortfalls included: a basic lack of data on dischargers; serious, unreported toxic discharges; incomplete identification of stormwater dischargers; enforcement actions delayed by a year or more following violations; and penalties that failed to recover the economic gains from noncompliance.[149] Nothing new here; the old patterns continue. Of more direct concern to the TMDL program, however, the report noted a lack of focus on all but major industrial point source dischargers, basic gaps in water quality data, incomplete compliance data, a lack of compliance data for watershed-based programs, and a "reluctance" on the part of states to address small business on the one hand and "economically vital business and industries" on the other.[150] The reader is left to wonder, with these categories excluded, what entities were getting addressed.

Two aspects of the Inspector General report are particularly relevant to TMDLs. The first is that much of the audit focused on point source dischargers, all of whom are covered by permit requirements designed to facilitate oversight and enforcement. The limits are fixed, derived from national standards, committed to writing, usually numerical, and compliance is self-reported and routine. From an enforcement standpoint, this is the easy stuff. Yet even in this universe, only 10 states reported a compliance rate of 90% or better with permit requirements during FY 2000; 20 states did not even reach 75% compliance, where a finding of noncompliance required 2 significant permit violations repeated within 2 consecutive quarters, i.e., egregious conduct.[151] In more than one-third of the states, over one-half of the facilities in significant violation in 1999 were significant violators in 2000.[152] Even for point source permitting, state enforcement is not securing compliance.[153]

Of equal relevance is the finding that, beyond major point source dischargers, there was less enforcement for several (more diffuse) categories of dischargers, including concentrated animal feeding operations (CAFOs) and urban runoff, that had received increased attention under the CWA because of their impacts on water quality.[154] Permit systems were in place but even basic monitoring and reporting was lacking.[155] The problem here was not a reluctance to sanction violators but, rather, an unwillingness even to find out who the violators were. CAFOs and urban stormwater are, of course, the two CWA permit categories most similar to the nonpoint runoff at issue with TMDLs.

Viewed as a whole, the Inspector General's report presages more trouble for an effective TMDL program. TMDLs are an ambient-based strategy whose enforcement depends not on self-reported compliance with numerical limits based on national standards but, rather, on management practices and impacts on receiving waters that are subject to interpretation and contest. If states as a whole have difficulty enforcing the NPDES program and the monitoring requirements contained in municipal stormwater and CAFO permits, it is not easy to see how they will do better with the more diffuse ambient game. Thirty years ago, the demands of proof inherent in ambient violations and the demands of political will led to little state enforcement at all.[156] Congress' answer in 1972 was to provide for EPA oversight and, with dramatic success, citizen enforcement as well.[157] Citizen suits are what brought the TMDL program out of remission.[158] It remains to be seen whether they will continue to exercise this same influence on its implementation.

EPA and the Regulatory Program

In August 2001, citing the need to build a "foundation of trust" among stakeholders and a "more workable program," EPA proposed to delay for 18 months the effective date of the final TMDL rule.[159] A new rule would be proposed in 2002 and adopted in 2003. Environmentalists booed. Agriculture cheered. Nobody was in the least surprised. It was a given to all concerned that with the arrival of a new Administration, the TMDL regulations as written were history and it was open season again on the issues involved.

☐ *The July 2000 Rule.* The Clinton Administration regulations might well be history, but they are also a useful benchmark from which to measure what will come. The final rule dropped required listings of "threatened" waters not yet fully impaired, listings of waters experiencing "pollution," e.g., from whatever cause, as opposed to those affected by "pollutants," e.g., only from discharges, pollution offsets for new dischargers into impaired waterways, separate forestry controls, and an administrative process for citizen challenges.[160] The periods for reporting were extended from 2 years to 4, and the deadlines for TMDL development were extended to up to 15 years.[161] EPA, further, would not act to develop a TMDL in the place of a defaulting state unless the state failed to show "reasonable progress" toward its development.[162] Each of these issues, some of which were vital to individual environmental organizations (and in particular the deadlines),[163] was conceded to states and discharger industries.

What the final rule retained was the core of the program the Agency had been shaping the previous decade: (1) TMDLs would cover nonpoint sources; (2) would include a plan for implementing the necessary load reductions; and (3) would include reasonable assurances that the proposed reductions would be implemented.[164] Such assurances could include voluntary market- and incentive-based initiatives, so long as they applied specifically to the water body at issue and would be implemented expeditiously, through reliable mechanisms, and with adequate funding.[165] Thus, the bones of contention would remain, as they had always been, nonpoint sources and implementation plans.

☐ *The Listening Sessions.* EPA's first action was to take the kettle off of boil. It set up a round of "listening sessions" in five major cities, ostensibly to elicit more "stakeholder perspectives" on "key issues" of the program.[166] While each session was associated with a set of themes, e.g., "are TMDLs appropriate for all impaired waters and pollutants?",[167] their panels and attendance were heavily weighted with state water program administrators and nonpoint industries who, whatever the assigned topic, produced familiar sounding recommendations, e.g., that EPA had no business regulating nonpoint sources; that TMDLs should not be implemented until other nonpoint programs had been given "time to work"; that TMDLs needed to avoid being "specific" and "inflexible"; that "functional equivalents" to TMDLs were sufficient; and that the process needed "off ramps" (a more expedited process) to delist impaired waters.[168] There were few new perspectives. It is hard to imagine, after all that TMDLs have been through, that there could be perspectives that were new. Viewed optimistically, the sessions served to blow off steam and provide an extra measure of participatory democracy for EPA's new program design. Viewed realistically, they provided a record, were any needed, for softening the program.

☐ *Monitoring and Assessment Guidance.* Concurrently EPA moved to propose new guidance to facilitate state acceptance of TMDLs, each containing a nugget of what is likely to appear in EPA's new program. In November 2001, the Agency issued the *2002 Integrated Water Quality Monitoring and Assessment Report Guidance*, intended, inter alia, to provide more flexibility for state listing decisions.[169] It allowed states to list several categories of impairment, including one for waters with "insufficient data" to determine impairment and another for those whose impairment is "not known."[170] Waters categorized with insufficient data or other unknowns would not require

TMDLs. Applauded by state agencies dealing with large numbers of waters and small amounts of data,[171] the guidance was viewed skeptically by environmentalists who envisioned a black hole for data-short, impaired waters into which many, if not most, polluted water bodies would fall.[172]

Removed from the final version of the guidance, but perking along on its own burner within the Agency, is the consolidated assessment and listing methodology (CALM), a recipe intended to provide more consistent and reliable data collection and reporting.[173] Originally presented as part of the guidance along with the carrot of an additional $25 million in state grants toward these ends,[174] CALM ran into rough sledding with state officials fearing that it could impose "baseline" conditions and, worse, include "requirements" for water quality monitoring programs.[175] The Association of State and Interstate Water Pollution Control Administrators issued a position statement that it did not support the use of "critical elements" as a "strict evaluation checklist" against which the "adequacy of monitoring programs is determined."[176] States to EPA: no requirements allowed.

☐ *The CWA §319 Program.* The most significant EPA action and the most indicative of its future intentions was its September 2001 Supplemental Guidelines for the Award of Section 319 Nonpoint Source Grants to States and Territories in FY 2002 and Subsequent Years, which was intended to provide a "concentrated focus" for its voluntary, grant-based, nonpoint source pollution control program.[177] The concentrated focus would be TMDLs. The memorandum began by reminding the states of their oft-stated position that §319 "provides an appropriate and effective programmatic framework" for nonpoint pollution and for the implementation of TMDLs.[178] TMDLs would provide the "analytical link" between "actions on the ground and the water quality results to be achieved."[179] The memorandum then dropped, or rather, phased in, a soft hammer: starting in FY 2002, and more fully effective in FY 2003, EPA would require the dedication of a significant portion of §319 funding to the development of nonpoint source TMDLs and to watershed plans implementing them.[180] Approved §319 plans would require "reasonable assurance" that the load allocations identified in the TMDLs would be achieved.[181] The TMDLs themselves would require a source-based quantification of load reductions, specified implementation measures, an identification of technical and financial assistance needed, a "reasonably expeditious" schedule for implementation, and a description of interim milestones, monitoring, and criteria to determine if "reasonable progress" is being made.[182] The ingredients should look familiar. These are, nearly jot-for-jot, the requirements of the suspended TMDL rule[183] transferred to the voluntary §319 program.

The American Farm Bureau was not pleased. In a stinging letter to EPA's Administrator in October 2001, the bureau protested that EPA had overstepped its bounds in using "the power of the purse" to force states to develop nonpoint source TMDLs.[184] The bureau found EPA's guidance "wholly inappropriate" given the litigation surrounding TMDLs and their application to nonpoint sources and indicated, joined by the National Cattlemen's Association and others, that a legal challenge to the guidance was a possibility.[185] It is clear that the agriculture industry, having stalled if not won the war on TMDLs and implementation plans for nonpoint sources under CWA §303(d), was now turning to fight TMDL-based grant-in-aid programs to states under §319. When you are a major polluter, the threats just keep on coming.

☐ *Trades and Markets*. On another front, by late 2001 and early 2002, EPA was preparing a new policy statement outlining market-based approaches, including a trading system, for CWA programs including TMDLs.[186]

Emissions trading is of course not new and was a central theme of the Clinton Administration. In 1996, EPA issued an *Effluent Trading in Watersheds Policy*[187] and a *Draft Framework for Watershed-Based Trading*[188] identifying, inter alia, the social benefits of trading as "encourag[ing] dialogue among stakeholders and foster[ing] concerted and holistic solutions."[189] The 1996 policy required trading to result in "an equivalent or better water pollutant reduction."[190] The Devil, of course, resides in the details.

EPA's renewed program is said to use state water quality standards as an emissions "cap" similar to the sulfur dioxide caps under the CAA acid rain program.[191] While any analysis of EPA's proposal needs a proposal to analyze, pollution control programs have sufficient experience with trading to know where the upsides and downsides lie. The upsides lie with cost savings, economies of scale, and political acceptance.[192] The downsides lie with what gets traded for what, in practice, and whether things really get cleaned up in the bargain.

A threshold question is who will want to trade, and the answer is those parties that would otherwise be compelled to expend greater costs in abating their pollution directly. In the current CWA scheme, those parties are industrial and municipal point sources operating under national technology standards. What they will be willing, indeed eager, to trade for is less-expensive abatement from nonpoint sources. Unless nonpoint sources are under a legal obligation to abate their discharges, however, these sources will have no incentive to buy less costly reductions from other nonpoint or point source players. Under a TMDL program that imposes no enforceable abatement requirements on nonpoint sources, therefore, trading only runs in one direction, from point to nonpoint sources. The danger is that the trades become escape hatches for point sources from having to meet the technology standards that have or that are being met by their competitors.[193] The only way to close such a hemorrhage would be to require full BAT compliance for point sources as a precondition for trading whatever *additional* compliance measures are imposed on them by TMDLs,[194] and to impose specific abatement obligations on nonpoint sources as well, something that EPA at the moment does not seem disposed to do.

A second difficulty with trading schemes is that, even for single-source pollutants, they often upon closer scrutiny turn out to be bogus.[195] In a practice so widespread that it has earned its own label—"gaming"—claims are made for wholly past reductions, for the same reductions several times, and for reductions that never happened, happened only ephemerally, or never will happen.[196] The monitoring, supervisory, and accounting costs of trading schemes are formidable and beyond the capacity of at least some states.[197] The state of Louisiana's accounting program for nonattainment ozone trading has become so hopelessly confused and so completely reliant on the accounting practices of industrial applicants for reduction credits that EPA was forced to disavow it[198]; the U.S. Department of Justice is currently auditing New Jersey's emissions trading program for possible CAA violations.[199] It should be kept in mind that these problems arose over emissions from discrete point sources, identifiable by concentration and volume, of single precursor pollutants. Tracking the reductions, proposed and real, from nonpoint sources across a watershed will present another order of difficulty.

One preview of this additional difficulty is the mitigation program under CWA §404[200] in which wetland values destroyed by development programs are to be offset by the acquisition and improvement of other wetlands.[201] Both nonpoint and §404 trading exchange "harm X" for "benefit Y"; the "X" is known but the "Y" is speculative and depends upon the on-the-ground application, success, and long-term maintenance of land use measures that will, in the one case, abate pollution and, in the other case, enhance wetlands values. In practice, the mitigation/trade measures—the improvement of streamside vegetation, for example—may be identical. As studies consistently show, the problem is that the Y mitigation is not implemented, does not work well, or does not work at all.[202] The success rate for wetland mitigation projects hovers near 50%.[203]

A final aspect of trading that glimmers within EPA's new trading initiative is its announcement of an "enhancement of economics" in its water programs.[204] What this term apparently includes is the economic valuation of aquatic resources—"what's a loon worth?" was offered as an example[205]—an exercise that has confounded resource economists since the 1970s and presents a significant problem in the natural resources damages programs of the U.S. Department of the Interior under the Comprehensive Environmental Response, Compensation, and Liability Act (CERCLA) [206]and the U.S. Coast Guard under the Oil Pollution Act.[207] Whatever a loon or a river is said to be worth in dollars, the inquiry in a permitting context opens a Pandora's box for decisions based not only on a comparison of costs to *impacts* but on a comparison of costs to *benefits*[208] that can never be adequately assessed.[209]

In short, while trading among sources has always been inherent in ambient-based management systems and indeed is touted as one of their major virtues, the formalization of a market in pollution rights raises serious issues of trading obligations, baselines, performance, and accountability that will need to be addressed. The war over permits and enforcement will not end; it will simply obtain new venues.

☐ *Water Quality Standards.* EPA is also pursuing several initiatives to shore up the foundation for the ambient water quality program—state water quality standards. It is a tricky problem. On the one hand, the existing standards are in most cases out of date and vary widely in their content and application.[210] Identical industries in adjoining states may face permit limits for the same pollutant that differ by more than 10,000 times.[211] Until recently these differences did not matter because water quality standards did not matter; few states bothered to apply them. TMDLs, however, now put pressure on the whole foundation. On the other hand, reopening water quality standards reopens questions of baselines, costs, and competing economic and political interests that could well weaken the criteria, standards, antidegradation policies, and other safeguards of the program.[212]

In 1998, the Agency issued a notice of proposed rulemaking on water quality standards across the board, asking a number of questions about the most critical issues with standards and criteria.[213] Perhaps realizing that the rulemaking had opened too large a can of worms, or perhaps overtaken by events more specifically related to TMDLs, this generic rulemaking has been on a slower track.[214] Spurred forward by the NRC report,[215] however, the new rules will likely facilitate, if not require, a wholesale, nationwide "use attainability" analysis for all impaired waters,[216] a recipe for accepting degradation that many states will not miss.[217] Unaddressed, meanwhile, are issues that have chronically plagued the CWA and its predecessors, including the high degree of play in mixing zones, application factors, variances, antidegradation policies, and enforcement.[218] There is no more uneven playing field in federal environmental law than water quality management. To the extent that EPA follows its current polestar of flexibility in state programs, the more that water quality standards matter the more this unevenness will increase.

These problems noted, a special challenge presented to water quality standards by TMDLs has been the absence of meaningful water quality criteria for the primary impacts of the primary pollution science, nutrient loadings from agriculture.[219] The question is difficult enough technically, as the relationship of loadings to impacts vary with local environments.[220] It is also difficult politically, as shown by the agriculture industry's effective resistance to measures to reduce nutrient loadings to the Mississippi River.[221] EPA's current nutrient guidance, issued informally over the last two years, provides for maximum state flexibility.[222] As with all other national water quality criteria, EPA developed suggested limits for nutrient-related pollutants, e.g., phosphorous, nitrogen, chlorophyll-a, and turbidity.[223] It then departed from its normal practice by dividing the nation into 14 "eco-regions," each to adopt its own criteria, from which the states would then derive their standards. States could adopt regional numerical criteria, narrative criteria, or any other "scientifically defensible" method. State standards were to be in place by 2004.

Obviously shy of creating another tempest, EPA will not require states to adopt nutrient management plans, although such plans were "strongly encouraged."[224] Whatever comes beyond "encouragement," therefore, will come from the TMDL program.

☐ *Focus Groups.* A reader diligent enough to have pursued the topic to this point is entitled to some lighter reading, and in this vein we consider the *EPA Nonpoint Source Pollution Focus Group Final Report*.[225] The report is an outgrowth of the Nonpoint Source Management Partnership, a collaboration between EPA and the states to "identify, prioritize and solve nonpoint source problems."[226] The problem here was image, and EPA turned to a consultant organization to get to the bottom of it.

The consultant organized focus groups in four major cities across the United States.[227] Two groups, divided by age, were assembled at each site and were asked to identify the visibility of nonpoint source pollution and to suggest measures to increase public awareness of the problem.[228] By overwhelming consensus, the groups concluded that nonpoint source pollution had near zero visibility, and that even the term "nonpoint source pollution" was a non-starter: "It doesn't tell you anything"; "[i]t sounds like there's nothing you can do."[229]

By way of remedy, the focus groups recommended a "bold, hard-hitting and provocative" advertising campaign featuring videos, music, and the tech-

niques of successful television advertisements.[230] Among the more specific
suggestions:

- Disgusting works; the grosser the better."[231]
- "Have Titanic hit a great big pile of trash, or
  oil cans."[232]
- "Britney Spears with a gas mask on."[233]
- "For me, everything today has to be hot girls: bathing suits,
  Maxim, and beer commercials."[234]

Exactly how EPA works these suggestions into its collaboration with
stakeholders and a more flexible, state-based TMDL program remains to
be seen.

☐ *The State of the Game.* As the year 2001 drew to a close, the states were
still using their approved 1998 lists of impaired waters identifying 36,000
water bodies that failed to meet water quality standards for at least one
pollutant.[235] Some states, spurred forward by environmental litigation,
had begun to make significant investments in TMDL implementation: $5
million in Iowa, $10 million in California.[236] Other states, as described in
an earlier article, have resorted to a variety of mechanisms to avoid their responsibilities, including revision of antidegradation policies, downgrading,
use unattainability, insufficient data, and this author's favorite, "swamp waters," to trim their workload.[237] For the waters remaining, EPA had approved almost 4,000 TMDLs submitted by the states, a pace of action that
will only accelerate.[238]

Of course, what matters more than the volume is the content. A review of
55 TMDLs by this author in 1998 found that the early approved submissions met few of the requirements of the statute and Agency guidelines and
regulations.[239] Variously, they did not quantify overall loadings, did not
quantify loadings from individual sources, neither identified nor quantified
nonpoint sources, focused almost exclusively on reductions from point
sources, and made little explicit provision either for margins of growth or
margins of error; only a few contained implementation plans, and none provided objective assurance that the necessary load reductions would be attained.[240] While a similar analysis of the second-wave TMDLs is beyond
the reach of this Article—and perhaps beyond the reach even of EPA—a
December 2001 study of TMDLs in West Virginia produced similar findings.[241] The study reviewed 25 TMDLs prepared by EPA and the state for a
range of point and nonpoint sources, among them current and abandoned
mining operations and agriculture.[242] Not surprisingly, the point sources
received specific abatement proposals while the nonpoint sources did not.
While new nonpoint source programs had been initiated in four impaired

watersheds, "no concrete steps toward implementation had been under-taken in the remaining seven watersheds."[243] No nonpoint source water TMDLs contained implementation plans.[244] Virtually all anticipated nonpoint source abatement was to be paid for through federal funding and supplemented by state funding.[245]

Large-scale water quality improvement projects show the same charac-teristics: long on goals, short on requirements and deadlines. Three of the most famous and ambitious restoration efforts in the country are those for the Florida Everglades, the Gulf of Mexico, and the Chesapeake Bay. In each case, years of planning has led to agreement on pollution reduction goals; a 40% reduction in nutrient loading in the case of the Chesa-peake,[246] and in the case of the Gulf of Mexico,[247] a desirable outcome of 30% reductions achieved by upstream states—the word "goal" was appar-ently too strong for the participants. Neither program contains enforce-able requirements or time lines.[248] In the case of the Everglades, the year 2002 saw the first regulations for a $7.8 billion, 30-year, federal-state res-toration plan criticized by environmentalists for its lack of specifics and praised by U.S. Sugar as "fluid."[249] By contrast, restoration planning for water quality in the San Joaquin delta of California has moved forward with significant abatement requirements from large irrigators and other dominant water users in the region.[250] Then again, the San Joaquin delta contains the Delta Smelt, an endangered species. When we have to, we get serious and abate.

What we have so far from §303(d) in practice, then, is a process in which TMDLs provide goals with varying levels of specificity. What we also have is a marked dichotomy between the treatment of point and nonpoint sources in the exigence of load reductions and in the question of who pays for them. For the life of water pollution control in this country, while public sewage treat-ment has been publicly funded, private industry point sources have paid their own abatement costs. Nonpoint source abatement, however, although private and including some of the largest corporations in America, is paid for largely by the government. The state of Wisconsin is in the final stages of adopting rules imposing mandatory controls on nonpoint source runoff but require the state to provide 70% of the costs.[251] The state of New York is providing over $14 million to farmers for runoff abatement,[252] and the city of New York is kicking in another $10 million to protect its drinking water resources.[253] The CWA, by creating a dichotomy between point and nonpoint sources, also cre-ated an attitude within the nonpoint industry of an entitlement to pollute akin to a property right. The attitude is that if you, the public, want to abate nonpoint pollution, then you, the public, will foot the bill.

Recent TMDL Litigation

TMDL litigation is undergoing a seismic shift from the offense to the defense, as federal and state programs come into rudimentary, facial compliance with §303(d) and as point and nonpoint sources see abatement requirements on the horizon. The litigation through the 1990s was brought almost exclusively by the environmental community trying to get the program in gear and, more specifically, requiring schedules for impaired water lists and TMDLs. As the lists and initial TMDLs appeared, nonpoint industries and municipal sewage treatment systems have reacted and have taken to court both the core concepts of the TMDL program and its application to particular sources. This litigation promises to be the wave of the future unless EPA relaxes the program's requirements, which it is in the process of doing. Relaxation at the federal level, however, will not wish away these issues at the state level, particularly in those states that continue to pursue abatement under the impetus of TMDLs.

Environmental litigation has continued to push the TMDL agenda forward. At the start of 2002, EPA was under court order by decision or consent decree in more than 20 states to establish TMDLs on timetables ranging from 6 to 12 years unless the states stepped forward.[254] Recent decisions and settlements in Hawaii, Iowa, and Tennessee kept this ball rolling despite minimal compliance by EPA and these states to list their waters and develop TMDLs.[255] On the other hand, an increasing number of courts are beginning to show a weariness in overseeing the process and are accepting an any-progress-is-sufficient-progress attitude toward this same low level of performance. Viewed on the "constructive submission" theory, courts in California, Maryland, and Oklahoma have recently held that the submission of something, anything, sufficed, and that it sufficed under the APA's "arbitrary and capricious" standard as well.[256] In the words of the California court, "California and the EPA have both been doing something about TMDLs, albeit not as rapidly as contemplated by the passage of the [CWA]."[257] The logic of these cases in giving EPA and the states, if they are intent on implementing the program, some leeway in going forward is difficult to gainsay. On the other hand, against a history of noncompliance and a recent, explicit federal policy change from hands-on to hands-off, more rigorous court review may be necessary to keep the program viable.

Environmental lawsuits have also challenged other compliance issues, particularly the exercise of EPA's discretion in approving the content of TMDLs and the question of permitting new activities in impaired waters for which TMDLs have not yet been prepared. In *Natural Resources Defense Council, Inc. v. Muszynski*,[258] the latest in a series of cases gigging TMDLs forward in the state of New York, the U.S. Court of Appeals for the Second

Circuit reversed and remanded EPA's approval of a TMDL based on "annual loadings," reasoning that limits based on seasonal variations of flow and temperature would make more sense.[259] The concept of "averaging" pollution loadings over long periods of time, high and low flows, and growing and nongrowing seasons is another way of gaming the TMDL program and, indeed, all ambient programs; the more averaging allowed, the more acceptable that periodic exceedances, even severe exceedances, become. Lawsuits in Maryland and Vermont have also raised the issue of permitting in the absence of TMDLs and appear to be headed toward allowing no new discharge, net, until TMDLs are prepared.[260] The content of TMDLs is also on appeal on the important question of whether TMDLs require an implementation plan. While EPA has done an abrupt about-face on this issue and is arguing, now, in the negative, the Agency had earlier represented to a court in Georgia that such plans were both required and going to be included in Georgia TMDLs, giving rise to an estoppel theory on which this case may be decided without reaching the general issue of whether such plans are required by law.[261] A similar case is pending in New Mexico, absent the estoppel argument but based on EPA guidance that required, for an approved TMDL, "reasonable assurance" that its load reductions would be accomplished.[262]

One more technical environmental challenge is pending against the state of Florida's adopted rules for determining water impairment, rules that formed the basis for much of the NRC report described above.[263] At bottom, Florida has provided a two-tiered approach to decisions on impairment and imposed a higher standard of proof for those waters subject to §303(d).[264] EPA has long required a minimum of three samples, 10% of which show impairment, for a decision to list and has accepted other data than sampling, such as fish kills and drinking water advisories, to serve as data sources as well. The Florida rule relegates all data other than monitoring to its initial candidate list.[265] It further requires greater certainty for waters that have fewer samples in order to correct for the possibility that these fewer samples might reflect unusual conditions.[266]

The state defends its rule as more objective and scientific than that formerly taken by EPA, and even predicts that its approach, although heavily favored by the sugar and pulp and paper industries, may lead to more listings than those currently named.[267] The reasons supporting this prediction are not obvious. If 100 samples are now required to match EPA's former threshold of 10% impairment, and less than 100 samples require a more than 10% showing, then unless the states do a lot more sampling waters are going to drop out of the program and into a limbo of the unproven. In terms of data requirements, taking the state of Maryland's list of 1,000-plus impaired waters as an easy number, and multiplying it by the 100 samples needed to prove it, yields 100,000 samples needed to maintain that state's list alone. Multiplying these samples by 50 states yields 5 million samples. Cutting these 5 million in half, to account for states with fewer waters, Oklahoma's 400 for example, yields a workload of 2.5 million samples. Those numbers are in the range of McDonald's hamburgers sold. Scientific confidence in an ambient-based system does not come cheap.

While the sum of the environmental litigation has been to continue to pressure the program forward, important litigation is brewing on the other side. The mega-action was filed in late 2000 against EPA's July 2000 TMDL rule by the American Farm Bureau Federation, the American Forest and Paper Association, the American Crop Protection Association, the National Pork Producers Council, the National Corn Growers Association, the National Chicken Council, the National Cattlemen's Beef Association, the National Cotton Council of America, the Fertilizer Institute, the Utility Water Act Group, and the TMDL Coalition, representing industrial dischargers and municipal publicly owned treatment works (POTWs).[268] Is there anyone whose name we have not yet called? On the environmental side are the Friends of the Earth and the Water Keeper Alliance. While the petitions for review in these cases raise a bevy of issues, at the heart of them are the two that have always drawn the fire of the nonpoint industries, the coverage of nonpoint sources and the requirement for implementation plans. The proceedings in the case have since been suspended with the consent of all parties while EPA reworks its way through these same issues.[269] As discussed below, it is likely that the Agency will, in the end, concede most if not all of the industry complaints.

Meanwhile, the defense bar is encouraging its clients to pool their resources to challenge individual TMDLs from start to finish, and predicting an "increase in challenges to lists of impaired water bodies and state methodology of establishing TMDLs."[270] POTWs, feeling the pinch of tightened permit requirements imposed by states unwilling to impose abatement requirements on nonpoint sources, are leading the way and have raised procedural issues that will add new layers of complexity to the program.[271]

A threshold issue is whether listings of impaired waters and TMDLs, at the state level, are decisions that require full notice-and-comment rulemaking.[272] Courts are arriving at opposite conclusions here, but the majority are answering in the affirmative, and the argument that these decisions are "statements of general applicability which impact, interpret, or prescribe law or policy" seems hard to gainsay.[273] The effect of these decisions will be, in theory, to provide review by both the environmental community and by affected sources. As a practical matter, however, setting aside the question of resources to litigate, in a program with so few affirmative requirements at the federal or state level the challenges will largely come in response to a state decision to list or impose TMDL allocations, i.e., from the affected discharge community. If full administrative process is required for all listings, TMDLs, state decisions "translating" state narrative criteria to TMDL allocations, and each plan of whatever nature to set allocations on whatever basis, including markets and trades for the estimated 40% of the nation's waters that are impaired and the 36,000 TMDL decisions awaiting them, we have a recipe for tying implementation in knots. Ambient-based management meets the APA.

Process issues aside, affected dischargers have also given more than notice of their intent to challenge the data and scientific underpinnings of TMDL decisions. Two cases on behalf of a Maryland POTW challenge the validity of the state's nutrient-related chlorophyll-a criterion and the calculations of a TMDL, e.g., "calibration runs of the model used to develop the TMDL predict impossible levels of dissolved oxygen" and "are irreconcilable with the available real world data."[274] Ambient-based management meets aggressive lawyering, an encounter it has often lost over the years.

Perhaps the safest conclusion from the current trend in TMDL litigation is that it is likely to grow and to contest every aspect of the program at the implementing state level. Ambient management is very much prove-it-or-lose-it and will lead, in the words of a defense lawyer, "to a diversion of a large amount of time and money into litigation of both regulated sources and the regulators."[275] The message from the defense is clear: we'll sue.

Prelude

When Congress adopted the TMDL program in 1972, it had a smaller job in mind.[276] Basing its approach to pollution control on national technology standards, it retained ambient-based management as a safety net, where technology-based permits would violate water quality standards, §303, and where residual pockets of pollution remained, §303(d): TMDLs. No one at the time believed that TMDLs would do more than come in late in the game and tidy up.[277]

Congress was half right. The national technology standards were more effective than it had reason to hope. Within the first years of application of BAT to industrial and municipal sources pollution loadings dropped precipitously,[278] in some industrial categories such as the pulp and paper industry they dropped by more than 90%.[279] Receiving water quality improved by 29%.[280] With later rounds of permitting, some industries and industrial categories have moved to closed system recycling of used waters, meeting the CWA's zero discharge goal.[281] Municipal treatment systems, meanwhile, dropped in pollution loadings by 50% while their populations served more than doubled.[282] Reviled by economists and the more hard-nosed industries as "inefficient," "dictatorial," and "one-size-fits-all," the NPDES system has had but one defense: it worked.[283]

Congress was also half wrong. Focused on evidence of poisoned lakes and rivers so contaminated by industrial chemicals that they were catching fire,[284] it failed to see the problem that nonpoint sources were to become. By the 1990s, these sources, primarily agriculture untouched by the NPDES program, had grown to elephantine proportions threatening waters the size of the Chesapeake Bay and the Gulf of Mexico and nearly one-half of all waters in between. Enter TMDLs, Congress' intended offense to handle the bits and pieces remaining after implementation of the NPDES program, suddenly facing a problem as large, varied, and intractable as industrial sources ever were. The question is whether the TMDL program will be up to the job.

Forward Into the Past

It is oft said that those who ignore history are doomed to repeat it. The inverse of the statement is only partially true. We may at times repeat history because we ignore the past. But we may also repeat history because other goals are more important to us, no matter what the lessons of the past. So it will be with TMDLs.

☐ *The Past as Prologue.* Ambient-based pollution control strategies have a strong grip on the American psyche.[285] They rely on science, an objective and steady guide. They conform to our desire for local government and local controls. And they are apparently rational, requiring abatement and cleanup only where contamination interferes with human uses. It is no surprise then that ambient strategies were at the heart of our first environmental legislation, our almost instinctual response to a pollution problem. They formed the basis for the Water Quality Act of 1965 and its predecessors.[286] They formed the basis of the CAA of 1970.[287] They were the guideposts for the Toxic Substances Control Act (TSCA), Resource Conservation and Recovery Act, Federal Insecticide, Fungicide, and Rodenticide Act, CERCLA, and the Safe Drinking Water Act.[288] Unfortunately, all of these statutes tripped over the same thresholds.

One difficulty is that ambient systems require more of science than it can deliver. The issues turn out to be more complex than imagined. They require extrapolations of causes and effects—be they over toxicity, carcinogenicity, persistence, bioaccumulation, exposure pathways, synergy, dilution, or distribution—that are rarely dispositive and highly susceptible to challenge.[289] The federal pesticide and toxic substances control programs bogged down under the number of subject chemicals and the burden of proving their effects.[290] The CAA hosts the same arguments over air pollutants, standards, transport, and attainment.[291] The Superfund has become a legend of litigation, a "full employment act for lawyers" over the issue of how clean is clean?[292] Setting safe levels even for known toxins has confounded the toxic emission programs of the Air and Water Acts,[293] and scientists are still arguing over dichlorodiphenyltrichloroethane (DDT), dioxin (a pollutant once characterized by the EPA as "by far the most potent carcinogen evaluated to date by this agency"),[294] and even the health effects of tobacco. Risk assessment may be science but it is anything but a steady guide.

No more steady a guide is risk management, which is frankly political and, in the case of air and water regulation, a decision conceived of as best lodged with state and local authorities who are said to be familiar with the problem and in tune with local needs.[295] In most states these needs are aligned with economic and development interests whose local influence—be it chickens in Arkansas, sugar in Florida, the timber industry in Idaho, wheat in Kansas, oil and gas in Louisiana, cattle in Nevada, coal in Wyoming, and real estate nearly everywhere—is magnified by being the dominant game in town. Trying to achieve a national interest in clean air or water through state and local governments, however appealing in theory, is like trying to encourage spaghetti through a keyhole.[296]

A third difficulty with ambient-based management is its insatiable demand for data, manpower, expertise, and detailed, site-specific analysis.[297] Every water segment has its own flow regime, natural and unnatural background levels of contaminants, contaminant-neutralizers, soils, subsoils, slope, streamside vegetation, rainfall, permeability, meanders, tides, pools and drops, flora, and fauna. One size does not fit all; each water body calls for separate analysis. The discovery of adverse impacts triggers even larger resource demands in identifying, and proving, the causes and their relative contributions to the problem. More data, more resources, more time.

Each of these factors plagued the ambient-based programs of the CWA and its predecessors.[298] In the 1950s and 1960s, many states did not even bother to set water quality standards, and those that did so kept an open eye toward encouraging economic development.[299] Enforcement was paralyzed by politics and lack of proof.[300] Federal-state abatement conferences for the Potomac River and Puget Sound went staggering into their second decade without a solution in sight.[301] By the late 1960s, meanwhile, municipalities were discharging untreated waste from 75 million people, and industrial sources more than doubled that figure in organic wastes alone, without beginning to account for heavy metals and hydrocarbons.[302] By 1971, after two decades of federal assistance to state water quality-based programs, more than 300,000 industrial sources were discharging 22 billion gallons of wastewater a year, less than one-third with any form of treatment.[303]

The years following the CWA of 1972 saw a repeat performance in the §208 program.[304] Section 208 provided assistance to states and local bodies for areawide water quality planning. In the most logical way, over many years, and through cooperating agencies, detailed investigations, and countless stakeholder meetings, the program undertook to identify all sources of pollution and develop plans to abate them.[305] It ate of millions of dollars, produced several hundred studies, and cleaned up very little water.[306] By the 1980s, the §208 program was quietly shelved. In its place, in 1987, came the §319 program[307] which attempted, through grants to participating states, to encourage nonpoint sources toward reducing their pollution loads.[308] As with §208, there were few standards and fewer sticks.[309] More studies ensued; nonpoint source pollution increased.[310]

We are now in the year 2002. The reports noted earlier in this Article tell us that states lack the basic tools for water quality management: monitoring, modeling, and site-specific analysis.[311] State water quality standards and application factors remain highly variable, with abundant opportunity to game the system.[312] State enforcement remains variable as well and influenced by interests of local importance.[313] As one indicator of political will, many states have adopted policies forbidding the imposition of environmental requirements more demanding than those required by federal law,[314] and more have enacted laws prohibiting the regulation of agriculture, and in some cases all nonpoint sources.[315] Nor do states have the money for increased water quality management responsibilities[316]; as of January 2002 nearly two-thirds were facing deficit budgets,[317] and that number is apparently growing. For the first time in years, the federal government is in deficit spending as well.[318] And the costs of this ambient program, by any measure, will be high.

These problems noted, EPA and the states continue to pronounce their faith in water quality standards-based management, seconded by the Congress, the scientific-consulting community, and, of course, regulated and nonregulated industry.[319] With all of these handicaps, and since none of them are secrets, one might well ask why ambient-based management would hold such sway? The answer is that it feeds into the primary agendas of many different constituencies for reasons other than the attainment of clean water:

- To the states, it offers the opportunity to regain authority over public policy;
- To water quality scientists, it offers a lead role in that policy and a continuous source of public funding;

- To water quality engineers, it returns water management, like the management of oil and gas, to logical outputs and human ends;
- To economists (somehow overlooking transaction costs)[320] it is efficiency, avoiding the sin of waters made too unpolluted;
- To federalists it is good government, as in the Articles of Confederation;
- To discharge industries, it puts water quality management back on the site-specific, prove-it-or-lose-it basis that worked so well for them before;
- To EPA, it is a way to share the burden of pollution control, a burden with few friends and many enemies;
- And to Congress it is a way of appearing to address an environmental problem while directing large amounts of money to agencies and institutions back home.

Ambient-based management may not work very well, but it is compatible with the pursuit of many different stars.

A current analogy may be useful. In the wake of the collapse of the Enron corporation in January 2002—produced, inter alia, by a lapse in federal regulation and a self-interested gaming of the system—it turned out that while most investment firms continued to promote Enron stock despite clear signals that the company was in trouble, at least one firm saw Enron failing and did otherwise. In order to proof-check that it had not misjudged Enron, the firm invited analysts from other firms to come in and tell it why its conclusions were wrong. "It's not that they didn't see what we saw," the firm's president is quoted as saying.[321] "They either chose to come to the wrong conclusion because it suited them for a variety of other reasons, or to put their faith in management."[322]

Everyone who looks knows the problems with ambient-based water quality management as well. We are, nonetheless, moved by other reasons.

☐ *The New TMDL Program.*

> I envision TMDLs to be a kind of information-based strategy which, if done properly, can inform, empower, and energize citizens, local communities and States to improve water quality at the local, watershed level. The basic information derived from a sound TMDL could liberate the creative energies of those most likely to benefit from reduced pollutant loadings to their own waters.

> —EPA Assistant Administrator for
> Water, November 2001[323]

EPA is redesigning a TMDL program that very much resembles the Water Quality Act of 1965 and §208 of the subsequent CWA—neither a marked success. Guided by the stated goals of "flexibility, cost-effectiveness, and efficiency,"[324] the new program will provide states the happy combination of increased federal funding and reduced federal oversight.[325] EPA's challenge, in a context in which the states and discharge industries hold all the important cards, is to come up with a program that is, on the one hand, acceptable to these same states and industries and, on the other hand, does not simply recreate a failed past.

The Agency has identified the key issues of its new rules and rulemaking to include: the listing of impaired waters; implementation plans and reasonable assurance of their implementation; time frames and deadlines; stakeholder involvement; and EPA's role in the process.[326] Not so identified, but very clearly at the threshold of these issues, is the coverage of nonpoint sources and nonpoint source contaminated waters.

☐ *Nonpoint Sources.* EPA has been committed to the view that CWA§303(d) includes nonpoint source pollution and pollution sources since its first program regulations in 1985.[327] As a practical matter, nonpoint sources are the dominant source of pollution in every state in the country, and the near exclusive sources in several western states.[328] An interpretation of §303(d) without nonpoint sources would be like an interpretation of Shakespeare without the plays, interesting poetry but not very important.

The nonpoint industries have taken the position that, since §303(d) speaks in terms of impairment remaining after the application of technology standards, it must contemplate only waters with point sources that are subject to technology standards, or, as a fallback, that it contemplates only waters that include point source discharges.[329] Such a reading of §303(d) is, of course, by no means compelled by its language; it is as easy to read the section as referring to *all* water impairment after the application of technology standards, not simply impairment in particular, point source-contaminated water bodies.[330] At best (or worst), the statute is ambiguous on the question, and the combination of EPA's inclusion of nonpoint source impairment in its regulations for nearly 20 years and the fact that this inclusion best furthers the CWA's clean water restoration goal should allow the Agency's interpretation to survive judicial review under *Chevron*[331] principles before even the most hostile court.

The inclusion of nonpoint source pollution remains a causa belli for the agriculture and timber industries, however, and statements from EPA officials indicate that the Agency is at least rethinking its position.[332] A compromise position that may appear at least as an option in the new regulations will be to include only those nonpoint sources to waters where point source pollution also exists, exempting thereby the so-called nonpoint-only waters.[333] Given the large number of nonpoint-only waters in the American West and the historic intransigence of nonpoint sources to abatement, this interpretation would reduce the impact of the TMDL program by as much as one-third, and by as much as 90% in some states—to state and industry opponents, a victory. A result so at odds with the Act's goals, the Agency's regulatory history, and the Agency's current view of TMDLs—as mere numerical targets, nonbinding calculations of load reductions to be achieved through other programs—will certainly be challenged in court. One would think such a challenge a clear winner until one recalled that the facts in *Chevron* were of a very similar pirouette by EPA, reversing its previous interpretation of a pollution control statute, which a majority of the Supreme Court found to be within its discretion.[334]

☐ *Listings.* The new rules will likely approve the five-part listing process described earlier, with only the fifth and last category identifying impaired waters that require TMDLs.[335] The fourth category, just below, will include waters that are impaired but that: (1) have TMDLs; (2) are impaired by pollution but not by a pollutant; or (3) are "expected to meet" water quality standards.[336] Although current Agency guidelines limit the expected-to-meet category to waters achieving standards within two years,[337] the Agency may well follow its rule of flexibility and allow expectations over longer periods of time and perhaps more based on hope than on performance.[338] One issue sure to arise in practice is the extent to which unproven "best management practices" by nonpoint sources will provide a reasonable basis to "expect" attainment over a given period of time.[339] Another issue is whether there will be a given period of time at all.[340]

Other approved listing categories will include "insufficient data" and "additional monitoring needed" waters, an approach that has already significantly reduced the lists of several states, and hence their workload in implementing the program.[341] How large a limbo of unproven impaired waters this approach creates remains to be seen, but EPA seems unlikely to impose deadlines for determinations under these lesser categories, or "hammer" provisions requiring full listing after fixed periods of time. According to an EPA spokesman, such time frames would "limit flexibility"; instead, per the Agency, compliance times should vary with the nature of the problem, local water conditions, existing abatement measures, etc.,[342] an approach that will invite case-by-case arguments in practice.

EPA also appears ready to approve, if not require, Florida's statistical threshold, described earlier, for determining impaired waters.[343] The data demands of this approach will almost certainly increase the list of unproven waters for which sufficient samples are lacking to establish the requisite certainty of impairment. Further, EPA has approved a Virginia program allowing the state, following listings, to delimit these same waters if voluntary efforts by sources in the watershed bring the water into compliance for two consecutive years.[344] Virginia officials see the program as an incentive for voluntary abatement measures, which it surely is.[345] Environmentalists see the program as an opportunity to delay working on TMDLs for two years or more, pending the development and then the assessment of the voluntary abatement measures[346]—which it also surely is.

In sum, the new listing process, while likely to focus initial cleanups on the most provable contaminated waters, is likely to lead as well to significant "gaming" toward the lesser and "expected to meet" categories, to postponement of the development of TMDLs, and to a large body of unproven waters which remain outside the system.

☐ *Source Loadings.* Section 303(d) requires states to derive the TMDLs of pollutants necessary to achieve water quality standards.[347] In its 1985 regulations, EPA defined "loading capacity" as the "greatest amount of loading that a water can receive" without violating these standards,[348] and TMDLs as the sum of individual wasteload allocations from nonpoint sources and load allocations, plus natural background levels, an allocation for future growth, and a margin of safety.[349] In its subsequent guidance and in its approvals of TMDLs since this time, EPA has, in theory at least, required not only the identification of an overall load but also the ascription of this load to contributing sources.[350] The question is whether the Agency will continue this approach, or, rather, will accept TMDLs that do no more than put all loadings in a single bucket, end of calculation.[351]

The question is both legal and practical. As a legal matter, the 1985 regulations require more than the bare language of the statute. If challenged, the Agency would have to rely on its historic interpretation and practice and its general rulemaking authority, which should suffice[352]; with the wide differences of opinion over the scope of agency discretion now found on the federal bench, however, any result is possible. As a practical matter, the identification of the loads of contributing sources is a vital tool to the next steps in the process, abatement planning and its implementation. The who-caused it question is a starting point for all remedial actions, including the well-known "whose mess is this in the kitchen?" To be sure, the relation between contribution and the ultimate cleanup responsibility may not be one-for-one in federal programs under CERCLA[353] or even the CAA,[354] but some relationship between causation and liability suits our sense of justice.

Identifying this relationship also provides a good basis for subsequent trading and for the application of other factors such as economic efficiency, i.e., tweaking cleanup responsibilities to favor the least expensive.[355] It, finally, provides a persuasive psychological handle over individual sources, particularly nonpoint sources over whom there is little other leverage, both in internal cleanup negotiations and in external publicity. If EPA wishes to rely on public pressure, the process needs to begin by fingering the blame.

☐ *Implementation Plans.* Assuming that EPA holds the line on nonpoint source coverage and the identification of individual source loadings in approved TMDLs, the next question is the explicit inclusion of implementation plans. Indeed, this is the mega-question of the program. The absence of effective and enforceable implementation mechanisms—and the consequent absence of implementation—was a key to the underperformance of all previous water quality programs. Even the most antagonistic states and industries to the TMDL program concede the importance of implementation to water quality improvement. They simply oppose being required and being reviewed. They contest the inclusion of implementation plans as part of TMDLs under §303(d) because the adequacy of these plans and their fulfillment would then be reviewable by EPA and, worse, at the behest of citizen groups, by courts of law.[356] For these reasons, implementation plans are both the most important and the most controversial part of the entire program.

The outcome on this issue is not in doubt. EPA will throw §303(d) implementation plans overboard, first thing out of port.[357] As described earlier, the Clinton Administration's TMDL rules, jettisoning nearly all else, hung on to §303(d) plans and required objective assurance of their fulfillment.[358] With these plans now eliminated, the TMDL process is reduced to a calculation of hypothetical load reductions that would be necessary to attain water quality standards, useful numbers for "an information-based strategy" in the words of the current EPA.[359]

A reviewing court's treatment of this administrative pirouette is more problematic. On its face, the statute refers implementation planning to §303(e),[360] and the Agency's explicit inclusion of this planning in the §303(d) context is relatively recent.[361] The Clinton Administration's decision to require §303(d) plans was supported both by the logic of the requirement in determining, as required by the statute, what load reductions were necessary, i.e., an ephemeral reduction from source "A" would make a greater reduction from "B" necessary, and by the Agency's generic authority to issue regulations necessary to carry out its functions.[362] As noted earlier, at least one federal court has ruled in favor of their inclusion,[363] but others lean in the opposite direction.[364] On balance, an administrative decision to jettison §303(d) implementation plans would be difficult to reverse.

In lieu of §303(d) implementation plans, EPA is now moving to vest implementation in §303(e), a never-never land of the CWA.[365] Section 303(e) requires a continuing planning process (CPP) approved by EPA that "will result in plans" that "include," among a variety of elements, TMDLs.[366] So far, then, we have a required "process" subject to federal review.[367] EPA regulations—understandably, given the hodge-podge nature of the statute—combine the planning processes of §303(e) (CPP plans), §208 (areawide waste treatment management plans), and §319 (nonpoint source plans) into water quality management plans (WQM plans), which are intended to "identify priority point and nonpoint water quality problems" and "control measures," including time frames and financing, necessary to "carry out the plan."[368] Among the WQM elements are said to be, without further elaboration, TMDLs.[369] Whatever its review authority in the planning process, EPA has no explicit review authority in its regulations over individual WQM plans, nor is the Agency authorized by the statute to promulgate plans should the states fail to do the job. In practice, state WQM plans are something of a misnomer and tend to consist of a series of publications on such elements as state water quality standards and the identification of impaired waters. The state of Louisiana's TMDL element, for example, simply lists impaired waters and summarizes state authority, e.g., permitting, to address the problem.[370] Small wonder, then, that TMDL implementation enters this land of no definition and gets lost.

The effect of reverting TMDL plans to §303(e) depends on what EPA now makes of the process. As presently structured and implemented, the section provides few standards for plans in general, none for TMDL implementation, and no process for either challenge or Agency or public review of individual plans. To those guided by the concept of states-rights—or those whose clients see advantages in a flexible program—this is a correct result.[371] It is also a facially legal result, given the shortage of statutory guidance. It is not, however, a necessary result. EPA has full authority to redefine implementation under §303(e), to include the implementation standards found in its July 2000 TMDL rule, and to include, as well, both as a condition of delegated programs and as a condition of CPP approval, a process for administrative decisionmaking at the state level based on these standards and subject to judicial review.[372] Whether the Agency has the heart and the political capital to do this, however, is an open question.

As we have earlier seen, EPA has moved to incorporate TMDL planning standards into its §319 program.[373] As also noted, this move has drawn vigorous protest from the agriculture industry[374] and its survival, and its rigor if it survives, is an open question. Certainly, if the inclusion of TMDL plans and assurances are incorporated into §319 they will improve the effectiveness of that program. Further, it could be argued that since EPA's primary leverage over nonpoint sources is essentially a power of the purse, vesting the plans under §319 preserves the same purse power through §319 or ancillary federal funding.

The argument overlooks two realities. The first is that the threat of withdrawing federal funds weakens leverage over nonperforming states. Federal funding for delegated programs under the CWA or under the similarly constructed Coastal Zone Management Act (CZMA) has not been withdrawn even in the face of dramatic state noncompliance, indeed, provocation.[375] Further, removing monies from states not interested in using them to abate pollution is a counterintuitive way to reach clean water.

The second reality allies to the first: the primary moving force in the §303(d) program for the past decade has been citizen enforcement of the section's requirements.[376] Complain as the Agency does about these suits as hindrances to rational administration of the statute—which they may be—they are also the primary reason the statute is being implemented at all. Were these suits removed, the TMDL program would fade as quietly into the night as its unsuccessful predecessors. Which may be no small part of the agenda. The worst fear of the nonpoint industry throughout the FACA and since has been that the program might lead to plans and abatement measures reviewable, first by the Agency, and then by a court of law.[377] It is also EPA's worst fear. Because listings and TMDL development were explicit requirements of §303(d), reviewable in a court of law, EPA, in effect, had to share enforcement authority over listings and TMDLs with environmentalists. By shifting implementation planning to §§303(e) and 319, without more, EPA regains control. In the shift, however, it loses the important, indeed essential, pressure that citizen enforcement provides.

☐ *Time Frames and Deadlines.* EPA believes in long time frames and few deadlines. It will combine listings under §§305(b) and 303(d) and extend the period of reporting to several more years, probably five.[378] The Agency will probably review the state §303(e) planning process on the same schedule, although exactly what the Agency will review it for, given the minimal requirements of the statute, is not clear. Deadlines for TMDL development may well be accelerated, given the fact that TMDLs will have no planning involved, although this acceleration is not certain.[379] On the other hand, courts for their part appear increasingly willing to accept any progress toward TMDL development as sufficient to comply with the statue.[380] The outlook is for ample flexibility in meeting whatever minimum requirements the new program entails.

□ *Stakeholder Involvement.* There are essentially three types of stake-holders in TMDL development: the states, the pollution sources, and citizens. The new rules will certainly provide for close collaboration among states and the point and nonpoint source communities over allocation issues and for the development of trading systems to achieve more cost-effective strategies. The more open question is how they will involve local citizens and environmentalists. On this issue, there appears to be a disconnect between the talk and the walk.

In testimony before Congress, EPA professes a desire to "empower and energize" citizens and local communities in the TMDL process, liberating "the creative energies of those most likely to benefit from reduced pollution loadings to their own waters."[381] By which beneficiaries the Agency must mean fishers, boaters, swimmers, paddlers, collectors, biologists, school kids, dreamers, and all the great number of Americans who care about clean water more than they care about clean anything else in the world. There are of course millions of them, many of them organized and almost all of them willing to get involved. They are for the most part volunteers, with a relatively few, low-paid, overextended professionals. The question is how they will be liberated and empowered to participate: as kibitzers, or as players.

EPA appears to imagine a world where TMDL information, in the hands of the public, will influence significant pollution reductions from nonpoint source industries, somewhat akin to the publicity effects of the toxic release inventory (TRI) list.[382] While the TRI is undoubtedly an effective tool, the Agency may be overlooking a significant difference in public perception between the release of toxins and the release of sediments. As EPA's own polling shows, the two are worlds apart.[383] EPA also overlooks the obvious fact that the practice of annual TRI disclosures has in no way obviated the continuing need to limit, monitor, and enforce compliance by the chemical industry.[384] The TRI is a complementary program; it is in no way the game-in-chief.

The basics to effective citizen participation in environmental programs are access to decisionmaking at all stages of the process, decisions based on objective standards, and the opportunity to have decisions reviewed when they depart from these standards or are based on demonstrably false information. The National Environmental Policy Act (NEPA)[385] works not because its standards are enforced by a supervising federal agency but rather by citizens and reviewing courts. The CWA NPDES program works the same way, a way explicitly promoted in the citizen suit provisions of the Act,[386] to the point that it is impossible to imagine the accomplishments of the Act without the constant pressure of citizen enforcement.[387] The genius of the Act was to invest enforcement at all three levels, federal, state, and citizen, in order to maximize the chances that at least one would get the job done.

EPA's current rules leave very little to which citizen involvement can attach. Access to TMDL calculations might be interesting information and the stuff of a good press release, but it is no substitute for an equal seat at the table. The Agency may aspire to liberated energy and community pressure rising up to secure clean water, but by the removal of implementation plans from §303(d) and the failure to recreate a similar process elsewhere, the Agency has, and one would have to say quite consciously, put that aspiration on short rations.

☐ *Summing Up.* EPA is moving toward a TMDL program that trades standards, oversight, and citizen enforcement for volunteerism, flexibility, and local decisionmaking. No one can gainsay the desirability of state leadership and voluntary participation in a program of this size and diversity. Nor can anyone gainsay the desirability of flexibility in designing solutions. The question is reasonable assurance that the solutions will work and the enforcement of their terms. At bottom, law is about rules, and any system that swaps rules for hope in dealing with actors who have historically refused to move forward is asking for failure.

One can imagine a scenario in which the TMDL program, made user-friendly and relieved of deadlines and enforcement, is accepted by the states with enthusiasm. Congress in turn funds it to the hilt, the post-September 11 economy and deficit budget notwithstanding. States, for their part, despite the fact that one-half are in deficit spending, more are heading in that direction, and nearly all have passed laws expressly prohibiting their regulation of agricultural and nonpoint sources, contribute a match in both funding and political will. Local governments hold the line on uses requiring clean water and maintain high water quality standards; a vast network of chemical monitors and biological surveys provides all necessary data; engineering models and scientific estimates provide persuasive, definitive answers to causes and impacts, fate and persistence, and the effectiveness of particular control measures; markets and trades take the sting out of abatement controls that, in turn, are scrupulously observed and self-enforced by dischargers, at which point the nonpoint industries, U.S. Sugar, Boise Cascade, Archer Daniels Midland, join in; those who do not are embarrassed into joining by adverse, TRI-like publicity; and we leave the lawyers and the environmental community for that matter looking for other things to do. We can imagine all this. EPA's new rules seem to. It would be a historic first. But anything is possible.

A more likely scenario is that the TMDL program bottomed on carrots, but far fewer than those needed, and will sputter forward unevenly even in the most well-intentioned and best-resourced states, which, in turn, are not legion. A program that simply provides a TMDL cap, or even load calculations, and leaves the rest to the states provides little backup for the hard decisions—hard in science, hard in proof at law, and hardest in politics—that will have to be made. Federal requirements may be a state governor's worst enemy, but they are a state environmental agency line player's best friend.[388] A program that depends, further, on the threat of EPA stepping in to do TMDLs should the states underperform, as many will surely do, depends largely on an illusion; through "conditional approvals" and other evasions already seen in EPA's responses to state failures in the CAA program,[389] this is one gorilla that simply does not come out of the closet.[390] The missing link of the new program is something in between: objective performance standards and the enfranchisement of citizens to secure compliance, the same ingredients that have brought the NPDES program home.

Forward Into the Future

The TMDL program needs help. As it is currently headed it will need a great deal of help, and this help will have to come from other, complementary approaches to pollution control.

There are at least three strategies for abating pollution.[391] One is to approach it from the backend, by its effects on the environment, ambient-based controls. Another is to approach it from the source, through technology and practice standards. A third is to approach it from the pollutant, either circumscribing or banning its use. With intractable problems—automobile emissions, for example—all three strategies are necessary to address the problem. We have ambient standards for the primary contaminants from automobile emissions[392] and highly complex requirements for abatement planning in nonattainment areas.[393] We have technology requirements as well,[394] technology-based emissions limitations,[395] fuel standards,[396] and low emission vehicles.[397] We have taken the third step, over time, of eliminating lead in gasoline altogether.[398]

The other lesson from the automobile, of course, is that where all three elements are not pursued vigorously the problems are forever managed and never solved. Each of these strategies is potentially available to the TMDL program. All three will be necessary for it to succeed.

☐ *Enhanced Ambient Management.* The TMDL program has often been described as an "air SIP," referencing the state implementation plan process under the CAA.[399] The analogy works in theory, but less well in practice and law. Unlike the TMDL program, added as a last-minute compromise to the CWA in 1972, the SIP program was intended to be the lead strategy for achieving national clean air. As such, Congress afforded it important federal, structural features not found in the CWA: uniform national ambient air quality standards (NAAQS)[400]; implementation plans with prescriptive standards for federal approval[401]; deadlines for their submission and review[402]; sanctions for underperformance and noncompliance[403]; and citizen suits with the potential of hounding the process forward.[404] If one were to imagine a program combining state management with close and rigorous federal supervision, this would be the one.

This said, one would not wish the CAA SIP program on one's worst enemy. The complexity of the system is mind-boggling and, in the view of many commentators, self-defeating.[405] NAAQS and their supporting science have been in controversy since day one, with few conclusive results.[406] Models of short- and long-range transport vary widely, at times in close coincidence with the interests that fund them.[407] Basic data and monitoring are spotty, selective, and widely unavailable.[408] Large airsheds remain in a limbo of insufficient information.[409] Delays in plan preparation, amendments, and approvals are multi-year.[410] Load allocations are unequally distributed, with demanding requirements on the more easily regulated point sources and almost hortatory planning provisions (e.g., "high occupancy lanes" for commuters, which in Louisiana means a second person in the car) for the diffuse sources that are often at the root of the problem.[411] The "adaptive management" required for changes in air quality and in source loadings is so constant that if a "plan" exists few even in the Agency know what and where it is.[412] Point sources are able to "game" the system at every point—monitoring,[413] false upgrades,[414] claimed reductions,[415] inspection and maintenance programs[416]—and trading systems add difficulties that confound both EPA and state administrators.[417] None of which should be news to the reader; the parallels with the CWA TMDL program are striking.

Prof. Robert Adler has written a thoughtful article on *Lessons From the Clean Air Act* for TMDLs in which, while recognizing essential differences between air and water quality management, he makes several recommendations for a strengthened TMDL program.[418] These include: consistency in water quality standards, monitoring, and listing; watershed, as airshed, planning areas; consolidated planning; implementation criteria and substantive implementation plans; attainment deadlines; and administrative review and enforcement authority.[419] In the end, however, he does not make them with great confidence in their effectiveness. While conceding that SIPs have succeeded "to some degree" in reducing air pollution, Professor Adler concludes that "[n]o one would propose to repeat the problems of delay, uncertainty, complexity and political divisiveness that have plagued the SIP process over the years."[420] He is not alone in this conclusion; nearly all commentators on the program agree.[421] So did Congress, which, by the late 1970s, began adding technology requirements to the CAA[422] and adopted them full bore in the Amendments of 1990.[423] Ambient standards remained in the mix, but they were no longer the main game.

Several years ago this author presented an examination question describing the plight of Mexico City, overrun at the time with smog and motor vehicles and without an air quality program. The proposal was, starting from scratch, to recommend an air pollution abatement strategy. Many students undertook to rewrite the SIP provisions of the CAA. They missed the obvious. The problem was not the absence of air standards and monitors, although one could doubtless spend considerable time and money on them. The problem was factories and cars.

☐ *Technology and Practice Standards*. To paraphrase a campaign slogan: "It's about agriculture, stupid!" The nonpoint source pollution that has swamped the nation's waters has many and diverse sources, but the lion's share are agricultural: crops and animals.[424] More than 50% of water impairment nationally comes from agricultural runoff.[425] In some western states dominated by cattle, the number reaches 90%.[426] More than 80% of the eutrophication of the Gulf of Mexico dead zone is attributable to farm loadings over 500 river miles away.[427] There is a time in the life of a household when one has looked at a messy room long enough and, without further dialogue about impacts and the rights of occupants, says the only reasonable thing: "Clean it up!" In the life of the CWA, that time has arrived for agriculture.

Agriculture is one of the largest industries in the United States, with a total production value of near $200 billion.[428] Its principle field crops are corn, soybeans, hay, and wheat[429]; it also produces on an annual basis 98 million cattle, 366 million egg-laying chickens, 6.75 billion meat chickens, and 61 million hogs.[430] It spends $18 billion on agricultural chemicals a year,[431] more than twice what it spends on gasoline[432] and electricity.[433] Its payroll reaches $16.9 billion in farm and contract employees.[434] Its larger operations are industrial, look industrial, and are managed as any national or multinational corporation.

The industry is both highly diverse and highly stratified, concentrating more by the year into large factory operations in which former individual farmers become sublet contractors or employees. The total number of American farmers has dropped from 7 million to 1.9 million in recent years.[435] Roughly one-half of this population, small farms, provide only

1.5% of total farm production value while, at the other end, 3.6% account for more than 50% of the total value.[436] The industry and its many subcategories are also highly subsidized by the federal government, at the rate of $20 billion per year, with the top 10% of farm operations receiving two-thirds of the benefits.[437] The industry is supported by federal and state agricultural research institutions and by entire universities.[438] It is also well defended through the American Farm Bureau Federation, a $200 million a year organization that produces another $18.5 billion through its insurance companies and provides aggressive campaign, political action, lobbying, and litigation services.[439]

With even this rudimentary understanding of the industry, the exemption of American agriculture from the CWA is either gross negligence or gross politics.[440] Whichever, few of the reasons that have been given for exempting farm sources from the NPDES program obtain today. Far from being trivial, they are mammoth. Far from being site-specific and local, their impacts are multi-state, regional, and even international. Far from being without available control technologies, the control strategies for nonpoint source pollution, e.g., shelterbelts, cover crops, and cattle fences, are orders of magnitude less complex and less costly than other industry controls. To be sure, farms are diverse, but they are no more diverse by crop and production method than the many categories and subcategories of pulp and paper manufacturers, petrochemicals, metals, rubber, and other industries subject to the NPDES program.[441] Nor is it a persuasive distinction that farm runoff does not emerge from a pipe. Construction, municipal, feedlot, and acid mine drainage do not emerge from pipes either. They all arise from identifiable technologies and practices. They all pollute. They should all share the burden of cleanup and this burden in America begins with adopting BAT. There is something wrong with a picture that regulates the discharges of small Pacific Coast canning factories[442] while Boise Cascade, U.S. Sugar, and Archer Daniels Midland walk free.

Prof. J.B. Ruhl has published a well-documented study of farm pollution, *Farms, Their Environmental Harms and Environmental Law*, suggesting a multifaceted strategy for imposing meaningful pollution controls.[443] His proposal relies on a mix of emissions trading, disclosure, taxes, and economic incentives familiar to any reader of the literature on reinventing environmental law.[444] His first and most persuasive strategy, however, and certainly the most concrete, is the application of technology standards to factory farm and large crop operations, what he calls the "agro-industry low-hanging fruit."[445] The proposal neatly severs the relatively few major farm players from the general population of farmers, subjecting only the former to federal regulation; such distinctions are already made in law between large and small municipalities[446] and large and small CAFOs.[447] There can be no doubt that sugar farming, rice farming, and other high-impact activities would benefit from the same multimedia, air, water, and waste analysis that EPA has provided for the pulp and paper industry.[448] Indeed, such analysis and abatement measures are already on hand in best practices manuals of the USDA, EPA, and many states.[449] They are undeniably effective.[450] The only question is whether they will, at last, be mandatory and, therefore, be implemented widely and evenhandedly across the country.

Of course, the proposal is heresy to the agriculture industry, which has tied up EPA's proposed BAT for CAFO's for several years[451] and is presently offering an alternative to technology standards based on "environmental management systems."[452] On the other hand, Congress and EPA have been nibbling around the edges of diffuse sources since the 1980s, bringing municipal runoff, construction runoff, and CAFOs under permit.[453] Environmental lawsuits are pushing the envelope farther with cases seeking permit controls for dairy farms,[454] stormwater runoff,[455] spraying of aquatic herbicides,[456] ballast waters,[457] and logging.[458] In the heat of battle, of course, EPA pulled back from further mention of the application of practice standards to logging roads,[459] but no reason in the world other than politics can distinguish between runoff from a construction site bulldozer, a forest road bulldozer, and a plow.

In short, technology controls were the genius of the CWA and have been the primary engine of its success. To continue to exempt agriculture from these controls requires an act of willful blindness. Whatever the reasons offered exempting agriculture in the past, those reasons no longer obtain. If we are truly serious about cleaning up the nation's waters, the agriculture industry should apply what everyone else is coming to apply: BAT.

☐ *Limiting the Pollutant.* Faced with an overload of mule pollution, one has several options. The first is an intensive examination of the Mule-Manure-Nitrogen-Cycle, followed by detailed studies of persistence, fate, and distribution, their relation to downstream algae blooms, and the post-baseline composition and distribution of aquatic communities. The second is to go to Best Available Mule Practices: we step 'em back from the creek. A third is to reduce the number of mules.

As a national environmental strategy, we have made such reductions before. We have eliminated chlorofluorocarbons (CFCs) and DDT. We have severely limited uses of lead, mercury, and polychlorinated biphenyls. We have learned two lessons from these experiences. The first is that when we limit the pollutants, the environment improves, dramatically.[460] Lead levels in urban air and in the bloodstreams of urban children dropped sharply[461]; the Brown Pelican and the American Bald Eagle, virtually exterminated by DDT and related pesticides, are coming off of the endangered species list.[462] The second lesson is that, no matter how loudly their manufacturers proclaimed that DDT, CFCs, and lead were indispensable, more benign alternatives were found that filled the niche.[463] Granted, these are drastic measures and ones limited to major, harmful chemical actors. They are also highly effective measures, and in terms of transaction costs, highly efficient as well.

The pollutant at issue in TMDLs is fertilizer.[464] To be sure, fertilizers are only part of the stew but they are the dominant man-made ingredient.[465] The contamination of the Louisiana dead zone is directly correlated to fertilizer use; the hypoxia has grown in direct proportion to fertilizer application upstream and rises seasonally with increased runoff.[466] This correlation is no secret to those working on cleanups for the Chesapeake Bay, the Apalachicola Bay, the Everglades, and many other anoxic bodies of water across the country.[467] If the primary proposition is: "It's about agriculture, stupid," then the sub-prime is: "It's about fertilizer."

More than 54 million tons a year—110 billion pounds—of commercial fertilizers and related liming materials are consumed in the United States.[468] Fertilizers with the primary nutrients—nitrogen, phosphorous, and potassium—account for 91% of the total.[469] The states of highest fertilizer consumption are, not surprisingly, agricultural states in the cornbelt and California.[470] While the potato crop is the most fertilizer-intensive for all primary nutrient fertilizers at 195 pounds per acre of nitrogen, 173 pounds per acre of phosphorous, and 139 pounds per acre of potassium . . . i.e., one-half ton of fertilizers per acre of crop[471] . . . corn, covering 70 million acres, leads the nation in total loadings.[472] Nearly 6 million tons of phosphates and nitrogen run back into the nation's waters.[473] Considering that almost one-half of the land mass of the United States is in field-crop agriculture,[474] what we have here is a very profitable business[475] and massive pollution.[476]

We also have, of course, a necessary ingredient to American farming and a principal factor in its success. On the other hand, fertilizers are over-marketed and overused in virtually every crop-growing sector,[477] not out of ignorance or low costs (indeed, fertilizers may be the largest cost in a growing season)[478] but because individual farmers find themselves in a prisoner's dilemma: if their neighbors do it, they cannot afford not to.[479] Meanwhile, of course, the environmental costs are "externalized," i.e., floated downstream to, say, Louisiana and the Chesapeake Bay. The question becomes, then, how to limit the application of fertilizers in a way that will not penalize those who are willing to restrict both their use and thus, to a degree, their production. At least three tools available for doing so.

The first is federal regulation to limit fertilizer application and use. In late 1985, EPA exercised its authority under TSCA to begin an investigation of fertilizers and the contamination of groundwater.[480] TSCA §8 was invoked to identify groundwater contamination problems,[481] §4 to test groundwater quality and health effect,[482] and §6 to determine appropriate controls.[483] The decisionmaking framework foresaw first-round controls—described as emphasizing "integrated problem solving," i.e., the one of best control, whether TSCA or another method, in 1988-1989, with further study leading to additional means as needed in the future.[484] Whether from the cumbersome nature of TSCA or the political force of the agriculture and fertilizer manufacturing industries, the initiative quickly died and has not reappeared.[485] The Agency is now looking in a more limited way at the impact of heavy metals from fertilizers, although it has proposed no strategy to deal with them.[486] This history notwithstanding, if ever there were a product with the type of multimedia impacts that TSCA was enacted to address, fertilizers certainly come to mind. The TSCA approach may not have died because it was a bad idea but, rather, precisely because it might have worked.

A second approach, developed by the USDA, several states, and the European Union (EU) and its Member countries are fertilizer/crop/soil ratios that determine optimal application regimes.[487] Yet a third approach, adopted by a few states and by several agriculture-intensive countries of the EU, is to impose fertilizer taxes, either across-the-board or in relation to optimal application standards.[488] The general question of pollution taxes is beyond the reach of this Article, but commentators note the difficulties they pose in calibrating the relationship of tax increases to a desired level of abatement, in fairness to smaller competitors, and more recently in environmental justice for communities impacted by larger competitors, e.g., the Louisiana chemical corridor.[489] The proposal here, however, is not to use taxes as a substitute for regulation—an approach considered and rejected by Congress in enacting the CWA of 1972—but, rather, as a supplement to incentivize abatement from its dominant and most intransigent source.

In 1992, the EU amended its organizing treaty to include a statement of environmental principles that would guide EU and Member State decisionmaking.[490] The first of these principles were: pollution should be rectified at the source, and the polluter pays.[491] Why not?

Reflections on the Emerging Program

The CWA was enacted with the mission of clean water. It was that simple, and it is still on the books. The approach was to clean up the country's major pollution sources through technology standards and to treat those remaining through federal-state, ambient-based programs: TMDLs. The technology standards—despite their subsequent compromises, litigation delays, loopholes, and enforcement lapses—worked remarkably well. What no one anticipated was that nonpoint sources would come along to eat up the gains. TMDLs are now facing a problem of a scale they were not designed to solve, and by themselves will never solve.

The emerging TMDL program, with its emphasis on incentives and voluntary measures, is based more on faith than on fact. In a previous series of articles on the TMDL program, this author concluded that, despite its indirectness, uncertainties, and steep maintenance costs, the program was worth the candle because it gave Americans who care about clean water the chance to make it happen.[492] The unstated corollary was that, absent an enforcement role for citizens, the program was more waste than product. While it is impossible to gainsay the need to involve state agencies in water pollution control, it is equally impossible to predict that—given the challenges in science, funding, and political will that this program faces—they will do the job any better than they have done for the past 50 years. The TMDL program needs carrots but it also needs consequences, and it could use help from other pollution control strategies that have proven themselves effective. With these additional points of leverage, TMDLs have the chance to make a significant contribution to clean water. Without them, all bets are off.

Notes to Chapter 6

1. TMDLs are referred to under §303(d) of the CWA, 33 U.S.C. §1313(d), ELR STAT. FWPCA §303(d).

2. Section 303(d) provides in relevant part:

> (d) Identification of areas with insufficient controls; maximum daily load; certain effluent limitations revision
>
> (1)(A) Each State shall identify those waters within its boundaries for which the effluent limitations required by section 1311(b)(1)(A) and section 1311(b)(1)(B) of this title are not stringent enough to implement any water quality standard applicable to such waters. The State shall establish a priority ranking for such waters, taking into account the severity of the pollution and the uses to be made of such waters.
>
> (B) Each State shall identify those waters or parts thereof within its boundaries for which controls on thermal discharges under section 1311 of this title are not stringent enough to assure protection and propagation of a balanced indigenous population of shellfish, fish, and wildlife.
>
> (C) Each State shall establish for the waters identified in paragraph (1)(A) of this subsection, and in accordance with the priority ranking, the total maximum daily load, for those pollutants which the Administrator identifies under section 1314(a)(2) of this title as suitable for such calculation. Such load shall be established at a level necessary to implement the applicable water quality standards with seasonal variations and a margin of safety which takes into account any lack of knowledge concerning the relationship between effluent limitations and water quality. . . .
>
> (2) Each State shall submit to the Administrator from time to time, with the first such submission not later than one hundred and eighty days after the date of publication of the first identification of pollutants under section 1314(a)(2)(D) of this title, for his approval the waters identified and the loads established under paragraphs (1)(A), (1)(B), (1)(C), and (1)(D) of this subsection. The Administrator shall either approve or disapprove such identification and load not later than thirty days after the date of submission. If the Administrator approves such identification and load, such State shall incorporate them into its current plan under subsection (e) of this section. If the Administrator disapproves such identification and load, he shall not later than thirty days after the date of such disapproval identify such waters in such State and establish such loads for such waters as he determines necessary to implement the water quality standards applicable to such waters and upon such identification and establishment the State shall incorporate them into its current plan under subsection (e) of this section.

3. *See infra* section entitled The Past as Prologue. *See also* WILLIAM H. ROGERS JR., ENVIRONMENTAL LAW (2d ed. 1994) 55-57 (risk-based management):

> The strategy of prospective regulation based on risk assessment has not been successful. Legislative deadlines are often missed. Regulatory endeavors often barely scratch the surface of the list of pollutant candidates. Known problem chemicals linger in commercial chemicals for years. The methodology demands more time, information, and bureaucratic effort than is available to devote to it. It requires a number of hard policy choices. It affords opportunities for refuge and obstructionism by parties not interested in cooperating.

161-64 (ambient air management), 342-52 (ambient water management), 741-45 (hazardous waste cleanup); Oliver Houck, *Of Bats, Birds, and B-A-T: The Convergent Evolution of Environmental Law,* 63 MISS. L.J. 403 (1994) (arguing that failure of ambient standards management has led to alternative standards in both pollution control and natural resources law).

4. For insight into the relative strength of EPA in the current Administration, see *Whitman Takes Back Seat to White House, OMB Policy Priorities,* INSIDE EPA, Jan. 4, 2002, at 15 ("The Bush Administration has centralized its environmental policymaking decisions in the White House more than virtually every previous administration, investing much more of the authority for broad environmental policy priorities with Office of Management and Budget (OMB) regulatory chief John Graham, observers say.").

5. *See New OMB List Targets Eight Major EPA Rules for Possible Rollback,* IN-SIDE EPA, Jan. 4, 2002, at 1.

6. U.S. EPA, Revisions to the Water Quality Planning and Management Regulation and Revision to the National Pollutant Discharge Elimination System Program in Support of Revision to the Water Quality Planning and Management Regulation, 65 Fed. Reg. 43586 (July 13, 2000).

7. EPA's first TMDL regulations were promulgated in 1978, U.S. EPA, Total Maximum Daily Loads Under the Clean Water Act, 43 Fed. Reg. 60664 (Dec. 28, 1978). They were amended in 1985 as part of the Agency's consolidated water quality management program, U.S. EPA, Water Quality Standards Regulation, 50 Fed. Reg. 1774 (Jan. 1, 1985), and again in 1992, 57 Fed. Reg. 33040 (July 24, 1992), following court decisions that were beginning to enforce TMDL requirements to impose deadlines for the submission of listed waters; no other deadlines nor substantive standards were provided for the TMDLs themselves. *See generally* Chapter 3, at 49-53.

8. *See id.* at 49-55.

9. *Id.* at 56-58, Chapter 4, at 77-82.

10. Chapter 3, at 57-58, Chapter 4, at 82-84.

11. *Id.* at 83-84.

12. Letter from John Barrett to Oliver A. Houck (Sept. 17, 1999) (on file with author). Mr. Barrett represented the American Farm Bureau Federation on the FACA and in subsequent lobbying against EPA's TMDL rules. In subsequent correspondence, Mr. Barrett has clarified that he was referring to the implementation of the §319 nonpoint source program, which he views as misplaced effort. Letter of John Barrett to Oliver Houck (Apr. 23, 2002) (on file with author).

13. J. Zane Walley, *The Water Wars*, RANGE MAG., Fall 1999, at 30.

14. *See* Chapter 4, at 76 (court-ordered schedules for TMDL preparation ranged from 12 years to as few as 5).

15. *See id.* at 77-82 (describing EPA guidance on listing and TMDL content).

16. 5 U.S.C. §553, *available in* ELR ADMIN. STAT. PROC. (notice-and-comment rulemaking requirements).

17. U.S. EPA, Proposed Regulations to the Water Quality Planning and Management Regulation, 64 Fed. Reg. 46012 (Aug. 23, 1999).

18. *See Water Quality Standards: Offset Requirements, Other Provisions Eliminated From TMDL Rule, EPA Says,* 31 Env't Rep. (BNA) 685 (Apr. 14, 2000).

19. U.S. EPA, Revisions to the Water Quality Planning and Management Regulations, 65 Fed. Reg. 43586, 43589 (July 13, 2000).

20. *See State Programs: Officials Want More Guidance, Flexibility, to Implement Programs, Subcommittee Told,* 33 Env't Rep. (BNA) n.p. (Mar. 2, 2001) (describing testimony from two state governors and two state agencies approving EPA TMDL rules); National Association of Convention Districts, *TMDL Update* (2000), at http://nacdnet.org/district/leader/ (describing agriculture interest lobbying).

21. T. Robert Braile, *Clean Water Bill by Smith Meets EPA Opposition*, BOSTON GLOBE, May 7, 2000 at 1.

22. *Water Quality Standards: Agency Accused of Secret Meetings, Shoddy Science in TMDL Proposed Rule,* 31 Env't Rep. (BNA) 1429 (July 7, 2000).

23. *Id.*

24. *See Notice and Comment,* ENVTL. F., Nov./Dec. 2000, at 17 ("A senior environmental official was stripped of power by a budget rider, reports the *Washington Post*. The measure, added to the Department of Agriculture spending bill, removes all authority for the under secretary responsible for the Forest Service and the Natural Resources Conservation Service, James Lyons, to run the two agencies.").

25. *Id.*

26. *See Water Quality Standards: Agency's Draft Final Regulation to Revise TMDL Program Sent for White House Review,* 31 Env't Rep. (BNA) 1325 (June 23, 2000).

27. *Id.*

28. *Id.*

29. *Id.*

30. *See* Claudia Copeland, *EPA's Total Maximum Daily Load (TMDL) Program: Highlights of the Final Revised Rule,* Cong. Research Serv., July 18, 2000, at 4, *available at* http://www.cnie.org/NLE/h2o-36.html (last visited Feb. 21, 2002); *see also Senate Bill Would Insure TMDL Funding, Delay EPA Implementation of Final Rule,* WATER ENV'T & TECH. NEWS WATCH (undated) (on file with author) (referencing EPA assurances to House Transportation and Infrastructure Committee Chairman Rep. Bud Shuster (R-Pa.)).

31. *See* comments of Earthjustice Legal Defense Fund representative on the proposed TMDL deadlines, *Water Quality Standards, supra* note 26 ("'Ten years plus five years is still 15 years,' she said. After that the 10 years states have to develop an implementation plan, and it pushes back the attainment of water quality standards even further, Mulhern said. Moreover, she added, the goal or attaining water quality standards is not enforceable. 'Fifty years from now, if the water is still not clean, will EPA still be on the hook to go and clean it up?' she asked.").

32. Personal conversation and e-mail correspondence with representatives of Earthjustice Legal Defense Fund, the Natural Resources Defense Council, Widener Law School Environmental Law Clinic, Southeastern Legal Foundation, Northwest Environmental Advocates, the National Wildlife Federation, the Sierra Club, and other national, state, and local citizen organizations throughout 1999-2000.

33. *See Water Quality Standards: EPA Plans to Move Forward With Issuance of TMDL Rule Despite Obstacles, Fox Says,* 31 Env't Rep. (BNA) 1123 (May 26, 2000).

34. Sen. Max Baucus (D-Mont.), for example, vowing to "reverse the [TMDL] decision at the earliest opportunity," characterized the rules as "roundly criticized by states, environmental groups, business organizations, and agricultural interests." *See Supplemental Spending Bill, infra* note 44.

35. *See States Split on Bush Review of Clinton-EPA Air, Water Initiatives,* INSIDE EPA, Aug. 31, 2001, at 1.

36. *See Nonpoint Sources Need to Be Included in TMDL Program, Treatment Officials Say,* 32 Env't Rep. (BNA) n.p. (Aug. 20, 2001) (questioning the General Counsel to her Association of Metropolitan Sewerage Agencies as stating: "What [the rule] did was to provide teeth to the program. . . . It made the program more meaningful.").

37. *See Water Quality Standards: Agency TMDL Proposal Costly, Technical, Unenforceable, Senate Chairman Tells Group,* 31 Env't Rep. (BNA) 389 (Mar. 3, 2000); Press Release, Office of Sen. Mike Crapo (R-Idaho), Senator Crapo's Floor Statement on S. 2417, The Water Pollution Program Enhancements Act of 2000 (undated), *available at* http://www.senate.gov/~Crapo/tmdl_floor_statement.htm.

38. *See Clean Water Network, Summary of Water Pollution Program Enhancement Act of 2000* (2000), *at* http://www.cwn.org/docs/programs/tmdl/s2417factsheet.htm.

39. *See* H.R. 3609, 106th Cong. (2000) and S. 2041, 106th Cong. (2000) (exempting silvicultural activities from the NPDES program); H.R.J. Res. 105, 106th Cong. (2000) (nullifying TMDL rules).

40. *See Water Quality Standards: Final TMDL Rule Signed by Browner, Styming Bid by Congress to Block Measure,* 32 Env't Rep. (BNA) 1468 (July 14, 2000) (quoting EPA Administrator Carol Browner: "It is up to the states to make the decisions. It is not a federal permitting program.").

41. H.R. 4425, 106th Cong. (2000). *See also* Copeland, *supra* note 30.

42. H.R. 4425; *see also* Copeland, *supra* note 30; *Water Quality Standards: Final TMDL Rule Signed by Browner, supra* note 40 (quoting EPA Administrator Browner: "It was put on the supplemental [appropriation to the military construction spending bill] late at night. It was a surprise, done very late at night, without public knowledge or public review.").

43. H.R. 4425; *see also infra* section entitled Supporting Science.

44. The bill funded, inter alia, funding for military activities in Kosovo, aid to Columbia, and domestic disaster relief. *Id. See also* Ground Water Protection Council, *Supplemental Spending Bill Approved by Congress Stops TMDL Rulemaking Effort* (2000), *at* http://gwpc.site.net/News/nws-tmdlrulemaking.htm.

45. For a discussion of the use and abuse of appropriations riders, see Sandra A. Zellmer, *Sacrificing Legislative Integrity at the Altar of Appropriations Riders: A Constitutional Crisis,* 21 HARV. L. REV. 457 (1998). In this case, President William J. Clinton complemented Congress for dropping "several anti-environmental riders," without mention of its rider blocking the TMDL rule—which he knew he could finalize before he signed the rider. *See* H.R. 4425. Such is the language of politics.

46. Seth Borenstein & Steven Chomma, *Clinton Hurries EPA to Beat Ban by Congress: Clean Water Bill Needs Signature by July 13,* TIMES PICAYUNE, July 6, 2000, at A-4.

47. *See Water Quality Standards: Final TMDL Rule Signed by Browner, supra* note 40.

48. 65 Fed. Reg. at 43585.

49. *See Water Quality Standards: Final TMDL Rule Signed by Browner, supra* note 40; *see also Copeland, supra* note 30, at 4.

50. For one criticism of Administrator Whitman's environmental record while governor of New Jersey, see RICHARD CAPLAN, POLLUTERS' PLAYGROUND: HOW THE GOVERNMENT PERMITS POLLUTION 10, 11 (U.S. PIRG Educ. Fund., May 2001).

> In her first budget, she cut more than 200 positions from the department. Other anti-enforcement actions included: eliminating the Office of Environmental Prosecutor and the [O]ffice of the Public Advocate; down-

sizing the DEP from 3,729 staff in 1992 to a low of 3,022 in 1998; eliminating the DEP lab; eliminating more than 100 stations that monitor water quality; removing more than 1,000 chemicals from the right-to-know list and thus placing them out of state inspection requirements; and conducting far fewer inspections by environmental regulators.

51. *See* Rena L. Steinzor, *EPA and Its Sisters at 30: Devolution, Revolution, or Reform?*, 31 ELR 11086 (Sept. 2001) ("As long as EPA . . . mollifies the states by turning the other way when they shove unpopular federal programs off the table, the faster the crises threatening the rule of law will grow.").

52. Chapter 5, at 131-41. *See also* WILLIAM H. ROGERS JR., ENVIRONMENTAL LAW 288-89 (1986).

53. *See* Oliver A. Houck, *The Regulation of Toxic Pollutants Under the Clean Water Act,* 31 ELR 10528 (Sept. 1991) (quoting floor statements of seven Senators and Representatives identifying weaknesses in the water quality standards program); *see also* the statement of the Senate conferencees on the 1972 Amendments to the CWA:

> The Committee adopted this substantial change because of the great difficulty associated with establishing reliable and enforceable precise effluent limitations on the basis of a given stream quality. Water quality standards, in addition to their deficiencies in relying on the assimilative capacity of receiving waters, often cannot be translated into effluent limitations—defendable in court tests, because of the imprecision of models for water quality and the effects of effluents in most waters.

S. REP. NO. 92-414 (1972), *reprinted in* 1972 U.S.C.C.A.N. 3675.

54. OFFICE OF WATER QUALITY, U.S. EPA, ASSESSMENT OF STATE NEEDS FOR TECHNICAL ASSISTANCE IN NPDES PERMITTING (1984).

55. OFFICE OF TECHNOLOGY ASSESSMENT, U.S. EPA, WATERS IN MARINE ENVIRONMENTS 206 (1987).

56. *Congress Lacks Conclusive Data Needed to Assess Water Act, Hydrologist Says,* 25 Env't Rep. (BNA) 3235 (Apr. 30, 1993); *see also* U.S. GAO, NATIONAL WATER QUALITY ASSESSMENT, GEOLOGICAL SURVEY, FACES FORMIDABLE DATA MANAGEMENT CHALLENGES (1993).

57. PUBLIC EMPLOYEES FOR ENVIRONMENTAL RESPONSIBILITY, MARKING WATERS, OFFICIAL WATER QUALITY REPORTS ARE ALL WET: AN INSIDE LOOK AT EPA'S IMPLEMENTATION OF THE CLEAN WATER ACT 2, 3, (1999).

58. *See* U.S. GAO, AIR POLLUTION: NATIONAL AIR MONITORING NETWORK IS INADEQUATE (1989).

59. U.S. GAO, KEY EPA AND STATE DECISIONS LIMITED BY INCONSISTENT AND INCOMPLETE DATA (2000) [hereinafter KEY EPA AND STATE DECISIONS].

60. *Id.* at 5.

61. *Id.* at 5-7. The Office of the Inspector General of EPA reaches the same conclusion in OFFICE OF INSPECTOR GENERAL, U.S. EPA, INCONSISTENCIES IN STATES' LISTINGS OF IMPAIRED WATER BODIES MAY DELAY TMDL DEVELOPMENT AND IMPLEMENTATION (2001).

62. U.S. GAO, KEY EPA AND STATE DECISIONS, *supra* note 59, at 9, fig. 2.

63. *Id.* at 8.

64. *Id.* at 28, 31, 45.

65. *Id.* at 7, fig. 7; *id.* at 43, 44.

66. *Id.*

67. *Id.*

68. *See* Chapter 2, at 11-34 (state efforts in the 1960s and 1970s); Chapter 5, at 133-34 (state efforts today).

69. Water quality-based management begins with the designation of a water "use," which determines water quality "standards," which determine, in turn, the amounts of pollution permissible. *See* 33 U.S.C. §1313(c)(2)(A), ELR STAT. FWPCA §303(c)(2)(A) (describing state designation of water uses); Mississippi Comm'n on Natural Resources v. Costle, 625 F.2d 1269, 10 ELR 20931 (5th Cir. 1980) (affirming broad state discretion in setting use-based standards).

70. *See* Donald W. Stever, *Waste Load Allocation, in* 2 LAW OF ENVIRONMENTAL PROTECTION 12-13 to 12-14 (Sheldon M. Novick et al. eds., 1998) ("the political difficulties interest in such a scheme are obvious. Given a choice between a sometimes intolerable burden on existing dischargers or saying 'no' to a new industry and its local economic benefits, the state agencies would be pressured to go along with a third alternative: reclassifying the stream segment to downgrade it.").

71. *See* Chapter 2, at 11-34. By imposing national technology standards, the CWA limited state authority to the application of these standards in state-delegated programs and to the imposition of additional water quality-based limits where necessary.

72. *Id.*

73. *Special Report, The Clean Water Act Amendments of 1987,* Daily Env't Rep. (BNA), Sept. 4, 1987, at 4 (quoting EPA Assessment Administrator for Water, Rebecca Hanmer).

74. Susan Bruninga, *TMDL Rule to Be Delayed Until April 2003; More Time Allowed for Impaired Waters Lists,* 32 Env't Rep. (BNA) 2065, Oct. 26, 2001.

75. *See* WATER SCIENCE AND TECHNOLOGY BOARD, NATIONAL RESEARCH COUNCIL, NATIONAL ACADEMY OF SCIENCE, SURVEY DATA, ASSESSING THE SCIENTIFIC BASIS OF THE TOTAL MAXIMUM DAILY LOAD APPROACH TO WATER POLLUTION

REDUCTION (undated) (on file with author) (identifying task as focused on "(1) what information is needed to determine TMDLs for impaired waters, (2) the sufficiency of knowledge about point and nonpoint sources of pollution, (3) the state of monitoring and modeling to assess and predict pollutant loads, and (4) the effectiveness of management approaches in controlling nonpoint source pollution").

76. Indeed, the NAS Staff Director of the study called the deadline "ungodly." Craig Pittman, *Was Panel on Water Cleanup Biased?*, ST. PETERSBURG TIMES, Sept. 3, 2001, at 1A.

77. NRC, ASSESSING THE TMDL APPROACH TO WATER QUALITY MANAGEMENT 3, 4, (June, 2001) [hereinafter NRC REPORT]. In subsequent testimony before Congress, the report panel chair, Dr. Kenneth Reckhow, summarized the report as finding that "we have the scientific capacity to identify the nation's polluted water and develop plans for their cleanup." National Association of Flood and Stormwater Management Agencies, *TMDL Hearing on Science Report: NRC Witnesses Stress That Science Exists to Identify Polluted Waters and Plan for Cleanup, But Improvements to TMDL Program Needed, at* www.nafsma.org/tmdlsciencereport.htm (last visited Feb. 13, 2002).

78. NRC REPORT, *supra* note 77, at 3.

79. Susan Bruninga, *Water Quality Standards: Agency TMDL Proposal Costly, Technical, Unenforceable, Senate Chairman Tells Group,* 31 Env't Rep. (BNA) n.p. (Mar. 3, 2000) (comments of Sen. Robert Smith of New Hampshire).

80. *See Pittman, supra* note 76 ("Whitman had the perfect excuse for postponing them [the TMDL rules]: The program had been criticized in a recent report by a panel from the prestigious National Academy of Sciences.").

81. NRC REPORT, *supra* note 77, at 81 (identifying "extremely large data requirements"), 82 (finding nonpoint source data "much less available and reliable" and "data generally unavailable" for the evaluation of the efficacy of nonpoint management controls).

82. *Id.* at 5.

83. *Id.* at 32-38.

84. For a discussion of the use of biological criteria, see Houck, *The Regulation of Toxic Pollutants Under the Clean Water Act, supra* note 53, at 10558-59. *See also* NRC REPORT, *supra* note 77, at 44-49.

85. NRC REPORT, *supra* note 77, at 33-38.

86. *Id.* at 41. How these two measuring sticks are applied together is an important question. If, for example, biological surveys are used to override chemical monitoring showing pollution, they will simply create one more loophole in the program. For this reason, the state of Ohio, a leader in biological assessment of water quality, only allows these assessments to upgrade control requirements, not both to lower them. See E-mail correspondence with Elaine Marsh, Project Director, Ohio Greenways (Jan. 17, 2002). Unfortunately, the Ohio program is "being systemati-

cally dismembered by budget cuts." E-mail correspondence with Michael Utt, President, Ohio Smallmouth Alliance (Jan. 15, 2000).

87. NRC REPORT, *supra* note 77, at 53-55. This approach is modeled after that proposed in Florida. *Id.*

88. NRC REPORT, *supra* note 77, at 53.

89. *Id.* at 58. *See also infra* section entitled Listings.

90. The report recommends, in this regard, that if a water body is not removed from the preliminary list at the end of a listing cycle, perhaps five years, it would automatically be placed on the TMDL list, a "hammer" provision seen in RCRA and other programs to action-force a decision. NRC REPORT, *supra* note 77, at 56. As a practical matter, whether such a redesignation could resist legal challenges on the basis of insufficient data, once the state had raised the data bar, is at least problematical. Also problematical, of course, is whether the states and EPA would ever accept such a regulatory hammer.

91. The report starts beating the drum for use-based management at the very beginning and continues the call throughout the report. Indeed, its first recommendation is that "the TMDL Program should focus first and foremost on improving the condition of waterbodies as measured by attainment of designated uses." *Id.* at 3. On page 6, it provides a flow chart that inserts a "Review Use/Standard" to the §303(d) process between listing and the development of TMDLs; such review is not contained in the statute or in EPA regulations or guidelines. On page 90, the report is still arguing that before a waterbody is listed, the state conduct a review of "the appropriateness of the water quality standard." *Id.* at 90. In short, in the mind-set of the report's authors, TMDLs are a drastic measure of last resort.

92. *Id.* at 49 (emphasis in the original).

93. *Id.* at 93.

94. *Id.* at 101.

95. *Id.*

96. *Id.*

97. *See* Pittman, *supra* note 76. The author of this instant Article has served on two NAS panels and has found this observation to be correct.

98. *See supra* note 76 and accompanying text.

99. *Id.* The committee's activism even brought it into conflict with congressional staff. *See* Susan Bruninga, *Scientists, Hill Staff Differ Over Charge of Science Panel Examining TMDL Program,* Envt Rep. (BNA) n p (Jan. 26, 2001).

100. *Id.*

101. Dr. Leonard Shabman, a professor of research and environmental emissions who was working with the NRC at the time, is credited as "having played a key role in drafting the text and developing the regulations." Pittman, *supra* note 76.

102. Kurt Stephenson & Leonard Shabman, *The Trouble Water Implementing TMDLs: A New Federal Rule Would Hurt Free Market Efforts to Protect Waterways*, REG., Spring 2001, at 28.

103. The report's concluding chapter is entitled "TMDL Implementation Challenges." NRC REPORT, *supra* note 77, at 97.

104. Stephenson & Shabman, *supra* note 102, at 29.

105. *Id.*

106. *Id.* at 32.

107. NRC REPORT, *supra* note 77, at 101.

108. The goal of the CWA, adopted in 1972 and maintained against heavy fire from states and industry, is "to restore and maintain the chemical, physical and biological integrity of the nation's waters." 33 U.S.C. §1251(a), ELR STAT. FWPCA §101(a). In order to achieve this end, "it is the national goal that the discharge of pollutants in the navigable waters be eliminated by 1985." *Id.* §1251(a)(1), ELR STAT. FWPCA §101(a)(1).

109. *See* U.S. EPA, THE NATIONAL COSTS OF THE TOTAL MAXIMUM DAILY LOAD PROGRAM (DRAFT REPORT) 1 (2001) (available from the ELR Document Service, ELR Order No. AD-4655) [hereinafter EPA COSTS REPORT]. The directive came as a "request" in the Conference Report on the VA/HUD and Independent Agencies Appropriations Act for FY 2001. *Id.*

110. *Id.* at 2. EPA's previous estimates of TMDL costs were widely criticized as incomplete and low-end. *See* U.S. GAO, CLEAN WATER ACT: PROPOSED REVISIONS TO EPA REGULATIONS TO CLEAN UP POLLUTED WATERS (2000). *See also* Copeland, *supra* note 30 (noting state criticisms of cost estimates).

111. EPA COSTS REPORT, *supra* note 109, at 2.

112. U.S. EPA, Notice of Availability of Draft Report on Costs Associated With the Total Maximum Daily Load Program and Request for Costs, 66 Fed. Reg. 41876 (Aug. 9, 2001).

113. EPA COSTS REPORT, *supra* note 109, at i, 12.

114. *Id.*

115. *Id.*

116. *Id.* at 16.

117. *Id.* at 12.

118. *Id.*

119. *Id.* at 13, tbl. IV-1.

120. *Id.*

121. *Id.* at ii, 15-21. The average costs per TMDL per pollutant was estimated at 28,000, with a typical range of $6,000 to $154,000. On a water body as opposed to

an individual pollutant basis, the costs were estimated at $52,000, with a range of $26,000 to $500,000. Complex TMDLs, characterized as "outliers," were estimated at up to $1 million.

122. *Id.* at iii.

123. *Id.* at 28-31.

124. *Id.* at 28, 29.

125. *Id.* at 29.

126. *Id.* at 30, 31.

127. *Id.* at 35, tbl. VI-1.

128. *Id.*

129. Susan Bruninga, *Water Pollution Costs of Implementing TMDL Regulation Underestimated in EPA Report, Groups Say,* Daily Env't Rep. (BNA), Dec. 14, 2001, at A-1.

130. *Id.*

131. *Id.*

132. *Id.* The comments were submitted by the Mercatus Center for Regulatory Studies at George Mason University. *Id.*

133. Susan Bruninga, *Agency Seeks Public Comment on Costs of Implementing Rule on Impaired Waters,* 32 Env't Rep. (BNA) n.p. (Aug. 10, 2001) (quoting Rick Parish of the Southern Environmental Law Center).

134. *See* Kenneth H. Reckhow, *Cuts in USGS Budget Undermine Sound Water Science, cited in* e-mail from river info-administrative river network.org (May 2, 2001).

135. OFFICE OF THE INSPECTOR GENERAL (OIG), EPA STATE ENFORCEMENT OF CLEAN WATER ACT DISCHARGERS CAN BE MORE EFFECTIVE 8 (2001) [hereinafter OIG REPORT].

136. A representative list of the more recent reports on enforcement include: U.S. GAO, ENVIRONMENTAL ENFORCEMENT: EPA CANNOT ENSURE THE RECOVERY OF SELF-REPORTED COMPLIANCE MONETARY DATA (1993); OFFICE OF ENFORCEMENT AND COMPLIANCE ASSURANCE, U.S. EPA, THE STATE OF FEDERAL FACILITIES (2000) (EPA 300 R-00-00); U.S. GAO, WATER POLLUTION: DIFFERENCES AMONG THE STATES IN ISSUING PERMITS LIMITING THE DISCHARGE OF POLLUTANTS (1996) (GAO/RCED-96-42); U.S. GAO, WATER POLLUTION: MANY VIOLATIONS HAVE NOT RECEIVED APPROPRIATE ENFORCEMENT ATTENTION 23 (1996) (GAO/RCED-96-23); Clifford Rechtschaffen, *Deterrence vs. Cooperation and the Evolving Theory of Environmental Enforcement,* 71 S. CAL. L. REV. 1181 (1998); John H. Cushman, *EPA and States Found to Be Lax on Pollution Law: Enforcement Is Faulted: Agencies Are Failing to Inspect, Issue Permits and Report Violations, Audit Says,* N.Y. TIMES, June 7, 1998, at 1.

137. David L. Markell, *The Role of Deterrence-Based Enforcement in a "Reinvented" State/Reduced Relationship: The Divide Between Theory and Reality,* 24 HARV. ENVTL. L. REV. 1, 55 (2000).

138. CAPLAN, *supra* note 50, at 5.

139. State agencies issue more than 90% of all CWA permits and conduct over 75% of CWA enforcement. OIG REPORT, *supra* note 135, at 6. *See also* R. Steven Brown, *The States Protect the Environment,* ECOSTATES MAG. (Summer 1999), *available at* http://www.sso.org/ecos/publications/statesarticle.htm ("A remarkable, and largely unnoticed, change in environmental protection has occurred over the past five to 10 years. The states have become the primary environmental protection agencies across the country."). Mr. Brown is Director of Research for the Environmental Council of the States.

140. *See Markell, supra* note 137; ENVIRONMENTAL LAW INST., REPORT OF THE COLLOQUIUM ON FEDERAL-STATE RELATIONS IN ENVIRONMENTAL ENFORCEMENT (1992); David R. Hodas, *Enforcement of Environmental Law in a Triangular Federal System: Can Three Not Be a Crowd When Enforcement Authority Is Shared by the United States, the States, and Their Citizens?,* 54 MD. L. REV. *1552* (1995).

141. *See* Clifford Rechtschaffen, *Competing Visions: EPA and the States Battle for the Future of Environmental Enforcement,* 30 ELR 10803 (Oct. 2002). Professor Rechtschaffen concludes: "Our experience to date . . . suggests that it would be ill-advised to make a wholesale shift away from deterrence-based practices." *Id.* at 10828.

142. 120 S. Ct. 693, 30 ELR 20246 (2000).

143. See the discussion of nonenforcement against Bethlehem Steel and Smithfield Farms in Steinzor, *supra* note 51, and Dereck Yeo & Roy A. Hogland, United States v. Smithfield: *A Paradigmatic Example of Lax Enforcement of the Clean Water Act by the Commonwealth of Virginia,* 23 WM. & MARY ENVTL. L. & POL'Y REV. *513* (1999). The same record of nonenforcement is found against the Exxon Mobil refineries in OMB Watch, *States Slack Off on Environmental Enforcement,* at http://www.ombwatch.org/execreport/enforcement.html (last visited Feb. 22, 2002). For a report of similar underperformance in Michigan, see Michigan Environmental Council, *Protect Our Children's Health,* at http://www.mecprotects. org/HEALTH.html (last visited Feb. 22, 2002).

144. *See* Robert Anderson, *Rollins Told to Close Site,* MINING ADVOC. (Baton Rouge), Aug. 7, 1985, at A1 (loss of controls at plant led to shutdown order); Bill Grady, *Former DEQ Chief Is Still in the Fight,* TIMES PICAYNE, June 1, 1992, at B-1.

145. A survey of Massachusetts environment enforcement officers reported that managers had "inappropriately intervened in a criminal investigation" and that nearly one-third "fear retaliation from [chain of command] for advocating strong environmental enforcement." Press Release, Public Employees for Environmental

Responsibilities, Environmental Cops Cannot Enforce the Law (Apr. 11, 2001), *cited in* CAPLAN, *supra* note 50, at 8.

146. OIG REPORT, *supra* note 135.

147. *Id.* at 8.

148. *Id.* at i-iii, 5-16, 36-42.

149. *Id.* at iii, 20-34, 43-50.

150. *Id.* at i, 5-13.

151. *Id.* at 17.

152. *Id.* at 43.

153. According to a study released in January 2002 by a Wisconsin environmental organization, the state lost between $14 and $248 million in 1998 by failing to prosecute water pollution law violations. Among the findings:

> • From 1990 to 1998, on average, the Department of Natural Resources (DNR) sent notices of violation to only 10% of all municipal and industrial facilities that were in significant noncompliance with their Wisconsin pollutant discharge elimination system (WPDES) permits.
> • During that same time period, the DNR only referred to the U.S. Department of Justice for prosecution 2.5% of all industrial and municipal facilities that were in significant noncompliance with their WPDES permits.
> • In 1999, the DNR failed to inspect 53% of all major industrial facilities with WPDES permits.
> • In 2000, only four industrial and municipal facilities were prosecuted for water pollution violations. Of these four, they paid only $212,217 dollars to the state in penalties.

Press Release, Midwest Environmental Advocates, Millions in State Revenues Lost Due to Lack of Enforcement of Water Laws (Jan. 28, 2002).

154. OIG REPORT, *supra* note 135, at 6-8. *See also* Chapter 4, at 88-94 (describing CAFO and municipal runoff programs).

155. OIG REPORT, *supra* note 135, at 20 ("The question, variety and complexity of the regulated community ha[d] greatly outstripped the system's capabilities. Dischargers not monitored by the [EPA compliance system] include: stormwater, [CAFOs], and sewer overflows."). Focused on the reporting and paperwork requirements for major dischargers, states tend to let the smaller discharges—which are precisely those at issue in nonpoint source positions—go unattended, even where they are purportedly regulated under the NPDES program. See the following notices of intent to file citizen suits of the Tulane Environmental Law Clinic:

> *Notice of Environmental Action Network re: General Animal Hospital, Inc.* (failure to operate and maintain pollution control equipment, and

to maintain effluent limitations) (Jan. 29, 2002).

Notice of Louisiana Environmental Action Network re: Bank One—Covington Banking Center (failure to operate and maintain pollution control equipment, and to maintain effluent limitations) (Jan. 29, 2002).

Notice of Louisiana Environmental Action Network re: Beau Amis Lounge, Inc. (failure to operate and maintain pollution control equipment and to maintain effluent limitations) (Jan. 29, 2002).

Notice of Louisiana Environmental Action Network re: Zelden Physical Therapy (failure to operate and maintain pollution control equipment and to file discharge monitoring reports to ensure compliance) (Jan. 25, 2002).

Notice of Louisiana Environmental Action Network re: Trinity Baptist Church (failure to operate and maintain pollution control equipment and to file discharge monitoring reports to ensure compliance) (Jan. 25, 2002).

Notice of Louisiana Environmental Action Network re: Gloria Coker, M.S. (failure to operate and maintain pollution control equipment and to file discharge monitoring reports to ensure compliance) (Jan. 23, 2002).

Notice of Louisiana Environmental Action Network re: Garrity, Sanders, Reed & Caire (failure to operate and maintain pollution control equipment and to file discharge monitoring reports to ensure compliance) (Jan. 23, 2002).

Notice of Louisiana Environmental Action Network re: Holton Enterprises of Covington, Inc. (failure to operate and maintain pollution control equipment and to file discharge monitoring reports to ensure compliance) (Dec. 6, 2001).

Notice of Louisiana Action Network re: Northlake Moving and Storage, Inc. (failure to operate and maintain pollution control equipment and to file discharge monitoring reports to ensure compliance) (Dec. 6, 2001).

Notice of Louisiana Environmental Action Network re: Plaza Professional Center, Inc. (failure to operate and maintain pollution control equipment and to file discharge monitoring reports to ensure compliance) (Dec. 6, 2001).

156. *See* Weyerhauser Co. v. Costle, 590 F.2d 1011, 9 ELR 20284 (D.C. Cir. 1978) (describing the ineffectiveness of water quality enforcement prior to the 1972 CWA Amendments).

157. 33 U.S.C. §1365, ELR Stat. FWPCA §505 (citizen suits). For the effectiveness of CWA citizen suits, see Hodas, *supra* note 140, at 1617-55; Jeffrey G. Miller, Citizen Suits: Private Enforcement of Federal Pollution Control Laws (1987).

158. *See* Chapter 3, at 55-56.

159. U.S. EPA, Delay of Effective Date of Revisions to the Water Quality Planning and Management Regulation, Notice of Proposed Rulemaking, 66 Fed. Reg. at 41877. The decision was made final in October. U.S. EPA, Effective Date of Revisions to the Water Quality Planning and Management Regulation, 66 Fed. Reg. 53044 (Oct. 18, 2001).

160. *See* Caplan, *supra* note 50, at 10, 11.

161. *Id.*

162. *Id.* at 12. The final rule defines "reasonable assurance" as "management means or other control actions (regulatory or voluntary)" that (1) apply specifically to the impaired water body, (2) will be accomplished through "reliable and effective" mechanisms, (3) will be implemented "as expeditiously as practicable," and (4) will be supported by "adequate funding." *Id.*

163. *See* comments of the Earthjustice Legal Defense Fund representative on the proposed TMDL deadlines, *Water Quality Standards: Agency's Draft Final Regulation, supra* note 26.

164. *See Copeland, supra* note 30, at 9-10.

165. *Id.*

166. Press Release, U.S. EPA, Public Meetings on the TMDL Program and Related Areas of the NPDES Program (undated), *available at* http://www.epa.gov/owow/tmdl/meetings/ (last visited Oct. 25, 2001).

167. The listening sessions took place in five cities, each with an ostensibly different theme: Chicago (nonpoint sources); Sacramento (TMDL content); Atlanta (EPA role, permitting); Oklahoma (listing); Washington, D.C. (all issues). Press Release, U.S. EPA, Meeting Dates, Times, Locations, and Meeting Themes (undated), *available* at http://www.epa.gov.owow/tmdl/meetings.html (last visited Oct. 25, 2001). In fact, the meetings were open to all comments and produced the same range of complaints heard since the days of the FACA. *See* Susan Bruninga, *Water Pollution: EPA Listening Sessions on TMDLs Covers Debate on Implementation, More Information,* 32 Env't Rep. (BNA) n.p. (Dec. 12, 2001).

168. Bruninga, *Water Pollution: EPA Listening Sessions, supra* note 167 (e.g., comments of Plum Creek Timber Company representative, "there are many ways to solve water quality problems, and the federal government should steer away

from an approach that is too prescriptive and inflexible"; discussion of deferring TMDLs until other nonpoint programs "have had the time to work").

169. Susan Bruninga, *Water Quality Standards: Monitoring Guidance Draws Support From Interested Parties; Categories Backed,* 32 Env't Rep. (BNA) 2309-10 (Nov. 30, 2001).

170. *Id. See also* Susan Bruninga, *Water Quality Standards: Draft Guidance on Integrating State Reports Defines Five Categories of Attainment States,* 32 Env't Rep. (BNA) 2062-63 (Oct. 26, 2001). The five categories are for waters:

> 1. attaining all water quality standards and no standards are threatened;
> 2. attaining some water quality standards, no standards are threatened, and insufficient data are available to determine if the remaining standards are met or threatened;
> 3. for which insufficient data are available to determine of water quality standards are met;
> 4. impaired or threatened for one or more water quality standards but not needing a [TMDL]; and
> 5. impaired or threatened for one or more water quality standards and a TMDL is needed.

Id. Only the last category requires a TMDL.

171. *Id.* ("This allows us to focus on waters that we really know are impaired, the industry official said.").

172. *Id.* ("This is the next step in a pattern developed by EPA of allowing, or encouraging, states to remove from the list waters requiring a TMDL, she said," quoting an attorney for Earthjustice.).

173. *See* Susan Bruninga, *EPA Draft Plan to Assist Streamlining in State Monitoring Program Expected Soon,* 32 Env't Rep. (BNA) 693 (Apr. 13, 2001). CALM elements include:

> • guidance or attainment and nonattainment of water quality standards;
> • comprehensive monitoring coverage;
> • presentation of data;
> • elements of an increasingly comprehensive state monitoring system;
> • causes and sources of impairment; and
> • sections of "discrete types" of pollutants such as pathogens, nutrients, sediments, and fish advisories.

Id. The director of Science and Technology in EPA's Office of Water is quoted as stating that these elements are "hugely underfunded." *Id.*

174. *See id. See also* Susan Bruninga, *Guidance to Integrate Water Act Reports Should Be Delayed, State Officials Tell EPA,* 32 Env't Rep. (BNA) 2116-17 (Nov. 2, 2001).

175. *See* Bruninga, *EPA Draft Plan, supra* note 173.

176. *Id.* Over the years, dealing with the Association of State and Interstate Water Pollution Control Administrators must appear to EPA like dealing with the teachers union in a problem-ridden public school system; at some point they become part of the problem. *See* Chapter 2, at 31-33.

177. U.S. EPA, Supplemental Guidelines for the Award of Section 319 Nonpoint Source Grants to States and Territories in FY 2002 and Subsequent Years, 66 Fed. Reg. 47653 (Sept. 13, 2001), *available at* http://www.epa.gov/owow/nps/cwact.html.

178. *Id.* at 47653.

179. *Id.* The "analytical link" language and role for TMDLs is identical to that of the Clinton Administration's Clean Water Action Plan. *See* Chapter 4, at 85-86.

180. 66 Fed. Reg. at 47654.

181. *Id.*

182. More specifically the new §319 TMDL guidance requires:

> a. An identification of the sources or groups of similar sources that will need to be controlled to achieve the load reductions established in the NPS [nonpoint source] TMDL (and to achieve any other watershed goals identified in the watershed-based plan);
> b. A description of the NPS management measures that will need to be implemented to achieve the load reductions established in the NPS TMDL (as well as to achieve other watershed goals identified in the watershed-based plan); an estimate of the load reductions expected to these management measures (recognizing the natural variability and the difficulty in precisely predicting the performance of management measures over time); and an identification of the critical areas in which those measures will need to be implemented to achieve the NPS TMDL;
> c. An estimate of the sources of technical and financial assistance needed, and/or authorities that will be relied upon, to implement the plan. As sources of funding, States should consider the use of their [§]319 programs, State Revolving Funds, USDA's Environmental Quality Incentives Program and Conservation Reserve Program, and other relevant Federal, State, local, and private funds that may be available to assist in implementing the plan;
> d. An information/education component that will be used to enhance public understanding of the project and encourage their participation in selecting, designing, and implementing the NPS management measures;
> e. A schedule for implementing the NPS management measures identi-

fied in the plan that is reasonably expeditious;

f. A description of interim, measurable milestones (e.g., amount of load reductions, or improvement in biological or habitat parameters), for determining whether NPS management measures or other control actions are being implemented;

g. A set of criteria that can be used to determine whether substantial progress is being made towards attaining water quality standards and, if not, the criteria for determining whether the NPS TMDL needs to be revised; and

h. A monitoring component to evaluate the effectiveness of the implementation efforts, measured against the criteria established under item (g) immediately above.

Id.

183. *See supra* section entitled July 2000 Rule. They are also, jot-for-jot, the requirements of 1997 EPA guidance entitled *New Policies for Establishing and Implementing Total Maximum Daily Loads (TMDLs)* (1997) (available from the ELR Document Service, ELR Order No. AD-3467). *See* Chapter 4, at 77-82.

184. *See Farm Groups Seek Major Revisions to Recent Water Grants Guidance,* INSIDE EPA, Oct. 26, 2001, at 20.

185. *Id.*

186. *See* Susan Bruninga, *Water Quality Standards, Draft Policy Statement Being Crafted by EPA on Market-Based Approaches,* 32 Env't Rep. (BNA) 2351 (Dec. 7, 2001).

187. U.S. EPA, Effluent Trading in Watersheds Policy Statement, 61 Fed. Reg. 4994 (Feb. 9, 1996).

188. U.S. EPA, Draft Framework for Watershed-Based Trading, 61 Fed. Reg. 29563 (June 11, 1996).

189. *Id.*

190. *Id.*

191. *See* Bruninga, *Water Quality Standards, Draft Policy Statement, supra* note 186, at 2352.

192. *See* 61 Fed. Reg. at 4994 (presenting advantages of trading programs).

193. "For instance, requiring point sources to obtain [NPDES] permit modification and requiring point source requirements to be incorporated into NPDES permits is not generally conducive to implementing market-based strategies." *See* Bruninga, *Water Quality Standards, Draft Policy Statement, supra* note 186 (quoting EPA Associate Administrator for Water). On the contrary, the case could be made that such permit requirements are indispensable to market-based strategies; without them, there is neither obligation nor accountability.

194. The Clinton Administration policy statement was clear on this point but, as with any policy, it is subject to change. *See EPA Eyes Replacing Facility Water Permits With Watershed Approach*, INSIDE EPA, Feb. 8, 2002.

195. *See* ROGERS, *supra* note 3, at 221-23; *see also* Citizens Against the Refinery's Effects v. EPA, 643 F. 2d 183, 11 ELR 20176 (4th Cir. 1981) (manipulation of air emission offsets); Bethlehem Steel Corp. v. EPA, 782 F.2d 645, 16 ELR 20268 (7th Cir. 1986) (same).

196. For a discussion of these difficulties in the CAA state implementation plan (SIP) program, see Robert W. Adler, *Integrated Approaches to Water Pollution: Lessons From the Clean Air Act*, 23 HARV. ENVTL. L. REV. 203, 243-45, 282. ("Critics charge that states produce 'cheater SIPs' that the state never intends to implement, and that emission inventories base attainment or maintenance predictions on unrealistically optimistic assumptions, questionable baselines, paper offsets or emission reductions that never materialize.") *Id.* at 245, citations omitted. The process is known as "gaming," described by a former EPA Administrator as "reaching the same high art of gamesmanship as lawyering." *Id.* (citing David Schoenbrod, *Goals or Rules Statutes, the Case of the Clean Air Act*, 32 UCLA L. REV. 740, 773 (1983).

197. *See* Adler, *supra* note 196, and Schoenbrod, *supra* note 196. *See also William F. Pedersen Jr.,* The Limits of Market-Based Approaches to Environmental Protection, 24 ELR 10173 (Apr. 1994).

198. *See* Joint Motion for Voluntary Remand, Louisiana Envtl. Action Network v. EPA, No. 99-60570 (5th Cir. Oct. 9, 2002). (Louisiana Department of Environmental Quality failed to assess validity of emission reductions credits).

199. *See DOJ Audit of New Jersey Trading Plan May Be Sign of CAA Violation*, INSIDE EPA, Jan. 18, 2002, at 14.

200. 33 U.S.C. §1344, ELR STAT. FWPCA §404.

201. *See* WILLIAM L. WANT, THE LAW OF WETLAND REGULATION §6.10 (1990).

202. *See* NRC, COMPENSATORY FOR WETLAND LOSSES UNDER THE CLEAN WATER ACT (2001) (severely criticizing administration and performance of mitigation under §404); *see also* U.S. GAO, WETLANDS PROTECTION: ASSESSMENTS NEEDED TO DETERMINE EFFECTIVENESS OF IN LIEU FEE MITIGATION (2001); J.B. Ruhl & R. Juge Gregg, *Integrating Ecosystem Services Into Environmental Law: A Case Study of Wetlands Mitigation Banking*, 20 STAN. ENVTL. L.J. *365 (2001); see* U.S. Army Corps of Engineers, Regulatory Guidance Letter, Guidance for the Establishment and Maintenance of Compensatory Mitigation Projects Under the Corps Regulatory Program Pursuant to Section 404(a) of the Clean Water Act and Section 10 of the Rivers and Harbors Act of 1999 (2001).

203. *See* Oliver A. Houck, *More Net Loss of Wetlands: The Army-EPA Agreement for Mitigation*, 20 ELR 10212 (June 1990). *See also* Endangered Species Coalition, GREENLines (Feb. 15, 2002) (citing a study by the Washington Department of Ecology concluding that "only about 13% of the man-made wetlands in Washington are fully successful").

204. *See* Bruninga, *Water Quality Standards, Draft Policy Statement, supra* note 186, at 2352.

205. *Id.*

206. 42 U.S.C. §9607(a)(4)(C), ELR Stat. CERCLA §107(a)(4)(C); *see also* 43 C.F.R. 11 (National Resource Damage Assessments). Ohio v. Department of the Interior, 800 F.2d 432, 19 ELR 21099 (D.C. Cir. 1989) (invalidating the U.S. Department of the Interior's original rule).

207. 33 U.S.C. §2706, ELR Stat. OPA §1006; *see also* 15 C.F.R. §990 (National Resource Damage Assessments); General Elec. Co. v. U.S. Department of Commerce, 128 F.3d 767, 28 ELR 20263 (D.C. Cir. 1997) (invalidating, in part, National Oceanic and Atmospheric Administration (NOAA) original rule).

208. *See* Bruninga, *Water Quality Standards, Draft Policy Statement, supra* note 186 (quoting EPA Assistant Administrator for Water's interest in the question of "natural capital and its benefits").

209. *See* Douglas R. Williams, *Valuing Natural Environments: Compensation, Market Norms, and the Ideal of Public Goods*, 27 Conn. L. Rev. 365 (1997).

210. *See* Robert W. Adler et al., The Clean Water Act 20 Years Later 118-28 (NRC 1993); *see also* Houck, *The Regulation of Toxic Pollutants, supra* note 53, at 10544-54.

211. *See* Houck, *The Regulation of Toxic Pollutants, supra* note 53, at 10549-54 (describing wide discrepancies in state water quality standards for dioxin). *See also* Zygmunt J.B. Plater et al., Environmental Law and Policy: Nature, Law, and Society 538-540 (2d ed. 1998) (describing differences in 775 times between New York and Pennsylvania emission limitations, also describing "play" in state management systems and "race of laxity" to lower standards); U.S. GAO, Differences Among the States in Issuing Permits Limiting the Discharge of Pollutants (1996).

212. Two key safeguards of the water quality program are restrictions on antidegradation (lowering existing water quality within a given use), 40 C.F.R. §131.12, and downgrading (lowering the use), 40 C.F.R. §131.10. Both restrictions contain escape hatches, however, where maintaining existing water quality and use would have significant economic and social impact. *Id.* §§131.12(a)(2), 131.10(g)(6). Needless to say, a state unwilling to maintain high water quality could drive a truck through these loopholes without scraping the fenders. The fact that unwilling states have not done so in a widespread fashion to date reflects more their failure to apply water quality standards at all than their resolve to hold the line. With the advent of TMDLs, these restrictions and loopholes will be put to the test.

213. *See* U.S. EPA, Advanced Notice of Proposed Rulemaking Water Quality Standards Regulation, 63 Fed. Reg. 36742 (July 7, 1998).

214. According to EPA's Office of Science and Technology within the water program, a new draft strategy would be developed in "early 2001 (sic)." Press Release, U.S. EPA, Strategy for Water Quality Standards and Guidance (Dec. 2001).

215. Telephone conversation of Andrew L. Adams with Fred Leutner, Chief, Office of Water, U.S. EPA (Jan. 19, 2002).

216. *See Upcoming EPA Water Use Guidance Sets Stage for Activist Fight,* INSIDE EPA, Feb. 8, 2002, at 3 ("EPA is preparing a new guidance for streamlining the process states use to downgrade water bodies' 'designated uses,' raising fears among environmentalists that the new process will significantly increase pollution discharges.").

217. *See supra* notes 91-93 and accompanying text. *See also Nonpoint Sources Need to Be Included in TMDL Program, Treatment Officials Say, supra* note 36 (citing Association of Municipal Sewer Authorities white paper "calling on states to review and revise as needed their designated uses and water quality criteria"); one can be sure that the Association of Municipal Sewer Authorities does not have upwards revisions in mind.

218. *See* Comments of Jacqueline Savitz, Coast Alliance et al., to Fred Leutner, Chief, Water Quality Standards Branch, Answers to Questions on Strategies for the Water Quality Standards Program (Sept. 18, 2001). *See also* Ohio Valley Envtl. Coalition v. EPA, No. 7:020059 (S.D. W. Va. Jan. 23, 2002) (citizen suit challenging alleged state weakening of antidegradation standards); Chapter 5, at 140-42.

219. *See* Chapter 5, at 151. *See also* U.S. Geological Serv., *National Water Quality Assessment Program, Nutrients in the Nation's Water Too Much of a Good Thing?,* at http://water.usgs.gov/nawqa/circ-1136/h8.html (last visited Feb. 21, 2002); Larry J. Puckett, U.S. Geological Serv., *National Water Quality Assessment Program, Nonpoint and Point Sources of Nitrogen in Major Watersheds of the United States,* at http://water.usgs.gov/nawqa/wri94-4001/wri94-4001main.html (last visited Feb. 21, 2002).

220. *See* Susan Bruninga, *Some Flexibility Afforded to States in Agency Guidance on Nutrient Criteria,* 32 Env't Rep. (BNA) 2252 (Nov. 23, 2001); U.S. EPA, Background Paper No. 4: Science and Technology, FACA Committee Meeting (Nov. 19-21, 1996).

221. *See* Chapter 5, at 144 (quoting Iowa Corn Growers Association President as saying: "It doesn't jive. Two and two is not adding up to four. Agriculture is being hung with the blame and we don't think it can be substantiated."). *See* Mark Schleifstein, *Panel Splits on River Dead Zone Goal,* TIMES PICAYUNE, June 16, 2000, at A-3 (quoting the Iowa Secretary of Agriculture as stating "before she could even consider [cleanup] goals, she will have to be shown direct benefits from the reduction of fertilizers to Iowa residents"); *Agriculture Department May Withhold Support of Gulf Hypoxia Study,* INSIDE EPA, Dec. 24, 1999, at 7 ("the [USDA] is threatening to withhold its approval of an interagency assessment of the cause of low water oxygen levels, or hypoxia, in the Gulf of Mexico unless other federal agencies delete language from the study"); the offending language was that suggesting a 20% cut in fertilizer use.

222. *See* Bruninga, *Some Flexibility, supra* note 220.

223. *Id.* The description of the nutrient standards program that follows is taken from this source. For a critique of the program, see Evan Hansen & Martin Christ, *EPA's Nutrient Criteria Recommendations and Their Application in Nutrient Eco Region XI* (May 20, 2001), at West Virginia Rivers Coalition, http://www.wvrivers.org (on file with author).

224. *See* Bruninga, *Some Flexibility, supra* note 220, at 2253.

225. U.S. EPA, EPA NONPOINT SOURCE POLLUTION FOCUS GROUPS FINAL REPORT (2001) (on file with author).

226. *Id.* at 2.

227. *Id.* at 3.

228. *Id.*

229. *Id.* at 4.

230. *Id.* at 1.

231. *Id.* at 7.

232. *Id.*

233. *Id.*

234. *Id.*

235. *See supra* section entitled Monitoring and Assessment Guidance.

236. *See* E-mail From Allene Levine, Marine Conservation Network, State Water Resources Declares TMDLs (Water Quality Control Pollution Programs) Highest Priority (Oct. 15, 2001); *see generally* Chapter 5, at 144 (describing positive initiatives in, inter alia, California, Missouri, and New York).

237. The Kansas Senate has recently enacted legislation requiring a cost-benefit analysis for designating state waters "primary contact recreation," and allowing downgrades to "secondary contract recreation" on the basis of denial of stream access by adjacent landowners. Communication with Charles M. Benjamin, Legislative Coordinator for Kansas Chapter of the Sierra Club, Lawrence, Kansas (Jan. 31, 2001); *see also* American Wildlands v. EPA, 260 F.2d 1192, 32 ELR 20860 (10th Cir. 2001) (approving Montana's exclusion of nonpoint sources from antidegradation review). Ohio Valley Envtl. Coalition v. Whitman, No. 3:02-0059 (S.D. W. Va. Jan. 23, 2002) (challenging West Virginia antidegradation program). *See generally* Chapter 5, at 144 (describing negative initiatives in other states). The state of Wyoming, for example, reduced its lists of over 400 impaired waters to 61, with 315 needing "further monitoring"; 275 of the 315 waters so delisted were impaired by nonpoint sources, primarily cattle. *See id.* at 138, 139. Of course, the relationship between the cattle industry and the deferred listings could be coincidental.

238. *See* EVAN HANSEN, TOTAL MAXIMUM DAILY LOADS IMPLEMENTATION IN WEST VIRGINIA: A STATUS REPORT 1 (Dec. 2001).

239. *See* Chapter 4, at 105-09, Appendix C, at 285-89.

240. Analysis of each TMDL for each factor is provided in Appendix C.

241. *See* HANSEN, *supra* note 238.

242. *Id.* at 2, 3.

243. *Id.* at 12.

244. *Id.* at 13.

245. *Id.* at 4. *See also* EPA Backs Innovative Virginia Program, *infra* note 344 ("The [Virginia] program will also target dischargers of nonpoint sources of pollution . . . in order to utilize state and federal grants for controlling contamination through best management practices."). The assumption is, for nonpoint source abatement, the government, i.e., the general public, pays. *See also infra* notes 251-53 and accompanying text.

246. Telephone conversation with Allison Wiedman, Chesapeake Bay Foundation (Feb. 18, 2002). Apparently, the 40% target is now being revised downwards. *Id.*

247. *See* MISSISSIPPI RIVER/GULF OF MEXICO WATERSHED NUTRIENT TASK FORCE, ACTION PLAN FOR REDUCING, MITIGATING, AND MANAGING HYPOXIA IN THE NORTHERN GULF OF MEXICO 21 (2001).

248. Telephone conversation with Wiedman, *supra* note 246 (Chesapeake Bay plan). The Gulf of Mexico "Action Plan" avoids even mentioning a "goal" of 30% reduction, stating instead that implementing strategies "should be aimed at" achieving this reduction, the goals for which begin with the following principle: "Encourage actions that are voluntary, practical and cost-effective." MISSISSIPPI RIVER/GULF OF MEXICO ACTION PLAN, *supra* note 247, at 21. In short, a plan it may be, but a plan of action it is not.

249. *See* Michael Grunwald, *Plan to Revive Everglades Brings Renewed Dispute: Environmentalists Say Draft Rules Offer No Gain*, WASH. POST, Dec. 29, 2001, at A-3. An attorney for the National Resources Defense Council is quoted as stating: "This is a joke . . . . They are basically saying let's keep doing everything the way it's been done in the past. That's what destroyed the Everglades in the first place." *Id.*

250. *See* Elizabeth Ann Rieke, *The Bay-Delta Accord: A Stride Toward Sustainability*, 67 U. COLO. L. REV. 341 (1996).

251. *See Landmark Nonpoint Rule Requires Wisconsin to Shoulder Most Costs*, INSIDE EPA, Jan. 18, 2002, at 1.

252. *See* Chapter 5, at 144.

253. *New York Farmers Paid to Shove Cows Off of City's Watershed*, N.Y. TIMES, Aug. 26, 1998, at B7.

254. Office of Water U.S. EPA, *TMDL Litigation by State, at* http://www.epa.gov/owow/tmdl/lawsuit1.html (last visited Nov. 5, 2001).

255. *See* Hihiwai Stream Restoration Coalition v. Whitman, No. 00-00477 (D. Haw. Sept. 5, 2001) (ordering EPA to comply with §303(d) and identify all of Hawaii's polluted streams and other water bodies); Save All Iowa Lakes, Oxbows,

Rivers & Streams v. EPA, No. C98-134 (D. Iowa Oct. 26, 2001) (consent decree requiring Iowa to complete TMDLs for 1998 lists within 10 years); Tennessee Envtl. Council v. EPA, No. 3-01-9932 (M.D. Tenn. May 10, 2001) (consent decree requiring Tennessee to set 7,890 TMDLs under a 10-year enforceable schedule).

256. *See* San Francisco Baykeeper v. Browner, 147 F. Supp. 2d 991 (M.D. Cal. 2001); Sierra Club v. EPA, 162 F. Supp. 2d 406 (D. Md. 2001); Hayes v. Whitman, 264 F.3d 969, 32 ELR 20043 (10th Cir. 2001). The constructive submission doctrine holds that EPA has an affirmative duty to treat a state's inaction with regard to prescribing TMDLs for impaired water bodies as an effective transfer of that authority to EPA. However, the doctrine is being narrowly defined so as to compel EPA action only when the state has done absolutely nothing regarding TMDL lists.

257. *San Francisco Baykeeper,* 147 F. Supp. at 1002.

258. 268 F.3d 91, 32 ELR 20203 (2d Cir. 2001).

259. *Id.* at 99, 32 ELR at 20207.

260. *See* In re Hannaford Bros. Co., No. WQ-01-01 (Vt. Water Resources Bd. June 29, 2001). *See also Water Permitting Dispute May Alter Rules Setting Discharge Limits,* INSIDE EPA, Mar. 2, 2001, at 18-19.

261. Sierra Club v. EPA, No. 01-145876gg (11th Cir. 2002) (oral argument set for Mar. 8, 2002).

262. Amigos Bravos v. Cook, No. 00-1615 (D.D.C. 2001) (before Judge Walton, no date set for oral argument).

263. Young v. Department of Envtl. Protection, No. 01-1462RP (Fla. Admin. Hearings 2002) (full history of the Administrative proceedings and the full text of documents can be accessed at http://www.cwn-se.org).

264. *See* Petition for Admin. Hearing, Young v. Department of Envtl. Protection, No. 01-1462RP (Fla. Admin. Hearings Apr. 13, 2001), at 150.

265. Identification of Impaired Surface Waters, 27 FLA. ADMIN. WKLY. 1395, at 62-303.300 et seq. (proposed Mar. 23, 2001).

266. The example of a flock of geese landing and dropping their waters is given. Thus, a water body with only 10 to 15 samples would require 3 positives, raising EPA's 10% from 20% to 30%, and requiring 100 samples before the 10% was statistically confirmed.

267. Telephone Interview with Jan Mandrup-Poulsen, Florida Department of Environmental Protection (Oct. 2001).

268. American Farm Bureau Fed'n v. Whitman, No. 00-1320 (D.D.C. July 18, 2000).

269. In October 2001, the lawsuit was suspended for 18 months at EPA's request so that it could consider potential revisions before issuing the final rule. *See Court Grants EPA Suspension of Lawsuit Over Impaired Waters Rule,* INSIDE EPA, Oct. 19, 2001, at 5-6.

270. John H. Stam, *Court-Ordered Deadlines for TMDLs Have Negative Consequences, ABA Told,* 32 Env't Rep. (BNA) 1589 (Aug. 10, 2001); *see also* Susan Bruninga, *Challenging TMDLs May Require Lawsuits, Alliances With Affected Parties, Lawyer Says,* 31 Env't Rep. (BNA) 1575-76 (July 28, 2000).

271. *See* Susan Bruninga, *Nonpoint Sources Should Not Be Excluded From TMDL Program, Government Argues,* 31 Env't Rep. (BNA) 547-48 (Mar. 24, 2000); *Suit Challenging EPA Authority to Set TMDLs for Nonpoint Sources Concerns Cities,* 30 Env't Rep. (BNA) 216 (June 4, 1999).

272. *See, e.g.,* Sierra Club v. EPA, 162 F. Supp. 2d 406 (D. Md. 2001); Western Carolina Reg'l Sewer Auth. v. DHEC, No. S.C. DHEC 98-ALJ-07-0267 (June 21, 1999); City of Anderson v. South Carolina Dep't of Health & Envtl. Control (discussed in *State Suit Will Decide Key Impaired Water Assessment Issues,* INSIDE EPA, Feb. 16, 2001, at 11-12); *but see Sacramento Reg'l County Sanitation Dist. v. State Water Resources Control Bd.,* No. 98C501702 (Cal. Super. Ct. Nov. 1, 2000).

273. *See, e.g., Sierra Club,* 162 F. Supp. 2d at 419-20.

274. Somerset County Sanitary Dist., Inc. v. Maryland Dep't of the Env't, No. 19-C-01-007932 (Md. Cir. Ct. May 11, 2001); City of Salisbury v. Maryland Dep't of the Env't, No. C-01-622 (Md. Cir. Ct. May 17, 2001).

275. Stam, *supra* note 270 (quoting Steven Koorse, attorney with Hunton & Williams, Richmond, Va.).

276. *See* Chapter 2, at 20-24.

277. *Id.* at 24 (House committee staff viewed §303 as a "game plan for the next generation"; a Senate staff member stated that, "we didn't take it seriously and thought it would be foolish for EPA to waste time and money to implement it"). The massive irony of §303(d) is that it was only written into the statute, as a last-minute compromise, at the insistence of the same states, industries, and trade associations who resist it today. *Id.* at 14-24.

278. *See* U.S. EPA, WATER QUALITY IMPROVEMENT STUDY (1989) (showing total loadings from industrial categories and quality of receiving waters before and after the application of the first BAT requirements).

279. *Id.* tbl. 1-2 (showing RAW (pre-BAT) pulp and paper industry emissions of total suspended solids at 10.8 million pounds (lbs.)/day and post-BAT at 0.89 million; the industry's organic priority pollutant discharger dropped from 32.8 thousand lbs./day to 3.3 thousand). Other industrial categories emissions fell dramatically as well, including:

			Priority Pollutant Loadings			
			(lbs./day)		(lbs./day)	
Industrial	Total Suspended Solids		Organics		Inorganics	
Categories	RAW	BAT	RAW	BAT	RAW	BAT

Coal Mining	224,011,488	1,672,001	400	133	134,373 7,401
Iron and	5,141,618	135,470	105,296	262	917,027 2,551
Metal Finishing	2,059,357	54,348	9,343	162	240,178 6,555
Petroleum Refining	239,004	67,957	17,119	103	4,077 796

280. *Id.* tbl. 3-1, which shows the following water quality improvement:

	Pre-Bat		Post Bat		Total River
	Not Complying	Complying	Not Complying	Complying	Miles Assessed
Pollutant	w/WQC	w/WQC	w/WQC	w/WQC	
Nickel	6,265.7	18,023.0	1,043.2	23,245.5	24,288.7
Lead	12,864.3	11,424.4	6,174.2	18,114.5	24,288.7
Zinc	9,748.1	14,540.6	2,469.0	21,819.7	24,288.7
Cyanide	12,916.3	11,372.4	4,562.1	19,726.6	24,288.7

281. *See* Chemical Mfrs. Ass'n v. EPA, 870 F.2d 177, 19 ELR 20989 (5th Cir. 1989), *cert. denied sub nom.* PPG Indus. v. EPA, 110 S. Ct. 1936 (1990) (requiring closed cycle recycling for some operations); Rybachek v. EPA, 904 F.2d 1276, 20 ELR 20973 (9th Cir. 1990) (zero discharge for placer mining).

282. *EPA Finds Significant Progress in Controlling Pollution of Water,* N.Y. TIMES, Feb. 12, 1984, at A-31 (claiming an improvement of 65% in POTW discharges in the first 10 years of the CWA POTW program, and that while the population served increased by 18 million people, total pollutants dischargers had stayed "roughly constant").

283. It has not worked completely, of course, and the later history of BAT and its application to large, rather-fight-than-switch industries led to compromised standards that abandoned the CWA's "action-forcing" and best achievable goals. *See Special Report, Effluent Guidelines Rulemaking Nears End: Litigation, Compliance Extensions Expected,* 15 Env't Rep. (BNA) 1629-30 (Jan. 21, 1983) (describing compromises in final rules for petroleum and leather tanning industrial categories). *See also Philip D. Reed, New BAT Standards: Lowering the Ceiling or Raising the Floor?,* 13 ELR 10002 (Jan. 1983) ("It can be argued that EPA has coupled relatively tough [best practical technology] with relatively lenient BAT.").

284. For the collapse of Lake Erie, see BARRY COMMONER, THE CLOSING CIRCLE 94-111 (1971); for rivers catching fire, see Patricia Howard, *A Happier Cleveland,* HOUS. POST, Oct. 24, 1990, at A2 (describing 1969 fire on the Cuyohoga River in Cleveland, Ohio).

285. For a general discussion of the theory and attractions of water quality-based regulation, see N. William Hines, *Nor Any Drop to Drink: Public Regulation of Water Quality Part I: State Pollution Control Programs,* 52 IOWA L. REV. 186 (1966); 2 WILLIAM H. ROGERS JR., ENVIRONMENTAL LAW: AIR AND WATER 242-53 (1986).

286. Water Quality Act, ch. 758, tit. III, §303, 62 Stat. 1155 (1948). For a history of federal water quality legislation prior to the 1972 Amendments, see Chapter 2, at 12-14.

287. 42 U.S.C. §§7408, 7409, ELR Stat. CAA §§108, 109; *see also infra* section entitled Enhanced Ambient Management.

288. Toxic Substances Control Act of 1976, Pub. L. No. 94-469, 90 Stat. 2003 (current version at 15 U.S.C. §§2601-2692, ELR Stat. TSCA §§2-412); Resource Conservation and Recovery Act, 42 U.S.C. §§6901-6992k, ELR Stat. RCRA §§1001-11011; Federal Insecticide, Fungicide, and Rodenticide Act of 1972, Pub. L. No. 92-516, 86 Stat. 987 (current version at 7 U.S.C. §§136-136y, ELR Stat. FIFRA §§2-34); Comprehensive Environmental Response, Compensation, and Liability Act of 1980, Pub. L. No. 96-510, 94 Stat. 2767 (current version at 42 U.S.C. §§9601-9675, ELR Stat. CERCLA §§101-405); Safe Drinking Water Act of 1974, Pub. L. No. 93-523, 88 Stat. 1660 (current version at 42 U.S.C. §§300f to 300j-26, ELR Stat. SDWA §§1401-1465).

289. For a view of these difficulties under the CWA, see Environmental Defense Fund v. EPA, 598 F.2d 62, 8 ELR 20765 (D.C. Cir. 1978) (upholding EPA extrapolations of human harm from tests on laboratory mice, stating, "as a practical matter, scientific knowledge about the effect of industrial chemicals cannot keep pace with the ability of industrial laboratories to create new ones," and "[w]hat scientists know about the causes of cancer is how limited is their knowledge"). *Id.* at 82, 8 ELR at 20780. *See also* Hercules, Inc. v. EPA, 598 F.2d 91, 8 ELR 20811 (D.C. Cir. 1978) (upholding EPA standards for the pesticides, derived through a complex mix of extrapolations and arbitrary safety factors).

290. *See* Environmental Defense Fund, Toxic Ignorance: The Continuing Absence of Basic Health Testing of Pop-Setting Chemicals in the United States (1997); Robert V. Percival et al., Environmental Regulation 522 (2d ed. 1996) ("Despite amendments to FIFRA, the process of canceling a pesticide remains fraught with considerable procedural difficulties.").

291. For difficulties in CAA standard setting, see Natural Resources Defense Council v. EPA, 824 F.2d 1146, 17 ELR 21032 (D.C. Cir. 1987) (vinyl chloride regulations); Natural Resource Defense Council v. EPA, 695 F.2d 48, 19 ELR 20344 (D.D.C. 1988) (benzene emissions). *See* Percival et al., Environmental Regulation, *supra* note 290, at 780 ("The regulatory burden in establishing a NAAQS is so demanding that EPA has strong incentives to avoid making frequent charges on such standards, much less to promulgate new ones."); *id.* at 822 ("Uncertainty over the causes and effects of acid deposition contributed to political gridlock.").

292. While an entire subject to itself, for a critical commentary on CERCLA risk-based decisionmaking, see Stephen Breyer, Breaking the Vicious Cycle (1993) (arguing for the creation of an independent science board to make correct and apolitical federal risk decisions); for a more technical walk through CERCLA's risk-assessment woods, *see* Lawrence E. Starfield, *The 1990 National Contingency Plan—More Detail and More Structure, But Still a Balancing Act,* 20

ELR 10222 (June 1990); Linda Malone, *Bioavailability: On the Frontiers of Science and Law in Cleanup Methodologies for Contamination,* 31 ELR 10800 (Aug. 2001).

293. *See supra* note 291 (air toxics); Houck, *The Regulation of Toxic Pollutants, supra* note 53 (water toxics).

294. U.S. EPA, INTEGRATED RISK ASSESSMENTS FOR DIOXINS AND FURANS FOR CHLORINE BLEACH IN PULP AND PAPER MILLS 1 (1990). For an update on the dioxin wars, see *Dioxin Litigants May File a Second Case Under New Data Guidelines,* INSIDE EPA, Jan. 11, 2002, at 14.

> Industry plaintiffs are considering dropping a portion of their current lawsuit challenging EPA's classification of dioxin as a known human carcinogen in its upcoming dioxin risk assessment of the chemical by-product, to instead file an additional lawsuit challenging the study under a newly released federal data quality guideline, sources say.

Id.

295. *See* NATIONAL WATER COMM'N, WATER POLICIES FOR THE FUTURE 105-06 (1973) (water pollution standards should be determined by local authorities).

296. To be sure, several states, most notably, California, have shown remarkable leadership and innovation in environmental protection, to the point of setting strict public health standards, requiring advanced control technologies, and resisting environmentally harmful federal proposals. To be equally sure, these states are in a clear minority and, when it comes to delegated water programs, have shown the same reluctance and underperformance of their colleagues. *See* San Francisco Baykeeper v. Browner, 147 F. Supp. 2d 991 (M.D. Cal. 2001) (California dragging its heels).

297. *See infra* section entitled Supporting Science.

298. *See* ROGERS, *supra* note 3; *see also* Chapter 5, at 131-34.

299. ROGERS, *supra* note 3; *see also* Chapter 5, at 131-34.

300. *See* S. REP. NO. 92-14 (1972), *reprinted in* 1972 U.S.C.C.A.N. 3671. *See also* Weyerhauser Co. v. Costle, 590 F.2d 1011, 9 ELR 20284 (D.C. Cir. 1978).

301. William H. Rogers Jr., *Industrial Water Pollution and the Refuse Act, A Second Chance for Water Quality,* 119 U. PA. L. REV. 761, 803 (1971).

302. *Id.* at 764-65.

303. *Id.* at 803.

304. 33 U.S.C. §1288, ELR STAT. FWPCA §208.

305. *See* JACKSON BATTLE & MAXINE LIPELES, WATER POLLUTION 538-40 (3d ed. 1998).

306. For a discussion of CWA §208 and its underperformance, *see id.; see also* ROGERS, ENVIRONMENTAL LAW: AIR AND WATER, *supra* note 285, at 319-30; ANDERSON ET AL., ENVIRONMENTAL PROTECTION LAW AND POLICY 384-86 (1990).

307. 33 U.S.C. §1329, ELR STAT. FWPCA §319.

308. *See* Chapter 2, at 30, 31.

309. Under §319, EPA does not review nonpoint plans but, rather, a state program to develop and implement them; EPA program disapproval, further, leads only to the possible loss of future grant funding. 33 U.S.C. §1329(h), ELR STAT. FWPCA §319(h). Senate leaders, in passing the measure, expressed their concern for lack of regulatory standards.

310. *See* David Zaring, *Agriculture, Nonpoint Source Pollution and Regulation, Catch the Clean Water Act's Bleak Present and Future,* 20 HARV. ENVTL. L. REV. 515 (1996) (concluding: "unfortunately, Section 319 has failed to reduce nonpoint source pollution. Its failings can be characterized as not enough carrot, not enough stick, and too much of the planning syndrome that had characterized Section 208"); George Gould, *Agriculture, Nonpoint Source Pollution, and Federal Law,* 23 U.C. DAVIS L. REV. 461 (1990) (ditto).

311. *See supra* section entitled State Capacity.

312. *See supra* section entitled Water Quality Standards.

313. *See supra* section entitled State Enforcement.

314. *See* ENVIRONMENTAL LAW INST., ENFORCEABLE STATE MECHANISMS FOR THE CONTROL OF NONPOINT SOURCE WATER, Appendix: State "No More Stringent" Laws (1997), *available at* http://www.eli.org.

315. *Id. at* 1 (Executive Summary) ("Some states . . . have adopted explicit statutory or regulatory exemptions for agriculture or forestry activities.").

316. *See States Back Revenues Needed to Implement TMDL Strategy, EPA Told,* Daily Env't Rep. (BNA), May 12, 1997, at A-8 (quoting Hawaii official: "In a period of declining state budgets . . . we do not expect to be able to obtain sufficient funding to establish scientifically-defensible numeric targets for polluted runoff control").

317. *See* Bruninga, *Water Quality Standards: Agency TMDL Proposal Costly, supra* note 79 (comments of Sen. Robert Smith of New Hampshire); Notes on *Hearings Before the Subcommittee on Water Resources and the Environment of the Committee on Transportation and Infrastructure,* U.S. House of Representatives, Nov. 15, 2001 (notes on file with author) (comments of Rep. Gene Taylor (R-Miss.)) (with three-fifths of the states in deficit spending, EPA should not expect additional state effort without funding support). State environmental agencies are, in turn, taking the largest budget cuts in a decade. *See* Greenwire (Feb. 15, 2002), *at* http://www.greenwire.com ("The economic downturn that blew in over the past year has chilled the budgets of many state environmental agencies, forcing

them to enact cuts not seen in a decade, and the outlook for the future is no brighter, according to a new report by the Environmental Council of the States."). *Id.* at 1. *See also* Press Release, Michigan Environmental Council, Engler Budget Cuts Fall Hard on MDEQ and MDNR (Nov. 7, 2001), *available at* http://www.mecprotects. org/pr11_06_01.html (citing a 24% cut in budget of the Michigan Department of Environmental Quality).

318. *See* David Broder, *Pretty Pictures Can't Hide the Red Ink,* TIMES PICAYUNE, Feb. 10, 2002, at A-7. The administration has proposed significant budget cuts for EPA in FY 2003, including CWA programs. *See also* Press Release, U.S. EPA, Administration Proposes $280 Million Cut in EPA's FY 03 Budget (Feb. 5, 2002), at 1.

319. *See* Chapter 2, at 31-33, Chapter 5, at 145-46; *see also* NRC REPORT, *supra* note 77.

320. *See* Howard Latin, *Ideal Versus Real Regulatory Efficiency: Implementation of Uniform Standards and "Fine Tuning" Regulatory Reforms,* 37 STAN. L. REV. 1267, 1270-71 (1985) ("The academic literature on regulatory reform reflects an excessive preoccupation with theoretical efficiency, while it places inadequate emphasis on actual decisionmaking costs and implementation constraints."); Daniel H. Cole & Peter Z. Grossman, *When Is Command and Control Efficient? Institutes, Technology, and the Comparative Efficiency of Alternative Regulatory Regimes for Environmental Protection,* 5 WIS. L. REV. 887, 935 (1999) ("specifically, standard economic accounts of the comparative efficiency of alternative regulatory regimes are insensitive to historical, institutional, and technological contexts. Most importantly, they tend to assume 'perfect (and, incidentally, costless) monitoring,' or they assume that monitoring costs are the same regardless of the control regime that is chosen").

321. Richard W. Steverman & Jeff Garth, *Web of Safeguards Failed as Energy Giant Fell,* TIMES PICAYUNE, Jan. 20, 2002, at A-23 (quoting Jim Chanos, President of Kynikos Associates).

322. *Id.*

323. Testimony of G. Tracy Mehan III, Assistant Administrator for Water, U.S. EPA, Before the Subcommittee on Water Resources and the Environment of the Committee on Transportation and Infrastructure, U.S. House of Representatives (Nov. 15, 2001), *available at* http://www.house.gov/transportation/water/11-15-01/ mehan.html.

324. Presentation of Charles Sutfin, U.S. EPA Office of Water, to ASIWPCA Meeting, Seattle, Washington, Jan. 14, 2002; *see also* testimony of G. Tracey Mehan, III, *supra* note 323 (describing EPA's efforts to provide greater flexibility).

325. *See EPA Preparing to Cede More Impaired Water Responsibility to States,* INSIDE EPA, June 29, 2001, at 1.

326. U.S. EPA Briefing Notes (on file with author), overhead 12, "Key Issues for Rulemaking" Including: 303(d) Listing; Implementation Plans; Reasonable An-

swer; Timeframes; Stakeholder Involvement; EPA TMDL Rule; and EPA Permitting Rule.

327. *See* Chapter 3, at 61.

328. *See infra* notes 424-27 and accompanying text; *see also* Chapter 4, at 95.

329. *See* Pronsolino v. Marcus, Nos. 00-16026, -16027 (9th Cir. May 31, 2002); *see also* American Farm Bureau Federation, Taking TMDLs Out of the Ivory Tower (unpublished) (on file with author). The Farm Bureau further argues that the addition of §319 to the CWA in 1987 confirms that nonpoint sources were previously exempt from the statute, and that the requirement of "daily" loads for TMDLs, by definition, excludes sporadic, weather-driven farm runoff. Id. The forestry industry has taken the same positions. *See* Chapter 3, at 61-62. These arguments were rejected in Pronsolino. *See also* Natural Resources Defense Council v. Muszynski, 268 F.3d 91, 32 ELR 20203 (2d Cir. 2001) (interpreting TMDLs to include, in some cases, seasonal loadings).

330. *See* Chapter 3, at 61-62. The statute reads in pertinent part: "Each state shall identify these sections within its boundaries for which the effluent limitations required by Section 1311(b)(1)(A) and Section 1311(b)(1)(B) of this title are not stringent enough to implement any water quality standard applicable to such waters." 33 U.S.C. §1313(d)(1)(A), ELR Stat. FWPCA §303(d)(1)(A).

331. Chevron, U.S.A., Inc. v. Natural Resources Defense Council, Inc., 467 U.S. 837, 14 ELR 20507 (1984) (announcing principle of deference to Agency interpretations of statutes).

332. Presentation of Sutfin, *supra* note 324 (indicating his personal agreement with the position not to list or require TMDLs for waters polluted by nonpoint sources only).

333. *Id.* This compromise was not stated, but is inferable from the previous comment cited.

334. *See Chevron,* 467 U.S. at 837, 14 ELR at 20507. The Court approved a turn-about by EPA on pollution abatement requirements in nonattainment areas under the CAA.

335. *See supra* section entitled Monitoring and Assessment Guidance.

336. *Id.; see also* Presentation of Sutfin, *supra* note 324.

337. *See* U.S. EPA, GUIDANCE FOR WATER QUALITY-BASED DECISIONS: THE TMDL PROCESS (1991) (available from the ELR Document Service, ELR Order No. AD-3550); *see also* U.S. EPA, NATIONAL CLARIFYING GUIDANCE FOR 1998 STATE AND TERRITORY SECTION 303(d) LISTING DECISIONS (1997) (available from the ELR Document Service, ELR Order No. AD-3504).

338. Presentation of Sutfin, *supra* note 324.

339. This issue is particularly relevant given EPA's recognition that the science is weak on the effectiveness of particular best management practice strategies. *Id.*

340. *Id.*

341. See the reduction in the impaired waters list for Wyoming, from over 400 waters to 61, with 315 now identified as requiring "further monitoring." Chapter 5, at 138.

342. *See* Presentation of Sutfin, *supra* note 324.

343. *See supra* section entitled Supporting Science.

344. *See EPA Backs Innovative Virginia Program to Avoid Setting TMDLs*, INSIDE EPA, Aug. 10, 2001.

345. *Id.*

346. *Id.*

347. *See supra* note 2.

348. 40 C.F.R. §130.2(c).

349. *Id.* §130.2(h). Hence the equation: TMDL = WLA (waste load allocation) + LA (load allocation) + BL (baseline condition) + MOS (margin of safety) + FG (future growth). *See* Adler, *supra* note 196, at n.113.

350. *See* U.S. EPA, GUIDANCE FOR WATER QUALITY-BASED DECISIONS, *supra* note 337.

351. *See EPA Preparing to Cede, supra* note 325 ("Other changes include lifting a requirement that TMDL discharge limits be set for certain point and nonpoint source dischargers, and instead would essentially alleviate the individual accountability of particular dischargers for controlling dischargers.").

352. *See* 33 U.S.C. §1361(a), ELR Stat. FWPCA §501(a) (EPA authority to adopt rules "as broad as necessary" to carry out its CWA responsibilities). This authority has been interpreted broadly in the past. *See* American Paper Inst. v. EPA, 890 F.2d 869, 875-878, 20 ELR 20482, 20485-86 (7th Cir. 1989); *see also* American Petroleum Inst. v. Knecht, 456 F. Supp. 889, 8 ELR 20853, *aff'd*, 609 F.2d 1306, 10 ELR 20083 (9th Cir. 1979) (upholding federal requirements under the Coastal Zone Management Act. "[U]nder our so called federal system . . . the federal bureaucracy is legally permitted to execute the congressional management with a high degree of befuddlement as long as it acts no more befuddled than the Congress must reasonably have anticipated." 456 F. Supp. at 931, 8 ELR at 20873).

353. CERCLA, a remedial statute seeking to spread the costs of cleanup beyond the general public, imposes joint and several liability for all (but minor) contributors. *See* Starfield, *supra* note 292, at 10226.

354. The CAA SIP process allows the state the freedom to allocate cleanup responsibilities among sources without regard to their contributions. *See* Union Elec. Co. v. EPA, 427 U.S. 246, 6 ELR 20570 (1976).

355. EPA has released model allocation options that are "efficient" and "equitable." E-mail correspondence with Merritt Frey, Clean Water Action Network, Boise, Idaho (Jan. 16, 2002).

356. *See* Chapter 4, at 84 (citing "some concerns that relevance on §303(d) could lead to judicial enforcement of TMDL plans in unexpected and unintended ways").

357. *See EPA Advances Set of Proposals for Upcoming Impaired Waters Rule,* IN-SIDE EPA, Aug. 17, 2001, at 11 (EPA is "looking at throwing out a requirement in the July 2000 rule that forced states to submit implementation plans with their impaired water lists").

358. *See supra* section II.B.1.

359. *See* Testimony of G. Tracy Mehan III, *supra* note 323.

360. "The state shall incorporate [TMDLs] into its current plan under subsection (e) of this section." 33 U.S.C. §1313(d)(2), ELR STAT. FWPCA §303(d)(2).

361. While EPA had required "reasonable assurance" as early as 1991, specific implementation plans were not required by the Agency until 1997. *See* Chapter 4, at 80-81.

362. *See supra* note 352.

363. *See* Sierra Club v. Hankinson, 939 F. Supp. 865, 27 ELR 20280 (N.D. Ga. 1996).

364. *See* Pronsolino v. Marcus, 91 F. Supp. 2d 1337, 30 ELR 20460 (N.D. Cal. 2000) (albeit dicta in the decision), *aff'd*, Nos. 00-16026, -16027 (9th Cir. May 31, 2002).

365. *See EPA Preparing to Cede, supra* note 325 ("The shift would move the agencies' oversight of state implementation plans from Section 303(d) of the Clean Water Act to Section 303(e) essentially throwing to state officials the responsibility for reviewing implementation plans, rather than EPA.").

366. 33 U.S.C. §1313(e), ELR STAT. FWPCA §303(e).

367. No one familiar with federal "process" review under, for example, the federal aid highway program or the coastal zone management program, can have much faith in its ability to provide environmentally protective results. *See* Oliver A. Houck & Michael Rolland, *Federalism in Wetlands Regulations,* 54 MD. L. REV. 1242, 1249-99 (1995) (describing spotty-at-best effectiveness of NOAA process review of state coastal management programs).

368. 40 C.F.R. §130.6.

369. *Id.* §130.6(1).

370. *See* Louisiana TMDL Program, at http://www.deq.state.la.us/technology/tmdl/index.htm (last visited Feb. 18, 2002). The state of Virginia has recently proposed to repeal all of its §303(e) plans as obsolete. Press Release, Virginia Department of Environmental Quality, Total Maximum Daily Loads—Proposed TMDL Planning Regulation (Jan. 18, 2001).

371. *See* NRC REPORT, *supra* note 77, at 101 (EPA should set "broad guidelines" and no more); Stevenson & Shabman, *supra* note 102 (ditto; then again, he drafted the report). *See supra* notes 101-07 and accompanying text.

372. *See supra* note 352.

373. *See supra* section entitled The CWA §319 Program.

374. *Id.*

375. *See* Houck & Rolland, *supra* note 367, at 1289-99 (describing EPA reluctance to sanction delegated NPDES programs and similar NOAA reluctance under the CZMA); Steinzor, *supra* note 51 (describing ineffectiveness of federal sanctions generally).

376. *See* Chapter 3, at 55-56, Chapter 4, at 75-77, and Oliver A. Houck, *TMDLs IV: The Final Frontier,* 29 ELR 10469, 10485-86 (Aug. 1999).

377. Chapter 4, at 84 (quoting concerns of the nonpoint source industries in the FACA "that reliance on §303(d) could lead to judicial enforcement of TMDL implementation plans in unexpected or unintended way" (citing the draft FACA report)), *id.* at 84 n.93.

378. *See EPA Advances Set of Proposals, supra* note 357.

379. *Id.*

380. *See supra* notes 257-58 and accompanying text.

381. *See* Testimony of G. Tracy Mehan III, *supra* note 323.

382. *See Mehan Says Toxics Inventory Holds Lessons for TMDL Program,* [20 Current Developments] Env't Rep. (BNA) 2400 (Dec. 14, 2001). The TRI is a requirement of the Emergency Planning and Community Right-To-Know Act, 42 U.S.C. §11001, ELR Stat. EPCRA §301, producing an annual record of industrial toxic dischargers nationwide. *Id.* §11023, ELR STAT. EPCRA §313.

383. *See* U.S. EPA, EPA NONPOINT SOURCE POLLUTION FOCUS GROUPS FINAL REPORT, *supra* note 225 and accompanying text.

384. Louisiana industries released, under permit, over 150 million pounds of toxins in 1999; the national total exceeded 7.5 billion pounds. U.S. EPA, *TRI Onsite and Offsite Releases by State, at* http://www.epa.gov/triinter/tridata/tri99/press/state_all.pdf (last visited Feb. 22, 2202).

385. 42 U.S.C. §4321, ELR STAT. NEPA §2.

386. 33 U.S.C. §1365, ELR STAT. FWPCA §505 (citizen suit provisions).

387. *See* Houck, *The Regulation of Toxic Pollutants, supra* note 53, at 10537 n.43 (recording the role of one citizen organization, the Natural Resources Defense Council, in the implementation of the Act. For a recent example of the action-forcing nature of a citizen lawsuit, see *Paper Mill Agrees to Pay $30 Million to Upgrade Plant, $2 Million for Restoration,* [32 Current Developments] Env't Rep. (BNA) 1685 (Aug. 24, 2001) (describing proposed settlement agreement in Pennsylvania in Public Interest Research Group of N.J. v. P.H. Glatfelter Co., No. 1 CV 99-09040 (M.D. Pa. Aug. 20, 2001); the pulp and paper plant at issue will, inter alia, eliminate dioxin-producing chlorine from its bleaching process, *id.,* a result that EPA has yet to achieve through regulation).

388. *See* Steve Novik & Bill Westerfield, *Whose SIP Is It Anyway? State-Federal Conflict in Clean Air Act Enforcement,* 18 WM. & MARY J. ENVTL. L. 215, 220 (1994) (quoting a Wisconsin air management official: "From direct personal experience I can tell you it is extremely difficult for a state to adopt and implement control measures which have not been specifically required by U.S. EPA.").

389. *See* THEODORE L. GARRETT & SONYA WINNER, CLEAN AIR DESKBOOK 16 (ELI 1992) (describing use of and court-imposed limits on EPA "conditional approvals" of state SIPs); in addition, partial and conditional approaches have subsequently been authorized by Congress, 42 U.S.C. §7410(k)(3), (4), ELR Stat. CAA §110(k)(3), (4).

390. *See* Steinzor, *supra* note 51. *See also* FREDERICK R. ANDERSON ET AL., ENVIRONMENTAL PROTECTION LAW AND POLICY 451-52 (3d ed. 1999) (federal implementation plans have been few, far between, and controversial).

391. Market-based approaches are not included in this analysis because they presuppose a target and an obligation to abate. *See* William F. Pedersen Jr., *Why the Clean Air Act Works Badly,* 129 PA. L. REV. 1059 (1981). Pollution trading in the context of the TMDL program is neither standard-setting nor obligation-imposing; rather, it is a potentially useful means of allocating abatement requirements.

392. 42 U.S.C. §7408, ELR STAT. CAA §108 (designation of criteria pollutants); §7409, ELR STAT. CAA §109 (establishment of national ambient air quality standards (NAAQS)). NAAQS have been established for, inter alia, nitrogen oxide and ozone.

393. *Id.* §7511, ELR STAT. CAA §181 (imposing more onerous SIP requirements in nonattainment areas according to severity of pollution); id. §7511(a), ELR STAT. CAA §181(a) (mandatory enhanced vehicle inspection and maintenance programs in more severely polluted nonattainment areas).

394. *Id.* §7521(m), ELR Stat. CAA §202(m) (emission control diagnostics).

395. *Id.* §7521(b)-(k), ELR STAT. CAA §202(b)-(k) (emissions standards).

396. *Id.* §7545, ELR STAT. CAA §211 (regulation of fuels).

397. *See* PERCIVAL ET AL., *supra* note 290, at 849-55 (discussing low-emission and zero-emission vehicle regulation).

398. *See* Amoco Oil Co. v. EPA, 501 F.2d 722, 4 ELR 20397 (D.C. Cir. 1972) (upholding regulations barring leaded gasoline in automobiles with catalytic converters, and requiring widespread marketing of unleaded gasoline); Ethyl Corp. v. EPA, 541 F.2d 1, 6 ELR 20267 (D.C. Cir. 1976) (en banc), *cert. denied,* 426 U.S. 941 (1976) (upholding phase-down in lead content in gasoline); 42 U.S.C. §7545(a), ELR Stat. CAA §211(a) (prohibiting the sale of leaded gasoline).

399. *See* Adler, *supra* note 196.

400. 42 U.S.C. §§7408, 7409, ELR STAT. CAA §§108, 109.

401. *Id.* §7410, ELR Stat. CAA §110; *see also* 40 C.F.R. §51.112 (spelling out SIP requirements more fully).

402. 42 U.S.C. §7410(a)(1), ELR Stat. CAA §110(a)(1) (the submissions are due within three years of the promulgation of a NAAQS).

403. EPA enforcement options include a federal SIP, 42 U.S.C. §7410(c), ELR Stat. CAA §110(c), and the withholding of federal highway monies and other federal assistance. *Id.* §7509, ELR Stat. CAA §109.

404. *Id.* §7604, ELR Stat. CAA §304. Approved SIPs, further, become enforceable by governments and citizens as a matter of federal law. *See* Adler, *supra* note 196, at 235 n.1902 and cases cited therein.

405. *See* U.S. Steel Corp. v. EPA, 444 U.S. 1035, 1078, 10 ELR 20081, 20082 (1980) (Rehnquist, J. dissenting) (the provisions of the CAA "virtually swim before one's eyes"). *See also* Adler, *supra* note 196, at 207-09; Pedersen, *supra* note 391; Schoenbrod, *supra* note 196; Arnold Rietze Jr., *A Century of Air Pollution Control Law: What's Worked; What's Failed; What Might Work,* 21 Envtl. L. 1549 (1991); John-Mark Stensvaag & Craig N. Oren, Clean Air Act: Law and Practice (1994).

406. *See* Rogers, *supra* note 3, at 161-68 ("consistently with their dignity as national health standards, the NAAQS have continued to be a tumultuous subject of public policy since their adoption in the early 1970s") *Id.* at 162. For a continuation of the controversy, see Whitman v. American Trucking Ass'n 121 S. Ct. 903, 31 ELR 20512 (2001) (ozone standards).

407. *See* Anderson et al., *supra* note 390, at 4545; Rogers, *supra* note 3, at 266-71. *See also* Air Pollution Control Dist. of Jefferson County v. EPA, 739 F.2d 1071, 14 ELR 20573 (6th Cir. 1984) (conflicts of modeling long-range transport).

408. *See* Rogers, *supra* note 3, at 269 ("the empirical bottom line on source monitoring is that it is a surprising no show; continuous monitoring is largely a fiction. It has been estimated that fewer than five percent of major air pollution sources have had their allowable emissions verified by stack testing").

409. The CAA provides a loophole of "unclassifiable" attainment for criteria pollutants based on insufficient information. 42 U.S.C. §7407(d)(1)(A)(iii), ELR Stat. CAA §107(d)(1)(A)(iii). This section has "apparently been abused to avoid more stringent source controls and has provided an incentive to avoid collecting the data needed to determine attainment." *See* Adler, *supra* note 196, at 233.

410. *See* Alder, *supra* note 196, at 241-42 and sources cited therein.

411. *Id.* at 294.

412. *See* Rogers, *supra* note 3, at 202-10 ("a SIP with pages turning, some on the shelf and some not yet arrived, hardly makes for ascertainable legal obligations"). *Id.* at 207.

413. *See* Lester B. Lave & Giberts Omenn, Cleaning the Air: Refining the Clean Air Act 42-43 (1981) (states discontinued monitoring in order to avoid

nonattainment designation); id. at 46 (attainment status depends on a monitoring system that is characterized by siting to avoid pollution sources, lax controls, and other manipulation to avoid nonattainment).

414. *See* Adler, *supra* note 196, at 282 and sources cited therein.

415. *Id.* at 233-34.

416. *See EPA Audits of State I/M Programs Reveals Series Enforcement Problems,* 16 Env't Rep. (BNA) 325 (1985) (noncompliance reaches 60% of inspection and maintenance facilities).

417. *See supra* notes 195-99 and accompanying text. *See also* Craig N. Oren, *Prevention of Significant Deterioration: Control Compelling Versus Site Shifting,* 74 Iowa L. Rev. 1, 5 (1988) (calling CAA prevention of significant deterioration trading an "elaborate regulatory hocus-pocus.") An enormous amount of resources have been spent on litigation simply attempting to keep the SIP process honest. *See* Rogers, *supra* note 3, at 204-10 and case cited therein.

418. Adler, *supra* note 196, at 250-75.

419. *Id.*

420. *Id.* at 294.

421. *See id.* and sources cited therein. *See also supra* note 415.

422. *See* 42 U.S.C. §7501(3), ELR Stat. CAA §171(3) (lowest achievable emission rate); *id.* §7502(c)(1), ELR Stat. CAA §172(c)(1) (reasonably available control technology); *id.* §7475(a)(4), ELR Stat. CAA §165(a)(4) (best available control technology).

423. 42 U.S.C. §§7661 et seq., ELR Stat. §§501 et seq.

424. Chapter 4, at 85-86 (identifying agriculture as the number one cause of impairment of the nation's rivers and lakes (citing the President's Clean Water Action Plan)), *id.* at 85 n.98.

425. *Id.*

426. *Id.*

427. *See* Donald A. Goolsby et al., Flux and Sources of Nutrients in the Mississippi-Atchafalaya River Basin 14 (1999) (attributing 90% of nitrogen and phosphorous loadings to nonpoint sources upstream); National Oceanic & Atmospheric Administration, *Hypoxia in the Gulf of Mexico, at* http://www.noaa.gov/products/pubs_hypox.html (principal Gulf hypoxia source areas Illinois, Indiana, Iowa, Minnesota, and Ohio).

428. National Agricultural Statistics Serv., U.S. Department of Agriculture, 1997 Census of Agriculture, *available at* http://www.nass.usda.gov/census/ [hereinafter Census], *cited in J.B. Ruhl,* Farms, Their Environmental Harms, and Environmental Law, 27 Ecology L.Q. 263 (2000). The agricultural data that follow are taken largely from this article.

429. *See* CENSUS, *supra* note 428, at 8, fig. 5.

430. *Id.* at 10, tbl. 1.

431. *Id.* at 23, tbl. 15.

432. *Id.* at 22, tbl. 14 (gasoline expenditures over $6 billion).

433. *Id.* at 100, tbl. 49 (electricity at our $2.75 billion).

434. *Id.*

435. *See Changing Rural America, in* VICKI MARKS, AMBER WAVES OF GRAIN 30 (Defenders of Wildlife 2000) (quoting a former Farm Bureau representative as having written that "in the past 50 years, farm numbers have dropped from 7 million to less than 2 million").

436. *See* CENSUS, *supra* note 428, at 6, fig. 2.

437. Elizabeth Becker, *Airing of Farm-Subsidy Details Cultivates Envy: Published Secrets Show Reliance on Government,* TIMES PICAYUNE, Dec. 28, 2001, at 11-13. A Republican state Senate candidate is quoted as saying: "You can see from the payment lists how the rich farmers can afford to buy up all the small ones like cannibals, all subsidized by the government." *Id.* (quoting candidate Rod Thorson). *See also* George Will, *Demos Head Into the Wild Blue Yonder,* TIMES PICAYUNE, Jan. 14, 2002, at B7 (two-thirds of farm subsidies go to 10% of the farming community, "most of whom earn more than $250,000 annually"—a phenomenon he then attributes to the Democratic Party).

438. There are 65 agricultural colleges and universities in the United States. Agriculture Colleges and Universities, *Agriculture Colleges and Universities Index, at* http://www.oneglobe.com/agriculture/agcolleg.html (last visited Feb. 19, 2001).

439. *See* MARKS, *supra* note 435 (detailing dominant insurance business of the Farm Bureau, and its political action, lobbying, and litigation initiatives).

440. Professor Ruhl characterizes the treatment of the agriculture industry as a series of "safe harbors" from environmental law and the CWA's treatment of nonpoint source pollution as a "classic example of passive nonregulation." Ruhl, Farms, *supra* note 428, at 293, 298. He is of course not the only one to note the anomaly. *See* John Davidson, *Conservation Agriculture: An Old New Idea,* 9 NAT. RESOURCES & ENV'T 20 (1995); C. Ford Runga, *Environmental Protection: From Farm to Market, in* THINKING ECOLOGICALLY: THE NEXT GENERATION OF ENVIRONMENTAL POLICY (Marion R. Chertow & David C. Esty eds., 1997); Tim Chen, *Get Green or Get Out: Decoupling Environmental From Economic Objectives in Agricultural Regulation,* 48 OKLA. L. REV. 333 (1995). Indeed, it is difficult to find any literature on agriculture and the environment that does not (1) note the anomaly and (2) conclude that the time has long come to end it.

441. For the diversity and complexity of industrial sources regulation under the NPDES program, see 40 C.F.R. §§401.10 et seq. (industrial category and subcategory technology-based emissions limitations).

442. *See* Association of Pac. Fisheries v. EPA, 615 F.2d 794, 10 ELR 20336 (9th Cir. 1990) (seafood processing standards will lead to closure of more than 10% of industry).

443. Ruhl, *Farms, supra* note 428, at 333.

444. *Id.*

445. *Id.* at 335-37.

446. *See* Chapter 4, at 92.

447. *Id.* at 89.

448. U.S. EPA, National Emission Standards for Hazardous Air Pollutants for Source Category: Pulp and Paper Production; Effluent Limitations Guidelines, Pretreatment Standards, and New Source Performance Standards, 63 Fed. Reg. 18504-751 (Apr. 15, 1998). The multimedia rule produced a 60% reduction in toxic air pollutants and a 96% reduction of dioxin discharges to waterways, leading to an "expedited cleanup" of 73 rivers and streams nationally. Press Release, U.S. EPA, EPA Eliminates Dioxin, Reduces Air and Water Pollutants From Nation's Pulp and Paper Mills (Nov. 14, 1997).

449. *See* Chapter 5, at 143.

450. *See id.* (describing a 40% drop within one year in nutrient loadings from Florida sugar farms through the requirement of best practices in the application of fertilizers).

451. *See EPA Data Appears to Undermine CAFO Rule,* INSIDE EPA, Nov. 26, 2001, at 1; *see also* Chapter 4, at 88.

452. *See Industry Pushes Regulatory Alternatives in EPA Feedlot Rule,* INSIDE EPA, Dec. 21, 2001, at 11.

453. *See* Chapter 4, at 87-99. *See also Construction Coalition Forms to Oppose Upcoming Effluent Rule,* INSIDE EPA, Jan. 4, 2002, at 5.

454. *See* Community Ass'n for Restoration of the Env't v. Henry Bosma Dairy, 52 ERC 1167 (E.D. Wash. 2001).

455. *See* Miccosukee Tribe v. Southern Fla. Water Mgmt. Dist., 49 ERC 2067 (11th Cir. 2002).

456. *See* Headwaters, Inc. v. Talent Irrigation Dist., 243 F.3d 526, 31 ELR 20535 (9th Cir. 2001).

457. *See* Northwest Envtl. Advocates v. EPA, No. Col1297-BZ (N.D. Cal. Apr. 2, 2001).

458. *See* Press Release, Cynthia Elkins & Alan Levine, Coast Action Group, Environmentalists Sue to Halt Federal Clean Water Violations by Pacific Lumber Company in Northern California (July 29, 2001).

459. *See supra* note 160 and accompanying text.

460. *See* B. Commoner, *Failure of the Environmental Effort,* 18 ELR 10195, 10197, tbl. III (June 1988) (showing reductions of 70 to 92% for lead, DDT, PCBs mercury, strantium 90, and phosphates).

461. *See* MARK SQUILLACE, ENVIRONMENTAL LAW: AIR POLLUTION 423 (1992) (ambient air levels of lead dropped sharply); Richard B. Alexander & Richard A. Smith, *Trends in Lead Concentrations in Major Rivers and Their Relation to Historic Changes in Gasoline-Lead Consumption,* 25 WATER RESOURCES BULL. 1275 (1989) (ambient water quality levels of lead dropped sharply as well).

462. *See* U.S. Department of the Interior, Proposed Rule to Remove the Bald Eagle in the Lower 48 States From the List of Endangered and Threatened Wildlife, 64 Fed. Reg. 36454 (July 6, 1999); 50 C.F.R. pt. 70 (removal of Brown Pelican from list); U.S. Department of the Interior, Final Rule to Remove the American Peregrine Falcon From the Federal List of Endangered and Threatened Wildlife, 64 Fed. Reg. 46542 (Aug. 25, 1999).

463. *See Moving Fast to Protect Ozone Layer,* N.Y. TIMES, May 15, 1991 (rapid progress in reducing CFCs in the electronic industry, despite industry claims that alternatives not available, and quoting an Apple Computer, Inc., chemist as stating: "If the federal government set a goal that there would be no fossil fuels sold by 1999, I bet you would see electric cars by then"). *See also* Houck, *The Regulation of Toxic Pollutants, supra* note 53, at 10554 (alternative bleaching agents replacing dioxin-producing chlorine in the pulp and paper industry). As for the economic impact of environmental requirements including these bans and reductions, between 1970 and 1990 the U.S. economy experienced a growth in real terms of 72% despite industry prophesies of lost jobs and economic doom. COUNCIL ON ECONOMIC QUALITY, 21ST ANNUAL REPORT 6-9 (1990).

464. Technically, the pollutants are phosphorous, nitrogen, and other components of fertilizers, but for the sake of convenience they are aggregated here as "fertilizers."

465. Commercial fertilizers are the leading cause of nitrate loadings in surface and groundwaters, *see* NATURAL RESOURCE CONSERVATION SERV., USDA, GEOGRAPHY OF HOPE 48 (1996), *cited in* Ruhl, *supra* note 428, at note 34. Fertilizer loadings increased by up to 10 times during the 20th century. *Id.* at 41-45.

466. NATIONAL SCIENCE AND TECHNOLOGY COMMITTEE ON ENVIRONMENT AND NATURAL RESOURCES, INTEGRATED ASSESSMENT OF HYPOXIA IN THE NORTHERN GULF OF MEXICO (2000), *available at* http://www.nosnoaa.gov/products/pubs hypox.html (last visited Feb. 22, 2002).

467. *See* Thomas E. Jordan et al., *Effects of Agriculture on Discharges of Nutrients From Coastal Plain Watersheds of Chesapeake Bay,* 26 J. ENVTL QUALITY 836 (1997). The correlation is found in Europe as well. *See EPA [European Protection Agency] Says Farm, Wastewater Practices at Fault in Eutrophication of North Seas,* 24 Int'l Env't Rep. (BNA) 969 (Nov. 7, 2001).

468. OFFICE OF POLLUTION PREVENTION AND TOXICS, U.S. EPA, BACKGROUND REPORT ON FERTILIZER USE, CONTAMINANTS, AND REGULATIONS i (1999) [hereinafter U.S. EPA, BACKGROUND REPORT].

469. *Id.*

470. *Id.*

471. *Id.*

472. *Id.*

473. *See* Ruhl, *Farms, supra* note 428, at 285, *citing* Charles M. Cooper & William M. Lipe, *Water Quality and Agriculture: Mississippi Experiences,* 47 J. SOIL & WATER CONSERVATION 221 (1992).

474. *See* Ruhl, *Farms, supra* note 428, at 272 n.20 (45% of the land mass of the United States is in field crop agriculture; another 30% is in silviculture and livestock).

475. In the late 1980s farmers were spending $6.7 billion on fertilizer alone; by the late 1990s they were spending $9.6 billion, an increase of nearly 50%. *See id.* at 113.

476. *See supra* note 474 and accompanying text. *See also* Ruhl, *Farms, supra* note 428, at 282-85, 287-91 (extent of farm runoff).

477. *See Less Fertilizer,* TIMES PICAYUNE, Apr. 3, 1998, at C1 ("the use of less fertilizer at precisely the right time can cut costs up to 17% for farmers in developing countries and reduce damage to the environment, according to a study of Mexican wheat").

478. *See supra* notes 431-33 and accompanying text (costs of agricultural chemicals as compared to costs for gasoline and electricity).

479. *See* Garrett Hardin, *The Tragedy of the Commons,* 83 SCIENCE 1234 (1968).

480. *See Groundwater: Draft Strategy Under TSCA Aims for Data on VOCs, Fertilizers, Septic System Additives,* [16 Current Developments] Env't Rep. (BNA) 1799 (Jan. 24, 1986).

481. 15 U.S.C. §2607, ELR STAT. TSCA §8. For a discussion of the (intended but little-used) TSCA mechanisms, see ROGERS, *supra* note 3, at 488-92.

482. 15 U.S.C. §2603, ELR STAT. TSCA §4.

483. *Id.* §2605, *ELR* STAT. TSCA §6.

484. *See Groundwater: Draft Strategy Under TSCA Aims for Data on VOCs, supra* note 480.

485. Telephone conversation of Andrew L. Adams with David Fagan, Office of Solid Waste, U.S. EPA (Jan. 30, 2002). Mr. Fagan was involved in the preparation of U.S. EPA BACKGROUND REPORT, *supra* note 468.

486. *See* U.S. EPA, BACKGROUND REPORT, *supra* note 468.

487. For an illustrative state program, see Pamela S. Clarke & Stacey M. Crank, *The Pennsylvania Nutrient Management Act: Pennsylvania Helps to "Save the Bay" Through Nonpoint Source Pollution Management,* 6 VILL. ENVTL. L.J. 319 (1995). For developments in the EU, see *New French Water Law to Extend Polluter-Pays Principle to Agriculture,* 24 Int'l Env't Rep. (BNA) 544 (July 4, 2001) (first-ever taxes on agriculture water use and runoff); Government Tells Commission It Will Hasten Efforts to Curb Nutrients to Meet EU Directive, [21 Current Developments] Env't Rep. (BNA) 1234 (Dec. 9, 1998) (EU directive imposes "nitrate accounts" and "nitrate crops"); Andrew P. Manale, *European Community Programs to Control Nitrate Emissions From Agriculture,* 14 Int'l Env't Rep. (BNA) 345 (June 19, 1991).

488. *See* MARC RIBARDO & DANETTE WOO, U.S. DEPARTMENT OF AGRICULTURE, SUMMARY OF STATE WATER QUALITY LAWS AFFECTING AGRICULTURE 54 (undated) (identifying fertilizer taxes in California, Iowa, South Dakota, and Wisconsin).

489. *See* JOHN-MARK STENSVAAG, MATERIALS ON ENVIRONMENTAL LAW 547-95 (1999); *see also* Pedersen, *supra* note 197, at 10173:
> The most potent signal alternative—imposing a tax on pollution—has thus far failed to be adopted widely. In addition, because the impact of a tax on pollution is hard to predict in advance, and because the government must also decide how to use the revenues collected, a tax raises policy and program design issues even more complicated than those that attend emissions trading.

Id. at 10173 n.4. These difficulties noted, states do impose permit fees based on the volume and toxicity of discharge, see LA. ADMIN. CODE tit. 33, §§1301-1313 (1988) (water program fee regulations), as do member countries of the EU. *See* Brennan & Johnson, *Pollution Control by Effluent Charges: It Works in the Federal Republic of Germany, Why Not in the U.S.,* 24 NAT. RESOURCES J. 929 (1984). For two symposia pushing the envelope on environment and taxation generally, see *Pollution Tax Forum: Colloquium,* 12 PACE ENVTL. L. REV. 1 (1994); Vermont Law School, The Third Annual Global Conference on Environmental Taxation (2002) (brochure) (on file with author).

490. Treaty on European Union: (Maastricht Treaty), Feb. 7, 1992, 31 I.L.M. 247, *available at* http://www.hri.org/docs/Maastrecht92.

491. *Id.* art. 130r(2) ("Action by the Commission, relating to the environment shall be based on the principles that preventative action should as a priority be rectified at the source, and that the polluter should pay.").

492. *See* Oliver A. Houck, *TMDLs, Are We There Yet? The Long Road Toward Water Quality-Based Regulation Under the Clean Water Act,* 27 ELR 10391, 10395 (Aug. 1997), Houck, *TMDLS IV, supra* note 376, at 10485-86. *See also* Chapter 7.

Chapter 7:
Concluding Thoughts

> Those who govern, having much business on their hands, do not generally like to take the trouble of considering and carrying into execution new projects. The best public measures are therefore seldom adopted from previous wisdom, but forced by the occasion.
>
> —Benjamin Franklin [1]

> You can get sucked into what the regulators tell you, but they don't live here, they don't love the river, and they're under tremendous pressure.
>
> —Housatonic River Initiative [2]

Something large is happening here. The nation is coming to grips with its huge, residual problem of water pollution, as it has with air pollution and, to an extent, with the use of the land itself—in much the same way. As has been observed elsewhere, TMDLs are the equivalent of clean air state implementation plans for water: [3] impact-based, chronically difficult mechanisms to induce states to induce polluting sources to respect baseline standards for human health and environmental quality. [4] They might also be analogized to endangered species habitat conservation plans: [5] impact-based mechanisms, chronically difficult in their science and their political science, to induce states and private parties to observe a baseline defined by the health, indeed the survival, of other living things. [6] Programs to restore and sustain the three great resources of the country—the air, the land, and the water—are now evolving convergently around the same principles, presenting the same heartaches, and limping toward the same overall goal.

One longs for a more direct approach. Wiggling backwards from water quality impacts to a multiplicity of pollution sources, each of which believes it is already doing more than its share (or has ample excuses not to do its share), through the complexity of modeling, on-site assessments, monitoring, surveillance, proof, counter-proof, never-sufficient-proof, jawboning and appeals, and through the medium of reluctant and at times even co-opted state agencies, is very much like pushing on a rope. [7] By contrast, the CWA's adoption of strike-to-the-heart, BAT standards for point source control was a stroke of genius whose effectiveness is proven not only by the stunning drop in point source loadings they produced—category by reluctant industrial category [8]—but by the stunning rate of imitation in other technology-based pollution control programs in the United States and abroad. [9] Why not for these other sources as well?

Congress could have done the same for nonpoint source pollution, but it deferred to the feeling that nonpoint sources were essentially small, local, not all that damaging, unmanageably diverse, and beyond remedy through simple technological controls. [10] Whatever its additional motives—and one suspects that in 1972 Congress had enough on its hands regulating discharges from industrial pipes without reaching for direct nonpoint controls as well—these reasons have not stood the test of time. It is now apparent that nonpoint source industries are anything but small, and in fact are led by multinational mining companies, timber corporations, agribusinesses the size of Archer Daniels Midland, and prominent members of the Fortune 500. It is also apparent that their contaminants make long journeys to both oceans, the Great Lakes, and the Gulf of Mexico, that they can be serious to the point of life-threatening, that they can wipe out entire fisheries and economies, that they are no more diverse than the several hundred categories and subcategories of point source industries regulated under the CWA, [11] and that they are far easier than most point source industries both technologically and economically to regulate—but not politically, and that is of course the rub.

It is not hard to imagine, were we starting from scratch and with the willingness of the 1972 Congress, measures even beyond national technology standards that could make significant inroads on nonpoint source pollution. Limiting inputs, such as fertilizers, comes to mind, and indeed a few states have begun to do just that, [12] as has the European Union. [13] Alternatively, the taxation of inputs [14] might come to mind for those who espouse letting "market forces" take the lead, but for the fact that the proponents of market forces always seem to disappear when it comes time to impose the volume caps, taxes, or other mechanisms that are necessary to put these forces into play; meanwhile, some of the nation's largest manufacturers of phosphate fertilizers [15] sit profitably along the lower Mississippi River selling their products to farmers upstream and watching the harmful effects of those products wash back down into the Gulf of Mexico dead zone, without paying a cent for their (considerable) environmental costs. Tax rebates for sound farm practices [16] could also help, as would more widespread cross-compliance mechanisms that have proven so successful in the U.S. Department of Agriculture swampbuster and sodbuster programs, tying federal farm subsidies to conservation goals. [17] All have been responsibly suggested, and one might dream on. But when one wakes up, it is to the expense and indirection and friction and snail's pace of TMDLs because they are the only game in town that nonpoint sources are required to play. [18]

Which leaves us with the ultimate question: Are TMDLs worth it? The jury has gone out on this question, once again. For all the reasons described in the preceding chapters, ambient-based controls have met with little success in environmental law. All the money and effort spent in calibrating loads and "proving" impacts could be better spent developing explicit technology-based best management practices, sweetening them through financial incentives, and enforcing them through the same permit mechanisms that have proven so successful in the CWA and other laws. Their consumption of resources aside, TMDLs also contain the threat of eroding the significant gains made in CWA point source controls by trading the certainty of point source permit emission limits for the amorphous and unenforceable content of state water quality and nonpoint source plans. [19] This risk is real, and rising. [20]

All of this said, TMDLs retain the upside potential for significant nonpoint source pollution control because they *sound* logical, they remain flexible, they defer largely to state prerogatives, and, most importantly, they, too, are enforceable.

The logic is political. As imperfect as their assessments may be—and all environmental assessments are imperfect—TMDLs provide both a bottom line and their own reason to get there, a reason that everybody can understand: the creek is dirty, so clean it up. The costs and difficulties of ambient standards are the price of political buy-in for parties that neither Congress nor state legislatures are otherwise willing to touch. [21] They are a means for previously unregulated sources to have their say, and for leveraging them to get beyond it. We are not "treating for treatment sake," as advocates of ambient approaches are quick to say; we are treating for something tangible that we all drink, fish, swim in, and simply look at with the pleasure of knowing that it is alive and well.

TMDLs, further, carry their own flexibility, with the potential for pollution trading and more cost-effective abatement, once all parties are firmly and inescapably (if unhappily) at the table. Positive effects from this leverage are beginning to surface in several states, with financial assistance from municipalities—which would otherwise incur significant treatment costs—for less expensive and more proactive land use controls upstream. [22]

Moreover, the states are indispensable players in an effort of this magnitude, and TMDLs respect state primacy for ambient-based water pollution control. [23] What §303(d) adds is a numerical goal, a few steps to get there that would be obvious to anyone genuinely trying, and an at times uncomfortable level of public review. These are, after all, state water quality standards, and the TMDLs will rely on whatever mix of implementation states and affected sources themselves select, a process virtually identical to the long-accepted process for CAA plans. Like air plans, they simply must contain reasonable assurance that the standards will be achieved. [24] Which is, of course, the point.

In the end, however, TMDLs are worth the effort because TMDLs, alone, have brought the same driving force into nonpoint source pollution that drove the CWA point source program toward meeting its own deadlines, promulgating its standards, issuing its permits, enforcing their provisions, and reducing pollution discharges: people who care about clean water. [25] There are a great many of them, as Congress in this decade learned. [26] There is a watchdog group in nearly every major watershed in the country, and there are many more formed around small streams and tributaries like the Hoosik River of New York and the Tangipahoa River of Louisiana that are not well known to the nation but that are cared for and defended as conscientiously as the borders of the United States. [27] It was these people whose lawsuits brought the TMDL program out of its 20-year slumber, and these same people are collecting samples on their waterways, reviewing the state data, [28] and commenting on inventories. They are ready and poised to do the same for TMDLs. [29]

These people will not be convenient for states, industry, or EPA. Some states, probably many states, will twist in several directions to minimize their TMDL responsibilities, reduce their listed waters, propose as few tangible solutions as possible, and defer implementation to the far horizon. Few TMDLs to date do otherwise. No EPA in the most willing of Administrations can bird-dog them all, and a willing Administration is never a given. At the baseline, every day, it is the Hudson Riverkeeper and SAILORS Inc. and volunteer groups like them that, in the best tradition of participatory democracy, advance the goals of law through the use of law, and no better illustration of the need for these groups exists than in the history of TMDLs.

For these reasons, TMDLs hold the best prospect of those now available for coming to grips with the last major, unregulated sources of water pollution in this country. They are not perfect mechanisms. They will require money, significantly more than we have committed to date, [30] but if America can't afford these resources while it is running its largest budget surplus of the century—as are many states—then it is hard to imagine when America can. They will require acknowledgement from nonpoint industries that they *are* the problem, cooperation from the states, staying power from the Administration, patience from Congress, and reinforcement by the courts, but if ever there were a program that fit the new millennium rhetoric of "stakeholder decisionmaking," this is the one. And if ever there were a stakeholder program likely to produce more results than bologna, it is §303(d). Because it has numerical targets and prescribed steps to achieve them, and because it empowers people with the energy and the ability in law to see that they take place.

Notes to Chapter 7

1. BENJAMIN FRANKLIN, AUTOBIOGRAPHY 212 (Yale Univ. Press 1964).

2. U.S. EPA, *Watershed Events—Fall 1998*, at 11 (visited May 20, 1999) http://www.epa.gov/owow/info/WaterEventsNews/eventf98.html (describing efforts of the Housatonic River Initiative in cleanup of the Housatonic watershed).

3. For discussion of similarities to CAA and possible implications for TMDLs, see Robert W. Adler, *Integrated Approaches to Water Pollution: Lessons From the Clean Air Act*, 23 HARV. ENVTL. L. REV. 203, 230 (1999).

4. For a discussion of difficulties in the CAA ambient-based state implementation plan (SIP) process, see Howard Latin, *Regulatory Failure, Administrative Incentives, and the New Clean Air Act*, 21 ENVTL. LAW. 1647, 1689, 1692-94 (1991):

> I believe there is a consensus among environmental analysts that the SIP process failed when the 1970 [CAA] was enacted, failed after the 1977 CAA Amendments, and was still failing to achieve attainment when the 1990 Amendments were enacted . . . . Fundamental characteristics of the SIP revision process—ambiguous institutional responsibilities, indefinite and inconsistent control requirements, uncertainty about the future effectiveness of diverse control measures, high decision making costs, bureaucratic vulnerability to interest-group criticisms and other political pressure—contributed directly to previous failures of this regulatory strategy and are still present in the new program.

See also Steve Novik & Bill Westerfield, *Whose SIP Is It Anyway? State-Federal Conflict in Clean Air Act Enforcement*, 18 WM. & MARY J. ENVTL. L. 245, 270-73 (1994):

> "From direct personal experience I can tell you it is extremely difficult for a state to adopt and implement control measures which have not been specifically required by U.S. EPA" [quoting the Director of Air Management of the Wisconsin Department of Natural Resources] . . . . State workshop participants . . . suggested that many state regulators face legislative prohibitions or political pressure not to adopt particular control measures unless they are clearly forced to by EPA . . . . State participants suggested that a second problem with models was that delegation of responsibility for applying models to the States provided them with ample opportunities to cheat in developing their implementation plans, a practice known as "gaming." States were able to choose favorable model assumptions and inputs to arrive at the least stringent predictions of emission reduction requirements [quoting from a study of the Congressional Office of Technology Assessment].

The implications of these conclusions for state implementation of TMDLs are (or should be) daunting.

5. 15 U.S.C. §1539, ELR STAT. ESA §10.

6. For a discussion of habitat conservation plans and their difficulties, see MICHAEL J. BEAN, THE EVOLUTION OF NATIONAL WILDLIFE LAW 364-65 (2d ed. 1983); Robert D. Thornton, *Searching for Consensus and Predictability: Habitat Conservation Planning Under the Endangered Species Act of 1973*, 21 ENVTL. L. 605, 606 (1991); J.B. Ruhl, *How to Kill Endangered Species Logically: The Nuts and Bolts of Endangered Species Act "HCP" Permits for Real Estate Development*, 5 ENVTL. LAW. 345 (1999).

7. Emerging from the similar morass of ambient-based regulation under the CAA, one former CAA litigator and current scholar has observed:

> [T]he Act's process is extremely complex, creating high transaction costs for governments and businesses. The Act's enforcement also requires more data about pollution effects and controls than science can provide, thereby allowing manipulation that undercuts achievement of the Act's ultimate goals, wastes resources and creates inequities . . . . It would be better for Congress to forego the theoretical benefits of fine-tuned pollution controls and instead prescribe emission limits for major industries.

David Schoenbrod, *Goals Statutes or Rules Statutes: The Case of the Clean Air Act*, 3 UCLA L. REV. 740, 743 (1983); *see also* Davis Clark, *What Went Right*, ENVTL. F., Mar./Apr. 1998, at 41:

> For anyone who doubts that goal-setting debates can be interminable, look how long the "how clean is clean" debate has been going. In contrast, look at how successfully California's Proposition 65 toxics law—with its legal hammers—has spurred business to seek action, demanding conclusive risk numbers so they can act to reduce their emissions to legally unassailable levels. For all its faults, the fragmented command-and-control regulatory system moves forward like a steamroller, motivating those in the way to hustle just to stay ahead and avoid being crushed.

8. EPA found an immediate 29% improvement in receiving water quality compliance when BAT regulations were imposed, as compared to pre-BAT conditions. U.S. EPA, REPORT TO CONGRESS: WATER QUALITY IMPROVEMENT STUDY 17 (1989).

9. This imitation, found in technology standards for CAA toxic emissions, 42 U.S.C. §7412, ELR STAT. CAA §112, Resource Conservation and Recovery Act "land ban" requirements, 42 U.S.C. §6924, ELR STAT. RCRA §3004, and other U.S. environmental programs, is discussed in Oliver Houck, *Of Birds, Bats and BAT: The Convergent Evolution of Environmental Law*, 63 MISS. L.J. 403 (1994); for the adoption of the CWA's technology standards in the European Union, see Council Directive 76/464 on Pollution Caused by Certain Dangerous Substances Discharged Into the Aquatic Environment of the Community, 1976 O.J. (L 129) 23 (providing technology-based emission limitations for toxic discharges, supplemented by a water quality standards approach).

10. *See* Oliver A. Houck, *TMDLs III: A New Framework for the Clean Water Act's Ambient Standards Program*, 28 ELR 10415, 10424 (Aug. 1998) [hereinafter *TMDLs III*]; *see also* Chapter 5, note 96 and sources cited therein.

11. *See* Effluent Guidelines and Standards, 40 C.F.R. ch. I, subch. N. (identifying technology standards for 65 major point source categories, each category containing several, and often many, subcategories).

12. *See* Marc RIBAUDO & DANETTE WOO, U.S. DEP'T OF AGRICULTURE, SUMMARY OF STATE WATER QUALITY LAWS AFFECTING AGRICULTURE 53 (undated). One would think that the costs of fertilizers alone—estimated at $320 million a year simply to offset fertilizer loss to runoff—would reduce the amounts applied, but for the fact that fertilizers do increase yields and until the costs of their application exceed the yields few farmers will unilaterally move to reduce them. *See* Garret Hardin, *The Tragedy of the Commons*, 83 SCIENCE 1234 (1968); *see also Less Fertilizer*, TIMES PICAYUNE (New Orleans), Apr. 3, 1998, at C1 ("the use of less fertilizer at precisely the right times can cut costs up to 17 percent for farmers in developing countries and reduce damage to the environment, according to a study of Mexican wheat"); Editorial, *Helping Clean the River*, TIMES PICAYUNE (New Orleans), Apr. 24, 1999, at B6 (describing reductions in fertilizer as necessary to restore the water quality of the Mississippi River).

13. The failure of member countries of the European Union (EU) to come to grips both with nonpoint source pollution and with ambient-based regulation of water quality more generally, *see* Turner T. Smith Jr. & Roszell D. Hunter, *The European Community Environmental Legal System, in* ENVIRONMENTAL LAW INST., EUROPEAN COMMUNITY DESKBOOK 22 (1992) (stating that the European Commission had initiated enforcement proceedings against all (then) 12 member states for failure to implement a water quality standards-based program), has driven both the EU and individual countries to require "nitrate accounts," impose nitrate caps, and set ambient nitrate concentration limits. *See Government Tells Commission It Will Hasten Efforts to Curb Nitrates to Meet EU Directive*, [21 Current Developments] Env't Rep. (BNA) 1234 (Dec. 9, 1998). Individual member countries have taken even more stringent measures to control agricultural nitrate sources. *See* Andrew P. Manale, *European Community Programs to Control Nitrate Emissions From Agriculture*, 14 Int'l Envtl. Rep. (BNA) 345 (June 19, 1991).

14. *See* RIBAUDO & WOO, *supra* note 12, at 54 (identifying fertilizer taxes in California, Iowa, South Dakota, and Wisconsin).

15. For a discussion of phosphate fertilizer manufacturing in Louisiana, see Alan Dean Weinberg & Dominic J. Gianna, *Whither Gypsum: The Mississippi River and the Threat of Toxic Pollution*, 3 TUL. ENVTL. L.J. 41 (1990).

16. *See* RIBAUDO & WOO, *supra* note 12.

17. The swampbuster provision of the 1990 Farm Bill dictates that federal farm subsidies cannot be used to fund wetland destruction. Linda A. Malone, *Reflections on the Jeffersonian Ideal of an Agrarian Democracy and the Emergence of an Agricultural and Environmental Ethic in the 1990 Farm Bill*, 12 STAN. ENVTL. L.J. 3

(1993). Under the sodbuster provision, all highly erodible land must be farmed according to an approved conservation plan to continue to receive federal farm benefits. Karen R. Hansen, *Agricultural Nonpoint Source Pollution: The Need for an American Farm Policy Based on an Integrated Systems Approach Recoupled to Ecology Stewardship*, 15 HAMLINE J. PUB. L. & POLICY 303 (1994). "The program has reduced soil erosion on these acres from an average of 17 tons per year to six tons per year." *Will Conservation Survive the 1995 Farm Bill?*, LAND LETTER, Dec. 31, 1994, at 5.

18. It is the fact of a requirement, of course, that is at issue. In the words of the California Research Bureau:

> Most nonpoint source representatives strongly oppose any program, whether it is a [waste discharge requirement], watershed management, TMDL, or other approach, that would set numeric limits on polluted runoff. They resist the imposition of specific management measures on individual landowners to comply with state or federal water quality guidelines. They fear that any such measures will lead to permits and actual enforcement of the numeric limits by water quality regulators.

JENNIFER RUFFOLO, CALIFORNIA RESEARCH BUREAU, TMDLs: THE REVOLUTION IN WATER QUALITY REGULATION 50 (Apr. 1999).

19. *See* WILLIAM H. RODGERS JR., ENVIRONMENTAL LAW 282 (2d ed. 1994) (stating that pollution sources long "for the day when the no discharge objective is abandoned in favor of basin level allocations of assimilative capacity").

20. E-mail Communication from Nora Chorover, Attorney, San Francisco Baykeeper, to Kathy Nemsick, Natural Resources Defense Council (Apr. 14, 1999) (on file with author) (describing regulators and regulatees in the San Francisco Bay/Delta area as viewing the TMDL process as "a vehicle for relaxing water quality based effluent limits on point source discharges."); *see also EPA to Launch Water Credit Trading Pullouts for Specific Watersheds*, INSIDE EPA WKLY. REP., Apr. 23, 1999, at 9 (the new system will enable a company to reduce discharges from another source and increase its own discharges of the same or even different pollutants).

21. For a broader discussion of these tradeoffs in environmental law, see Richard Stewart, *Pyramids of Sacrifice*, 86 YALE L.J. 1196 (1977).

22. For example, see Andrew Revkin, *U.S. to Pay Farmers to Shoo Cows Off City's Watershed*, N.Y. TIMES, Aug. 26, 1998, at B3; *see also* WASHINGTON DEP'T OF ECOLOGY & REGION X, U.S. EPA, CLEAN WATER ACT SECTION 303 ASSURANCES FOR FORESTRY MODULE (undated) (on file with author) (deferring TMDLs for the adoption of state forestry practices); see also Chelsea H. Congdon et al., *Economic Incentives and Nonpoint Source Pollution: A Case Study of California's Grasslands Region*, 2 HASTINGS W.-NW J. ENVTL. L. & POL'Y 185 (1995) (discussing the potential for nonpoint source pollutant emission caps and trading).

23. The CWA is ambiguous on the issue of primacy. *Compare* 33 U.S.C. §1251(b), ELR Stat. FWPCA §101(b) ("It is the policy of the Congress to recognize, preserve and protect the primary responsibilities and rights of States to prevent, reduce, and eliminate pollution") *with id.* §1251(a), ELR Stat. FWPCA §101(a)(1) ("[I]t is the *national* goal that the discharge of pollutants into the navigable waters be eliminated by 1985" (emphasis added)), and *id.* §1251(a), ELR Stat. FWPCA §101(a)(3) ("[I]t is the *national* policy that the discharge of toxic pollutants in toxic amounts be prohibited" (emphasis added)). In practice, the national pollutant discharge elimination system program has been driven by federal technology standards while the ambient standards program, under federal supervision to be sure, has been a state responsibility, in most states as we have seen a responsibility only lightly exercised, if that.

24. *TMDLs III, supra* note 10; for the requirement of reasonable assurances under the CAA, see 42 U.S.C. §7410, ELR Stat. CAA §110.

25. This phenomenon and the role of citizen suits in producing it is discussed in Oliver A. Houck, *TMDLs, Are We There Yet?: The Long Road Toward Water Quality-Based Regulation Under the Clean Water Act*, 27 ELR 10391, 10395 (Aug. 1997). The momentum continues. *See* Natural Resources Defense Council v. Fox, No. 94 Civ. 8424 (S.D.N.Y. filed Nov. 1994) (ongoing litigation); Hayes v. Browner, No. 97CV1090BU (J) (N.D. Okla. filed Nov. 1997) (ongoing litigation); Defenders of Wildlife v. Browner, No. 93-234 TUC ACM (D. Ariz. Apr. 22, 1997) (consent decree entered); Ohio Valley Envtl. Coalition, Inc. v. Browner, No. 2:95-0529 (S.D. W. Va. filed July 1995) (settled). As of March 30, 1999, EPA had listed 13 states with consent orders to establish TMDLs, 16 more states with TMDL cases pending, 5 more states with notices of intent to sue to establish TMDLs, and 6 more states with notices of intent to sue to establish 1998 lists of impaired waters. U.S. EPA, *Total Maximum Daily Load (TMDL) Program: TMDL Litigation by State* (last visited Mar. 30, 1999), *at* http://www.epa.gov/owow/tmdl/lawsuit1.html.

26. Legislation of the 104th Congress designed to relax CWA requirements met with strong public opposition and was widely perceived as a political mistake by parties on all sides of the issue. *See* Oliver A. Houck, *TMDLs: The Resurrection of Water Quality Standards-Based Regulation Under the Clean Water Act*, 27 ELR 10329, 10343-44 (July 1997).

27. One such recently formed organization is SAILORS Inc., short for Save All Iowa Lakes, Oxbows, Rivers and Streams Inc; any group with this level of imagination in its name holds the promise for follow through. In November 1998, SAILORS filed suit over the adequacy of Iowa's TMDL program. E-mail Communication from Regina Thiry, SAILORS Inc., to Oliver Houck (Apr. 15, 1999) (on file with author).

28. *See* Comments of Alliance for Wild Rockies and the Lands Council, on the 1998 Idaho 303(d) List (Feb. 15, 1999) (on file with author) (a detailed critique of Idaho's most recent submission of impaired waters). While the critique is doubtless subject to criticism in its own right, the fact of this and similar critiques feeding into state and federal decisions is as important—indeed vital—to the success of the

CWA as it is to the success of the National Environmental Policy Act and to all American environmental law.

29. The judicial review and enforceability of TMDLs by citizen groups remain an open question. EPA approval of a state TMDL is judicially reviewable in federal court and, if the TMDL includes an implementation plan, the plan will be reviewable as well. This review is, of course, the reason for industry resistance to §303(d) generally and to inclusion of such a plan in TMDLs. Once a state TMDL-cum-plan is approved, however, the enforcement of its conditions will depend in the first instance on review by state courts and state law. The difference between the enforcement of TMDLs and existing state "water management plans" in state court, of course, is that TMDLs hold the promise of containing objective (i.e., reviewable) requirements. EPA's continuing leverage and, indirectly that of citizen groups, will be through the more general review of state-delegated programs and through other funding and permitting authority. *See TMDLs III, supra* note 10, at 10420-21. Exercising this authority under the CWA, which lacks the sanction found in the CAA, for example, of reducing state transportation funding for inadequate state plans, 42 U.S.C. §7509, ELR STAT. CAA §179 (sanctions and consequences of failure to attain), will be a continuing challenge to the Agency and will likely result in even more "negotiated" TMDLs than similarly negotiated CAA implementation plans.

30. EPA has recently estimated expenditures of $9.4 billion in annual nonpoint pollution control costs. *See Congress to Investigate Nonpoint Pollution Activities, Cost Estimates*, INSIDE EPA WKLY. REP., Mar. 19, 1999, at 11. Another report places the sum at $100 billion over the next 20 years. *EPA Seeks Nonpoint Source Authority*, INSIDE EPA WKLY. REP., May 7, 1999, at 4. These costs appear to be both low and high. Both the U.S. GAO and a prominent House committee chair have criticized EPA's estimates as under inclusive. *Id; see also* U.S. GAO, *Water Quality: Federal Role in Addressing and Contributing to Nonpoint Source Pollution*, GAO/RCED-99-45, ch. 0:3 (Feb. 26, 1999) http://www.gao.gov/AIndexFY99/abstracts/rc99045.htm; Rep. Sherwood L. Boehlert, Statement Before the Water Resources and Environmental Subcommittee Hearing on Governors' Perspectives on the Clean Water Act (Feb. 23, 1999) ("I believe that EPA will be the first to admit that its estimates of nonpoint are unrealistically low."). On the other hand, the great majority of expenditures EPA claims for nonpoint source pollution controls are the expenses of other federal programs, the majority being those of the USDA, with other primary (e.g., soil conservation) objectives. *Id.* ch. 0:4.1. Meanwhile, the NOAA Administrator has announced a budget of $22 million in fiscal year 2000 (an increase of $5.8 million) for nonpoint pollution abatement. *See* OFFICE OF PUBLIC AND CONSTITUENT AFFAIRS, NATIONAL OCEANIC & ATMOSPHERIC ADMINISTRATION, NOAA's CLEAN WATER INITIATIVE (undated) (on file with author); *see also* Susan Bruninga, *Browner Defends Proposed SRF Cuts, Seeks New Clean Water Law, Funding Plan*, [29 Current Developments] Env't Rep. (BNA) 2480 (Apr. 19, 1999) (describing a proposed $550 million reduction in the clean water state revolving fund, monies traditionally used for sewage treatment construction but more recently made available for nonpoint

source controls as well). Obviously, the supply side of the clean water equation has yet to meet the demand side.

Appendices

Appendix A
Clean Water Act §§303(d)-(e) and 319

Federal Water Pollution Control Act
33 U.S.C. §§1313(d)–(e) and 1329

(commonly known as the Clean Water Act §§303(d)–(e) and 319)

§1313 [FWPCA §303]
Water quality standards and implementation plans

. . .

(d) Identification of areas with insufficient controls; maximum daily load; certain effluent limitations revision

(1)(A) Each State shall identify those waters within its boundaries for which the effluent limitations required by section 1311(b)(1)(A) and section 1311(b)(1)(B) of this title are not stringent enough to implement any water quality standard applicable to such waters. The State shall establish a priority ranking for such waters, taking into account the severity of the pollution and the uses to be made of such waters.

(B) Each State shall identify those waters or parts thereof within its boundaries for which controls on thermal discharges under section 1311 of this title are not stringent enough to assure protection and propagation of a balanced indigenous population of shellfish, fish, and wildlife.

(C) Each State shall establish for the waters identified in paragraph (1)(A) of this subsection, and in accordance with the priority ranking, the total maximum daily load, for those pollutants which the Administrator identifies under section 1314(a)(2) of this title as suitable for such calculation. Such load shall be established at a level necessary to implement the applicable water quality standards with seasonal variations and a margin of safety which takes into account any lack of knowledge concerning the relationship between effluent limitations and water quality.

(D) Each State shall estimate for the waters identified in paragraph (1)(B) of this subsection the total maximum daily thermal load required to assure protection and propagation of a balanced, indigenous population of shellfish, fish, and wildlife. Such estimates shall take into account the normal water temperatures, flow rates, seasonal variations, existing sources of heat input, and the dissipative capacity of the identified waters or parts thereof. Such estimates shall include a calculation of the maximum heat input that can be made into each such part and shall include a margin of safety which takes into account any lack of knowledge concerning the development of thermal water quality criteria for such protection and propagation in the identified waters or parts thereof.

(2) Each State shall submit to the Administrator from time to time, with the first such submission not later than one hundred and eighty days after the date of publication of the first identification of pollutants under section 1314(a)(2)(D) of this title, for his approval the waters identified and the loads established under paragraphs (1)(A), (1)(B), (1)(C), and (1)(D) of this subsection. The Administrator shall either approve or disapprove such identification and load not later than thirty days after the date of submission. If the Administrator approves such identification and load, such State shall incorporate them into its current plan under subsection (e) of this section. If the Administrator disapproves such identification and load, he shall not later than thirty days after the date of such disapproval identify such waters in such State and establish such loads for such waters as he determines necessary to implement the water quality standards applicable to such waters and upon such identification and establishment the State shall incorporate them into its current plan under subsection (e) of this section.

(3) For the specific purpose of developing information, each State shall identify all waters within its boundaries which it has not identified under paragraph (1)(A) and (1)(B) of this subsection and estimate for such waters the total maximum daily load with seasonal variations and margins of safety, for those pollutants which the Administrator identifies under section 1314(a)(2) of this title as suitable for such calculation and for thermal discharges, at a level that would assure protection and propagation of a balanced indigenous population of fish, shellfish, and wildlife.

(4) Limitations on revision of certain effluent limitations

(A) Standard not attained

For waters identified under paragraph (1)(A) where the applicable water quality standard has not yet been attained, any effluent limitation based on a total maximum daily load or other waste load allocation established under this section may be revised only if (i) the cumulative effect of all such revised effluent limitations based on such total maximum daily load or waste load allocation will assure the attainment of such water quality standard, or (ii) the designated use which is not being attained is removed in accordance with regulations established under this section.

(B) Standard attained

For waters identified under paragraph (1)(A) where the quality of such waters equals or exceeds levels necessary to protect the designated use for such waters or otherwise required by applicable water quality standards, any effluent limitation based on a total maximum daily load or other waste load allocation established under this section, or any water quality standard established under this section, or any other permitting standard may be revised only if such revision is subject to and consistent with the antidegradation policy established under this section.

(e) Continuing planning process

(1) Each State shall have a continuing planning process approved under paragraph (2) of this subsection which is consistent with this chapter.

(2) Each State shall submit not later than 120 days after October 18, 1972, to the Administrator for his approval a proposed continuing planning process which is consistent with this chapter. Not later than thirty days after the date of submission of such a process the Administrator shall either approve or disapprove such process. The Administrator shall from time to time review each State's approved planning process for the purpose of insuring that such planning process is at all times consistent with this chapter. The Administrator shall not approve any State permit program under subchapter IV of this chapter for any State which does not have an approved continuing planning process under this section.

(3) The Administrator shall approve any continuing planning process submitted to him under this section which will result in plans for all navigable waters within such State, which include, but are not limited to, the following:

(A) effluent limitations and schedules of compliance at least as stringent as those required by section 1311(b)(1), section 1311(b)(2), section 1316, and section 1317 of this title, and at least as stringent as any requirements contained in any applicable water quality standard in effect under authority of this section;

(B) the incorporation of all elements of any applicable area-wide waste management plans under section 1288 of this title, and applicable basin plans under section 1289 of this title;

(C) total maximum daily load for pollutants in accordance with subsection (d) of this section;

(D) procedures for revision;

(E) adequate authority for intergovernmental cooperation;

(F) adequate implementation, including schedules of compliance, for revised or new water quality standards, under subsection (c) of this section;

(G) controls over the disposition of all residual waste from any water treatment processing;

(H) an inventory and ranking, in order of priority, of needs for construction of waste treatment works required to meet the applicable requirements of sections 1311 and 1312 of this title.

§1329 [FWPCA §319]
Nonpoint source management programs
(a) State assessment reports
(1) Contents

The Governor of each State shall, after notice and opportunity for public comment, prepare and submit to the Administrator for approval, a report which—

(A) identifies those navigable waters within the State which, without additional action to control nonpoint sources of pollution, cannot reasonably be expected to attain or maintain applicable water quality standards or the goals and requirements of this chapter;

(B) identifies those categories and subcategories of nonpoint sources or, where appropriate, particular nonpoint sources which add significant pollution to each portion of the navigable waters identified under subparagraph (A) in amounts which contribute to such portion not meeting such water quality standards or such goals and requirements;

(C) describes the process, including intergovernmental coordination and public participation, for identifying best management practices and measures to control each category and subcategory of nonpoint sources and, where appropriate, particular nonpoint sources identified under subparagraph (B) and to reduce, to the maximum extent practicable, the level of pollution resulting from such category, subcategory, or source; and

(D) identifies and describes State and local programs for controlling pollution added from nonpoint sources to, and improving the quality of, each such portion of the navigable waters, including but not limited to those programs which are receiving Federal assistance under subsections (h) and (i) of this section.

(2) Information used in preparation

In developing the report required by this section, the State (A) may rely upon information developed pursuant to sections 1288, 1313(e), 1314(f), 1315(b), and 1324 of this title, and other information as appropriate, and (B) may utilize appropriate elements of the waste treatment management plans developed pursuant to sections 1288(b) and 1313 of this title, to the extent such elements are consistent with and fulfill the requirements of this section.

(b) State management programs
(1) In general

The Governor of each State, for that State or in combination with adjacent States, shall, after notice and opportunity for public comment, prepare and submit to the Administrator for approval a management program which such State proposes to implement in the first four fiscal years beginning after the date of submission of such management program for controlling pollution added from nonpoint sources to the navigable waters within the State and improving the quality of such waters.

(2) Specific contents

Each management program proposed for implementation under this subsection shall include each of the following:

(A) An identification of the best management practices and measures which will be undertaken to reduce pollutant loadings resulting from each category, subcategory, or particular nonpoint source designated under paragraph (1)(B), taking into account the impact of the practice on groundwater quality.

(B) An identification of programs (including, as appropriate, nonregulatory or regulatory programs for enforcement, technical assistance, financial assistance, education, training, technology transfer, and demonstration projects) to achieve implementation of the best management practices by the categories, subcategories, and particular nonpoint sources designated under subparagraph (A).

(C) A schedule containing annual milestones for (i) utilization of the program implementation methods identified in subparagraph (B), and (ii) implementation of the best management practices identified in subparagraph (A) by the categories, subcategories, or particular nonpoint sources designated under paragraph (1)(B). Such schedule shall provide for utilization of the best management practices at the earliest practicable date.

(D) A certification of the attorney general of the State or States (or the chief attorney of any State water pollution control agency which has independent legal counsel) that the laws of the State or States, as the case may be, provide adequate authority to implement such management program or, if there is not such adequate authority, a list of such additional authorities as will be necessary to implement such management program. A schedule and commitment by the State or States to seek such additional authorities as expeditiously as practicable.

(E) Sources of Federal and other assistance and funding (other than assistance provided under subsections (h) and (i) of this section) which will be available in each of such fiscal years for supporting implementation of such practices and measures and the purposes for which such assistance will be used in each of such fiscal years.

(F) An identification of Federal financial assistance programs and Federal development projects for which the State will review individual assistance applications or development projects for their effect on water quality pursuant to the procedures set forth in Executive Order 12372 as in effect on September 17, 1983, to determine whether such assistance applications or development projects would be consistent with the program prepared under this subsection; for the purposes of this subparagraph, identification shall not be limited to the assistance programs or development projects subject to Executive Order 12372 but may include any programs listed in the most recent Catalog of Federal Domestic Assistance which may have an effect on the purposes and objectives of the State's nonpoint source pollution management program.

(3) Utilization of local and private experts

In developing and implementing a management program under this subsection, a State shall, to the maximum extent practicable, involve local public and private agencies and organizations which have expertise in control of nonpoint sources of pollution.

(4) Development on watershed basis

A State shall, to the maximum extent practicable, develop and implement a management program under this subsection on a watershed-by-watershed basis within such State.

(c) Administrative provisions

(1) Cooperation requirement

Any report required by subsection (a) of this section and any management program and report required by subsection (b) of this section shall be developed in cooperation with local, substate regional, and interstate entities which are actively planning for the implementation of nonpoint source pollution controls and have either been certified by the Administrator in accordance with section 1288 of this title, have worked jointly with the State on water quality management planning under section 1285(j) of this title, or have been designated by the State legislative body or Governor as water quality management planning agencies for their geographic areas.

(2) Time period for submission of reports and management programs

Each report and management program shall be submitted to the Administrator during the 18-month period beginning on February 4, 1987.

(d) Approval or disapproval of reports and management programs

(1) Deadline

Subject to paragraph (2), not later than 180 days after the date of submission to the Administrator of any report or management program under this section (other than subsections (h), (i), and (k) of this section), the Administrator shall either approve or disapprove such report or management program, as the case may be. The Administrator may approve a portion of a management program under this subsection. If the Administrator does not disapprove a report, management program, or portion of a management program in such 180-day period, such report, management program, or portion shall be deemed approved for purposes of this section.

(2) Procedure for disapproval

If, after notice and opportunity for public comment and consultation with appropriate Federal and State agencies and other interested persons, the Administrator determines that—

(A) the proposed management program or any portion thereof does not meet the requirements of subsection (b)(2) of this section or is not likely to satisfy, in whole or in part, the goals and requirements of this chapter;

(B) adequate authority does not exist, or adequate resources are not available, to implement such program or portion;

(C) the schedule for implementing such program or portion is not sufficiently expeditious; or

(D) the practices and measures proposed in such program or portion are not adequate to reduce the level of pollution in navigable waters in the State resulting from nonpoint sources and to improve the quality of navigable waters in the State;

the Administrator shall within 6 months of the receipt of the proposed program notify the State of any revisions or modifications necessary to obtain approval. The State shall thereupon have an additional 3 months to submit its revised management program and the Administrator shall approve or disapprove such revised program within three months of receipt.

(3) Failure of State to submit report

If a Governor of a State does not submit the report required by subsection (a) of this section within the period specified by subsection (c)(2) of this section, the Administrator shall, within 30 months after February 4, 1987, prepare a report for such State which makes the identifications required by paragraphs (1)(A) and (1)(B) of subsection (a) of this section. Upon completion of the requirement of the preceding sentence and after notice and opportunity for comment, the Administrator shall report to Congress on his actions pursuant to this section.

(e) Local management programs; technical assistance

If a State fails to submit a management program under subsection (b) of this section or the Administrator does not approve such a management program, a local public agency or organization which has expertise in, and authority to, control water pollution resulting from nonpoint sources in any area of such State which the Administrator determines is of sufficient geographic size may, with approval of such State, request the Administrator to provide, and the Administrator shall provide, technical assistance to such agency or organization in developing for such area a management program which is described in subsection (b) of this section and can be approved pursuant to subsection (d) of this section. After development of such management program, such agency or organization shall submit such management program to the Administrator for approval. If the Administrator approves such management program, such agency or organization shall be eligible to receive financial assistance under subsection (h) of this section for implementation of such management program as if such agency or organization were a State for which a report submitted under subsection (a) of this section and a management program submitted under subsection (b) of this section were approved under this section. Such financial assistance shall be subject to the same terms and conditions as assistance provided to a State under subsection (h) of this section.

(f) Technical assistance for States

Upon request of a State, the Administrator may provide technical assistance to such State in developing a management program approved under subsection (b) of this section for those portions of the navigable waters requested by such State.

(g) Interstate management conference

(1) Convening of conference; notification; purpose

If any portion of the navigable waters in any State which is implementing a management program approved under this section is not meeting applicable water quality standards or the goals and requirements of this chapter as a result, in whole or in part, of pollution from nonpoint sources in another State, such State may petition the Administrator to convene, and the Administrator shall convene, a management conference of all States which contribute significant pollution resulting from nonpoint sources to such portion. If, on the basis of information available, the Administrator determines that a State is not meeting applicable water quality standards or the goals and requirements of this chapter as a result, in whole or in part, of significant pollution from nonpoint sources in another State, the Administrator shall notify such States. The Administrator may convene a management conference under this paragraph not later than 180 days after giving such notification, whether or not the State which is not meeting such standards requests such conference. The purpose of such conference shall be to develop an agreement among such States to reduce the level of pollution in such portion resulting from nonpoint sources and to improve the water quality of such portion. Nothing in such agreement shall supersede or abrogate rights to quantities of water which have been established by interstate water compacts, Supreme Court decrees, or State water laws. This subsection shall not apply to any pollution which is subject to the Colorado River Basin Salinity Control Act [43 U.S.C. 1571 et seq.]. The requirement that the Administrator convene a management conference shall not be subject to the provisions of section 1365 of this title.

(2) State management program requirement

To the extent that the States reach agreement through such conference, the management programs of the States which are parties to such agreements and which contribute significant pollution to the navigable waters or portions thereof not meeting applicable water quality standards or goals and requirements of this chapter will be revised to reflect such agreement. Such management programs shall be consistent with Federal and State law.

(h) Grant program

(1) Grants for implementation of management programs

Upon application of a State for which a report submitted under subsection (a) of this section and a management program submitted under subsection (b) of this section is approved under this section, the Administrator shall make grants, subject to such terms and conditions as the Administrator considers appropriate, under this subsection to such State for the purpose of assisting the State in implementing such management program. Funds reserved pursuant to section 1285(j)(5) of this title may be used to develop and implement such management program.

(2) Applications

An application for a grant under this subsection in any fiscal year shall be in such form and shall contain such other information as the Administrator may require, including an identification and description of the best management practices and measures which the State proposes to assist, encourage, or require in such year with the Federal assistance to be provided under the grant.

(3) Federal share

The Federal share of the cost of each management program implemented with Federal assistance under this subsection in any fiscal year shall not exceed 60 percent of the cost incurred by the State in implementing such management program and shall be made on condition that the non-Federal share is provided from non-Federal sources.

(4) Limitation on grant amounts

Notwithstanding any other provision of this subsection, not more than 15 percent of the amount appropriated to carry out this subsection may be used to make grants to any one State, including any grants to any local public agency or organization with authority to control pollution from nonpoint sources in any area of such State.

(5) Priority for effective mechanisms

For each fiscal year beginning after September 30, 1987, the Administrator may give priority in making grants under this subsection, and shall give consideration in determining the Federal share of any such grant, to States which have implemented or are proposing to implement management programs which will—

(A) control particularly difficult or serious nonpoint source pollution problems, including, but not limited to, problems resulting from mining activities;

(B) implement innovative methods or practices for controlling nonpoint sources of pollution, including regulatory programs where the Administrator deems appropriate;

(C) control interstate nonpoint source pollution problems; or

(D) carry out groundwater quality protection activities which the Administrator determines are part of a comprehensive nonpoint source pollution control program, including research, planning, groundwater assessments, demonstration programs, enforcement, technical assistance, education, and training to protect groundwater quality from nonpoint sources of pollution.

(6) Availability for obligation

The funds granted to each State pursuant to this subsection in a fiscal year shall remain available for obligation by such State for the fiscal year for which appropriated. The amount of any such funds not obligated by the end of such fiscal year shall be available to the Administrator for granting to other States under this subsection in the next fiscal year.

(7) Limitation on use of funds

States may use funds from grants made pursuant to this section for financial assistance to persons only to the extent that such assistance is related to the costs of demonstration projects.

(8) Satisfactory progress

No grant may be made under this subsection in any fiscal year to a State which in the preceding fiscal year received a grant under this subsection unless the Administrator determines that such State made satisfactory progress in such preceding fiscal year in meeting the schedule specified by such State under subsection (b)(2) of this section.

(9) Maintenance of effort

No grant may be made to a State under this subsection in any fiscal year unless such State enters into such agreements with the Administrator as the Administrator may require to ensure that such State will maintain its aggregate expenditures from all other sources for programs for controlling pollution added to the navigable waters in such State from nonpoint sources and improving the quality of such waters at or above the average level of such expenditures in its two fiscal years preceding February 4, 1987.

(10) Request for information

The Administrator may request such information, data, and reports as he considers necessary to make the determination of continuing eligibility for grants under this section.

(11) Reporting and other requirements

Each State shall report to the Administrator on an annual basis concerning (A) its progress in meeting the schedule of milestones submitted pursuant to subsection (b)(2)(C) of this section, and (B) to the extent that appropriate information is available, reductions in nonpoint source pollutant loading and improvements in water quality for those navigable waters or watersheds within the State which were identified pursuant to subsection (a)(1)(A) of this section resulting from implementation of the management program.

(12) Limitation on administrative costs

For purposes of this subsection, administrative costs in the form of salaries, overhead, or indirect costs for services provided and charged against activities and programs carried out with a grant under this subsection shall not exceed in any fiscal year 10 percent of the amount of the grant in such year, except that costs of implementing enforcement and regulatory activities, education, training, technical assistance, demonstration projects, and technology transfer programs shall not be subject to this limitation.

(i) Grants for protecting groundwater quality

(1) Eligible applicants and activities

Upon application of a State for which a report submitted under subsection (a) of this section and a plan submitted under subsection (b) of this section is approved under this section, the Administrator shall make grants under this subsection to such State for the purpose of assisting such State in carrying out groundwater quality protection activities which the Administrator determines will advance the State toward implementation of a comprehensive nonpoint source pollution control program. Such activities shall include, but not be limited to, research, planning, groundwater assessments, demonstration programs, enforcement, technical assistance, education and training to protect the quality of groundwater and to prevent contamination of groundwater from nonpoint sources of pollution.

(2) Applications

An application for a grant under this subsection shall be in such form and shall contain such information as the Administrator may require.

(3) Federal share; maximum amount

The Federal share of the cost of assisting a State in carrying out groundwater protection activities in any fiscal year under this subsection shall be 50 percent of the costs incurred by the State in carrying out such activities, except that the maximum amount of Federal assistance which any State may receive under this subsection in any fiscal year shall not exceed $130,000.

(4) Report

The Administrator shall include in each report transmitted under subsection (m) of this section a report on the activities and programs implemented under this subsection during the preceding fiscal year.

(j) Authorization of appropriations

There is authorized to be appropriated to carry out subsections (h) and (i) of this section not to exceed $70,000,000 for fiscal year 1988, $100,000,000 per fiscal year for each of fiscal years 1989 and 1990, and $130,000,000 for fiscal year 1991; except that for each of such fiscal years not to exceed $7,500,000 may be made available to carry out subsection (i) of this section. Sums appropriated pursuant to this subsection shall remain available until expended.

(k) Consistency of other programs and projects with management programs

The Administrator shall transmit to the Office of Management and Budget and the appropriate Federal departments and agencies a list of those assistance programs and development projects identified by each State under subsection (b)(2)(F) of this section for which individual assistance applications and projects will be reviewed pursuant to the procedures set forth in Executive Order 12372 as in effect on September 17, 1983. Beginning not later than sixty days after receiving notification by the Administrator, each Federal department and agency shall modify existing regulations to allow States to review individual development projects and assistance applications under the identified Federal assistance programs and shall accommodate, according to the requirements and definitions of Executive Order 12372, as in effect on September 17, 1983, the concerns of the State regarding the consistency of such applications or projects with the State nonpoint source pollution management program.

(l) Collection of information

The Administrator shall collect and make available, through publications and other appropriate means, information pertaining to management practices and implementation methods, including, but not limited to, (1) information concerning the costs and relative efficiencies of best management practices for reducing nonpoint source pollution; and (2) available data concerning the relationship between water quality and implementation of various management practices to control nonpoint sources of pollution.

(m) Reports of Administrator

(1) Annual reports

Not later than January 1, 1988, and each January 1 thereafter, the Administrator shall transmit to the Committee on Public Works and Transportation of the House of Representatives and the Committee on Environment and Public Works of the Senate, a report for the preceding fiscal year on the activities and programs implemented under this section and the progress made in reducing pollution in the navigable waters resulting from nonpoint sources and improving the quality of such waters.

(2) Final report

Not later than January 1, 1990, the Administrator shall transmit to Congress a final report on the activities carried out under this section. Such report, at a minimum, shall—

(A) describe the management programs being implemented by the States by types and amount of affected navigable waters, categories and subcategories of nonpoint sources, and types of best management practices being implemented;

(B) describe the experiences of the States in adhering to schedules and implementing best management practices;

(C) describe the amount and purpose of grants awarded pursuant to subsections (h) and (i) of this section;

(D) identify, to the extent that information is available, the progress made in reducing pollutant loads and improving water quality in the navigable waters;

(E) indicate what further actions need to be taken to attain and maintain in those navigable waters (i) applicable water quality standards, and (ii) the goals and requirements of this chapter;

(F) include recommendations of the Administrator concerning future programs (including enforcement programs) for controlling pollution from nonpoint sources; and

(G) identify the activities and programs of departments, agencies, and instrumentalities of the United States which are inconsistent with the management programs submitted by the States and recommend modifications so that such activities and programs are consistent with and assist the States in implementation of such management programs.

(n) Set aside for administrative personnel

Not less than 5 percent of the funds appropriated pursuant to subsection (j) of this section for any fiscal year shall be available to the Administrator to maintain personnel levels at the Environmental Protection Agency at levels which are adequate to carry out this section in such year.

(June 30, 1948, ch. 758, title III, §319, as added Feb. 4, 1987, Pub. L. 100-4, title III, §316(a), 101 Stat. 52.)

References In Text

Executive Order 12372, referred to in subsecs. (b)(2)(F) and (k), is Ex. Ord. No. 12372, July 14, 1982, 47 F.R. 30959, as amended, which is set out under section 6506 of Title 31, Money and Finance.

Appendix B

TMDL LITIGATION BY STATE[1]

States in which EPA is under court order to establish TMDLs if states do not establish TMDLs

Alabama (1998 consent decree)
Alaska (1992 consent decree)
Arkansas (2000 consent decree)
Calif. (LA) (1999 consent decree)
Calif. (North Coast)
   (1997 consent decree)
Calif. (Newport Bay)
   (1997 consent decree)
Delaware (1997 consent decree)
District of Columbia
   (2000 consent decree)
Florida (1999 consent decree)
Georgia (1997 consent decree)
Hawaii (2001 partial consent decree)

Iowa (2001 consent decree)
Kansas (1998 consent decree)
Louisiana (2002 consent decree)
Mississippi (1998 consent decree)
Missouri (2001 consent decree)
Montana (2000 consent decree)
New Mexico (1997 consent decree)
Oregon (2000 consent decree)
Pennsylvania (1997 consent decree)

Tennessee (2001 consent decree)
Virginia (1999 consent decree)
Washington (1998 consent decree)
West Virginia (1997 consent decree)

States with respect to which plaintiffs have filed litigation seeking to compel EPA to establish TMDLs

California
Idaho
Nevada
Ohio
Wyoming

---

1   Source: U.S. EPA, June 24, 2002.

State in which notices of intent to sue have been filed seeking court orders for EPA to establish TMDLs

Arizona

Cases dismissed without orders that EPA establish TMDLs (some cases were resolved with settlement agreements)

Arizona (EPA completed all consent decree obligations; decree terminated July 17, 2000)

Colorado (joint motion for administrative closure filed Aug. 24, 1999; parties signed settlement agreement in which EPA agreed to establish TMDLs if state did not)

Idaho (EPA motion to dismiss granted 1997)

Lake Michigan (WI, IL, IN, MI) (Scott case—final order 1984; related NWF case challenging EPA actions in response to Scott order—case dismissed in 1991)

Minnesota (dismissed in 1993)

Maryland (dismissed in 2001)

New Jersey (dismissed in 2002)

New York (EPA motion to dismiss granted on all but one claim on May 2, 2000)

North Carolina (joint stipulation of dismissal filed June 1998; EPA agreed by letter to ensure development of a TMDL for the Nuese River by certain date)

Oklahoma (Tenth Circuit upheld dismissal of case on Aug. 29, 2001)

South Dakota (dismissed without prejudice on Aug. 27, 1999)

APPENDIX C

Summary of Illustrative Total Maximum Daily Load Determinations, April 1998

The summary that follows tracks the steps of the Clean Water Act §303(d) and of EPA regulations and guidance for their implementation. In brief, a TMDL is the sum of those waste load allocations (WLAs) of a given pollutant from point sources, load allocations (LAs) from nonpoint sources, margins of safety (MOS) to reflect uncertainty in the calculations, and margins to accommodate discharges from future development (MFDs) that are necessary to reduce their total in order for the receiving water to meet a state water quality standard. EPA's equation simply captures the obvious: TMDL = WLA + LA + MOS + MFD. Logically, a TMDL will first identify the total current loadings of an offending pollutant, then the total (lesser) loadings necessary to meet water quality standards, and the necessary allocations and margins and, at least in some fashion, a mechanism for their implementation. These were the points of focus for the analysis below. A further description of this analysis and its conclusions is contained in the preceding text.

Location (by EPA Region)	Source	Pollutants of Concern	Pre-TMDL Load	Gross Load Cal. (TMDL)	TMDL Allocation (PS/NPS)	Implementation	Margin of Safety	Future Dev. Margin	Projected NPS Reduction
Region 1									
Willimantic River, Connecticut	PS	NH3-N, DO, Phosphorus, TSS	no	PS only	PS: quantified	WLA: NPDES	no	no	no
Lake Champlain, NY, VT, Quebec	PS/NPS	Phosphorus	quantified	quantified	PS: quantified NPS: quantified only	WLA: NPDES LA: BMPs	quantified	quantified	yes
Flints Pond Hollis, NH	NPS	Phosphorus, Chlorophyll-a	quantified	quantified	NPS: quantified	LA: zoning, BMPs	no	no	yes
Lamprey River Epping, NH	PS/NPS	NH3-N, DO, CBOD, Phosphorus	not quantified	quantified (seasonal)	PS: quantified NPS: quantified	WLA: NPDES LA: none	quantified	no	no
Saco River Estuary, Maine	PS	DO, BOD	quantified	quantified in part	PS: quantified	WLA: NPDES	quantified	no	no
Region 2									
Bog Brook Reservoir, NY	PS, NPS	Phosphorus	quantified	quantified	PS: quantified NPS: quantified	WLA: NPDES LA: BMP (reserved)	quantified	quantified	no (deferred)
East Branch Reservoir, NY	PS, NPS	Phosphorus	quantified	quantified	PS: quantified NPS: quantified	WLA: NPDES LA: BMP (reserved)	quantified	not quantified, mentioned	no (deferred)

Location (by EPA Region)	Source	Pollutants of Concern	Pre-TMDL Load	Gross Load Cal. (TMDL)	TMDL Allocation (PS/NPS)	Implementation	Margin of Safety	Future Dev. Margin	Projected NPS Reduction
Croton Falls Reservoir, NY	PS, NPS	Phosphorus	quantified	quantified	PS: quantified NPS: quantified	WLA: NPDES LA: BMP (reserved)	quantified	not quantified, mentioned	no (deferred)
Diverting Reservoir, NY	PS, NPS	Phosphorus	quantified	quantified	PS: quantified NPS: quantified	WLA: NPDES LA: BMP (reserved)	quantified	not quantified, mentioned	no (deferred)
Middle Branch Reservoir, NY	PS, NPS	Phosphorus	quantified	quantified	PS: quantified NPS: quantified	WLA: NPDES LA: BMP (reserved)	quantified	not quantified, mentioned	no (deferred)
Region 3									
Apoquinimink River, DE	PS, NPS	Phosphorus, CBOD, BOD	quantified	quantified	PS: quantified NPS: quantified	WLA: NPDES LA: not specified	not quantified, mentioned	no	yes (but unspecified)
Upper Blackwater River, VA	PS, NPS	CBOD, NBOD	quantified	quantified	PS: quantified NPS: quantified	WLA: NPDES LA: not specified	not quantified, mentioned	no	yes (but unspecified)
South Fork Branch Potomac River, WV	PS, NPS	Fecal coliform	quantified	quantified	PS: quantified NPS: quantified	WLA: NPDES LA: not specified	not quantified, mentioned	no	yes (but unspecified)
Region 4									
Tar-Pamlico Basin, NC	PS, NPS	Nitrogen, Phosphorus	quantified	quantified	PS: quantified NPS: no	PS/NPS Trading Program	not quantified, mentioned	not quantified, mentioned	yes
Roanoke River, NC***	PS	Dioxin	quantified	quantified	PS: quantified	yes	no	no	no
Lake Wylie, NC	PS, NPS	Chlorophyll-a	quantified	quantified	PS: quantified NPS: no	WLA: NPDES LA: BMP	not quantified, mentioned	quantified	no

Location (by EPA Region)	Source	Pollutants of Concern	Pre-TMDL Load	Gross Load Cal. (TMDL)	TMDL Allocation (PS/NPS)	Implementation	Margin of Safety	Future Dev. Margin	Projected NPS Reduction
Region 5									
Roberts Creek Brownsdale, MN	PS, NPS	CBOD, DO, NH3-N	no	quantified	PS: quantified NPS: not quantified	WLA: NPDES LA: no	no	no	no
Center Creek Fairmont, MN	PS	TSS, DO, CBOD, NH3-N, Fecal coliform	quantified	for NH3-N (seasonal)	PS: quantified NPS: not quantified	WLA: NPDES LA: no	no	no	no
Penobscot Creek Hibbing, MN	PS	DO, NH3-N, Temperature	quantified	no	PS: quantified (seasonal) NPS: not quantified	WLA: NPDES LA: no	no	no	no
Sycamore Creek Ingham Co., MI	NPS	Sediment, TSS	quantified	quantified	NPS: quantified	LA: BMP	no	no	no
Lower Minn. River, MN	PS, NPS	CBOD, Ammonia	quantified	quantified (seasonal)	PS: quantified NPS: quantified	WLA: NPDES LA: BMP	no	no	yes
Region 6									
North Canadian River, OK	PS	CBOD	quantified	quantified (seasonal)	PS: quantified NPS: quantified	WLA: NPDES LA: BMP	quantified	no	no
Coal Creek Okamulgee, OK	PS	DO, CBOD, NH3-N, TSS, BOD	no	quantified	PS: quantified	WLA: NPDES	no	no	no
Otter Creek E. Otter, OK	PS	CBOD, NH3-N	no	quantified	PS: quantified	WLA: NPDES	quantified	no	no
Arkansas River, OK	PS	DO	no	quantified	PS: quantified	WLA: NPDES	quantified	no	no
Vermillion River, LA	PS	DO, Fecal coliform, Mercury, CBOD, TSS	no	no	PS: quantified	WLA: NPDES	no	no	no
Bayou Yarbor Opelousas, LA	PS	DO, CBOD, NH3-N	no	quantified	no	no	no	no	no

Location (by EPA Region)	Source	Pollutants of Concern	Pre-TMDL Load	Gross Load Cal. (TMDL)	TMDL Allocation (PS/NPS)	Implementation	Margin of Safety	Future Dev. Margin	Projected NPS Reduction
Foxskin Bayou Bossier Parish, LA	PS	DO, BOD, TSS, NH3-N	quantified	quantified	PS: quantified NPS: quantified	WLA: NPDES LA: no	no	no	no
W. Pearl River Pearl River LA	PS	DO, BOD, TSS, NH3-N	quantified	quantified	PS: quantified	WLA: NPDES	quantified	no	no
Bayou Teche, LA	PS	CBOD, TKN, DO	quantified	quantified	PS: quantified	WLA: NPDES	no	no	no
Hominy Creek Osage Co., OK	PS	DO, CBOD, NH3-N	quantified	quantified	PS: quantified	WLA: NPDES	quantified	no	no
Region 7									
No TMDLs available									
Region 8									
W. Fork Clear Creek, CO	PS, NPS	Toxins, Metals	not quantified	quantified (seasonal)	PS: quantified NPS: quantified	WLA: NPDES LA: BMPs	quantified	not quantified, mentioned	no
Boulder Creek, CO	PS, NPS	NH3-N, Nutrients	quantified	quantified	PS: quantified NPS: quantified	WLA: NPDES LA: BMP (phased)	no	quantified	no
Deep Creek, MT	NPS	TSS	quantified	quantified	no	Monitoring only	no	no	no
Lake Poinsett, SD	NPS	Nutrients, TSS, Fecal coliform	quantified	quantified	no	WLA: no LA: BMP	no	no	no
Upper Big Sioux, SD	NPS	Nutrients, TSS	quantified	quantified	no	LA: BMP, control mechanisms	no	no	no
Region 9									
Truckee River, NV	PS, NPS	Nitrogen, Phosphorus, TSS	quantified	quantified	PS: quantified NPS: quantified	WLA: NPDES LA: stormwater permitting	not quantified, mentioned	not quantified, mentioned	no

Location (by EPA Region)	Source	Pollutants of Concern	Pre-TMDL Load	Gross Load Cal. (TMDL)	TMDL Allocation (PS/NPS)	Implementation	Margin of Safety	Future Dev. Margin	Projected NPS Reduction
Laguna de Santa Rosa, CA	PS, NPS	Ammonia, DO	quantified	quantified	PS: quantified NPS: quantified	WLA: NPDES LA: stormwater permitting	not quantified, mentioned	not quantified, mentioned	no
Region 10									
Salmon River, ID	NPS	Sediments	quantified	not quantified	NPS: not quantified (25% goal)	LA: BMP	not quantified, mentioned	not quantified, mentioned	yes
Columbia River Basin, WA, OR, ID	PS, NPS	Dioxin	quantified	quantified	PS: quantified NPS: quantified	WLA: NPDES LA: BMP	quantified	quantified	no
Lake Chelan, WA	PS, NPS	Phosphorus, Bacteria	no	quantified	PS: quantified NPS: quantified	WLA: NPDES LA: quality committee	not quantified, mentioned	quantified	yes
Tualatin River, OR	PS, NPS	Phosphorus	quantified	quantified	PS: quantified NPS: quantified	WLA: NPDES LA: future BMPs	quantified	no	no (deferred)
Vanderbilt Creek, AL	NPS	TSS, Turbidity	quantified	quantified	NPS: quantified	LA: BMP (phased)	quantified	no	yes
Upper Birch Creek, AL	NPS	TSS, Turbidity	quantified	quantified	PS: quantified NPS: quantified	WLA: NPDES LA: BMP	quantified	no	yes
Lemon Creek, AL	NPS	TSS, Turbidity	quantified	quantified	NPS: quantified	LA: BMP	quantified	quantified	yes

Key:

PS = point source
NPS = nonpoint source
WLA = waste load allocation
LA = load allocation
NPDES = national pollutant discharge elimination system
BMP = best management practices plan

NH_3-N = nitrogen
DO = dissolved oxygen
TSS = total suspended solids
BOD = biological oxygen demand
CBOD = carbonaceous biochemical oxygen demand
TKN = total Kjeldahl nitrogen

For a full description of these terms, categories, and analysis see preceding text.

Appendix D

EPA TMDL Regulations

On July 13, 2000, EPA promulgated final regulations for the TMDL program. The regulations themselves are relatively brief, fewer than 10 pages of the *Federal Register*, and are presented in a novel, question-and-answer format, e.g., What data and information do you need to assemble and consider to identify and list impaired waterbodies? The preamble to the regulations, on the other hand, responding to the large volume of comments received in the rulemaking process, runs 75 pages in the *Federal Register*, 3 columns per page, and provides detail explanations for each policy issue raised and choice made. It would serve little purpose to reproduce this document here. It is useful, however, to appreciate the comprehensive scope and analysis of the issues resolved in the final rules, and for that reason the opening sections of the preamble are reproduced below. These rules are, of course, about to be changed again, and rather dramatically. EPA's analysis of July 2000 provides a useful backdrop for these changes, because however one Administration or another choose to address them, the issues at the heart of a TMDL process will not go away.

Environmental Protection Agency
40 CFR Parts 9, 122, 123, 124, and 130, 65 Fed. Reg. 43586 (July 13, 2000)

Revisions to the Water Quality Planning and Management Regulation and Revisions to the National Pollutant Discharge Elimination System Program in Support of Revisions to the Water Quality Planning and Management Regulation

B. Table of Contents of This Preamble

A. Regulatory Flexibility Act (RFA) as amended by the Small Business Regulatory Enforcement Fairness Act of 1996 (SBREFA), 5 U.S.C. 601 *et seq.*

B. Regulatory Planning and Review, Executive Order 12866

C. Unfunded Mandates Reform Act

D. Paperwork Reduction Act

E. Federalism, Executive Order 13132

F. Consultation and Coordination with Indian Tribal Governments, Executive Order 13084

G. Protection of Children from Environmental Health Risks and Safety Risks, Executive Order 13045

H. National Technology Transfer and Advancement Act

I. Congressional Review Act

Entities Potentially Regulated by the Final Rule

State, Territorial or authorized Tribal Governments.

States, Territories and authorized Tribes.

This table is not intended to be exhaustive, but rather provides a guide for readers regarding entities likely to be regulated by this action. This table lists the types of entities that EPA is now aware could potentially be regulated by this action. Other types of entities not listed in this table could also be regulated. To determine whether you are regulated by this action, you should carefully examine the applicability criteria in §130.20. If you have questions regarding the applicability of this action to a particular entity, consult one of the persons listed in the **FOR FURTHER INFORMATION CONTACT** section.

Response to Comments

This preamble explains in detail the elements of the final TMDL regulations and the amendments which EPA is making to the NPDES program in order to support implementation of the TMDL program. EPA has made changes to its proposal in response to comments received on the proposed rules. EPA has evaluated all the significant comments it received including comments submitted after the close of the comment period and prepared a Response to Comment Document containing EPA's response to those comments. This document complements discussions in this preamble and is available for review in the Water Docket.

Before Reading This Preamble, You Should Read the Final Rule

I. Introduction

A. *Background*

1. What are the Water Quality Concerns Addressed by this Rule?

The CWA includes a number of programs aimed at restoring and maintaining water quality. These include national technology-based effluent limitation guidelines; national water quality criteria guidance; State, Territorial and authorized Tribal water quality standards; State, Territorial and authorized Tribal nonpoint source (NPS) management programs; funding provisions for municipal wastewater treatment facilities; State, Territorial and authorized Tribal water quality monitoring programs; and the NPDES permit program for point sources. These programs have produced significant and widespread improvements in water quality over the last quarter-century, but many waterbodies still fail to attain or maintain water quality standards due to one or more pollutants.

The National Water Quality Inventory Report to Congress for 1998 indicates that of the 23 percent of the Nation's rivers and streams that have been assessed, 35 percent do not fully support water quality standards or uses and an additional 10 percent are threatened. Of the 32 percent of estuary waterbodies assessed, 44 percent are not fully supporting water quality standards or uses and an additional 9 percent are threatened. Of the 42 percent of lakes, ponds, and reservoirs assessed (not including the Great Lakes), 45 percent are not fully supporting water quality standards or uses and an additional 9 percent are threatened. The report also indicates that 90 percent of the Great Lakes shoreline miles have been assessed, and that 96 percent of these are not fully supporting water quality standards and an additional 2 percent are threatened. The report indicates that pollutants in rainwater runoff from urban and agricultural land are a leading source of impairment. Agriculture is the leading source of pollutants in assessed rivers and streams, contributing to 59 percent of the reported water quality problems and affecting about 170,000 river miles. Hydromodification is the second leading source of impairment, and urban runoff/storm sewers is the third major source, contributing respectively 20 percent and 12 percent of reported water quality problems. EPA recognizes that a large percentage of streams has not been assessed but believes that there is sufficient information in hand to warrant concern over those unassessed waters and the slow pace at which many waters are attaining water quality standards.

The 1998 section 303(d) lists of impaired waterbodies submitted by States and Territories provided additional information. The section 303(d) lists relied, in part, on information in the section 305(b) reports. The States and Territories identified over 20,000 individual waterbodies including river and stream segments, lakes, and estuaries that do not attain State water quality standards despite 28 years of pollution control efforts. These impaired waterbodies include approximately 300,000 miles of river and shoreline and approximately 5 million acres of lakes. Approximately 210 million people live within 10 miles of these waterbodies. State and local governments also reported that they issued 2,506 fish advisories and closed 353 beaches in 1998.

EPA believes that a significant part of the response to these problems must be a more rigorous implementation of the TMDL program. EPA believes that today's rule will provide the tools for States, Territories and authorized Tribes to bring the assessment and restoration authorities provided by section 303(d) into greater use and result in significant improvements in the quality of the Nation's waterbodies.

2. What are the Current Statutory Authorities That Support This Final Rule?

The goal of establishing TMDLs is to assure that water quality standards are attained and maintained. Section 303(d) of the CWA which Congress enacted in 1972 requires States, Territories and authorized Tribes to identify and establish a priority ranking for waterbodies for which technology-based effluent limitations required by section 301 are not stringent enough to attain and maintain applicable water quality standards, establish TMDLs for the pollutants causing impairment in those waterbodies, and submit, from time to time, the list of impaired waterbodies and TMDLs to EPA. EPA must review and approve or disapprove lists and TMDLs within 30 days of the time they are submitted. If EPA disapproves a list or a TMDL, EPA must establish the list or TMDL. In addition, EPA and the courts have interpreted the statute as requiring EPA to establish lists and TMDLs when a State fails to do so. Furthermore, the requirement to identify and establish TMDLs for waterbodies exists regardless of whether the waterbody is impaired by point sources, nonpoint sources or a combination of both. *Pronsolino v. Marcus*, 2000 WL 356305 (N.D. Cal. March 30, 2000.)

Listing impaired waterbodies and establishing TMDLs for waterbodies impaired by pollutants from nonpoint sources does not mean any new or additional implementation authorities are created. Once a TMDL is established, existing State, Territorial and authorized Tribal programs, other Federal agencies' policies and procedures, as well as voluntary and incentive-based programs, are the basis for implementing the controls and reductions identified in TMDLs.

CWA Section 402 establishes a program, the NPDES Program, to regulate the "discharge of a pollutant," other than dredged or fill materials, from a "point source" into "waters of the United States." The CWA and NPDES regulations define a "discharge of a pollutant," "point source," and "waters of the United States." The NPDES Program is administered at the federal level by EPA unless a State, Tribe or U.S. Territory assumes the program after receiving approval by the federal government. Under section 402, discharges of pollutants to waters of the United States are authorized by obtaining and complying with the terms of an NPDES permit. NPDES permits commonly contain numerical limits on the amounts of specified pollutants that may be discharged and specified best management practices (BMPs) designed to minimize water quality impacts. These numerical effluent limitations and BMPs or other non-numerical effluent limitations implement both technology-based and water quality-based requirements of the Act. Technology-based limitations represent the degree of control that can be achieved by point sources using various levels of pollution control technology. If necessary to achieve compliance with applicable water quality standards, NPDES permits must contain water quality-based limitations more stringent than the applicable technology-based standards.

3. What is the Regulatory Background of Today's Action?

a. What are the Current Requirements?

EPA issued regulations governing identification of impaired waterbodies and establishment of TMDLs, at §130.7, in 1985 and revised them in 1992. These regulations provide that:

• State, Territorial and authorized Tribal lists must include those waters still requiring TMDLs because technology based effluent limitations required by the CWA or more stringent effluent limitations and other pollution controls (e.g., management measures) required by local, State, or Federal authority are not stringent enough to attain and maintain applicable water quality standards;

• State, Territorial and authorized Tribal lists must be submitted to EPA every two years, beginning in 1992, on April 1 of every even-numbered year;

• The priority ranking for listed waters must include an identification of the pollutant or pollutants causing or expected to cause the impairment and an identification of the waterbodies targeted for TMDL development in the next two years;

• States, Territories and authorized Tribes, in developing lists, must assemble and evaluate all existing and readily available water quality-related data and information;

• States, Territories and authorized Tribes must submit, with each list, the methodology used to develop the list and provide EPA with a rationale for any decision not to use any existing and readily available water quality-related data and information; and

• TMDLs must be established at levels necessary to implement applicable water quality standards with seasonal variations and a margin of safety that takes into account any lack of knowledge concerning the relationship between effluent limitations and water quality.

The regulations define a TMDL as a quantitative assessment of pollutants that cause water quality impairments. A TMDL specifies the amount of a particular pollutant that may be present in a waterbody, allocates allowable pollutant loads among sources, and provides the basis for attaining or maintaining water quality standards. TMDLs are established for waterbody and pollutant combinations for waterbodies impaired by point sources, nonpoint sources, or a combination of both point and nonpoint sources. Indian Tribes may be authorized to establish TMDLs for waterbodies within their jurisdiction. To date, however, no Tribe has sought or received CWA authority to establish TMDLs.

The NPDES regulations, in several provisions and under certain circumstances, allow the permitting authority and/or EPA to subject certain previously non-designated sources to NPDES program requirements. EPA established these jurisdictional regulations in 1973 when the Agency and the States focused permitting resources primarily on continuous discharges, for example, industrial and municipal sources. Also, in the early stages of CWA implementation, the Agency and the States focused on implementation of technology-based standards. At that time, EPA attempted to limit the scope of the NPDES permitting program to certain types of point sources. The D.C. Circuit rejected that attempt, however, and explained that EPA could not exempt point sources from the NPDES program. *NRDC v. Costle*, 568 F.2d 1369, 1377 (D.C. Cir. 1977). Although the Court rejected this attempt, it did recognize the Agency's discretion to define "point source" and "nonpoint source." The existing NPDES regulations identifying animal production and silvicultural sources represents an early attempt to do so.

Also, under the NPDES program regulations, a Regional Administrator may review and object to State-issued NPDES permits. The procedures by which a Regional Administrator may review and object to these permits are found in §123.44. The existing objection authority, under section 402(d) of the Act, grants EPA 90 days within which to object to a proposed State permit that fails to meet the guidelines and requirements of the Act. If a State fails to respond to an EPA objection within 90 days of objection, exclusive authority to issue the NPDES permit to that discharger passes to EPA.

b. What Changes Did EPA Propose in August 1999?

In 1996, the Office of Water determined that there was a need for a comprehensive evaluation of EPA's and State, Territorial and authorized Tribal implementation of section 303(d) requirements. EPA convened a committee under the Federal Advisory Committee Act (TMDL FACA committee) to undertake such an evaluation and make recommendations for improving implementation of the TMDL program, including recommendation for revised regulations and guidance. The TMDL FACA committee included 20 individuals with diverse backgrounds, including agriculture, forestry, environmental advocacy, industry, and State, local, and Tribal governments. On July 28, 1998, the committee submitted its final report to EPA which contained more than 100 consensus recommendations, a subset of which recommended regulatory changes. The TMDL FACA committee recommendations helped guide the development of the revisions which EPA proposed in August 1999.

In proposing revisions to the regulations governing TMDLs, EPA also relied upon the past experience of States and Territories. EPA's proposal recognized and responded to some of the issues raised by stakeholders regarding the effectiveness and consistency of the TMDL program. EPA also proposed changes intended to resolve some of the issues and concerns raised by litigation concerning the identification of impaired waterbodies and the establishment of TMDLs. Finally, EPA proposed changes to the NPDES permitting regulations to assist in the establishment and implementation of TMDLs and to better address point source discharges to waters not meeting water quality standards prior to establishment of a TMDL.

Key elements of the changes proposed in August, 1999 include:

• State, Territorial, and authorized Tribal section 303(d) listing methodologies would become more specific, subject to public review, and provided to EPA for review prior to submission of the list.

• States, Territories and authorized Tribes would develop a more comprehensive list of waterbodies impaired and threatened by pollution, organize it into four parts, and submit it to EPA.

• States, Territories and authorized Tribes would establish TMDLs only for waterbodies on the first part of the list.

• States, Territories and authorized Tribes would keep waterbodies on the lists until water quality standards were achieved.

• States, Territories and authorized Tribes would establish and submit to EPA schedules to establish all TMDLs within 15 years of listing.

• States, Territories, and authorized Tribes would rank TMDLs into high, medium or low priority.

- TMDLs would include 10 specific elements, one of which is an implementation plan.

- States, Territories, and authorized Tribes would notify the public and give them the opportunity to comment on the methodology, lists, priority rankings, schedules, and TMDLs prior to submission to EPA.

- New and significantly expanded discharges subject to NPDES permits would need to obtain an offset for the increased discharge before being allowed to discharge the increase.

- Certain point source storm water discharges from silviculture would be required to seek a permit if necessary to implement a TMDL.

- EPA could designate certain animal feeding operations and aquatic animal production facilities as sources subject to NPDES permits in authorized States.

- EPA could object to expired and administratively continued State-issued NPDES permits.

- Regulatory language would codify requirements pertaining to citizens' rights to petition EPA.

c. What has EPA Done to Gather Information and Input as it Developed This Final Rule?

EPA published the proposed rule on August 23, 1999, and provided for an initial 60 day comment period, which was later extended to a total of 150 days. EPA received about 34,000 comments on the proposal comprised of about 30,500 postcards, 2,700 letters making one or two points, and 780 detailed comments addressing many issues. EPA has reviewed all these comments as part of the development of today's final rule.

EPA also engaged in an extensive outreach and information-sharing effort following the publication of the proposed rule. The Agency sponsored and participated in six public meetings nationwide, to better inform the public on the contents of the proposed rules, and to get informal feedback from the public. These meetings took place in Denver, Los Angeles, Atlanta, Kansas City, Seattle, and Manchester, New Hampshire. In addition, EPA participated in numerous other meetings, conferences and information-sharing sessions to discuss the proposed rule and listen to alternative approaches to achieving the nation's clean water goals.

The Agency has had an ongoing dialogue with State and local officials and their national/regional organizations throughout the development of this rule. EPA has met with organizations representing State and local-elected officials including: the National Governors' Association, the Western Governors' Association, the National Conference of State Legislatures, the National Association of Counties, the National League of Cities and EPA's State and Local Advisory Group. Many discussion sessions were held with officials who administer State and local programs related to water quality, agriculture, forestry, and harbors. Discussions were held with such organizations as the Environmental Council of the States, the Association of State and Interstate Water Pollution Control Administrators, the Association of Municipal Sewerage Agencies, the Association of Municipal Water Agencies, the National Association of State Agricultural Departments, the National Association of State Foresters, the Western States Water Council, the Association of State Drinking Water Administrators, the National Association of Flood and Storm Water Management Agencies, the Interstate Conference on Water Policy, and the Western States Land Commissioners

EPA met with groups representing business, industry, agriculture, and forestry interests, including the Electric Power Research Institute, the Utility Water Action Group, American Water Works Association, the American Forest and Paper Association, the Family Farm Alliance, the National Association of Conservation Districts, a number of State Farm Bureaus, corn and soybean grower organizations and forestry associations. EPA also met with environmental and citizen groups including the Natural Resources Defense Council, Sierra Club, Friends of the Earth and Earth Justice. EPA participated in numerous Congressional briefings and hearings held in Washington and in several field locations. The results of these meetings and discussions are reflected in today's rule.

B. What are the Significant Issues in Today's Rule?

1. What are EPA's Objectives for Today's Rule?

States, Territories, and authorized Tribes are essential in carrying out a successful program and EPA looks forward to working with them in developing this program. Further, we believe that, ultimately, any successful effort depends on a cooperative approach that pulls together the variety of entities and stakeholders involved in the watershed. EPA through this rulemaking seeks to provide a framework that facilitates this approach.

EPA received many comments regarding the overall purpose of the proposed rule. Many commenters expressed concerns that EPA was putting too much emphasis on TMDLs and ignoring other programs and initiatives under the CWA which are also aimed at restoring or maintaining water quality. A common theme through many comments was that the Agency should not attempt to force-fit clean up of every impairment through the TMDL process. EPA agrees with the commenters that for some waterbodies and watersheds, existing plans and agreements may accomplish much of what this rule intends. However, EPA believes that identifying waterbodies that are impaired and establishing TMDLs is both statutorily required and will help focus ongoing activities for more efficient attainment of water quality standards.

The CWA requires TMDLs for pollutants in impaired waterbodies if implementation of technology-based effluent limitations is not sufficient to attain water quality standards. Today's rule clarifies this concept to require that TMDLs be established for all pollutants in impaired waterbodies unless enforceable Federal, State, Territorial or authorized Tribal controls will result in attainment of water quality standards by the time the next list in the listing cycle is required.

EPA recognizes that watershed or other plans developed under other State, Territorial or authorized Tribal programs or by other Federal agencies, such as wet weather flow plans, Coastal Zone Management plans, or conservation plans administered by the Natural Resources Conservation Service, have the same goal as a TMDL. EPA believes that these other activities are crucial to the attainment of water quality standards either because they will result in attainment of water quality standards before a TMDL is established or because they are the basis for implementation of the controls required by TMDLs. Thus, today's rule provides a role for the various programs aimed at improving water quality—both as an alternative to developing a TMDL in certain circumstances, and a means for implementing TMDLs.

Many commenters also perceived EPA's proposal as an attempt to supplant State, Territorial or authorized Tribal primacy. Today's rule preserves the primary responsibilities of States, Territories and authorized Tribes and clarifies EPA's responsibilities under the CWA. EPA believes that today's rule provides greater clarity regarding the requirements for States, Territories and authorized Tribes and EPA's own responsibilities for the TMDL program. EPA believes that today's rule establishes a framework for effective, cooperative efforts between State, Territorial, authorized Tribal governments, individuals, local governments and other Federal agencies.

EPA is also conscious of the need for adequate resources. EPA has sought to increase funding for development and implementation of TMDLs in both the FY 2001 Federal budget and prior budgets. In the FY 2001 Federal budget the Agency has requested an additional $45 million in CWA Section 106 grants specifically for the TMDL program. In FY 2001, EPA requested $250 million for section 319 nonpoint source grants, an increase of $50 million (25%) over FY 2000. In addition, the FY 1999 and FY 2000 budgets of $200 million per year for section 319 grants represented a doubling (100% increase) of the prior section 319 funding. To further support State nonpoint source implementation, EPA has proposed an FY 2002 budget that gives States and Territories the option to reserve up to 19% of their Clean Water

State Revolving Fund capitalization grants to provide grants for implementing nonpoint source and estuary management projects.

2. What Are the Key Differences Between the Proposal and Today's Final Rule?

This section summarizes the significant changes EPA has made in the rule adopted today compared to the proposed rule. A more detailed discussion of all the changes is included in the specific sections for these changes in this preamble.

a. Threatened waterbodies. EPA proposed that threatened waterbodies be listed on Part 1 of the list, meaning that TMDLs would have to be established for them as for impaired waters. After carefully considering comments, particularly the concerns raised by commenters regarding the technical difficulties inherent in determining when water quality trends are declining and the difficulty in making listing decisions, EPA is not requiring that States, Territories or authorized Tribes list threatened waterbodies on the section 303(d) list or that TMDLs be prepared for these waterbodies. States, Territories and authorized Tribes retain, at their discretion, the option to list threatened waterbodies on their section 303(d) list and establish TMDLs for these waterbodies.

b. The four-part 303(d) list. EPA proposed that the section 303(d) list include all impaired waterbodies, sorted into four parts, and a priority ranking for those waterbodies with respect to establishing TMDLs. Part 1 of the list would include impaired waterbodies for which TMDLs would be required to be established within 15 years. Part 2 of the list would include waterbodies impaired by pollution that is not caused by a pollutant. TMDLs would not be required for these waterbodies. Part 3 of the list would include waterbodies for which TMDLs had been established but water quality standards not yet attained. Part 4 would include waterbodies for which technology-based controls or other enforceable controls would attain water quality standards by the next listing cycle. Today's final rule adds a clarification that if during the development of each list, a waterbody previously listed on Part 3 of the list has not made substantial progress towards attainment of water quality standards, it must be moved to Part 1 and a new TMDL must be established. Today's rule also allows States, Territories and authorized Tribes to submit their list in different formats. EPA will still approve all four parts of the list, but States, Territories and authorized Tribes may submit lists in any of three formats. Lists may be submitted to EPA as described in the proposal—that is, as one four-part list published by itself, as part of the section 305(b) water quality report, or with Part 1 submitted separately to EPA as a section 303(d) submission and Parts 2, 3 and 4 submitted to EPA as a section 303(d) component of the section 305(b) water quality report.

c. Inclusion of schedules in the section 303(d) list. EPA proposed that States, Territories and authorized Tribes should submit the list and priority rankings to EPA for approval, and should separately submit a schedule for establishing TMDLs which would not be subject to EPA approval. Today's rule requires States, Territories, and authorized Tribes to submit a prioritized schedule for establishing TMDLs for waterbodies listed on Part 1. Further, as suggested by some commenters, the final regulations require that TMDL establishment be scheduled as expeditiously as practicable and within 10 years of July 10, 2000, or 10 years from the due date for the first list on which the waterbody appeared, whichever is later, rather than the 15 year period EPA proposed. However, the schedule can be extended for up to 5 years when a State, Territory, or authorized Tribe explains that despite expeditious action establishment of TMDLs within 10 years is not practicable.

d. Implementation plan. EPA proposed that TMDLs must contain an implementation plan as a required element for approval. Today's rule, like the proposal, requires an implementation plan as a mandatory element of an approvable TMDL, and includes substantial changes to the reasonable assurance and implementation plan requirements in response to the comments received. The implementation plan requirements differ depending on whether waterbodies are impaired only by point sources subject to an NPDES permit, only by other sources (including nonpoint sources), or by both. EPA is also adding specificity regarding when the NPDES permits implementing wasteload allocations must be issued. Finally EPA is establishing a goal of 5 years for implementing management measures or control actions to achieve load allocations, and a goal of 10 years for attaining water quality standards.

e. Reasonable assurance. EPA proposed that States, Territories and authorized Tribes provide reasonable assurance that the wasteload and load allocations reflected in TMDLs would be implemented. Today's final rule clarifies how reasonable assurance can be demonstrated for waterbodies impaired by all pollutant sources, and provides additional detail on how reasonable assurance can be demonstrated for nonpoint sources. These changes reflect and seek to address the uncertainties inherent in dealing with nonpoint pollutant sources and recognize the importance of voluntary and incentive-based programs. Finally, today's rule specifies how EPA will provide reasonable assurance when it establishes TMDLs.

f. The petition process. EPA proposed to codify requirements applicable to petitions which can be filed with the Administrator by citizens who believe that EPA has failed to comply with its TMDL responsibilities under the CWA. Today's rule does not include requirements codifying the petition process. EPA notes, however, that eliminating the proposed petition process from the rule does not change the fact that any person is entitled, under the

Administrative Procedure Act (APA), to petition EPA to take specific actions regarding identification of impaired waterbodies and establishment of TMDLs.

g. Offsets. EPA proposed to require new and significantly expanded discharges subject to the NPDES permit program to obtain an offset for their increased load before being allowed to discharge the increase. Today's rule does not include any requirement for an offset.

h. Silviculture, Animal Feeding Operations, and Aquatic Animal Production Facilities. EPA proposed to allow EPA and States to designate certain point source storm water discharges from silviculture as subject to the NPDES permitting program. EPA also proposed to allow EPA to designate certain animal feeding operations and aquatic animal production facilities as point sources in NPDES authorized states. EPA has decided to withdraw this proposal.

II. Changes to Part 130

This section explains in detail the elements of the final Part 130 TMDL regulations and how these regulations differ from the proposal. EPA has made several significant changes to the proposal, clarified other requirements, and rewritten and reorganized the regulatory language. Most of these changes have been made in response to comments received on the proposed rule.

A. What Definitions are Included in This Final Rule? (§130.2)

Today's final action revises the definitions of load (or loading), load allocation, wasteload allocation, and TMDL, and adds definitions for the terms pollutant, total maximum daily thermal load, impaired waterbody, thermal discharge, reasonable assurance, management measures, waterbody, and list. In addition, for reasons explained in detail later in this section EPA has decided not to promulgate definitions which were not proposed but were suggested by the commenters.

1. What Definitions are Added or Revised?

a. New Definition of Pollutant (§130.2(d))

What did EPA propose? On August 23, 1999, EPA proposed to add a definition for "pollutant" that was the same as the definition in the CWA at section 502(6). EPA also proposed to clarify that, in EPA's view, the definition of pollutant would encompass drinking water contaminants that are regulated under section 1412 of the Safe Drinking Water Act and that may be discharged to waters of the U.S. that are the source water of one or more public water systems. EPA was proposing to clarify that drinking water contaminants that meet these criteria are pollutants as defined in the CWA.

What comments did EPA receive? EPA received many comments on this proposed definition which are addressed fully in the Response to Comment Document included in the Docket. Most commenters offered suggestions as to which particular substances (particularly naturally occurring pollutants, FIFRA registered pesticides, and flow) may or may not be pollutants, and requested specific recognition of these substances in the definition. Others objected to inclusion of drinking water contaminants in the definition, believing that they were better addressed by the Safe Drinking Water Act requirements. In addition, EPA received several requests for more examples to help clarify the distinction between pollutants and pollution. Some commenters understood EPA to propose that "pollutant" includes non-point source pollution while others did not. Others gave examples of situations where they believed it would be impossible to decide whether a waterbody was impaired by pollution or a pollutant. Examples given included: biological impairment due to displacement of bedload sediment during high intermittent streamflow caused by increased impervious surface, and impairment due to low dissolved oxygen levels in hydropower releases.

What is EPA promulgating today? EPA is promulgating a definition of pollutant that is identical to the definition in EPA's current NPDES regulations. That definition is identical to the CWA definition except that it excludes certain radioactive materials from the definition. *Train v. Colorado Public Int. Research Group*, 426 U.S. 1, 25 (1976) (Congress did not intend for materials governed by the Atomic Energy Act to be included in the category of pollutants subject to regulation by EPA under the CWA). In recognition that the CWA definition does not expressly discuss drinking water contaminants, EPA is not including a reference to drinking water contaminants in the final language. However, EPA interprets the CWA definition of pollutant to include, in most cases, drinking water contaminants that are regulated under section 1412 of the Safe Drinking Water Act (SDWA). This interpretation is consistent with both the language and the intent of the CWA. First, drinking water contaminants fall within the meaning of one or more of the terms used by Congress to define pollutant. Second, the term "public water supplies" is listed under CWA section 303(c)(2)(A) as a potential beneficial use to be protected by water quality standards. EPA expects that virtually all drinking water contaminants that are regulated in the future will be encompassed by one of or more of the terms used to define pollutants.

EPA wishes to clarify the relationship between pollutants and pollution for purposes of section 303(d). Pollution, as defined by the CWA, and the current regulations is "the man-made or man-induced alteration of the chemical, physical, biological, and radiological integrity of a waterbody." This is a broad term that encompasses many types of changes to a waterbody, including alterations to the character of a waterbody that do not result from the introduction of a specific pollutant or the presence of pollutants in a waterbody at a level that causes an impairment. In other words, all waterbodies which are impaired by human intervention suffer from some form of pollution. In some cases, the pollution is caused by the presence of a pollutant, and a TMDL is required. In other cases it is caused by activities other than the introduction of a pollutant.

The following are two examples of pollution caused by pollutants. The discharge of copper from an NPDES regulated facility is the introduction of a pollutant into a waterbody. To the extent that this pollutant alters the chemical or biological integrity of the waterbody, it is also an example of pollution. (Copper is not likely to cause an alteration to the water's physical integrity.) Similarly, landscape actions that result in the introduction of sediment into a waterbody constitute pollution when that sediment (which is a pollutant) results in an alteration of the chemical, physical, or biological integrity of the waterbody. TMDLs would have to be established for each of these waterbodies.

Degraded aquatic habitat is evidence of impairment which may be caused solely by channelization of a stream's bottom. In this case the waterbody would be considered impaired by pollution that is not a result of the introduction or presence of a pollutant. However, if the channelization also caused the bottom to become smothered by excessive sediment deposition, then the waterbody impairment is caused by a pollutant (sediment) and a TMDL would be required.

Based on data contained in the 1998 section 303(d) lists, EPA believes that many waterbodies that fail to attain water quality standards, fail to do so because a specific substance or material, a pollutant, has been or is being introduced into the waterbody. EPA believes the vast majority of impairments are caused by the introduction of pollutants and does not anticipate large numbers of waterbodies to be identified as impaired only by pollution. Of the top 15 categories of impairment identified on the 1998 section 303(d) lists, 11 categories are directly or indirectly associated with pollutants: sediments, pathogens, nutrients, metals, low dissolved oxygen, temperature, pH, pesticides, mercury, organics, and ammonia. Together, these categories account for 77% of the total impairments listed. In comparison, three of the top 15 categories either are not associated with pollutants or the link to pollutants is generally unknown: habitat alterations, impaired biologic communities and flow alterations. These categories account for only 12% of the total number of listed impairments.

While TMDLs are not required to be established for waterbodies impaired by pollution but not a pollutant, they nonetheless remain waterbodies which fail to attain or maintain water quality standards. EPA believes that States, Territories and authorized Tribes should use approaches and institute actions other than TMDLs to begin the task of returning these waterbodies to full attainment of water quality standards. As explained later in the preamble, one of the reasons for including these waterbodies on Part 2 of the list is to ensure that they remain in the public's eye and are not simply ignored.

Another frequently asked question concerns pollutants that are "natural." Water quality standards often fail to distinguish between pollutants that are introduced into a waterbody as the result of some human activity and those that are present in a waterbody due to natural processes such as weathering of metals from geologic strata. Where a natural pollutant occurs along with an anthropogenic pollutant, they both must be accounted for within the TMDL so that the TMDL is established at a level that will implement the water quality standards. For example, cadmium originating from the natural weathering of a geologic outcrop, as well as cadmium from a mine tailings pond, must be accounted for in the wasteload allocation of a TMDL to ensure that the wasteload allocation is properly set to achieve water quality standards. EPA recognizes that there may be instances where the introduction of natural substances alone may cause the waterbody to exceed the water quality standards unless the standard contains an exception for addressing such situations. In those circumstances, EPA encourages States, Territories, and authorized Tribes to revise their water quality standards to reflect and recognize the presence and effect of substances that occur naturally.

EPA does not believe that flow, or lack of flow, is a pollutant as defined by CWA Section 502(6). Some commenters have urged EPA to revise the proposed regulations to require TMDLs for all forms of pollution, including hydromodification, which reduce the amount of water flowing through a river or stream. They argue that since low flow can lead to non-attainment of water quality standards, *e.g.*, use as a fishery, waterbodies impacted by low flow should be listed on Part 1 and have TMDLs established for them. While EPA believes that waterbodies which do not attain and maintain water quality standards solely because of low flow must be identified on Part 2 of a State's section 303(d) list, it does not believe section 303(d)(1)(C) requires that States must establish TMDLs for such waters. This is because EPA interprets section 303(d)(1)(C) to require that TMDLs be established for "pollutants" and does not believe "low flow" is a pollutant. Section 303(d)(1)(C) provides that States shall establish TMDLs "for those pollutants" which the Administrator identifies as suitable for such calculation. In 1978, EPA said that all pollutants under proper technical permit conditions were suitable for TMDL calculations. However, low flow is not a pollutant. It is not one of the items specifically mentioned in the list of pollutants Congress included at section 502(6) of the CWA. Nor does it fit within the meaning of any of those terms.

Instead, low flow is a condition of a waterbody (*i.e.*, a reduced volume of water) that when man-made or man-induced would be categorized under the CWA as pollution, provided it altered the physical, biological and radiological integrity of the water. Many forms of human activity, including the introduction of pollutants, can cause water pollution. Not all pollution-causing activities, however, must be analyzed and allocated in a TMDL. Section 303(d) is a mechanism that requires an accounting and allocation of pollutants introduced into impaired waters (whether from point or nonpoint sources). If low flow in a river, even if man-induced, exacerbates or amplifies the impairing effect of a pollutant in that river by increasing its concentration, that factor is to be accounted for and dealt with in the TMDL by calculating and allocating the total pollutant load in light of, among other things, seasonal variations in flow. However, where no pollutant is identified as causing an exceedance of water quality standards, EPA does not believe the CWA requires a TMDL to be established.

The Supreme Court's decision in *PUD. No 1 of Jefferson County et al. v. Washington Dept. of Ecology et al.*, 511 U.S. 700 (1994), does not compel a different result. In that case a city and local utility district wanted to build a dam on the Dosewallips river in Washington State. The project would divert water from the river to run the dam's turbines and then return the water to the river below the dam. To protect salmon populations in the river, the state imposed a minimum flow requirement as part of its CWA section 401 certification of the project. The Court determined that compliance with section 303(c) water quality standards is a proper function of a section 401 certificate. Accordingly, the Court concluded that pursuant to section 401, the state may require the dam project to maintain minimum stream flow necessary to protect the river's designed use as salmon habitat.

The Supreme Court in *Jefferson County* did not interpret section 303(d) and did not hold that TMDLs had to be established for flow-impacted waters. The Court did reject petitioner's claim that the CWA is only concerned with water "quality" and does not allow the regulation of water "quantity." Like EPA, it recognized that water quantity may be closely related to water quality and that reduced stream flow may constitute "pollution" under the Act. However, in holding that section 401 certification applied to dam projects as a whole—including pollution-causing water withdrawals—and not just discharges of pollutants, the Court did not decide that a section 303(d) TMDL must be established for low flow-impaired waterbody. This is because *Jefferson County* did not decide that low flow was a pollutant. Under section 303(d) it is pollutants, not pollution, for which TMDLs must be established.

However, EPA recognizes that there will be cases where flow or lack thereof will enhance the ability of a pollutant to impair a waterbody. EPA has provided for this eventuality by requiring that States, Territories and authorized Tribes consider seasonal variations, including flow, when establishing TMDLs. (See discussion at §130.32(b)(9).)

Also, EPA declines at this time to define "chemical wastes" as that term appears in the definition of "pollutant" to exclude pesticides designated for aquatic uses. EPA recognizes that the requirements of section 303(d) and this rule may lead to waterbodies being listed due to the presence of pesticides registered under the Federal Insecticide, Fungicide and Rodenticide Act (FIFRA) because water quality standards for that chemical are exceeded. EPA will continue to evaluate the interface between its regulatory responsibilities under FIFRA and the CWA.

Note: EPA erroneously listed "pollution" as a proposed new definition in the preamble to the proposal. In fact, the definition of pollution is included in the current rules and has been revised by simply adding a citation of the CWA section defining that term.

b. Revised Definition of Loading (§130.2(e))

What did EPA propose? EPA proposed to make a grammatical revision to the definition of "load or loading" by using the words "loading of pollutant" to clarify that loading is the introduction of a pollutant whether man-made or naturally-occurring rather than as a parenthetical explanation of what is man-caused loading. EPA did not consider this change substantive and did not discuss it in the preamble to the proposed rule.

What comments did EPA receive? Some commenters expressed concern about perceived inconsistencies between (1) the proposed definition of loading and the expression of a TMDL at proposed §130.34 and (2) between this definition and the proposed definition of a TMDL at §130.2(h)(2). Other commenters requested revisions to clarify that the load describes when the water quality standard is attained, that the definition does not apply to nonpoint sources, or that ambient temperature increases are not a load. Another commenter suggested that EPA include the definition of load capacity included in the current requirements which EPA did not include in the proposal.

What is EPA promulgating today? EPA has carefully considered these comments but is promulgating this definition as proposed. EPA does not believe that there are inconsistencies between the definition and the manner in which TMDLs may be expressed pursuant to §130.33. EPA does not interpret the final rule to require that TMDLs be always expressed as the load or load reduction of the pollutant causing the impairment. The final rule at §130.33(b)(4) preserves the flexibility to express the TMDL as a quantitative expression of a modification to a characteristic of the waterbody that results in a certain load or load reduction. Similarly, EPA does not believe there are inconsistencies between the proposed definition of load as a substance or matter introduced in a waterbody and the proposed definition of a TMDL at §130.2(h)(2) which would have required identification and quantification of the load "that may be present" in the waterbody. TMDLs are generally established using the principle of mass balance, which is the core principle of water quality modeling. The mass of a pollutant in a waterbody is a function of the mass introduced into the waterbody and the mass that flows out of the waterbody. The same principle applies for thermal energy.

EPA sees no inconsistency between describing loading as an introduction of a substance or matter into a waterbody and requiring identification of the pollutant load present within the waterbody for the purpose of establishing TMDLs. The characterization of a mass of material as a load into, or a load within, a waterbody will depend in some instances on how the State, Territory, or authorized Tribe decides to frame the TMDL.

EPA is not revising the definition of load to suggest that the load describes when the water quality standard is attained. The definition of "load or loading" merely refers to the quantity of matter or thermal energy introduced into a waterbody; it is not intended to include an interpretation of the environmental consequence of that load. It is the calculation of the TMDL and the resulting allocations which establish the loading targets necessary to achieve water quality standards.

EPA is not revising the definition of load or loading to exclude nonpoint sources. As noted above, EPA believes that section 303(d) applies to all sources including nonpoint sources, and that all sources are considered when allocations needed to attain or maintain water quality standards are established. EPA has consistently required the inclusion of pollutants from nonpoint sources in estimates of loading. By defining "load allocations" which pertain to nonpoint sources as "best estimate of loadings," the language of the current regulations clearly demonstrates that EPA intended for pollutants from nonpoint sources to be included in the definition of load and loading. Therefore, EPA believes it is simply a continuation of its policy to consider the definition of loads to apply to nonpoint sources.

Similarly, EPA is not revising the definition of load or loading to exclude increases in temperature due to solar input. EPA does not believe that the source of a load should disqualify it from being a load. What needs to be done to mitigate heat load from solar input will be addressed by a State, Territory, or authorized Tribe when it establishes the TMDL.

Finally, EPA is not including the definition of load capacity contained in the existing regulations. EPA proposed to delete the definition of "load capacity" because retaining a separate definition of load capacity would only add confusion as to whether a TMDL consisted merely of the load capacity or the ten elements of the TMDL. The loading capacity is found as element three in the eleven elements of the TMDL. EPA continues to believe that retaining a separate definition of load capacity would only add confusion as to whether a TMDL consisted merely of the load capacity or the ten elements of the TMDL promulgated in today's regulation.

c. Revised Definition of Load Allocation (§130.2(f))

What did EPA propose? EPA proposed to simplify the existing definition of "load allocation" by defining it as simply the part of the total load in a TMDL that is allocated to nonpoint sources, including atmospheric deposition, or natural background sources, as opposed to wasteload allocation to point sources. In proposing this change, EPA moved the substantive requirement of how a load allocation is determined from the definition of load allocation to the description of a TMDL in proposed §130.33(b).

What comments did EPA receive? EPA received a large number of comments with regard to its definition of load allocations, covering a range of issues. Again, many commenters asserted that EPA did not have the statutory authority to address pollutant loadings from nonpoint sources because Congress intended the TMDL provisions of the CWA to apply only to waterbodies impaired by point sources or waterbodies where control of point sources alone would result in attainment of water quality standards.

In contrast, many commenters supported the inclusion of pollutant loadings from nonpoint sources in the TMDL program. A frequently-cited reason for the need for such an approach was the commenters' belief that existing nonpoint source programs had so far failed to adequately address nonpoint source pollution. Numerous commenters urged EPA to require quantitative estimates of pollutant loadings from nonpoint sources, while acknowledging that doing so would be more difficult than for point sources.

Some commenters suggested that EPA retain the existing definition of load allocation, along with the definitions of wasteload allocation, loading capacity, and TMDL. These commenters believed that the current definitions provide more clarity as to how loadings are defined and allocated than did the proposed definitions.

Other commenters suggested that the definition of load allocation should not include specific reference to atmospheric deposition or natural background. These commenters contended that the technical uncertainties in linking atmospheric deposition sources to water quality and the lack of Clean Air Act authority to control atmospheric loadings would make it difficult to calculate and implement load allocations. Furthermore, the commenters contended that natural background cannot be reduced and therefore should not be part of the load allocation.

Several comments called for including point sources not covered by the NPDES permit program (such as certain types of storm water sources) under the load allocation portion of the TMDL, rather than the wasteload allocation portion.

What is EPA promulgating today? In response to comments, EPA is clarifying that pollutants from storm water runoff not regulated under NPDES must be accounted for in the load allocation. EPA is also clarifying that pollutants from other sources, such as groundwater, air deposition or background pollutants from upstream sources must be accounted for in the load allocation.

For the reasons discussed earlier in today's preamble, EPA continues to believe that the CWA requires TMDLs to consider loadings from nonpoint sources. For these reasons, EPA rejects the suggestions that EPA delete the definition of load allocation, and consider the TMDL to consist only of wasteload allocations for point sources regulated by NPDES permits. EPA also continues to believe that load allocations must reflect contributions from atmospheric deposition. Where these loads exist, they contribute to the overall load of a pollutant within a waterbody and must be accounted for in the TMDL. Otherwise, the sum of load and wasteload allocations will exceed the amount necessary for the waterbody to attain water quality standards. For these reason and the reasons expressed in the Response to Comment Document, EPA believes that load allocations must include pollutant loads from all sources not already reflected in the wasteload allocations.

EPA believes that, at a minimum, it is possible to determine the total of aggregated loadings from air deposition to a particular waterbody. As a result, EPA expects that States, Territories and authorized Tribes will initially develop load allocations based on nationwide reductions expected as a result of programs developed under the Clean Air Act, and any State-required reductions in emission from local sources. As techniques improve to quantify the relative contributions of different sources, EPA expects that States, Territories and authorized Tribes will more specifically identify air sources and the expected reduction from these sources.

EPA does not consider a loading to surface water from groundwater to necessarily be part of the background loading. The background loading in a TMDL is generally either the loading from upstream of the waterbody for which the TMDL is being established, or else is a loading to the waterbody that originates from natural, not anthropogenic, sources. Pollutants entering a waterbody from groundwater can originate from either natural or anthropogenic sources. For example, the chlorides in groundwater that seep into a waterbody can originate from the geological rock formations or from brine seeping from oil production wells. In either case, the load allocation will address these loadings as part of the load allocation.

EPA recognizes that by moving some of the details from the current definition of load allocation into the TMDL regulatory requirements of

§130.32, it has shortened the definition of load allocation in the current rule. EPA believes this is appropriate because the new §130.32 provides sufficient additional information about the nature of a load allocation (and a wasteload allocation). EPA believes it is better to include this information in one place, and has selected to do so in §130.32.

d. Revised Definition of Wasteload Allocation (§130.2(g))

What did EPA propose? EPA proposed to simplify the existing definition of "wasteload allocation" by defining it as simply the part of the total load in a TMDL that is allocated to a point source. In proposing this change, EPA moved the substantive requirement of how a wasteload allocation is determined into the description of a TMDL in proposed §130.33(b).

What comments did EPA receive? Some commenters said that wasteload allocations should include only loads from point sources covered by the NPDES permit program, but not include loads from point sources not covered by NPDES, such as some types of storm water. Other commenters indicated that all point sources should be included in the wasteload allocation, regardless of their status with regard to NPDES.

A significant number of commenters said EPA should retain language in the existing definition which states that wasteload allocations are a form of effluent limits. One commenter noted that wasteload allocations should be defined as allocated to individual, classes or groups of sources.

What is EPA promulgating today? Today's rule clarifies that only point sources subject to an NPDES permit need to be included in the wasteload allocation. All other sources of a pollutant, be they point source or nonpoint sources, are included in the load allocation. In 1985, when EPA published the definition contained in the existing regulations, all point source discharges were subject to an NPDES permit. The Water Quality Act of 1987, however, provided that not all storm water discharges from point sources were subject to NPDES permits. As a result, today some storm water discharges through point sources are not subject to NPDES requirements. Generally, these are storm water discharges that do not fall into the eleven categories of storm water associated with industrial activities or that are below the threshold of the storm water phase II regulations. To continue this approach, EPA is clarifying that wasteload allocations apply only to point source discharges which are or can be subject to an NPDES permit.

Also, EPA is clarifying that for waterbodies impaired by both point and nonpoint sources, anticipated load reductions from nonpoint sources may be taken into account in calculating the wasteload allocation. EPA received a number of comments stating that in such cases implementation of the TMDL may proceed on different schedules for point and nonpoint sources and supporting the recognition in the final rule of a such a phased approach to implementation of TMDLs (*i.e.*, "phased TMDLs"). EPA interprets the term "phased TMDLs" to describe TMDLs where the wasteload allocations are based on expected reductions from sources other than those regulated by NPDES permits. A phased TMDL includes wasteload allocations that are based on those expected load allocations and includes a monitoring plan to verify the load reductions. See Guidance for Water Quality-Based Decisions: The TMDL process, EPA 440/4-91/001. EPA considers that the combination of requirements for reasonable assurance and the implementation plan in today's rule provide the structure for phased TMDLs. The definition of reasonable assurance provides the basis by which a State, Territory, or authorized Tribe can demonstrate that the load allocations in the TMDL are likely to occur. The implementation plan also requires that the TMDL establish a schedule or timetable which includes a monitoring or modeling plan to measure the effectiveness of point and nonpoint source control measures. Such a plan would include data collection, the assessment for water quality standards attainment, and, if needed, additional predictive modeling.

EPA recognizes it is difficult to ensure with precision that implementing nonpoint source controls will achieve expected load reductions. For example, management measures for nonpoint sources may not perform according to expectations to achieve expected pollutant load reductions despite best efforts. EPA believes that an important part of the phased approach, as discussed above, is the recognition that ultimate success in achieving water quality standards for nonpoint sources may depend upon an iterative approach. States, Territories and authorized Tribes may determine to what extent nonpoint source management measures are meeting the performance expectations on which they are based and implement improved management measures, designs or operations and maintenance procedures. Today's rule at §130.32(c)(2)(v) provides for interim, measurable milestones for determining whether management measures or other action controls are being implemented, and a process for implementing stronger and more effective management measures if necessary. EPA recognizes that this type of approach might involve very long time-frames before water quality standards are eventually realized. EPA also expects that information on actual performance of management measures may lead to questions concerning the appropriateness of the water quality standards and that, in some cases, States, Territories and authorized Tribes may initiate use attainability analyses to determine the appropriate use and, possibly, revise the use on the basis of the information gathered during implementation phase of the TMDL.

EPA is deleting the sentence in the current definition that defines a wasteload allocation as a type of water quality[-]based effluent limitation. EPA acknowledges that water quality-based effluent limitations that derive from a TMDL are based on the TMDL wasteload allocation, but does not believe that wasteload allocations serve as water quality based effluent limits. EPA explained this in its 1991 "Technical Support Guidance for Water Quality-based Toxics Control." Wasteload allocations reflect the mass load of a pollutant that allows a waterbody to attain water quality standards based on the averaging period of the water quality standard. For example, a wasteload allocation based on attaining the 4-day average water quality criterion for copper reflects a 4-day mass load. Effluent limitations reflect periods established by NPDES regulations: generally weekly and monthly limits for publicly owned treatment works and daily and monthly limits for other facilities (see §122.45(d)) and therefore are not the strict equivalent of a wasteload allocation.

e. Revised Definition of TMDL (§130.2(h))

What did EPA propose? EPA proposed to define a "TMDL" as a written plan and analysis established to ensure that an impaired waterbody attains and maintains water quality standards in the event of reasonably foreseeable increases in pollutant loads. Under the proposed revisions, a TMDL would also have had to include ten basic elements, which were described in §130.33(b) and are listed in section I.A.3.b. of this preamble. EPA's proposal was meant to amplify the existing regulatory definition that a TMDL is the sum of load and wasteload allocations and a margin of safety, taking into consideration seasonal variations.

What comments did EPA receive? EPA received numerous comments regarding its proposed changes to the definition of TMDLs. Specific comments regarding the ten proposed elements of a TMDL are addressed later in the discussion of §130.32(b) of today's rule. Some commenters expressed concerns that the proposed definition expanded the concept of a TMDL beyond that mandated by section 303(d). Additional commenters suggested that section 303(d) requires TMDLs only for point sources, and suggested that the TMDL definition reflect this. Others interpreted the proposed definition as going beyond the statutory concept of a TMDL as simply a calculation of the total load necessary to attain and maintain water quality standards. Further comments suggested that the proposed definition was too vague. All these commenters recommended that the existing definition be retained.

Some commenters supported the proposed definition and agreed that it was consistent with section 303(d). These commenters suggested that EPA clarify how the ten elements of the TMDL achieve the statutory concept, *i.e.*, quantify the sum of load and wasteload allocations with a margin of safety and take into consideration seasonal variations.

Further comments expressed concern that the proposed definition required a separate TMDL analysis for each pollutant causing an impairment and for each waterbody. Several commenters believed EPA has no authority to require TMDLs to address growth and recommended that references to growth be stricken from the definition.

What is EPA promulgating today? Today's rule modifies the proposal in a number of ways. EPA is adding the word "quantitative" to the final definition at §130.2(f) to clarify that the TMDL must contain a quantified plan for allocating pollutant loads to attain and maintain water quality standards. EPA is also clarifying that a TMDL must assure that water quality standards are attained and maintained throughout the waterbody and in all seasons of the year. EPA believes this revision clarifies that the TMDL quantifies how water quality standards will be attained and maintained. As proposed and promulgated, the total effect of all the elements of the TMDL require a quantification of the sum of load and wasteload allocations, along with a margin of safety and consideration of seasonal variations, and EPA believes that the definition in the final rule is consistent with section 303(d). Also, EPA has reorganized the provisions of two of the elements and split one, such that there are now eleven elements of a TMDL; this change is discussed in the preamble discussion of §130.32(b).

EPA declines to use the existing regulatory definition of TMDL as suggested by many comments for several reasons. Based on its experience in reviewing and approving TMDLs, EPA continues to believe that the TMDL elements in the final rule definition specify in appropriate detail the information EPA considers necessary to quantify loadings and determine whether the loadings, once implemented, would result in attainment of water quality standards in the waterbody. They will also provide EPA with an element missing from the current regulations, *i.e.*, assurance that the TMDL will in fact be implemented. EPA believes that this information will allow the Agency to make timely and appropriate decisions on TMDLs submitted for review. It will also provide certainty to States, Territories and authorized Tribes on what an approvable TMDL is. Furthermore, as previously discussed in today's preamble, section 303(d) applies to both point sources and nonpoint sources.

EPA is deleting the reference to reasonable foreseeable increases in pollutant loads from the proposed introductory paragraph in the definition, because these increases are addressed in the element of the TMDL that pertains to increases in pollutant loading. EPA addresses other comments and concerns about how TMDLs consider increases in pollutant loads in the Response to Comments document and in today's preamble discussion about §130.32(b).

Finally, in the promulgated definition, EPA is clarifying that it considers a TMDL to apply to one pollutant in a waterbody. However, this does not mean that EPA requires a separate data collection, data analysis, or report for each TMDL. Instead, EPA encourages States, Territories, and authorized Tribes to establish TMDLs on a coordinated basis for a group of waterbodies within a watershed, and that a single analysis can be conducted for several pollutants, instead of for only a single pollutant. EPA does not construe the new definition of waterbody at §130.2(q) to limit the ability of States, Territories and authorized Tribes to establish TMDLs on a watershed basis. In fact, EPA encourages coordinating the establishment of TMDLs on a watershed basis. Also, EPA did not intend to require that States, Territories, and authorized Tribes conduct a separate TMDL analysis for each pollutant in a waterbody or watershed. EPA wants to provide States, Territories and authorized Tribes the flexibility to develop and focus their TMDLs as appropriate, *i.e.*, to address single or multiple impairments in a waterbody, in part of a waterbody, or in multiple waterbodies.

f. New Definition of TMDTL (§130.2(i))

EPA is promulgating a definition of the term "total maximum daily thermal load" or TMDTL to help promote clarity with respect to the requirements which apply to TMDTLs. A TMDTL is a TMDL for a waterbody impaired by thermal discharge(s). In general, the same requirements for an approvable TMDL also apply to TMDTLs, since they are a subset of TMDLs. However, waterbodies with a thermal discharge will be evaluated for listing based on whether the waterbody is supporting a balanced, indigenous population of shellfish, fish, and wildlife. If such waters are listed, they will receive a TMDTL which must be calculated to assure protection and propagation of such a population.

g. New Definition of Impaired Waterbody (§130.2(j))

What did EPA propose? EPA proposed a definition of "impaired waterbody" to define precisely waterbodies which should be considered as not attaining water quality standards and proposed to include within that definition waterbodies impaired by unknown causes.

What comments did EPA receive? Many commenters objected to that part of the definition which required them to account for waterbodies impaired by unknown causes. They believed that the concept was too vague and too broad. They were concerned that some would argue that certain waterbodies should be deemed impaired when there was no evidence of impairment.

What is EPA promulgating today? In response to the comments, EPA is making a change to the proposed definition to clarify its intent regarding waterbodies impaired by unknown causes. EPA does not intend for States, Territories, and authorized Tribes to list waterbodies in the absence of any information demonstrating an impairment. Rather, by proposing to require listing of impaired waters even if the pollutant causing the impairment is unknown, EPA wanted to ensure that lack of information regarding the specific pollutant would not be a reason for not listing an impaired water. After consideration of the comments received, EPA has decided to modify the proposed provision. In situations where the specific pollutant is unknown, but there is information showing impairment, such information tends to consist of biological information (*e.g.*, information showing a water is not supporting a designated or existing aquatic life habitat use). Therefore, EPA is replacing the reference to unknown causes of impairments in the proposal with a provision requiring that waterbodies be considered impaired (and thus listed) when biological information indicates that they do not attain and maintain water quality standards. Prior to developing a TMDL for such waters, the State, Territory, or authorized Tribe would need to identify the particular pollutant causing the impairment. EPA is aware that in past lists, some States, Territories, and authorized Tribes have identified broad categories of pollutants, such as metals or nutrients, as the cause of impairments. Under today's regulation, the only situation in which the State may identify the pollutant as unknown until such time that the TMDL is developed is for waters where the only information demonstrating impairment is biological information. EPA is developing guidance to assist States, Territories, and authorized Tribes to identify the causes of a biological impairment. See draft "Stressor Identification Guidance," April 28, 2000. Otherwise, EPA expects that States will be able to identify the particular metal, nutrient, or other pollutant causing the impairment.

EPA is also modifying the definition of impaired waterbody to include waters that fail to attain and maintain water quality standards. EPA is using the phrase "attain and maintain" to mean that the waterbody must consistently continue to meet water quality standards throughout the waterbody in order to be considered not impaired. Any failure to meet an applicable standard would mean that the waterbody should be listed and a TMDL should be developed if it is listed on Part 1. The use of the phrase "attain and maintain" can be distinguished from the proposed requirement to list threatened waters, which is not included in today's action. Threatened waters are those that are meeting standards, but exhibit a declining trend in water quality such that they would likely exceed standards in the future. Such waters are not required to be included on the section 303(d) list though States can do so. By waters that do not attain and maintain standards, EPA intends to ensure that States, Territories, and authorized Tribes list waters that may occasionally meet an applicable standard, but fail to consistently do so. As in the proposal, the Agency is including in the promulgated definition language from section 303(d)(1)(B) which establishes the standard for considering a waterbody impaired by thermal discharges, *i.e.*, the waterbody does not have or maintain a balanced indigenous population of shellfish, fish and wildlife. As discussed in the preamble to the proposed rule (64 FR 46021-46022, August 23, 1999) and later in today's preamble, EPA interprets section 303(d) to require TMDLs only for waterbodies impaired by pollutants.

Finally, EPA believes that the term impaired waterbodies is a plain language definition of the pre-existing regulatory term water quality limited segment which derived from the CWA. EPA interprets section 303(d) as pertaining to parts of or complete waterbodies that do not attain and maintain water quality standards. For these waterbodies technology-based controls are insufficient to attain water quality standards and water quality-based controls are required, *i.e.*, they are water-quality limited. Also in today's rule, EPA defines waterbody to include one or multiple segments of rivers, lakes, estuaries, etc. Thus, EPA believes that the term "impaired waterbodies" is analogous to the term water-quality limited segment and more understandable to the general public.

h. New Definition of Management Measures (§130.2 (m))

What did EPA propose? EPA did not propose a definition for "management measures." Instead, the proposed regulations used the term Best Management Practices (BMPs), a definition of which was carried over in the proposal from the current requirements.

What comments did EPA receive? Commenters pointed out that the definition of BMPs in the current regulations refers only to nonpoint sources, and they suggested that it should be revised to refer to all sources to which BMPs could be applied. These would include some point sources such as certain storm water discharges. Commenters also were concerned that the reference to BMPs as being selected by an agency would limit the applicability of certain BMPs in the context of establishing TMDLs.

What is EPA promulgating today? EPA agrees with the commenters that it intended the term BMPs in the proposal to include the management of sources other than nonpoint sources. However, rather than modify the pre-existing definition of BMP to accomplish that result, which could have unforeseen impacts on other Agency programs which use this term, EPA is including a definition of "management measures" in today's regulation. This term and definition retain those concepts in the current definition of BMPs which are applicable to TMDLs but eliminate the references to nonpoint sources and selection by an agency. EPA believes the definition of "management measure" is a logical outgrowth of the proposed definition of "BMP" and a reasonable response to the above-referenced comments.

i. New Definition of Thermal Discharge (§130.2(o))

What did EPA propose? EPA proposed adding the definition of "thermal discharge" to clarify the meaning of the term for the purpose of identifying impaired waterbodies and establishing Total Maximum Daily Thermal Loads (TMDTLs) pursuant to section 303(d). EPA proposed to define the term as "the discharge of heat from a point source." EPA believed that the definition was important since waterbodies impaired by thermal discharge are subject to section 303(d) listing and TMDTL requirements, and furthermore, the test for measuring successful implementation is different than for other pollutants.

What comments did EPA receive? EPA received several comments on this definition. Some comments requested clarification of whether EPA meant discharge of heat from all point sources. Other comments suggested that the definition be revised to include nonpoint sources of heat.

What is EPA promulgating today? EPA is promulgating the proposed definition with a minor change to clarify that it applies to only those point sources "that are required to have NPDES permits." EPA provided detailed explanations in the preamble to the proposal regarding its interpretation of the statute as it pertains to inclusion of thermal discharges in the TMDL program. (64 FR 46017 August 23, 1999). As discussed in the preamble to the proposed rule, EPA believes the CWA reference to "balanced, indigenous population of shellfish, fish and wildlife" refers only to those discharges subject to sections 301 and 306, which relate to point sources subject to NPDES permits. Therefore EPA is not expanding the definition of thermal discharge to include nonpoint sources. EPA acknowledges that nonpoint sources and other sources not subject to NPDES permits can introduce heat into a waterbody. However, for reasons discussed in the preamble to the proposed rule, EPA believes that the CWA requires that TMDLs rather than TMDTLs be established for these waterbodies if they are impaired solely by these sources and that they must attain water quality standards, and not just a balanced, indigenous population of shellfish, fish and wildlife.

j. New Definition of Reasonable Assurance (§130.2(p))

What did EPA propose? EPA proposed to define "reasonable assurance" as a demonstration that wasteload allocations and load allocations in a TMDL would be implemented. EPA proposed that each TMDL provide reasonable assurance that allocations contained in a TMDL would, in fact, be implemented to attain and maintain water quality standards in the waterbody. EPA incorporated the term in proposed §130.33(b)(10)(iii) dealing with TMDL implementation plans to emphasize that implementation of the allocations in TMDLs is critical to the ultimate attainment of standards in impaired waterbodies across the country.

What comments did EPA receive? EPA received a number of comments generally opposing the concept of reasonable assurance. Some commenters believe that EPA does not have the authority to require States, Territories or authorized Tribes to demonstrate reasonable assurance, and that the definition of reasonable assurance was too prescriptive. EPA also received comments generally in support of the reasonable assurance provision, noting that it is important to have assurance that implementation will occur and that water quality standards will be met.

EPA received many comments on specific aspects of the proposed definition of reasonable assurance. A major theme was that the proposed definition did not recognize that State, Territorial and authorized Tribal nonpoint source programs are largely voluntary. Furthermore, many commenters noted that States may have limited regulatory authority to address nonpoint sources, and perceived the definition of reasonable assurance as forcing States to adopt regulatory controls on nonpoint sources. Many commenters urged that voluntary, incentive-based programs should be acceptable as reasonable assurance. Conversely, a number of commenters believed that regulatory controls for nonpoint sources were necessary to provide reasonable assurance, or that, in order to provide reasonable assurance, implementation plans needed to be enforceable. A few commenters suggested that States, Territories and authorized Tribes need to have regulatory authority to control pollutants from nonpoint sources in the event that voluntary programs do not succeed.

Numerous commenters expressed concern about the funding component of reasonable assurance. A frequently-cited concern was that States would not be able to guarantee full funding to implement the TMDL at the time a TMDL was established. Some commenters also believed that the funding provision was not well-defined, and that, when reviewing TMDLs, EPA would not be able to evaluate whether the State had demonstrated "adequate funding." Others noted that States, Territories and authorized Tribes lack adequate funding and staff to establish and implement TMDLs and that EPA needs to ensure adequate funding through the section and other programs.

EPA received some comments regarding the ability of existing State and Federal authorities and programs to satisfy the reasonable assurance provision. Some commenters suggested that approval of a State, Territorial or authorized Tribal nonpoint source program or nonpoint source management plan should by itself, constitute reasonable assurance. Other commenters disagreed and said that reference to existing programs by itself is not adequate, and that control actions assuring TMDL implementation must be specific to the source and the waterbody. Some commenters urged flexibility in allowing for a variety of implementation mechanisms to satisfy reasonable assurance such as other Federal and State forest and land management programs. Several comments pointed out that it would be difficult to provide reasonable assurance, given the challenge of aligning multiple State and Federal agencies, and multiple watershed groups.

Some commenters suggested that EPA needs to better define what it means that procedures and mechanisms relating to nonpoint sources of a pollutant must be implemented expeditiously, or specify a particular timeframe for their implementation. A few commenters believed that EPA was not in a position to evaluate what constitutes expeditious, and that the term should be eliminated.

A few commenters questioned EPA's authority to provide reasonable assurance when it establishes a TMDL for nonpoint sources. Some also questioned EPA's authority to condition section 319 grant funds as a way of providing reasonable assurance. Conversely, a few commenters supported EPA's full use of its authorities to implement TMDLs, or to condition section 319 funds, as necessary.

What is EPA promulgating today? Today's rule contains a revised definition of reasonable assurance. Reasonable assurance continues to mean a demonstration that TMDLs will be implemented through regulatory or voluntary actions, by Federal, State or local governments, authorized Tribes or individuals.

Reasonable assurance is a demonstration that a TMDL's implementation plan will indeed be implemented. (See §130.32(c).) EPA believes that it has the authority to require the demonstration of reasonable assurance as part of the implementation plan. Section 303(d) requires that a TMDL be established at a level necessary to implement water quality standards and requires EPA to review and either approve or disapprove the TMDL. CWA section 501(a) also authorizes EPA to adopt regulations as necessary to implement the Act. To approve a TMDL, EPA believes it is necessary to determine whether a TMDL is in fact established at a level necessary to attain water quality standards. For EPA to determine that the TMDL will implement water quality standards, there must be a demonstration in the TMDL of reasonable assurance that the TMDL's load and wasteload allocations will be implemented. Otherwise, the allocations presented in a TMDL lack a necessary link to anticipated attainment of water quality standards.

Reasonable Assurance for Point Sources for Which an NPDES Permit is Required

Reasonable assurance for point sources for which an NPDES permit is required means that States, Territories and authorized Tribes must identify procedures that will ensure that permits will be modified, issued or reissued as expeditiously as practicable to incorporate effluent limits consistent with the wasteload allocations. For these demonstrations of reasonable assurance, the phrase "as expeditiously as practicable" means in general that the permitting authority, either an authorized State, Territory, or Tribe, or EPA, will issue the permit as follows. For facilities receiving a permit for the first time, "as expeditiously as practicable" means that the permitting authority must issue the permit that implements the wasteload allocation before the facility begins to discharge. Under EPA's current NPDES rules, a facility may only discharge pollutants from point sources into waters of the United States as authorized by an NPDES permit (§122.1). New facilities must receive their permit before they can lawfully discharge pollutants. Also, current NPDES regulations require that NPDES effluent limitations be consistent with the applicable wasteload allocation in an approved TMDL (§122.44(d)(1)(vii)(B)). Therefore, EPA believes that its interpretation of "as expeditiously as practicable" for facilities receiving their first permit is consistent with the current practice of the NPDES permit program. For facilities currently permitted, "as expeditiously as practicable" means that the permitting authority will reissue the permit as soon as it can after the permit expires, taking into account factors such as available permitting resources, staff and budget constraints, other competing priorities, and watershed efficiencies. Alternatively, the permitting authority, may choose to modify the permit prior to expiration in accordance with the permitting authority's modification requirements.

The phrase "as expeditiously as practicable" adds a time element to the word "expeditiously," which was used in the proposal. The dictionary definition of "expeditiously" is fast or rapidly. EPA received comments about "how fast is fast," and whether any factor governed how quickly EPA expected a permitting authority to issue or reissue NPDES permits. EPA intended that permitting authorities would not delay their normal issuance or reissuance of permits and would modify the permits when they contained a reopener provision allowing modification of the permit conditions on the basis of new information. EPA is using the phrase "as expeditiously as practicable" in the final rule to clarify further what EPA means by the word "expeditiously" used in the proposal. This clarification should allow permit authorities to schedule permit issuance and reissuance actions consistent with the relevant factors discussed above.

Reasonable Assurance for Sources for Which an NPDES Permit is Not Required

For all other sources, including nonpoint sources, storm water sources for which an NPDES permit is not required, atmospheric deposition, groundwater and background sources, reasonable assurance means that actions implementing the load allocations meet a four-part test. The control actions or management measures must be (1) specific to the pollutant and waterbody for which the TMDL is being established, (2) implemented as expeditiously as practicable, (3) accomplished through reliable delivery mechanisms, and (4) supported by adequate funding. For these sources, each TMDL must meet each one of these tests prior to EPA approval.

(1) Specific to the pollutant and waterbody. The first part of the four part test for reasonable assurance is that the management measure or control be specific to the pollutant and waterbody. By this, EPA means that the State, Territory, or authorized Tribe knows of, and can point to, information showing that the management measure relied upon to achieve the reduction in the loading can reduce that pollutant. By "specific," EPA does not intend that States, Territories or authorized Tribes collect new or additional site-specific information, but rather that they provide EPA existing data that relates to the specific waterbody and pollutant. For example, a State may rely on a program that installs buffer strips to demonstrate reasonable assurance. In this example, the State would point to National Resource Conservation Service information showing that buffer strips are effective in mitigating erosion and thus can reduce loadings of the specific pollutant, *i.e.*, sediment. Also, the State would need to show which waterbodies within the watershed would receive buffer strips and explain the characteristic of these buffer strips. In this way, the State may fulfill the requirements of this part of the four part test. For atmospheric deposition, where the controls will result from Clean Air Act regulations, reference to current or anticipated Clean Air Act regulations should explain how those regulations relate to the specific pollutant of concern.

(2) As expeditiously as practicable. EPA intended that States, Territories, and authorized Tribes would implement management measures as quickly as they reasonably could in light of other water quality needs. For the reasons discussed above, EPA is using the phrase "as expeditiously as practicable" in the final rule to clarify the word "expeditiously" as used in the proposal. EPA expects that States, Territories, and authorized Tribes will make nonpoint source controls implementing a TMDL for which there are no point sources subject to NPDES permits a high priority for nonpoint source program funding. Scheduling of nonpoint source controls is also discussed in section II.P. of this preamble. For atmospheric deposition, adoption of Clean Air Act regulations and implementation of those regulations pursuant to the provisions of the Clean Air Act would satisfy the reasonable assurance requirement that implementation will occur as expeditiously as practicable.

(3) Reliable delivery mechanisms. EPA did not include the concept of "reliable delivery mechanism" in the proposed definition of reasonable assurance. EPA did discuss this concept in the preamble discussion of the definition. (64 FR 46033, August 23, 1999). Reliable delivery mechanism means the programmatic and administrative means by which the manage-

ment measures and control actions will be implemented and monitored. Several comments expressed concern that the preamble discussion was not reflected in the rule language, and suggested that this preamble phrase should be included in the definition. EPA was persuaded by the comments that it should do this.

EPA is also adding the word "effective" to modify "reliable delivery mechanism." EPA believes that this concept is a logical outgrowth of the preamble to the proposed rule. There, EPA discussed that voluntary and incentive-based programs may be used to demonstrate reasonable assurance. It goes without saying that these programs must be "effective" in order to provide reasonable assurance. Nevertheless, to avoid confusion, EPA decided to be clear and add the word "effective" to the final rule.

Some existing nonpoint source related programs may also be reliable and effective delivery mechanisms specific to the waterbody and pollutant for purposes of providing reasonable assurance. Programs, procedures or authorities including State, Territorial or authorized Tribal programs approved under section 319 of the CWA or existing conservation or water quality protection programs administered by the United States Department of Agriculture which have demonstrated success in delivering water quality improvements in the past may be reliable delivery mechanisms for the purpose of §130.2(p). State, Territories and authorized Tribes will need to explain how these programs will be implemented in the specific impaired waterbody and how they address the pollutant causing the impairment. For atmospheric deposition, implementation of the Clean Air Act regulatory program could provide the necessary reliable delivery mechanism.

(4) Adequate funding. Finally, today's rule clarifies what EPA considers to be "adequate funding" for the purpose of demonstrating reasonable assurance. In response to comments, EPA is including in the final rule the funding language from the proposed rule preamble, and providing a more detailed discussion of this term below. (64 FR 46033 to 46034, August 23, 1999). EPA believes that adequate funding means that existing water quality funds have been allocated to implement load allocations to the fullest extent practicable and in a manner consistent with the effective operation of the clean water program in the State, Territory, or authorized Tribe. EPA believes that implementing TMDLs is a central part of water quality management. At the same time EPA recognizes that effective water quality programs are comprised of many different activities which must be carried out concurrently. It would make no sense to fund only TMDL activities and eliminate other important activities. For atmospheric deposition, where controls will be required by Clean Air Act regulations, the process for adoption and implementation of those regulations should satisfy the requirement for adequate funding.

Today's rule requires that States, Territories and authorized Tribes identify adequate clean water program funding to implement load allocations. Clean water program funding includes Federal funding through the CWA and some related Federal, State, Territorial or authorized Tribal funding. In the event that funding is not currently adequate to implement the TMDL, EPA may approve the TMDL if the State, Territory, or authorized Tribe provides an explanation of when adequate funds will be available and a schedule by which these funds will be obtained and used to implement the TMDL. EPA believes that such a schedule identifying when load allocations will be implemented as funding becomes available is necessary to provide reasonable assurance that load allocations will be achieved where adequate funding is not currently available. As indicated in implementation plans provisions, such a schedule must assure that implementation will be as expeditious as practicable (*i.e.*, within 5 years when practicable) for waterbodies impaired only by sources which are not subject to NPDES permits, including nonpoint sources.

Use of Existing Programs

EPA believes that existing nonpoint source programs can provide the suite of control actions and management measures for States to rely on when meeting the reasonable assurance test. Examples of voluntary and incentive-based actions or existing programs include State, Territorial or authorized Tribal programs to audit implementation of agricultural management measures and memoranda of understanding between State, Territorial and authorized Tribal governments and organizations that represent categories, subcategories or individual sources which assure implementation and effectiveness of management measures.

A State, Territory, or authorized Tribe may need to consider other programs to address pollutants introduced in a waterbody by atmospheric deposition or groundwater. For example, the State, Territory, or authorized Tribe could rely on scheduled reductions in atmospheric sources under the Clean Air Act or similar State authority. Likewise, it could rely on reduced groundwater loadings as a result of remedial actions under the Resource Conservation and Recovery Act (RCRA) or similar State authority. If these programs cannot provide reasonable assurance that the pollutant loads will be reduced, the load reduction will have to be assigned to other sources.

Generally, a State, Territory, or authorized Tribe will demonstrate reasonable assurance for the part of the load allocation that addresses the loading of pollutants contributed by background sources by quantifying the loading so that it can be included in the calculation of the total loading in a waterbody. In these situations, this background loading would be presumed to be constant and load reductions will be assigned to other sources. However, if a State, Territory, or authorized Tribe expects that the background loadings will decrease as a result of some action and is relying on this decrease in the calculation of wasteload and load allocations, then the State, Territory, or authorized Tribe will need to apply the four-part test to demonstrate the reasonable assurance for this expected reduction.

The test of reasonable assurance in today's rule is not met simply by having programs, authorities or voluntary measures described in the definition of reasonable assurance in place. In order for such programs, authorities or measures to provide reasonable assurance each one of the four parts of the test must be satisfied. For example, if a State offers a particular voluntary program approved under section 319 as proof of reasonable assurance, EPA will review the program information to see whether it specifically addresses the waterbody/pollutant of concern, includes actions that will be implemented as expeditiously as practicable, will be accomplished through a reliable delivery mechanism with a good track record of success and meet the adequate funding test.

Reasonable Assurance When EPA Establishes TMDLs

In some cases, EPA will have to disapprove a State's TMDL and establish the TMDL. When establishing a TMDL, EPA will also have to provide reasonable assurance as required by §§130.32(c) and 130.2(p). In providing reasonable assurance, EPA may rely on various statutory or regulatory authorities to meet the four-part test which applies to load allocations for sources not subject to an NPDES permit. EPA cannot, of course, require States, Territories or authorized Tribes to use their own statutory or regulatory authorities to provide reasonable assurance for EPA. EPA may, however, condition some or all CWA grants to the fullest extent practicable and in a manner consistent with the effective operation of other CWA programs in order to meet the adequate funding part of the four-part reasonable assurance test. Such action would by itself serve to satisfy that part of the reasonable assurance test when EPA establishes a TMDL. For example, EPA may condition section 319 grants such that States can only use some or all of these funds to implement management measures in watersheds where EPA has established a TMDL that includes load reductions for nonpoint sources. Similarly, EPA may condition section 106 grants to States such that some of the funds for monitoring can only be used to support the monitoring specified in TMDL implementation plans. EPA may also use its voluntary, incentive-based programs, such as section 104(b)(3) demonstration grants for watershed restoration, to ensure that management measures are funded and implemented. EPA may provide reasonable assurance for wasteload allocations by issuing NPDES permits within the time frames prescribed by §130.32(c)(1)(ii) where EPA is the permitting authority, or by objecting to expired State-issued permits so that new permits will be issued to implement wasteload allocations from approved TMDLs.

By requiring such a demonstration of reasonable assurance before it may approve or establish a TMDL, EPA does not intend to create a mandatory duty or legal obligation that either the State, Territory, authorized Tribe or EPA implement those actions identified as providing reasonable assurance. The reasonable assurance demonstration is a "snapshot-in-time" identification of those voluntary and regulatory actions that the State, Territory, authorized Tribe or EPA intends to take to ensure that the nonpoint source load allocations assigned in the TMDL will be realized. If such demonstration is deemed satisfactory at the time the TMDL is being reviewed or developed by EPA, the TMDL may be approved or established. If in the future, the State, Territory, authorized Tribe or EPA determines that the TMDL is not being implemented, or that the implementation plan needs to be revised, the State, Territory, authorized Tribe or EPA may take action, as appropriate under existing State, Territorial, Tribal or Federal legal authority, to effect implementation or revise the TMDL. Nothing in this rule, however, creates in EPA or the States new legal authority beyond that provided by existing State, Territorial, Tribal or Federal law to implement load allocations for nonpoint sources or creates for EPA, States, Territories or authorized Tribes a mandatory duty to do so.

k. New Definition of Waterbody (§130.2(q))

What did EPA propose? EPA proposed a definition of the new term "waterbody" to codify EPA's interpretation of the term for the purposes of TMDLs. The proposed definition would have provided States, Territories, and authorized Tribes more flexibility than the current regulation which refers to segments and would have allowed States, Territories, and authorized Tribes to tailor the geographical size of the watershed for which the TMDL was being established to match the pollutants and nature of impairment.

What comments did EPA receive? EPA received a number of comments on this definition. Most commenters suggested that the definition exclude ephemeral streams and wetlands. These commenters expressed concern over the application of water quality standards to these waterbodies, and thus suggested that TMDLs should not be established for them. Other comments expressed concern that the definition would prevent establishment of a TMDL for one segment of a river.

What is EPA promulgating today? After review of comments, EPA is promulgating the proposed definition with two minor changes. First, EPA is revising the proposed language to recognize that waterbodies can be made up of one or more segments of rivers, streams, lakes, wetlands, coastal waters or ocean waters. EPA did not intend to require that a TMDL consider the full geographic extent of a waterbody. Rather EPA intended to give States, Territories and authorized Tribes the flexibility to establish TMDLs for one or more segments. Second, EPA is adding a recommendation to the rule that the use of segments should be consistent with the use of segments in a State's water quality standards. EPA is making this recommendation to help promote consistency between how TMDLs are developed and how water quality standards are expressed.

EPA does not believe that the nature of a waterbody, such as an ephemeral stream or a wetland, and the challenge that nature may pose to establishing a TMDL, should preclude it from being defined as a waterbody. EPA believes that this is a water quality standard issue and that the appropriate forum for resolving questions about water quality standards is in the development of the standards themselves, and not in the application of the standards in a TMDL context.

1. New Definition of List (§130.2(v))

What did EPA propose? EPA proposed to include a new definition to refer to the four elements of the list and the prioritized schedule. EPA proposed this revision to expedite reference to the four elements and schedule within the rule.

What comments did EPA receive? EPA received no substantial comments unique to this definition. Some commenters did offer suggestions on what are acceptable elements of a list; these comments are addressed in parts of today's preamble that address these elements.

What is EPA promulgating today? EPA is revising the proposed definition of "list of impaired waterbodies" to make it consistent with other provisions of the final rule. First, EPA is clarifying that the list consists of all four parts of the required submission. This is to ensure that there is no confusion over whether certain parts of the list that may be submitted along with the State's section 305(b) report are in fact part of the section 303(d) list. In addition, the definition states that Part 1 of the list includes both waterbodies identified for TMDL development and the prioritized schedule for those waterbodies. This revision makes the definition consistent with the requirement to submit the prioritized schedule as part of the list itself, subject to EPA approval or disapproval, rather than as a separate document with the list submission that EPA will review but not take action on.

2. Response to Requests for New Definitions

What did EPA propose? EPA's proposal of August 23, 1999, requested comments on all aspects of adding new definitions.

What comments did EPA receive? EPA received comments suggesting that EPA add several definitions for terms used in the proposed rule or discussed in comments which requested additions to the requirements of the final rule.

What is EPA promulgating today? EPA has decided not to add other definitions to §130.2. EPA is not adding a definition of "balanced indigenous population of fish, shellfish, and wildlife." There is an existing regulatory definition of the term "balanced indigenous population" in §125.70 that, although it explicitly applies only to the regulations implementing section 316(a), provides the Agency's interpretation of this term for purposes of identifying impaired waterbodies and establishing TMDLs pursuant to section 303(d).

EPA is not adding a definition of "watershed." The term is not used within the final rule to trigger a regulatory provision, and thus does not require definition. EPA prefers to allow States, Territories, and authorized Tribes the flexibility to define a watershed within the context of their own programs. However, EPA encourages the use of the hydrologic unit codes for watersheds defined by the U.S. Geologic Survey since they are a uniform system of watershed identification that will clearly identify to other States, Territories, Tribes, EPA and the public the boundaries of watersheds defined by the States in the context of their water quality programs.

EPA is not including a specific definition in the final rule for "trading" and thus declines to add trading-related definitions for "real," "quantifiable" or "surplus" as suggested by some comments as being necessary if EPA included regulatory provisions for trading.

EPA is not adding a definition of "existing and readily available," "man-made or man-induced," "point source," "nonpoint source," and "waters of the contiguous zone." This final rule at §130.22(b) already provides a definition of existing and readily available water-quality related data and information by enumerating particular categories of water-quality related data and information that must be considered. The regulations clearly state that this list is not exhaustive, but rather is intended to identify specific kinds of water quality-related data and information that will be considered existing and readily available, in addition to water-quality related data and information in other relevant categories that are not explicitly listed in the regulations. EPA does not believe it can accurately identify each and every type of water-quality related data and information that should be considered in every state's listing process, in light of the broad variety of relevant water-quality related data and information that is and will be available. Therefore, it is appropriate to list specific categories that are likely to exist for every state, and leave it to the States, Territories, and authorized Tribes to collect and evaluate other relevant information.

The CWA itself uses the term "man-made or man-induced" within the statutory definition of pollution; EPA believes this term is very clear and needs no further clarification. The CWA already defines "point source" and EPA does not believe that today's rule needs to reiterate this definition. EPA interprets "nonpoint source" to apply to all sources that do not meet the statutory definition of a point source. Finally, the CWA at section 502(a) already defines the term "contiguous zone" and EPA does not believe that it needs to reiterate this definition in today's final rule.

EPA disagrees that it should add a definition of "sensitive aquatic species." This term was used in the proposal merely to indicate a factor that States, Territories and authorized Tribes should consider when establishing priorities for TMDLs. Since this is a discretionary practice in the final rule, EPA believes that it need not define the term.

EPA also disagrees that it should add a definition of "seasonal variations." This term originates in CWA section 303(d)(1)(C). EPA believes it means seasonal variation in environmental conditions which affect a waterbody's character, *e.g.*, variations in a waterbody's temperature, flow rate, or dissolved oxygen level. EPA does not believe the term needs a separate regulatory definition. Further, §130.32(b)(9) provides sufficient explanation of what is to be included in the assessment of seasonal variation.

EPA disagrees that it should add a definition of "comprehensive watershed management plan." This term is not used in the final rule, and thus does not require definition.

EPA disagrees that it should add a definition of "natural sources/causes" or "ephemeral stream." EPA believes these terms are best defined in State, Territorial and authorized Tribe's water quality standards. The term "natural sources/causes" was suggested to clarify how a TMDL would address impairments caused by natural sources or causes. EPA believes this question is best addressed when a State, Territory, or authorized Tribe decides the appropriate water quality criteria for that waterbody. The term "ephemeral stream" was suggested to identify a type of waterbody for which special water quality standards would be necessary. Again, EPA believes this question is best addressed when a State, Territory, or authorized Tribe decides the appropriate water quality criteria for that waterbody.

Lists of Subjects

40 CFR Part 9

Reporting and recordkeeping requirements.

40 CFR Part 122

Environmental protection, Administrative practice and procedure, Confidential business information, Hazardous substances, Reporting and recordkeeping requirements, Water pollution control.

40 CFR Part 123

Environmental protection, Administrative practice and procedure, Confidential business information, Hazardous substances, Indians—lands, Intergovernmental relations, Penalties, Reporting and recordkeeping requirements, Water pollution control.

40 CFR Part 124

Environmental protection, Administrative practice and procedure, Hazardous substances, Indians—lands, Reporting and recordkeeping requirements, Water pollution control, Water supply.

40 CFR Part 130

Environmental protection, Reporting and recordkeeping requirements, Water pollution control.

Dated: July 11, 2000.

Carol Browner,
Administrator.

For the reasons set forth in the preamble, EPA amends 40 CFR parts 9, 122, 123, 124, and 130 as follows:

PART 9—OMB APPROVALS UNDER THE PAPERWORK REDUCTION ACT

1. The authority citation for part 9 continues to read as follows:

Authority: 7 U.S.C. 135 *et seq.*, 136-136y; 15 U.S.C. 2001, 2003, 2005, 2006, 2601-2671; 21 U.S.C. 331j, 346a, 348; 31 U.S.C. 9701; 33 U.S.C. 1251 *et seq.*, 1311, 1313d, 1314, 1318, 1321, 1326, 1330, 1342, 1344, 1345 (d) and (e), 1361; E.O. 11735, 38 FR 21243, 3 CFR, 1971-1975 Comp. p. 973; 42 U.S.C. 241, 242b, 243, 246, 300f, 300g, 300g-1, 300g-2, 300g-3, 300g-4, 300g-5, 300g-6, 300j-1, 300j-2, 300j-3, 300j-4, 300j-9, 1857 *et seq.*, 6901-6992k, 7401-7671q, 7542, 9601-9657, 11023, 11048.

2. In §9.1, amend the table by removing the entries "130.6-130.10" and "130.15," and adding new entries in numerical order under the indicated heading to read as follows:

§9.1 OMB approvals under the Paperwork Reduction Act.
*   *   *   *   *

40 CFR citation	OMB control No.
* * * * *	
Water Quality Planning and Management	
130.7 ·	2040-0071
130.11 ·	2040-0071
130.20-130.37 · · · · · · · · · · · · · · ·	2040-0071
130.51 ·	2040-0071
130.60-130.61 · · · · · · · · · · · · · · ·	2040-0071
130.64 ·	2040-0071

*   *   *   *   *

PART 122—EPA ADMINISTERED PERMIT PROGRAMS: THE NATIONAL POLLUTANT DISCHARGE ELIMINATION SYSTEM

1. The authority citation for part 122 continues to read as follows:
Authority: The Clean Water Act, 33 U.S.C. 1251 *et seq.*

2. Amend §122.44 to revise paragraphs (d) introductory text and (d)(1) introductory text to read as follows:

§122.44 Establishing limitations, standards, and other permit conditions (applicable to State NPDES programs, see §123.25).
*   *   *   *   *

(d) *Water quality standards and State requirements:* any requirements in addition to or more stringent than promulgated effluent limitations guidelines or standards under sections 301, 304, 306, 307, 318 and 405 of CWA necessary to:

(1) Achieve water quality standards established under section 303 of the CWA, including State narrative criteria for water quality and State antidegradation provisions.

*   *   *   *   *

PART 123—STATE PROGRAM REQUIREMENTS

1. The authority citation for part 123 continues to read as follows:

Authority: The Clean Water Act, 33 U.S.C. 1251 *et seq.*

2. Amend §123.44 to add paragraph (k) to read as follows:

§123.44 EPA review of and objections to State permits.

*   *   *   *   *

(k)(1) Where a State fails to submit a new draft or proposed permit to EPA within 90 days after the expiration of the existing permit, EPA may review the administratively-continued permit, using the procedure described in paragraphs (a)(1) through (h)(3) of this section, if:

(i) The administratively-continued permit allows the discharge of pollutant(s) into a waterbody for which EPA has established or approved a TMDL and the permit is not consistent with an applicable wasteload allocation; or

(ii) The administratively-continued permit allows the discharge of a pollutant(s) of concern into a waterbody that does not attain and maintain water quality standards and for which EPA has not established or approved a TMDL.

(2) To review an expired and administratively-continued permit under this paragraph (k) EPA must give the State and the discharger at least 90 days written notice of its intent to consider the expired permit as a proposed permit. At any time beginning 90 days after permit expiration, EPA may submit this notice.

(3) If the State submits a draft or proposed permit for EPA review at any time before EPA issues the permit under paragraph (h) of this section, EPA will withdraw its notice of intent to take permit authority under this paragraph (k) and will evaluate the draft or proposed permit under this section.

PART 124—PROCEDURES FOR DECISIONMAKING

1. The authority citation for part 124 continues to read as follows:

Authority: Resource Conservation and Recovery Act, 42 U.S.C. 6901 *et seq.*; Safe Drinking Water Act, 42 U.S.C. 300f *et seq.*; Clean Water Act, 33 U.S.C. 1251 *et seq.*; Clean Air Act, 42 U.S.C. 7401 *et seq.*

2. Revise §124.7 to read as follows:

§124.7 Statement of basis.

(a) EPA shall prepare a statement of basis for every draft permit for which a fact sheet under §124.8 is not prepared. The statement of basis shall briefly describe the derivation of the conditions of the draft permit and the reasons for them or, in the case of notices of intent to deny or terminate, reasons supporting the tentative decision. In particular, the statement of basis shall include:

(1) In cases where a TMDL has not been established for an impaired waterbody, an explanation of how permit limits and/or conditions were derived for all pollutants in the discharger's effluent for which the waterbody is impaired; and

(2) In cases where a TMDL has been established for an impaired waterbody, any TMDL that has been established for a pollutant contained in the discharger's effluent; the applicable wasteload allocation derived for the pollutant in the TMDL for that discharger; and an explanation of how permit limits for the pollutant of concern were derived as well as how those limits are consistent with the applicable wasteload allocation.

(b) The statement of basis shall be sent to the applicant and, on request, to any other person.

3. Amend §124.8 by adding paragraphs (b)(4)(i) and (b)(4)(ii) to read as follows:

§124.8 Fact sheet.

*   *   *   *   *

(b) * * *

(4) * * *

(i) In cases where a TMDL has not been established for an impaired waterbody, an explanation of how permit limits and/or conditions were derived for all pollutants in the discharger's effluent for which the waterbody is impaired; and

(ii) In cases where a TMDL has been established for an impaired waterbody, any TMDL that has been established for a pollutant contained in the discharger's effluent; the applicable wasteload allocation derived for the pollutant in the TMDL for that discharger; and an explanation of how permit limits for the pollutant of concern were derived as well as how those limits are consistent with the applicable wasteload allocation.

*   *   *   *   *

PART 130—WATER QUALITY PLANNING AND MANAGEMENT

1. The authority citation for part 130 continues to read as follows:
Authority: 33 U.S.C. 1251 *et seq.*

2. Redesignate §§130.4 through 130.6, and 130.8 through 130.15 as follows: *§§130.4 through 130.15 [Redesignated]*

Old section	New section
130.4..	130.10
130.5..	130.50
130.6..	130.51
130.8..	130.11
130.9..	130.60
130.10..	130.61
130.11..	130.62
130.12..	130.63
130.15..	130.64

§130.3 [Removed]

3. Section 130.3 is removed.

§§130.0 through 130.2 and §130.7 [Redesignated as Subpart A]

4. Sections 130.0 through 130.2 and 130.7 are designated as Subpart A and a subpart heading is added to read as follows:

Subpart A—Summary, Purpose and Definitions

§§130.10 and 130.11 [Redesignated as Subpart B]

5. Sections 130.10 and 130.11 are designated as Subpart B and a subpart heading is added to read as follows:

Subpart B—Water Quality Monitoring and Reporting

§§130.50 and 130.51 [Redesignated as Subpart D]

6. Sections 130.50 and 130.51 are designated as Subpart D and a subpart heading is added to read as follows:

Subpart D—Water Quality Planning and Implementation

§§130.60 through 130.64 [Redesignated as Subpart E]

7. Sections 130.60 through 130.64 are designated as Subpart E and a subpart heading is added to read as follows:

Subpart E—Miscellaneous Provisions
8. Amend §130.1 to revise paragraph (a) as follows:

§130.1 Applicability.
(a) This part applies to all State, eligible Indian Tribe, interstate, areawide and regional and local CWA water quality planning and management activities undertaken on or after February 11, 1985 including all updates and continuing certifications for approved Water Quality Management plans developed under sections 208 and 303 of the Act.

*   *   *   *   *

9. Amend §130.2 to revise paragraphs (c) (d), (e), (f), (g), (h), (i), (j), and (m), and add paragraphs (o), (p), (q), and (r) as follows:

§130.2 Definitions.
*   *   *   *   *

(c) *Pollution.* The man-made or man-induced alteration of the chemical, physical, biological, and radiological integrity of water. (See Clean Water Act section 502(19).)

(d) *Pollutant.* Dredged spoil, solid waste, incinerator residue, sewage, garbage, sewage sludge, munitions, chemical wastes, biological materials, radioactive materials (except those regulated under Atomic Energy Act of 1954, as amended (42 U.S.C. 2011 *et seq.*)), heat, wrecked or discarded equipment, rock, sand, cellar dirt, and industrial, municipal, and agricultural waste discharged into water. This term does not mean: "sewage from vessels" within the meaning of section 312 of the Clean Water Act; or water, gas, or other material that is injected into a well to facilitate production of oil or gas, or water derived in association with oil or gas production and disposed of in a well, if the well used either to facilitate production or for disposal purposes is approved by authority of the State in which the well is located, and if the State determines that such injection or disposal will not result in the degradation of ground or surface water resources. (See Clean Water Act section 502(6).)

(e) *Load or loading.* An amount of matter or thermal energy that is introduced into a receiving water; to introduce matter or thermal energy into a receiving water. Loading of pollutants may be either man-caused or natural (natural background loading).

(f) *Load allocation.* The portion of a TMDL's pollutant load allocated to a nonpoint source, storm water source for which a National Pollutant Discharge Elimination System (NPDES) permit is not required, atmospheric deposition, ground water, or background source of pollutants.

(g) *Wasteload allocation.* The portion of a TMDL's pollutant load allocated to a point source of a pollutant for which an NPDES permit is required. For waterbodies impaired by both point and nonpoint sources, wasteload allocations may reflect anticipated or expected reductions of pollutants from other sources if those anticipated or expected reductions are supported by reasonable assurance that they will occur.

(h) *Total maximum daily load (TMDL)*. A TMDL is a written, quantitative plan and analysis for attaining and maintaining water quality standards in all seasons for a specific waterbody and pollutant. TMDLs may be established on a coordinated basis for a group of waterbodies in a watershed. TMDLs must be established for waterbodies on Part 1 of the list of impaired waterbodies and must include the following eleven elements:

(1) The name and geographic location of the impaired waterbody;

(2) Identification of the pollutant and the applicable water quality standard;

(3) Quantification of the pollutant load that may be present in the waterbody and still ensure attainment and maintenance of water quality standards;

(4) Quantification of the amount or degree by which the current pollutant load in the waterbody, including the pollutant load from upstream sources that is being accounted for as background loading, deviates from the pollutant load needed to attain and maintain water quality standards;

(5) Identification of source categories, source subcategories or individual sources of the pollutant;

(6) Wasteload allocations;

(7) Load allocations;

(8) A margin of safety;

(9) Consideration of seasonal variations;

(10) Allowance for reasonably foreseeable increases in pollutant loads including future growth; and

(11) An implementation plan.

(i) *Total Maximum Daily Thermal Load (TMDTL)*. A TMDTL is a TMDL for impaired waterbodies receiving a thermal discharge.

(j) *Impaired waterbody*. Any waterbody of the United States that does not attain and maintain water quality standards (as defined in 40 CFR Part 131) throughout the waterbody due to an individual pollutant, multiple pollutants, or other causes of pollution, including any waterbody for which biological information indicates that it does not attain and maintain water quality standards. Where a waterbody receives a thermal discharge from one or more point sources, impaired means that the waterbody does not have or maintain a balanced indigenous population of shellfish, fish, and wildlife.

*   *   *   *   *

(m) *Management measures*. Best practical and economically achievable measures to control the addition of pollutants to waters of the United States

through the application of nonpoint pollution control practices, technologies, processes, siting criteria, operating methods, best management practices, or other alternatives.
*   *   *   *   *

(o) *Thermal discharge.* The discharge of the pollutant heat from a point source that is required to have an NPDES permit.

(p) *Reasonable assurance.* Reasonable assurance means a demonstration that TMDLs will be implemented through regulatory or voluntary actions, including management measures or other controls, by Federal, State or local governments, authorized Tribes, or individuals.

(1) For point sources regulated under section 402 of the Clean Water Act, the demonstration of reasonable assurance must identify procedures that ensure that NPDES permits will be issued, reissued, or revised as expeditiously as practicable to implement applicable TMDL wasteload allocations for point sources.

(2) For nonpoint sources, storm water sources for which an NPDES permit is not required, atmospheric deposition, ground water or background sources of a pollutant, the demonstration of reasonable assurance must show that management measures or other control actions to implement the load allocations contained in each TMDL meet the following four-part test: they specifically apply to the pollutant(s) and the waterbody for which the TMDL is being established; they will be implemented as expeditiously as practicable; they will be accomplished through reliable and effective delivery mechanisms; and they will be supported by adequate water quality funding.

(i) Adequate water quality funding means that the State, Territory, or authorized Tribe has allocated existing water quality funds from any source to the implementation of the TMDL load allocations to the fullest extent practicable and in a manner consistent with the effective operation of its clean water program. In the event that existing funding is not adequate to fully implement the TMDL load allocations, you may satisfy the funding requirement of reasonable assurance by including an explanation of when adequate funds will become available and the schedule by which these funds will be used to implement the TMDL load allocations. When EPA establishes a TMDL, EPA must show there is adequate funding. It may do so by conditioning Clean Water Act grants to the fullest extent practicable and in a manner consistent with effective operation of other Clean Water Act programs.

(ii) Voluntary and incentive-based actions, or existing programs, procedures or authorities are acceptable means of demonstrating reasonable assurance if they satisfy the four-part test. Examples of voluntary and incentive-based actions include: State, Territorial, or authorized Tribal programs to audit implementation of agricultural or forestry best management practices; memoranda of understanding between States, Territories, authorized Tribes, and organizations representing categories, subcategories, or individual sources; or State-, Territory-, or authorized Tribe-approved programs for categories, subcategories or individual sources to ensure effectiveness of best management practices.

(iii) Examples of existing programs, procedures or authorities that may be reliable delivery mechanisms include State, Territorial, and authorized Tribal programs approved by EPA under section 319 of the Clean Water Act; participation in existing United States Department of Agriculture conservation or water quality protection programs; participation in existing programs under the Coastal Zone Act Reauthorization Amendments; regulations; local ordinances; performance bonds; contracts; cost-share agreements; memoranda of understanding; site-specific or watershed-specific voluntary actions; and compliance audits of best management practices.

(q) *Waterbody.* A geographically defined portion of navigable waters, waters of the contiguous zone, and ocean waters under the jurisdiction of the United States, made up of one or more of the segments of rivers, streams, lakes, wetlands, coastal waters and ocean waters. Identifications of waterbodies should be consistent with the way in which segments are described in State, Territorial, or authorized Tribal water quality standards.

(r) *List of Impaired Waterbodies or "List."* The list of all impaired waterbodies submitted by a State, Territory, or authorized Tribe. This list consists of Parts 1, 2, 3, and 4 described in §130.27 and the prioritized schedule described in §130.28. Part 1 of the list consists of the identification of the waterbodies for which TMDLs must be established and a prioritized schedule for establishing TMDLs.

10. Revise §130.7 as follows:

§130.7 Total maximum daily loads (TMDL) and individual water quality-based effluent limitations.

(a)-(b) [Reserved]

(c) *Development of TMDLs and individual water quality based effluent limitations.* This paragraph will expire January 11, 2002 or nine months from the effective date of this rule, whichever occurs later.

(1) Each State shall establish TMDLs for the waterbodies identified at §130.27(a) and in accordance with the priority ranking. For pollutants other than heat, TMDLs shall be established at levels necessary to attain and maintain the applicable narrative and numerical WQS with seasonal variations and a margin of safety which takes into account any lack of knowledge concerning the relationship between effluent limitations and water quality. Determinations of TMDLs shall take into account critical conditions for stream flow, loading, and water quality parameters.

(i) TMDLs may be established using a pollutant-by-pollutant or biomonitoring approach. In many cases both techniques may be needed. Site-specific information should be used wherever possible.

(ii) TMDLs shall be established for all pollutants preventing or expected to prevent attainment of water quality standards as identified pursuant to §130.27(a). Calculations to establish TMDLs shall be subject to public review as defined in the State CPP.

(2) Each State shall estimate for the waterbodies identified at §130.27(a) that require thermal TMDLs, the total maximum daily thermal load which cannot be exceeded in order to assure protection and propagation of a balanced, indigenous population of shell-fish, fish and wildlife. Such estimates shall take into account the normal water temperatures, flow rates, seasonal variations, existing sources of heat input, and the dissipative capacity of the identified waters or parts thereof. Such estimates shall include a calculation of the maximum heat input that can be made into each such part and shall include a margin of safety which takes into account any lack of knowledge concerning the development of thermal water quality criteria for protection and propagation of a balanced, indigenous population of shellfish, fish and wildlife in the identified waters or parts thereof.

11. Amend newly designated §130.10 in paragraph (a) by adding a note to the paragraph, and revise paragraph (b) as follows:

§130.10 Water quality monitoring.

(a) * * *

Note to paragraph (a): EPA recommends that you use "Policy and Program Requirements to Implement the Mandatory Quality Assurance Program," EPA Order 5360.1, April 3, 1984, as revised July 16, 1998, or subsequent revisions.

(b) The State's water monitoring program shall include collection and analysis of physical, chemical and biological data and quality assurance and control programs to assure scientifically valid data. The uses of these data include determining abatement and control priorities; developing and reviewing water quality standards, total maximum daily loads, wasteload allocations and load allocations; assessing compliance with National Pollutant Discharge Elimination System (NPDES) permits by dischargers; reporting information to the public through the section 305(b) report and reviewing site-specific monitoring efforts and source water assessments conducted under the Safe Drinking Water Act.

12. Amend newly designated §130.11 to revise paragraph (a) as follows:

§130.11 Water quality report.

(a) Each State shall prepare and submit biennially to the Regional Administrator a water quality report in accordance with section 305(b) of the Act. The water quality report serves as the primary assessment of State water quality. Based upon the water quality data and problems identified in the 305(b) report, States develop water quality management (WQM) plan elements to help direct all subsequent control activities. Water quality problems identified in the 305(b) report should be analyzed through water quality management planning leading to the development of alternative controls and procedures for problems identified in the latest 305(b) report. States may also use the 305(b) report to describe ground-water quality and to guide development of ground-water plans and programs. Water quality problems identified in the 305(b) report should be emphasized and reflected in the State's WQM plan and annual work program under sections 106 and 205(j) of the Clean Water Act and where the designated use includes public water supply, in the source water assessment conducted under the SDWA.

*   *   *   *   *

13. Add Subpart C consisting of §§130.20 through 130.37 as follows:

Subpart C—Identifying Impaired Waterbodies And Establishing Total Maximum Daily Loads (TMDLs)

What This Subpart Covers
Sec.
130.20 Who must comply with subpart C of this part?
130.21 What is the purpose of this subpart?

Listing Impaired Waterbodies, and Documenting Your Methodology for Making Listing Decisions
130.22 What data and information do you need to assemble and consider to identify and list impaired waterbodies?
130.23 How do you develop and document your methodology for considering and evaluating all existing and readily available data and information to develop your list?
130.24 When must you provide your methodology to EPA?
130.25 What is the scope of your list of impaired waterbodies?
130.26 How do you apply your water quality standards antidegradation policy to the listing of impaired waterbodies?
130.27 How must you format your list of impaired waterbodies?
130.28 What must your prioritized schedule for submitting TMDLs to EPA contain?
130.29 Can you modify your list?

Subpart C—Identifying Impaired Waterbodies And Establishing Total Maximum Daily Loads (TMDLs)

What This Subpart Covers

§130.20 Who must comply with subpart C in this part?

(a) Subpart C applies to States, Territories, and authorized Tribes. The term "you" in this subpart refers to these three governmental entities.

(b) Portions of this subpart apply to the United States Environmental Protection Agency (EPA). When this is the case, the rule specifies EPA's responsibilities and obligations.

§130.21 What is the purpose of this subpart?

(a) This subpart explains how to identify and list impaired waterbodies and establish TMDLs in accordance with section 303(d) of the Clean Water Act. The subpart also explains how EPA reviews and approves or disapproves your lists and TMDLs. Specifically, the subpart explains how to:

(1) Assemble all existing and readily available water quality-related data and information;

(2) Document your methodology for considering and evaluating all existing and readily available water quality-related data and information to make decisions on your list and provide the methodology to EPA and the public;

(3) Identify impaired waterbodies to be included on the list and decide which of those waterbodies will have TMDLs established for them;

(4) Identify the pollutant or pollutants causing the impairment for all waterbodies on Part 1 of your list;

(5) Develop a prioritized schedule for establishing TMDLs for waterbodies on Part 1 of your list;

(6) Establish TMDLs for waterbodies on Part 1 of your list and submit them to EPA for review;

(7) Provide public notice and an opportunity for public comment on your methodology, your list, and TMDLs prior to final submission to EPA.

(b) It also explains how EPA must:

(1) Review and approve or disapprove your list of impaired waterbodies;

(2) Develop a list where you fail to do so or if EPA disapproves your list;

(3) Review and approve or disapprove your TMDLs;

(4) Establish TMDLs if you have not made substantial progress in establishing TMDLs in accordance with your approved schedule, or if EPA disapproves your TMDLs.

Listing Impaired Waterbodies, and Documenting Your Methodology for Making Listing Decisions

§130.22 What data and information do you need to assemble and consider to identify and list impaired waterbodies?

(a) You need to assemble and consider all existing and readily available water quality-related data and information when you develop your list of impaired waterbodies.

(b) Existing and readily available water quality-related data and information includes at a minimum the data and information in and forming the basis for the following:

(1) Your most recent EPA approved section 303(d) list;

(2) Your most recent Clean Water Act section 305(b) report;

(3) Clean Water Act section 319 nonpoint source assessments;

(4) Drinking water source water assessments under section 1453 of the Safe Drinking Water Act;

(5) Dilution calculations, trend analyses, or predictive models for determining the physical, chemical or biological integrity of streams, rivers, lakes, and estuaries; and

(6) Data, information, and water quality problems reported from local, State, Territorial, or Federal agencies (especially the U.S. Geological Survey National Water Quality Assessment (NAWQA) and National Stream Quality Accounting Network (NASQAN)), Tribal governments, members of the public, and academic institutions.

§130.23 How do you develop and document your methodology for considering and evaluating all existing and readily available data and information to develop your list?

(a) Your methodology needs to explain how you will consider and evaluate all existing and readily available water quality-related data and information to determine which waterbodies you will include on Parts 1, 2, 3, and 4 of your list, and to determine how you will prioritize your schedule for establishing TMDLs for waterbodies on Part 1 of your list. You must develop a draft methodology and notify the public of the availability of the draft methodology for review and comment. You should notify directly those who submit a written request for notification. You must provide the public an opportunity to submit comments on the draft methodology for no less than 60 days. You must provide a summary of all comments received and your responses to significant comments when you provide a copy of the final methodology to EPA, as required by §130.24 of this subpart. You must make your final methodology available to the public when you provide a copy to EPA.

(b) The methodology should explain how you will consider and evaluate the following types of data and information when you make listing decisions and develop your prioritized schedule for TMDL establishment:

(1) Physical data and information;

(2) Chemical data and information;

(3) Biological data and information;

(4) Aquatic and riparian habitat data and information; and

(5) Other data and information about waterbody impairments, including drinking water susceptibility analyses.

(c) Your methodology should, at a minimum, identify those types of data and information that you will treat as "existing and readily available" and explain how you consider the following factors in making listing decisions and in developing your prioritized schedule for TMDL establishment:

(1) Data quality and age;

(2) Degree of confidence you have in the information you use to determine whether waterbodies are impaired, including a description of the quality assurance/quality control factors you will apply to data and information; and

(3) Number and degree of exceedances of numeric or narrative criteria and periods of nonattainment of designated uses or other factors used to determine whether waterbodies are impaired.

(d) Your methodology should describe the procedures and methods you will use to collect ambient water quality information.

(e) Your methodology should, at a minimum, also include the following:

(1) A description of the selection factors you will use to include and remove waterbodies from your list;

(2) A process for resolving disagreements with other jurisdictions involving waterbodies crossed by State, Territorial, Tribal or international boundaries; and

(3) A description of the method and factors you will use to develop your prioritized schedule for establishing TMDLs.

§130.24 When must you provide your methodology to EPA?

(a)(1) If this section is not effective by May 1, 2001, you must provide to EPA a description of the methodology used to develop your 2002 list and a description of the data and information used to identify waters (including a description of the existing and readily available data and information used by the State, Territory, and authorized Tribe) by April 1, 2002. The provisions of §130.23(b) through (e) do not apply to this methodology.

(2) If this section is effective on or before May 1, 2001, you must provide your final methodology for your 2002 list and a summary of public comments on your methodology by November 1, 2001. This methodology will apply to the list required in 2002.

(b) You must provide to EPA the final methodology and a summary of public comments for your 2006 and subsequent lists submitted under §130.30(a) no later than two years before you submit your next list, beginning in the year 2004. For example, you provide to EPA the methodology for your 303(d) list for 2006 on or before April 1, 2004. When providing final methodologies to EPA, you need to provide only the parts of the previous methodology you are revising; however, prior to submitting your final methodology to EPA, the entire methodology must be available to the public.

(c) EPA will review your final methodology and will provide you with comments within 60 days of receiving it. EPA will not approve or disapprove your methodology. EPA will consider your methodology in its review and approval or disapproval of your next list.

§130.25 What is the scope of your list of impaired waterbodies?

(a) Your approvable list of impaired waterbodies includes, based on all existing and readily available water quality-related data and information using appropriate quality assurance/quality control:

(1) Waterbodies that are impaired by individual pollutants, multiple pollutants, or pollution from any source, including point sources, nonpoint sources, storm water sources for which a National Pollutant Discharge Elimination System (NPDES) permit is not required, ground water, and atmospheric deposition.

(2) Waterbodies for which biological information indicates that they do not attain and maintain water quality standards.

(3) Waterbodies that are impaired by point sources only, nonpoint sources only, or by a combination of point and nonpoint sources.

(b) Your list may include, at your option, waterbodies that are not impaired, but which, based on expected changes in loadings or conditions, you anticipate will become impaired in the next four years.

§130.26 How do you apply your water quality standards antidegradation policy to the listing of impaired waterbodies?

(a) Water quality standards as defined at 40 CFR Part 131 include several requirements, including one for a State antidegradation policy. Your list must include waterbodies consistent with your antidegradation policy as described below.

(1) Any waterbody is impaired if it is not maintaining a designated use or more protective existing use that was attained on or after November 28, 1975.

(2) Any Tier 3 waterbody is impaired when the level of water quality that existed at the time the waterbody was designated as Tier 3 has declined. Tier 3 waters are waters you have designated as outstanding national resource waters.

(b) [Reserved]

§130.27 How must you format your list of impaired waterbodies?

(a) Your list of impaired waterbodies must include the following four parts:

(1) *Part 1.* Waterbodies impaired by one or more pollutant(s) as defined by §130.2(d), unless listed in Part 3 or 4. Waterbodies identified as impaired through biological information must be listed on Part 1 unless you know that the impairment is not caused by one or more pollutants, in which case you may place the waterbody on Part 2 of the list. Where the waterbody is listed due to biological information, the first step in establishing the TMDL is identifying the pollutant(s) causing the impairment. Waterbodies must also be included on Part 1 where you or EPA have determined, in accordance with §§130.32(c)(1)(v), (2)(vii), and (3)(i), that a TMDL needs to be revised. Waterbodies that you chose to list pursuant to §130.25(b), because you anticipate that they will become impaired by one or more pollutant(s), must be included on Part 1 of your list. A TMDL is required for waterbodies on Part 1 of the list.

(2) *Part 2.* Waterbodies impaired by pollution as defined by §130.2(c) but not impaired by one or more pollutants. A TMDL is not required for waterbodies on Part 2 of the list.

(3) *Part 3.* Waterbodies for which EPA has approved or established a TMDL and water quality standards have not yet been attained. The waterbody must be placed on Part 1 of the list and scheduled for establishment of a new TMDL if you or EPA determine that substantial progress towards attaining the water quality standard is not occurring.

(4) *Part 4.* Waterbodies that are impaired, for which the State, Territory, or authorized Tribe demonstrates that water quality standards will be attained by the date of submission of the next list as a result of implementation of technology-based effluent limitations required by sections 301(b), 306, or 307 of the Clean Water Act or other controls enforceable by State, Territorial or authorized Tribal or Federal law or regulation (including more stringent water quality-based effluent limitations in NPDES permits). A TMDL is not required for waterbodies on Part 4. If a waterbody listed on Part 4 does not attain water quality standards by the time the next list is required to be submitted to EPA, such waterbody must be included on Part 1 unless you can demonstrate that the failure to attain water quality standards is due to failure of point source dischargers to comply with applicable NPDES permit effluent limitations, which are in effect. TMDLs for waterbodies moved from Part 4 to Part 1 of the list must be scheduled for establishment in accordance with the requirements of §130.28(b).

(b) You must identify:

(1) The pollutant or pollutants causing the impairment for each waterbody on Part 1 of the list, or for waterbodies for which the impairment is a result of biological information, the pollutant or pollutants if known.

(2) The type of pollution causing the impairment for each waterbody on Part 2.

(3) The geographic location of each waterbody on the list, using the National Hydrography Database or subsequent revisions, or a compatible georeferenced database.

(c) Any one of the three reporting formats described in this paragraph are acceptable.

(1) *Separate section 303(d) list.* You may submit your list as a separate four-part section 303(d) list.

(2) *Consolidated section 303(d) list and section 305(b) report.* You may submit your list as a component of your water quality report (section 305(b) report). You must clearly identify the parts of your water quality report you are submitting as your four-part section 303(d) list.

(3) *Part 1 waterbodies in section 303(d) report and Parts 2, 3, and 4 waterbodies in section 305(b) report.* You may submit Part 1 of your list as a separate section 303(d) list, provided you include Parts 2, 3, and 4 of your list as a component of your section 305(b) water quality report and clearly

identify the parts of your water quality report that you are submitting as Parts 2, 3, and 4 of your section 303(d) list.

(d) EPA will approve or disapprove your four-part section 303(d) list regardless of the reporting format that you use.

§130.28 What must your prioritized schedule for submitting TMDLs to EPA contain?

(a) Your list must include a prioritized schedule for establishing TMDLs for all waterbodies and pollutant combinations on Part 1 of your list.

(b) You must schedule establishment of TMDLs:

(1) as expeditiously as practicable, evenly paced over the duration of the schedule;

(2) no later than 10 years from July 10, 2000, if the waterbody and pollutant was listed on any part of the list before that date or 10 years from the due date of the first subsequent list after July 10, 2000, on which the waterbody and pollutant is initially included. You may extend the schedule for one or more TMDLs by no more than five years if you explain to EPA as part of your list submission that, despite expeditious actions, establishment of all TMDLs on Part 1 of your list within 10 years is not practicable.

(c) You must identify each specific TMDL you intend to establish and the one year period during which it is scheduled to be established. Your schedule should provide for the coordinated establishment of TMDLs within a watershed to the fullest extent practicable.

(d) You must:

(1) explain how you considered the severity of the impairment and the designated use of the waterbody in prioritizing waterbodies for TMDL establishment on your schedule.

(2) Identify waterbodies:

(i) That are designated in water quality standards as a public drinking water supply, or are used as a source of drinking water, and are impaired by a pollutant that is contributing to a violation of a national primary drinking water regulation (NPDWR) by a public water system or causes a public water system to be vulnerable to a violation of a NPDWR; or

(ii) Where species listed as threatened or endangered under section 4 of the Endangered Species Act are present in the waterbody.

(3) Waterbodies identified in this subsection must be given a higher priority unless you explain why a different priority is appropriate.

(e) When identifying and scheduling your waterbodies for TMDL establishment, you may also consider the presence of sensitive aquatic species and other factors such as the historical, cultural, economic and aesthetic uses of the waterbody. You may consider other factors in prioritizing your schedule, including the value and vulnerability of particular waterbodies;

the recreational, economic, and aesthetic importance of particular waterbodies; TMDL complexity; the degree of public interest and support; State, Territorial and authorized Tribal policies and priorities; national policies and priorities; or the efficiencies that might result from coordinating the establishment of TMDLs for multiple waterbodies located in the same watershed. If you are using a rotating basin approach, you may take that approach into account when prioritizing waterbodies on your schedule because of the inherent efficiencies of such an approach.

(f) If you consider other factors, you should identify each factor and explain how you used each factor in prioritizing your schedule.

§130.29 Can you modify your list?

(a) You may modify your list at times other than those required by §130.30, in accordance with this section. If you modify your list and prioritized schedule, you must submit your list to EPA as a modification to your list under this section and follow the public participation requirements of §130.36, except that such requirements shall apply only to waterbodies and issues addressed by the modification. The requirements of subsections (b), (c), (d), and (e) of this section apply to lists submitted under §130.30(a) or at any other time.

(b) You must keep each impaired waterbody on your list for a particular pollutant until it is attaining and maintaining applicable water quality standards for that pollutant.

(c) You may remove a listed waterbody for a particular pollutant if new data or information indicate that the waterbody is attaining and maintaining the applicable water quality standards for that pollutant.

(d) You may add a waterbody to your list if you have data or information indicating that it is impaired.

(e) You may modify your prioritized schedule for establishing TMDLs in accordance with §130.28 based on new information provided that the modification does not reduce the number of TMDLs scheduled for completion during the first four years of the current approved schedule.

(f) EPA must issue an order approving or disapproving the modification of your list or prioritized schedule in accordance with §130.30(b).

(g) EPA may also issue an order modifying a list consistent with the provisions of paragraphs (c), (d) and (e) of this section, after providing notice and an opportunity for public comment.

§130.30 When must you submit your list of impaired waterbodies to EPA and what will EPA do with it?

(a) You must submit your list of impaired waterbodies to EPA by April 1 of every fourth year, beginning in the year 2002.

(b) EPA must:

(1) Issue an order approving or disapproving your list or modification of your list, within 30 days of receipt, in whole or in part if it is not consistent with the requirements of §§130.25 through 130.29.

(2) By order, within 30 days of disapproval, issue a new list consistent with §§130.25 through 130.29 if EPA disapproves or partially disapproves your list or modification of your list.

(3) Publish the order required by paragraph (b)(2) of this section in the **Federal Register** and a general circulation newspaper in your State, Territory, or where your Tribe is located and request public comment for at least 30 days.

(4) Issue a subsequent order revising the new list after the close of the public comment period, as appropriate, if EPA revises its initial order required by paragraph (b)(2) of this section based on public comment.

(5) Send you a copy of its order(s).

(6) Establish a list of impaired waterbodies for your State, Territory, or authorized Tribe consistent with §§130.25 through 130.29 if you fail to do so by April 1 of every fourth year.

(c) EPA may establish lists of waterbodies that do not attain and maintain Federal water quality standards.

(d) You must incorporate into your water quality management plan those portions of your list that EPA approves or establishes.

Establishment and EPA Review of TMDLs

§130.31 Which waterbodies need TMDLs?

(a) You must establish TMDLs for all waterbodies and pollutant combinations on Part 1 of your list in accordance with your approved schedule and submit the TMDLs to EPA.

(b) You do not need to establish TMDLs for waterbodies on Parts 2, 3, and 4 of your list.

§130.32 What are the minimum elements of a TMDL submitted to EPA?

(a) A TMDL is a written, quantitative plan and analysis for attaining and maintaining water quality standards in all seasons for a specific waterbody and pollutant. TMDLs may be established on a coordinated basis for a group of waterbodies in a watershed. A TMDL provides the opportunity to compare relative contributions of pollutants from all sources and consider technical and economic trade-offs between point and nonpoint sources.

(b) You must include the following minimum elements in any TMDL submitted to EPA:

(1) The name and geographic location, as required by §130.27(b)(3), of the impaired waterbody for which the TMDL is being established and, to the extent known, the names and geographic locations of the waterbodies upstream of the impaired waterbody that contribute significant amounts of the pollutant for which the TMDL is being established;

(2) Identification of the pollutant and the applicable water quality standard for which the TMDL is being established;

(3) Quantification of the pollutant load that may be present in the waterbody and still ensure attainment and maintenance of water quality standards;

(4) Quantification of the amount or degree by which the current pollutant load in the waterbody, including the pollutant load from upstream sources that is being accounted for as background loading, deviates from the pollutant load needed to attain and maintain water quality standards;

(5) Identification of source categories, source subcategories, or individual sources of the pollutant consistent with the definitions of load and wasteload allocation in §§130.2(f) and (g), respectively, for which the wasteload allocations and load allocations are being established;

(6) Wasteload allocations assigned to point sources permitted under section 402 of the Clean Water Act discharging the pollutant for which the TMDL is being established that will, when implemented in conjunction with assigned load allocations, if any, result in the attainment and maintenance of water quality standards in the waterbody. Wasteload allocations that reflect pollutant load reductions for point sources needed to ensure that the waterbody attains and maintains water quality standards must be expressed as individual wasteload allocations for each source. Wasteload allocations that do not reflect pollutant load reductions from point sources needed for the waterbody to attain and maintain water quality standards may be expressed as an individual wasteload allocation for a source or may be included within a wasteload allocation for a category or subcategory of sources. Wasteload allocations for sources subject to a specified general permit, regardless of whether they reflect pollutant reductions, may be allotted to categories of sources. You should submit supporting technical analyses demonstrating that wasteload allocations, when implemented in conjunction with necessary load allocations, will result in the attainment and maintenance of the water quality standard(s) applicable to the pollutant for which the TMDL is being established;

(7) Load allocations, ranging from reasonably accurate estimates to gross allotments, for nonpoint sources of a pollutant, storm water sources for which an NPDES permit is not required, atmospheric deposition, ground water or background sources of a pollutant that, when implemented in conjunction with assigned wasteload allocations, if any, result in the attainment

and maintenance of water quality standards in the waterbody. If feasible, a separate load allocation must be allocated to each source of a pollutant. Where this is not feasible, load allocations may be allocated to categories or subcategories of sources. Pollutant loads from sources that do not need to be reduced for the waterbody to attain and maintain water quality standards may be included within a category of sources or subcategory of sources. You should submit supporting technical analyses demonstrating that load allocations, when implemented in conjunction with necessary wasteload allocations, will result in the attainment and maintenance of water quality standards applicable to the pollutant for which the TMDL is being established;

(8) A margin of safety that appropriately accounts for uncertainty related to the TMDL, including uncertainties associated with pollutant loads, modeling water quality, and monitoring water quality. A margin of safety may be expressed as unallocated assimilative capacity or conservative analytical assumptions used in establishing the TMDL;

(9) Consideration of seasonal variations, stream water flow levels, and other environmental factors that affect the relationship between pollutant loadings and water quality impacts, such that the allocations will result in attainment and maintenance of water quality standards in all seasons of the year and during all flow conditions;

(10) Allowance for reasonably foreseeable increases in pollutant loads including future growth; and

(11) An implementation plan which meets the requirements of paragraph (c) of this section.

(c) The purpose of the implementation plan is to provide a description, in a level of detail appropriate to the circumstances, of actions necessary to implement the TMDL so that the waterbody attains and maintains water quality standards. EPA does not expect the implementation plan to be a complex, lengthy document.

(1) For waterbodies impaired only by point sources for which NPDES permits will implement the TMDL, an implementation plan must include:

(i) An identification of the wasteload allocation(s) that the effluent limitation(s) must be consistent with pursuant to §122.44(d)(1)(vii)(B) in the NPDES permit(s) that will be issued, reissued, or revised. In all instances, the NPDES permit effluent limitation(s) must be consistent with the applicable wasteload allocation(s). You must identify:

(A) The point sources that are or will be regulated by individual permits and the categories or subcategories of point sources that are or will be regulated by general permits that will be subject to such effluent limitations.

(B) The permit, if you intend to implement the wasteload allocation by requiring a point source to apply for coverage under an existing NPDES general permit.

(C) The elements of the general permit necessary to ensure implementation of the wasteload allocation, if you intend for a point source to be regulated by a new general permit.

(ii) A schedule for issuing, reissuing or revising the NPDES permit(s) as expeditiously as practicable to include effluent limits consistent with the wasteload allocation(s) in the TMDL. EPA must:

(A) Reissue or revise the permit(s) within two years after the establishment of the TMDL where EPA is the NPDES permitting authority.

(B) Notify the NPDES Director of EPA's intent to object to the permit pursuant to the provisions of §123.44(k) within one year after expiration of the permit term, or where the permit term expired prior to the establishment of the TMDL, within one year from establishment of the TMDL where the State is the NPDES permitting authority, and the permit term has expired.

(C) Issue an NPDES permit that incorporates effluent limitations based on wasteload allocation(s) in the TMDL within one year thereafter where the State has not done so. Nothing in this paragraph (c)(1)(ii) limits EPA's authority to reissue a permit after the expiration of the two-year time frame set forth in this paragraph (c)(1)(ii), or invoke the mechanism described in §123.44(k) after the expiration of either of the one-year time frames set forth in this paragraph (c)(1)(ii).

(iii) The date by which the implementation plan will result in the waterbody attaining and maintaining applicable water quality standards and the basis for that determination;

(iv) A monitoring and/or modeling plan designed to measure the effectiveness of the controls implementing the wasteload allocations and the progress the waterbody is making toward attaining water quality standards; and

(v) The criteria you will use to determine that substantial progress toward attaining water quality standards is being made and if not, the criteria for determining whether the TMDL needs to be revised.

(2) For waterbodies impaired only by nonpoint source(s), storm water sources for which an NPDES permit is not required, atmospheric deposition, ground water or background sources of a pollutant where no NPDES permit will implement the TMDL, the implementation plan must include:

(i) An identification of the source categories, source subcategories, or individual sources of the pollutant which must be controlled to implement the load allocations;

(ii) A description of specific regulatory or voluntary actions, including management measures or other controls, by Federal, State or local governments, authorized Tribes, or individuals that provide reasonable assurance, consistent with §130.2(p), that load allocations will be implemented and achieve the assigned load reductions. Your selection of management measures for achieving the load allocation may recognize both the natural variability and the difficulty in precisely predicting the performance of management measures over time;

(iii) A schedule, which is as expeditious as practicable, for implementing the management measures or other control actions to achieve load allocations in the TMDL within 5 years, when implementation within this period is practicable;

(iv) The date by which the implementation plan will result in the waterbody attaining and maintaining applicable water quality standards, and the basis for that determination;

(v) A description of interim, measurable milestones for determining whether management measures or other control actions are being implemented;

(vi) A monitoring and/or modeling plan designed to measure the effectiveness of the management measures or other controls implementing the load allocations and the progress the waterbody is making toward attaining water quality standards, and a process for implementing stronger and more effective management measures if necessary; and

(vii) The criteria you will use to determine that substantial progress toward attaining water quality standards is being made and if not, the criteria for determining whether the TMDL needs to be revised.

(3) For waterbodies impaired by both point sources and nonpoint sources where NPDES permits and management measures or other control actions for nonpoint or other sources will implement the TMDL, the implementation plan must include:

(i) The elements of paragraphs (c)(1) and (2) of this section; and

(ii) A description of the extent to which wasteload allocations reflect expected achievement of load allocations requiring reductions in loadings.

(4) For all impaired waterbodies, the implementation plan must be based on a goal of attaining and maintaining the applicable water quality standards within ten years whenever attainment and maintenance within this period is practicable.

(d) TMDTLs must meet all the requirements of paragraphs (b) and (c) of this section, except that, rather than estimating a TMDTL at a level necessary to attain and maintain water quality standards, you must estimate the TMDTL as required by statute at a level necessary to ensure protection and propagation of a balanced indigenous population of shellfish, fish, and wildlife, taking into account the normal water temperatures, flow rates, seasonal variations, existing sources of heat input, and dissipative capacity of the waterbody for which the TMDTL is being established. Estimates for those waterbodies must include a calculation of the maximum heat input and a margin of safety that takes into account any lack of knowledge concerning the development of thermal water quality criteria.

(e) A TMDL must not be likely to jeopardize the continued existence of an endangered or threatened species listed under section 4 of the Endangered Species Act or result in the destruction or adverse modification of its designated critical habitat.

§130.33 How are TMDLs expressed?

(a) A TMDL must contain a quantitative expression of the pollutant load or load reduction necessary to ensure that the waterbody will attain and maintain water quality standards, or, as appropriate, the pollutant load or load reduction required to attain and maintain aquatic or riparian habitat, biological, channel or geomorphological or other conditions that will result in attainment and maintenance of water quality standards.

(b) As appropriate to the characteristics of the waterbody and pollutant, the pollutant load or load reduction may be expressed in one or more of the following ways:

(1) The pollutant load that can be present in the waterbody and ensure that it attains and maintains water quality standards;

(2) The reduction from current pollutant loads required to attain and maintain water quality standards;

(3) The pollutant load or reduction of pollutant load required to attain and maintain aquatic, riparian, biological, channel or geomorphological measures so that water quality standards are attained and maintained;

(4) A quantitative expression of a modification of a characteristic of the waterbody, e.g., aquatic and riparian habitat, biological, channel, geomorphological, or chemical characteristics, that results in a pollutant load or reduction of pollutant load so that water quality standards are attained and maintained; or

(5) In terms of either mass per time, toxicity or other appropriate measure.

§130.34 What actions must EPA take on TMDLs that are submitted for review?

(a) EPA must:

(1) Review each TMDL you submit to determine if it meets the requirements of §§130.31, 130.32 and 130.33 and issue an order approving or disapproving each TMDL you submit within 30 days after you submit it.

(2) Disapprove the TMDL if it does not meet all those requirements.

(3) Issue an order establishing a new TMDL for a waterbody and pollutant within 30 days of EPA's disapproval or determination of the need for revision, if EPA disapproves a TMDL you submit or determines that an existing TMDL needs to be revised.

(4) Publish this order in the **Federal Register** and a general circulation newspaper and request public comment for at least 30 days.

(5) Issue a subsequent order revising the TMDL after the close of the public comment period, as appropriate, if EPA revises its initial order based on public comment.

(6) Send you the final TMDL EPA establishes. You must incorporate any EPA-established or EPA approved TMDL into your water quality management plan.

(b) When EPA establishes a TMDL it must provide reasonable assurance. It may satisfy the adequate funding requirement of reasonable assurance by conditioning Clean Water Act grants to the fullest extent practicable and in a manner consistent with effective operation of other Clean Water Act programs.

(c) EPA may also use any of its statutory or regulatory authorities and voluntary, incentive-based programs, as it determines appropriate, to supplement conditioning Clean Water Act grants in demonstrating reasonable assurance.

§130.35 How will EPA assure that TMDLs are established?

(a) EPA must assure that TMDLs for waterbodies and pollutants identified on Part 1 of your list are established. EPA must do this by:

(1) Working with you to assure that TMDLs are established in accordance with your schedule; and

(2) Establishing a TMDL if you have not made substantial progress in establishing the TMDL in accordance with your approved schedule. Substantial progress means that you have established a TMDL not later than the end of the one-year period during which it was scheduled to be established. EPA must establish the TMDL within two years of the date on which you fail to make substantial progress. The Administrator may extend this period for no more than two years on a case-by-case basis if there is a compelling need for additional time. Notice of such extension shall be published in the **Federal Register**.

(b) EPA may establish TMDLs under other circumstances including:

(1) You request that EPA do so; or

(2) EPA determines it is necessary to establish a TMDL for an interstate or boundary waterbody or to implement Federal water quality standards.

(c) In establishing any TMDL pursuant to this section, EPA shall provide notice and an opportunity for public comment on such order.

Public Participation

§130.36 What public participation requirements apply to your lists and TMDLs?

(a) You must provide public notice and allow the public no less than 30 days to review and comment on your list of impaired waterbodies and TMDLs prior to submission to EPA. You should notify directly those who submit a written request for notification.

(b) At the time you make your submission to EPA, you must provide EPA with a summary of all public comments received on your list and TMDLs and your response to all significant comments, indicating how the comments were considered in your final decision.

(c) Prior to your submission to EPA, and at the time that you provide the public the opportunity to review and comment on your list and TMDLs:

(1) You must provide a copy of each of these documents to EPA, the U.S. Fish and Wildlife Service, and to the National Marine Fisheries Service where appropriate (*e.g.*, coastal areas), unless you request EPA to provide these documents to the Services, in which case EPA will do so.

(2) You are encouraged to establish processes with both the U.S. Fish and Wildlife Service and the National Marine Fisheries Service that will provide for the early identification and resolution of threatened and endangered species concerns as they relate to your list and TMDLs. To facilitate consideration of endangered and threatened species in the listing and TMDL process, EPA will ask the U.S. Fish and Wildlife Service and the National Marine Fisheries Service, where appropriate, to provide you and EPA with any comments that they may have on your lists and TMDLs.

(3) You must consider any comments from EPA, the U.S. Fish and Wildlife Service, or the National Marine Fisheries Service in establishing your list and TMDLs and document your consideration of these comments in accordance with paragraph (b) of this section.

(d) EPA will review any comments submitted by the U.S. Fish and Wildlife Service or the National Marine Fisheries Service and consider how you addressed these and EPA's comments prior to EPA's approval or disapproval of your submission.

TMDLs Established During the Transition

§130.37 What is the effect of this rule on TMDLs established during the transition?

(a) EPA will approve any TMDL submitted to it for review before January 11, 2002 or nine months from the effective date of this rule, whichever occurs later, if the TMDL meets either the requirements in §130.7 in effect prior to July 13, 2000 or the requirements in §§130.31, 130.32 and 130.33 of this Subpart C.

(b) EPA will establish TMDLs before Janaury 11, 2002 or nine months from the effective date of this rule, whichever occurs later, either according to the requirements in §130.7 in effect prior to July 13, 2000 or the requirements in §§130.31, 130.32 and 130.33 of this Subpart C.

14. Amend newly designated §130.50 to revise paragraph (b) introductory text and (b)(3) as follows:

§130.50 Continuing planning process

*   *   *   *   *

(b) *Content.* The State may determine the format of its CPP as long as the minimum requirements of the CWA and this regulation are met. A State CPP need not be a single document, provided the State identifies in one document (i.e., an index) the other documents, statutes, rules, policies and guidance that comprise its CPP. The following processes must be described in each State CPP and the State may include other processes, including watershed-based planning and implementation, at its discretion.

*   *   *   *   *

(3) The process for developing total maximum daily loads (TMDLs) and individual water quality based effluent limitations for pollutants in accordance with section 303(d) of the Act and §§130.31 through 130.36 of this Part.

*   *   *   *   *

15. Amend newly designated §130.51 to revise paragraphs (a), (c)(1), and (f) as follows:

§130.51 Water quality management plans

(a) *Water quality management plans.* You must base continuing water quality planning on initial water quality management plans produced in accordance with sections 208 and 303(e) of the Clean Water Act and certified and approved updates to those plans. Your annual water quality planning should focus on priority issues and geographic areas identified in your latest section 305(b) reports and have a watershed focus. Water quality planning should be directed at the removal of conditions placed on previously certified and approved water quality management plans and updates to support the implementation of wasteload allocations and load allocations contained in TMDLs.

*   *   *   *   *

(c) * * *

(1) *Total Maximum Daily Loads.* TMDLs in accordance with section 303(d) and (e)(3)(C) of the Act and §§130.2 and 130.31 through 130.36;

also lists of impaired waters in accordance with §§130.2 and 130.22 through 130.30.

*   *   *   *   *

(f) *Consistency.* Construction grant and permit decisions must be made in accordance with certified and approved WQM plans as described in §§130.63(a) and (b). Likewise, financial assistance under the State water pollution control revolving funds may be made only to projects which are in conformity with such plans as specified in section 603(f) of the Act.

*   *   *   *   *

§130.61 [Amended]

16. Amend newly designated §130.61 to remove and reserve paragraph (b)(2), and remove paragraph (d).

17. Revise newly designated §130.64 as follows:

§130.64 Processing application for Indian Tribes

The Regional Administrator shall process an application of an Indian Tribe submitted under §130.51(d) in a timely manner. He shall promptly notify the Indian Tribe of receipt of the application.